Second Homes For Dummies®

D0598474

Keep In Touch with the Important People

You want to enlist the help of others when buying, operating, and maintaining your second home. Use this helpful list to keep track of these important people and/or companies:

Important Contact Info

	Name	Telephone Number	Cell Number	E-Mail Address
Property Manager				
Real Estate Agent				
Landscaper				
House Cleaner				
Handyman				
Plumber				
HVAC Repairman				
Electrician				
Home Inspector				
Attorney				
Neighbor #1				
Neighbor #2				

Maintaining Your Home from a Distance

Keeping tabs on a property from afar can be a challenge, but it doesn't have to be insurmountable. Here are a few pointers for those of you who are more than a few hours' drive time away from your second homes:

- **Accept the fact that you can't control everything:** Try as you might, things are bound to come up when you're not *right there* to quickly nip them in the bud. Accept the fact that you can't control everything that comes up with your second home, and prepare for whatever eventualities come your way.

- **Rely on people who can help:** Some of these souls will do it for free (like friendly neighbors); others charge a fee (like property managers); and all are good candidates for the second-home owner looking for assistance in managing a far-off property.

- **Visit as often as you can:** If you opt not to rent out your home — or if you're only renting it on a short-term basis — be sure to get as much enjoyment out of it as you can.

- **Follow the rules:** Even though you're not there to be annoyed by knee-high grass, the lawn still needs to be cut, and the home needs to be kept in good condition. If you can't do it yourself, get some help.

- **Tackle problems as they come up:** Little problems can easily turn into enormous ones when they're left unattended.

For Dummies: Bestselling Book Series for Beginners

Second Homes For Dummies®

Cheat Sheet

Steps to Narrowing Down Potential Renters

Did you buy a second home for investment purposes? If so, you made a smart move. And one way to maximize your return on your investment is to rent it. That way, you can use the rental money to pay the house's mortgage, removing some of the financial burden and making the home a more equitable investment. Keep the following in mind when searching for renters: You don't want people living in your second home who will *lower* your home's value.

1. **Ask prospective renters to fill out a written rental application.**

2. **Ask to see a valid, current, photo identification card.**

3. **Follow the Fair Housing Act.**

   This act mandates that landlords can't deny anyone housing based on race, religion, or similar factors.

4. **Perform a background check.**

   Doing so is particularly important for landlords in search of long-term renters.

5. **Run a credit check to find out about their payment history.**

   Remember, though, that you'll need their permission and their Social Security number. (Also, this may spook some prospective renters who don't want you to dig that deep into their lives. If they resist, you'll need to decide if a credit report is a make-or-break condition.) One place to start is at the online credit-check provider Youcreditcheck.com (www.you creditcheck.com), which charges $9.95 for instant credit reports.

6. **Call one or more previous landlords and ask how well the prospective tenant paid for and kept up the property.**

   To ensure that you're actually speaking to the landlord (and not someone's girlfriend posing as a landlord), inquire about the property, where it's located, how big it is, and how much it rents for per month. An owner will have all this info in his head and will be able to answer immediately.

7. **Meet the prospective renters in person.**

   Schedule a time to get together and meet face to face. If they're moving from a distance, doing so may not be feasible. If they're local, a get-together can help you get a true sense of them.

Checking In on Your Home: A Checklist

Whether you live 15 minutes away from your second home or 15 hours doesn't matter. You want to be sure that you always keep a close eye on your second home. After all, your second home is a valuable investment that you want to protect. If you live farther away and can't make a regular check-in, ask a close friend to drop in and make the inspection.

During your (or whoever's) inspection, work your way through the following list. Make a photocopy of this list and carry it with you every time you check on your home.

❏ **HVAC system:** Make sure it's at the right temperature. In hot climates, set the thermostat at about 78 to 80 degrees. In cold climates, keep it at 55 degrees.

❏ **Toilets:** Make sure that none are running excessively, clogged, or overflowing.

❏ **Kitchen and bathroom faucets:** Make sure they're all turned off and not leaking. To winterize the plumbing so the pipes don't freeze, leave at least one faucet dripping at a very low level to keep the water flowing through them.

❏ **Outdoor faucets, hoses, and receptacles:** Make sure water sources are turned off and not leaking. Make sure trash cans and lids are secured.

❏ **Lawn and landscaping:** Make sure someone is trimming grass and pruning bushes like they're supposed to be doing.

❏ **Pools and hot tubs:** Make sure their water levels are sufficient or drained and that the chemicals are balanced.

❏ **All doors:** Make sure they're locked.

❏ **Windows:** Make sure they're not open, unlocked, or broken.

❏ **Any outdoor or indoor lights that should be left on:** Make sure the bulbs aren't burned out.

❏ **The monitored security alarm system:** Make sure it's active and working — and be sure not to trip it yourself!

❏ **Any other areas of the home that are of particular concern:** This includes driveways, where those "free" newspapers can quickly pile up and make it look like the home is vacant.

For Dummies: Bestselling Book Series for Beginners

by Bridget McCrea
Former real estate agent and writer
with
Stephen Spignesi
author of more than 40 books

BICENTENNIAL
1807
WILEY
2007
BICENTENNIAL

Wiley Publishing, Inc.

Second Homes For Dummies®

Published by
Wiley Publishing, Inc.
111 River St.
Hoboken, NJ 07030-5774
www.wiley.com

WILEY

About the Authors

Bridget McCrea is a former real estate agent who, for the last 12 years, has run her own Florida-based freelance writing company, Expert Writing Services, Inc. She specializes in business topics and, because of her background, spends a good deal of her time writing about real estate–related topics for magazines such as *REALTOR Magazine, Florida Realtor, The Residential Specialist,* and *Log Home Living.*

Bridget has also penned a few books along the way, including *The Real Estate Agent's Field Guide, The Home Buyer's Question and Answer Book, The Real Estate Agent's Business Planner,* and the *RE/MAX Guide to Buying a Home.*

She's shared her home-buying expertise on various radio programs and Web sites, and is herself a homeowner who, until recently, also owned a rental home out of state.

Hunkered down in her Florida home office for most of the day and night, Bridget does break away from her desk now and then to work out at the gym and run 5K road races on a regular basis. She's now thinking seriously about training her 12-year-old daughter, Catie, to take over her business so she can put down the pen, turn off the computer, buy a vacation home on Maui, and get a life outside of work. So far, Catie has been somewhat noncommittal about giving up soccer and homework to be a CEO.

Stephen Spignesi is a full-time writer and editor and the author of 40 nonfiction books and one acclaimed debut novel, *Dialogues* (Bantam). His books include *The New York Times* bestseller, *J.F.K. Jr.,* five books about Stephen King, three books about the Beatles, and several books about world and American history, pop culture, the paranormal, true crime, TV, movies, cooking, natural disasters, Italian historical figures, cats, and contemporary fiction. Stephen's most recent book is *George Washington's Leadership Lessons* (published by Wiley), written with James Rees, the executive director of George Washington's Mount Vernon. Stephen lives in New Haven, Connecticut, with his wife, Pam, and their beloved and brilliant cat, Carter.

Author's Acknowledgments

I'd like to thank the team at Wiley for giving me the opportunity to write this book, and for hooking me up with one of the most prolific "dummifiers" ever bred, Stephen Spignesi. Also, special thanks to project editor Chad Sievers, copy editor Vicki Adang, and acquisitions editor Mike Lewis.

Huge thanks also to my agent, Marilyn Allen of the Allen O'Shea Literary Agency, for introducing me to the project in the first place, and to my daughter, Catie, for putting up with me while I holed myself up in my office in order to be able to do the best job possible on this book.

Publisher's Acknowledgments

We're proud of this book; please send us your comments through our Dummies online registration form located at www.dummies.com/register/.

Some of the people who helped bring this book to market include the following:

Acquisitions, Editorial, and Media Development

Project Editor: Chad R. Sievers

Acquisitions Editor: Michael Lewis

Copy Editor: Vicki Adang

Technical Editor: Pat Persiano

Editorial Manager: Michelle Hacker

Editorial Assistants: Erin Calligan Mooney, Joe Niesen, Leeann Harney

Cover Photos: © Shaun Egan/The Image Bank/ Getty Images

Cartoons: Rich Tennant (www.the5thwave.com)

Composition Services

Project Coordinator: Jennifer Theriot

Layout and Graphics: Carl Byers, Denny Hager, Joyce Haughey, Shane Johnson, Stephanie D. Jumper, Heather Ryan

Proofreaders: Aptara, John Greenough, Todd Lothery

Indexer: Aptara

Anniversary Logo Design: Richard Pacifico

Publishing and Editorial for Consumer Dummies

> **Diane Graves Steele,** Vice President and Publisher, Consumer Dummies

> **Joyce Pepple,** Acquisitions Director, Consumer Dummies

> **Kristin A. Cocks,** Product Development Director, Consumer Dummies

> **Michael Spring,** Vice President and Publisher, Travel

> **Kelly Regan,** Editorial Director, Travel

Publishing for Technology Dummies

> **Andy Cummings,** Vice President and Publisher, Dummies Technology/General User

Composition Services

> **Gerry Fahey,** Vice President of Production Services

> **Debbie Stailey,** Director of Composition Services

Contents at a Glance

Table of Contents

Introduction

Are you interested in finding your own getaway somewhere other than in your hometown? Or perhaps you want to purchase a second home as an investment, rent it on a year-round or short-term basis to others for profit, and then sell it? Or maybe you want to buy a second home, hang onto the property for a few years, rent it for profit, and then sell your primary home and move into the second home during retirement? Or do you want to brag about owning two homes or having a home on the shore where you spend your summers?

If you fit into any of these categories — or a combination of them — then *Second Homes For Dummies* is for you. Long term, real estate has always been a great investment. A second home can serve not only as a delightful vacation spot for you and yours, but can also make you some money. Best of both worlds, right?

With this book in your hands, you'll be well prepared to handle the entire second-home buying process, from concept to completion. No matter how you want to use your second home — as a vacation spot, as an investment (rental property), or as a future retirement home — or where you want your second home to be located, I talk about some of the challenges and problems you may encounter. Danger signs are identifiable, though, and I help you keep a wary eye.

About This Book

With the ranks of second-home owners growing in leaps and bounds (check out Chapter 1 for specific statistics), there's no time like the present to jump into the second-home game. On the other hand, buying a second home — and paying for it — can be tricky and fraught with challenges that tend to rear their heads at the worst possible times.

Although I can't predict every single challenge or obstacle that will crop up in your own second-home buying adventure, I can cover the bases and the basics by helping you prepare for what may very well be the second biggest financial transaction — after your primary home purchase, of course — of your lifetime.

Second Homes For Dummies serves as an adjunct to your own knowledge — that potpourri of information you've accumulated over the years about homes and real estate and plumbing and taxes and . . . well, you get the point. I present all this info in a logical and modular format so you can find just what you need on the subjects that interest you.

This book also can bolster the info you receive from any professionals and advisors you choose to work with. Real estate agents, attorneys, property managers, and even friends and family (especially those who already own second homes) can really be gold mines of info for you and can serve as a strong support team during this process.

Conventions Used in This Book

I use the following conventions in this book to help you navigate your way:

- ✔ I *italicize* all new words and terms that are defined.
- ✔ I **boldface** all text to indicate the action part of numbered lists and for keywords in bulleted lists.
- ✔ I use `monofont` for all Web addresses and e-mail addresses.

Also, I alternate references between male and female when discussing the different professionals in this book because your property inspector, real estate agent, or whomever may be a woman or man.

What Not to Read

Of course I want you to read everything that I've written in this book. However, I also realistically know that you're a busy person and only want to read just what you need to know to help you buy a second home. So feel free to skip the sidebars. These shaded boxes appear here and there. These sidebars often contain related but nonessential info, often about my personal experiences with real estate and second homes. Although this info is interesting, it's not essential for you to read to find and buy a second home.

Foolish Assumptions

In writing this book, I make a few assumptions about you, my dear reader, to whittle down the info and make it as useful as possible. I can assure you that you've picked up the right home-buying guide for your adventure. The assumptions I make include

✔ You already own a primary home.

✔ You're seriously considering purchasing a second home, and you want just the need-to-know info before you proceed.

✔ You've already been through at least one home purchase transaction involving a mortgage, and you've survived a closing.

✔ You're looking for a getaway that's at least a few hours away (driving time) from your primary residence.

✔ You want to use your second home solely for your own personal use, or use it yourself in between renting it out for short-term stints to others (for profit).

✔ You want to buy a second home as an investment property. For now, you plan on renting it long term, but eventually you plan on making it your primary residence.

✔ You'll likely retire to your second home someday.

✔ You're a take-control type of person, and you'll refer to this book again and again as you figure out whether you want to buy a second home, where you want to buy, and how you want to use the property.

How This Book Is Organized

Like every *For Dummies* book, *Second Homes For Dummies* has chapters with self-contained info, so you can read the chapters that interest you the most. I organize this book into five parts. Here's what you find in each:

Part 1: Seeing a Second Home in Your Future

In this first part, I cover the high-level info that can help you determine if second-home ownership is right for you. I discuss the basics of buying a second home, and who's out there in the marketplace doing it right along with you — and possibly competing with you for the choice properties. This part also answers the all-important "can I afford it?" question for you and walks you through the myriad options available to you as a second-home buyer.

Part II: Searching for Your New Home and Sealing the Deal

This part gets into the basics of finding the perfect home, whether you're doing it on your own or with the help of a real estate agent. I discuss everyone's role in the game, including real estate agents, loan officers, title companies, accountants, and so on, and advise you on how you can fit these pros into your own game plan. And because financing tends to be the most challenging aspect of the purchase process, you also find in this section a slew of information on that topic.

If you're considering purchasing a second home overseas, this part has an entire chapter that deals with the many issues you may face and what you can do to make the process less stressful.

Part III: Making Your Second Home a Smart Investment

Whether you're looking to rent out your home or just keep it for yourself, you'll want to do whatever you can to ensure that it remains a sound, growing investment. What you *don't* want to happen is to fall into the trap of neglecting your property and, thus, reducing its value, as well as your equity in the place. I show you how to increase your home's value in this section, how to rent your home, how to make smart renovations, and how to handle the maintenance and upkeep on your new home.

Part IV: Home, Sweet Home: Retiring to Your Second Home

This part helps you make the transition from landlord or vacationer to full-time resident of your second home. Here you can discover how to tell when the time is right to make the move, what steps need to be taken to ensure a smooth transition, and how to fix up the home to make it suitable for year-round living. You also can read about retirement and estate planning.

Part V: The Part of Tens

Every *For Dummies* book has this fun part with short chapters full of interesting tidbits. This part contains important information presented in a compact list format that you can read quickly. This part boils down some of the most important aspects of second-home buying, including ten great locations, ten ways to make your home first-rate, and ten rules to lay down when friends and family use your home.

Icons Used in This Book

You can find helpful hints sprinkled throughout every chapter of this book. I identify them with icons, odd-looking symbols that appear occasionally in the margin next to the text that can help you easily identify this useful information. *Second Homes For Dummies* includes the following icons:

These are ideas and, sometimes, tricks of the trade that can save you time, energy, and headaches during the second-home buying process. Who needs added frustration in their lives, right? These tips alleviate some of the pressure.

These are pitfalls that you can avoid during just about every aspect of the process. This information can help you *not* make the mistakes many who came before you have already made.

This icon points out info that's worth remembering.

This icon points you to anecdotal information from real folks who own their own second homes and who have been through illustrative experiences that can be useful for buyers like you.

Where to Go from Here

In a perfect world where no one had jobs, children to care for, obligations to handle, and (of course) TV shows to watch, you would read this book in its entirety from cover to cover.

Because I'm as busy and distracted as you are, I know that's probably not going to happen. The great thing about this and every other *For Dummies* book, however, is that you can pick it up and flip through it for the information that you need *right now,* and then go back to the other sections later as issues crop up, or as you need more background on certain areas of the process. If you're not entirely sure what topics you want to read, flip through the Table of Contents or the Index. Locate the topics that interest you, and then peruse those chapters or sections that apply to your present situation. Customized for use by busy home buyers, this book serves as your trustworthy guide as you make your way through your second-home buying venture.

After you read this book, I hope you're able to purchase a second home in the perfect location and make many memorable memories there with your friends and loved ones.

Part I

Seeing a Second Home in Your Future

"Robert's always dreamt of having a second home — or a bigger tree."

In this part . . .

*H*ave you often dreamed of owning a second home in an ideal location where you and your family can escape for family vacations and where you hope to retire someday? Maybe you and your significant other have started thinking about how you can afford a second home? Be honest, now. It has crossed your mind, right? And I don't blame you one whit. It's a lovely dream — and one you can make a reality, too.

If you see a new second home in your future, you've come to the right place. In this part, I discuss the basics of second-home ownership, cover the various home types you can choose from, and help you figure out whether you can afford a second home — and give you some alternatives if you can't. The final chapter in this part discusses location (location, location), and what to look for when you're shopping for a great place for your second home.

Chapter 1

The Lowdown on Buying and Owning a Second Home

In This Chapter

▶ Preparing to join millions of other second-home owners

▶ Buying, selling, and investing in real estate

▶ Managing your second home from a distance

▶ Living in your second home after retirement

*W*elcome to the world of second-home ownership! If you're considering buying a second home, you've come to the right place. Here, you can discover how wonderful it is to have a second home to run away to, how gratifying it is to rent your place for extra income (if you choose to do so), and how comforting it is to know that you'll retire there at some point in your life if you so choose.

A large number of people — many of whom have been disenchanted with low stock market gains over the past few years — have turned to investing in second homes. This strategy is twofold: Grab a nice slice of paradise while also putting money in a place where, thanks to the wonders of housing appreciation, it will (ideally) grow steadily over time.

Owning a second home can be a fun adventure, but it isn't free of some ups and downs. This chapter gives you an overview of what you can expect when you buy and own a second home. I explain why people buy second homes and discuss the second-home market. I also show you the good, the bad, and the ugly of owning a second home (and, yes, there's always a little of each), and I help you avoid making mistakes when searching for the perfect second home. Finally, I help you get into the "real estate investor" mind-set, and I explain the roles that you the home buyer, your trusted real estate agent, and those unknown home *sellers* play in the process.

Identifying Why People Buy a Second Home

People purchase second homes for various reasons, and you're likely to relate to at least one of them. Perhaps you want to be able to get away at the drop of a hat and know that you have somewhere to go that isn't a hotel room, a rented condominium, or your in-laws' sleeper sofa.

Second homes are commonly located in vacation-oriented areas and can be a great escape for you, as well as for your friends and family who are invited to make use of the place and its facilities and amenities (if, of course, things like a pool and tennis courts came along with the purchase). Or perhaps you simply want a fairly safe investment and plan to rent the property to make some extra bucks.

This section gives you a brief rundown of some of the main reasons why people buy second homes. Keep in mind that this section is simply a quick glance. Check out Chapter 3 for more discussion on the pros and cons of buying and owning a second home.

A vacation getaway

Who loves taking a vacation? Raise your hand. Of course, you have your hand up, right? Vacations allow you to take time off from work to escape the daily grind and relax and unwind. You can decompress from the stress of work, spend time with your family, and enjoy your surroundings.

Many people buy second homes so they have a reason to take a few days off to get away and visit it! If you can make the time, a vacation spot is ready and waiting for you. Especially for hardworking people who tend to burn the candle at both ends (doesn't that sound like you?), a second home is a great place for some downtime. Think about it: If you know that you have an empty, available beach home a mere five hours away, won't you be more apt to go there, visit, and just relax? I know I would!

A place for family and friends to visit

Whether you bring friends and family along on vacation, or let them use your digs on their own, friends and relatives will love the fact that you have a pad for them to use away from home — and that you're such a generous sort that you don't mind them enjoying it.

Many people enjoy using their second homes as a gathering spot for friends and family. No matter if you're at the second home with your kith and kin socializing for a getaway weekend or holiday, or some of your extended family is using your home for their own little getaway, a second home is a great way to bring your loved ones together. This book offers plenty of tips and advice on how to deal with these types of guests. For example, should you charge them rent (check out Chapter 11)? And how do you ask them to follow the house rules (check out Chapter 20)?

An investment (in the form of rent money)

Some people purchase second homes for investment purposes. Rather than spend their vacations there, they rent the property with the intention of making some money. In doing so, they begin to build equity in yet another home, thus forming the foundation for a retirement nest egg that at some point can be sold to a third party or willed to an heir.

By renting your place for more than 14 days per year, you not only can collect rent checks, but you can also gain tax advantages that owners who opt not to rent simply don't have. (Refer to Chapter 14 for the specific IRS rules and regulations for renting your second home.)

Just the stats, please: Why people buy second homes

According to the National Association of Realtors (NAR), sales of second homes, in the form of vacation homes and investment homes, set records in 2005. In fact, the combined total of second-home sales accounted for 4 out of 10 residential transactions.

The NAR reports that 27.7 percent of all homes purchased in 2005 were for *investment,* and another 12.2 percent were purchased for use as *vacation homes.* Altogether, 3.34 million second homes were sold in 2005, up 16.0 percent over 2004 — more than 9,000 second homes were bought and sold every day of the year!

The NAR determined the reasons vacation-home buyers wanted a second home:

- ✔ 41 percent purchased their dwellings to use for vacations.

- ✔ 31 percent purchased a place to use as a family retreat.

- ✔ 28 percent bought to diversify their investment portfolio.

For investment-home buyers:

- ✔ 55 percent said rental income was the primary factor for buying.

- ✔ 35 percent wanted to diversify their investments.

Part III of this book covers everything you need to know about renting your home, including finding renters, hiring a property manager, remodeling your home, maintaining your home, and paying the appropriate taxes on a rental property.

A space to peacefully retire to

Knowing that you actually own a delightful place on a gorgeous beach in Maui, and that it's just sitting there waiting for you to come and live there full time, may be reason enough for you to purchase a second home. In fact, many people buy second homes with retirement in mind.

Whether you plan to retire in 5 years or 25 years, you can purchase a second home and use it as an incentive to work hard and look forward to the golden years when you can relax. If you do purchase a second home for retirement, it doesn't have to sit empty until you're ready to move in permanently. You can use it as a vacation destination for yourself or friends, or you can rent it. Even if you have to rent it seasonally or full time in the interim, the home is still there (and still appreciating in value) while you put in those additional years of work and plan for the day when you can retire and enjoy it *fully* — and *full time*. (Refer to Part IV for more in-depth info about retiring to your home.)

Understanding the Second-Home Market

Remember when having more than one house was a really big deal? Yes, there was a time when owning a second home was considered a luxury only afforded by the affluent, with everyone else content to stay in hotels or rented spaces while on vacation.

The perception of second-home owners being King Midas has changed dramatically over the last few years. Low mortgage interest rates and an often uncertain and fluctuating stock market have pushed more people to consider real estate as an investment, rather than a necessity, or even a luxury. But do you wonder if you fit in the second-home market? If you want to see how you compare with these second-home buyers, this section can help you understand the second-home market a bit better.

Who is the second-home buyer?

The second-home buyer can be the person who is looking for a monthly escape of her own in a neighboring town or hundreds of miles away. The second-home buyer can be the shrewd investor who wants to add a few rental properties to his retirement portfolio. The second-home buyer can be the wealthy family that has always wanted to own their own chalet on the countryside in France. Knowing who's buying second homes is useful in that you can easily tell if you fit into one of these categories, and this knowledge (combined with other considerations, such as what type of homes they're buying and what amenities and features they're looking for; check out Chapter 3) can help you decide if a second home is right for you.

REAL LIFE EXAMPLE

An agent picks his clients' brains

One Chicago real estate agent I know does a good 5 to 10 percent of his annual business with second-home buyers eager to purchase property in the city's downtown Streeterville neighborhood. That's where theaters, opera houses, restaurants, and Navy Pier are flanked by one- and two-bedroom condos priced in the $200,000 to $300,000 range.

Before the agent takes them out to look at properties, though, he first probes into the buyers' wants and needs by asking questions like:

✔ What will you use the property for?

✔ What amenities or features are you looking for?

✔ How long do you plan to own this property?

✔ Would you be willing to upgrade it to maximize its value?

✔ Would you rather spend more money on a finished condo unit, or would you prefer buying something that you can work on?

Why all the questions?

According to the agent, buying a second, in-town home in Chicago is about convenience as much as it is about property appreciation. His second-home customers include folks ranging from investors looking for a city getaway, to parents who are purchasing homes for their college-age children attending school in the area. Most of his clients come to him through word-of-mouth referrals from bankers and lawyers, as well as through his firm's excellent relocation department. (For more on working with a real estate agent, flip to Chapter 6.)

And most of my friend's clients are also thinking about exit strategies before they even sign on the dotted line. According to the agent, he often finds himself answering one simple question time after time: "If I needed to sell right away, how quickly could I do so?"

In 2005, the profile for a typical second-home buyer who uses the home for vacations was as follows:

- ✔ He was 52 years old.
- ✔ She had an annual income of $82,800.
- ✔ He purchased a property that was a median of 197 miles from his primary residence. Also, 47 percent of these homes were less than 100 miles away, and 43 percent were 500 miles or more.

In 2005, the profile of the typical second-home buyer who uses the home as an investment was as follows:

- ✔ She was 49 years old.
- ✔ He had an income of $81,400.
- ✔ She bought a home that was relatively close by — a median of 15 miles from her primary residence.

More than three-fourths of people who bought second homes for vacations have no interest in renting their property, and 21 percent said it would become a primary residence on retirement, compared with only 2 percent of people who purchased a second home as an investment. Furthermore, 14 percent of investment buyers and 6 percent of vacation-home buyers purchased a property that their son or daughter could occupy while in school.

Where do you fit in? People of all ages and walks of life purchase second homes. If you're paying your bills and enjoying life, and can afford the out-of-pocket expenses — down payment, closing costs, and other outlays associated with buying a home — the odds are you can purchase and use a second home — as a vacation home, a full-time rental, a future retirement home, or a place where you and your family can spend every weekend if you want to.

Location is everything

The National Association of Realtors asked second-home buyers which characteristics they sought out and valued most about their property.

Here's what they said about location. (Check out Chapter 4 for more on why location is important when buying a second home.)

- ✔ 40 percent said close to an ocean, river, or lake
- ✔ 34 percent said close to family members
- ✔ 27 percent said close to preferred recreational activities
- ✔ 27 percent said close to their primary residence
- ✔ 26 percent said close to mountains
- ✔ 24 percent said close to a preferred vacation area
- ✔ 17 percent said close to a job or school

And you don't have to spend millions of dollars to get into your second home of choice. Many of today's buyers are spending reasonable amounts of money to buy second homes. The median price of a vacation home in 2005 was $204,100, up 7.4 percent from $190,000 in 2004. The typical investment property cost $183,500 in 2005, up 24.0 percent from $148,000 in 2004.

Where are people buying second homes?

Knowing where the second home hot spots are can help you pinpoint the best place for yours, particularly if you don't already have a specific city, state, or county in mind. By keeping an eye on where others are flocking to, you can get a great sense of where the best values, amenities, and attractions are without having to get on an airplane and see for yourself.

People are purchasing second homes in various regions of the United States. According to the National Association of Realtors (NAR), in 2005, here's how the second-home-sales buying pattern shakes out (in order of popularity):

- ✔ **The Midwest:** 33 percent
- ✔ **The South:** 30 percent
- ✔ **The West:** 20 percent
- ✔ **The Northeast:** 17 percent

When you're ready to pick the place where you want to purchase your second home, Chapters 4 and 18 have some useful advice you can apply to your search. Some people are also buying homes abroad. Check out Chapter 9 for more about buying a second home overseas.

Getting in on the Second-Home Boom: Are You Ready?

Turning your dream of owning two homes into a reality requires careful consideration, despite the allure of low mortgage interest rates and that extra cash lying around waiting to be invested.

As you decide whether a second home is right for you, take a few moments and consider the following pointers and reminders:

- ✔ **Thoroughly review your ability to pay for a second home.** Asking yourself if you can afford a second home is particularly important if you're already carrying a mortgage on your first home and you don't plan to generate rental income from your second home. Check out Chapter 2 for more info about whether you can afford a second home.

✔ **While figuring out your financials, keep in mind the investment potential of the new home.** If your second home is in a coastal area where property appreciation is consistent and high (say, in the 15 to 25 percent range annually or every couple of years), for example, the financial returns may be significant. Also your home's rental potential can increase its value. If you so desire, rent can start pouring in during those months when you're not using the place. (See Chapter 11 to read more about renting a second home.)

✔ **Understand the main financial differences of buying a second home compared to your first home.** Most second-home loans require down payments of 15 to 20 percent, and some mortgage companies require higher down payments on second homes, compared to first homes. I've heard of lenders demanding up to 50 percent of the total sales price. How much you'll be asked to come up with depends in large part on your credit rating. (Check out Chapter 8 for more info on financing differences and credit scores.)

✔ **Know that after the sale closes, you need to be able to afford the monthly mortgage payment, utilities, and any additional upkeep or related fees.** Remember, owning and maintaining a property isn't cheap. You must maintain the property. (Check out Chapter 13 for more on the upkeep of a second home.)

✔ **Factor in tax obligations.** Have a financial advisor or accountant clearly explain the tax considerations you'll incur well ahead of your closing day. If you decide to rent the unit when you're not using it, you need to know how all that additional taxable income will affect your financial picture. (See Chapter 14 for more info on sending Uncle Sam his due.)

✔ **Look for a home and area that boasts the kinds of amenities that will make you and yours happy and comfortable.** Are there certain activities that you can't live without, even when you're on vacation? (Did I just hear someone shriek the word "golf"?) The key is to make sure you know which amenities you want *before* you buy, and only look for those homes that have the features or that provide easy access to them. For example, you may desire a house with a pool and basement game room, and your spouse may want nearby shopping malls.

✔ **Think about your social and family lifestyle.** If having friends and family — a built-in community — close by is important, consider areas that you have frequented over the years.

✔ **Choose a climate that matches your needs.** My favorite season is summer. My friend Steve's is, too. If you're planning on using your second home year-round, be sure that the location experiences the weather you enjoy throughout the year. (See Chapter 4.)

✔ **Figure out the ideal travel distance, by car or plane, to your second home.** How often do you plan on visiting your second home? If, for example, you detest flying, choose somewhere within a few hours' drive. If, on the other hand, driving is your nemesis, then go for something very close to home or far enough away to justify the cost of a plane trip. (Check out Chapter 4.)

✔ **Think about your second home's long-term use.** Will you be renting it? Then make it easy on yourself and pick a place that's popular for vacationers and renters. Will you retire to the home? Then make sure the home and its surroundings feature all the amenities and extras that you need to be comfortable and content.

Finding and Purchasing a Second Home: On Your Own or with an Agent

Do you want to buy a second home for your family to use on vacations? Are you considering expanding your investment portfolio with a second home? No matter the reason, if you want to purchase a second home, you first have to know where to find one. Where do you start? You have two choices when it comes to buying a second home:

✔ **Shop around on your own, decide on a home, and handle the details of the purchase by yourself.** Handling the deal on your own may not be easy, but if you've been through real estate transactions before, and if you know what to expect, then you know it's doable. The upside is that you're in control. The downside is that it's a huge amount of work. See Chapter 5 for details on how to go about buying a second home on your own.

✔ **Use a real estate agent to help you buy your second home.** Because agents typically collect commissions from the seller side of the transaction, you have nothing to lose when you hire an agent to help you purchase your home. The pluses include having a pro and all the knowledge and resources she brings to the table. The negatives include not having total control and having to depend on the agent to find what you're looking for. See Chapter 6 for the nitty-gritty on how to select and work with an agent.

What Kind of Second Home to Avoid

If you're seriously considering buying a second home, you can't just buy the first home you see. Make sure you're not buying a property that you'll later ask yourself why the heck you bought it. If you're working with a real estate agent, rely on her expertise to help you find the home that's right for you. If you're not using a real estate agent, make sure you know what you're buying. (For example, an inspector can help you if you notice a structural problem with a home; see Chapter 7 for more info.)

The following list points out a few types of houses you may want to stay away from:

- ✔ A home that doesn't meet your specific needs, or that of your family.

- ✔ A house that's located in an area of the country that you don't particularly care for (or even loathe with the heat of a thousand suns).

- ✔ A dwelling located in an area where the amenities you really want are few and far between.

- ✔ A home that's obviously overpriced (comparatively speaking) in a declining market. (This is a sure sign that you could lose money on your investment.)

- ✔ A house that you want to buy *right now* because you really like the way it looks. Doing so is called *buying on emotion,* and no second-home owner should get sucked into this situation. You'll live to regret it. I've seen it happen.

- ✔ An abode that needs entirely too much work to get into shape for comfortable living. This type of home is considered a *fixer-upper.*

- ✔ A home that's not located in an area where others want to visit. This is especially important if you plan on renting it on a seasonal or annual basis.

- ✔ A house that's too far away for you to get to on a regular basis, say, once a month, or once every other month — unless, of course, you're buying overseas and are aware of the fact that it will be far away regardless of where you buy.

This list is a good starting point. Feel free to add to it, based on your own circumstances. By selecting a home that meets your needs, as well as one that's a good investment, you'll be much happier with your choice.

Are You Saying I'm a Real Estate Investor with Only Two Houses? Yes!

Real estate is a game of sorts and, as a primary homeowner, you're already playing it. And, like every game, real estate buying and selling has rules, winners, losers, and a multitude of ways to play. When you become a second-home buyer, you officially move into the "investor" category of game player. Why? Because you now have a bit more skin in the game. Plus, you've shown that you have a true interest in putting your money into real estate — even if it's just for the sake of having a fun vacation every month, which is fine.

This section gives you a quick overview of each person's role in the real estate game, and how you can put their expertise and experience to work in making your real estate transaction successful and smooth, as well as how to score the best deal possible. Keep in mind that these concepts are discussed at length elsewhere in the book, too. Check out Chapter 6 for more on who does what, and to whom, and for whom!

The seller's game

The seller probably has the easiest job: Get the highest possible price for her home in the shortest amount of time. Period.

To make this happen,

- **She sets an asking price that's higher than what she thinks she'll get.** Very few prices these days are really and truly firm.

- **She negotiates hard on all points.** You can expect one of three things to happen if you insist on knocking off a significant amount from her price because of a faulty dishwasher or a carpet you feel needs to be replaced.

  - She'll give you an outright, "No, thanks."

  - She'll be willing to discuss a compromise.

  - She won't even dignify your offer with a response.

- **She refuses to settle until she knows she's getting a good deal for her home.** Sellers rarely agree to a sale if they feel they're not getting what they deserve.

Of course, the *motivated seller,* a subspecies of the seller, is slightly different. How? She's much more flexible on all aspects of the sale, and for one good reason: She's eager to sell. For whatever reason, she can't allow the house to sit on the market for weeks or even months. This type of situation can be a real opportunity for the serious buyer.

But if a seller is *not* in a hurry, and she knows what the house is worth and has decided that that's the amount she wants, no matter what, then it'll take the First Cavalry to move her. (For more insights into negotiating with a seller, see Chapter 5.)

The buyer's game

The buyer — and for purposes of this book (except for Chapter 16, where you're the seller), that's *you* — is out to pay the lowest possible price for the home that meets his needs in as many ways as possible. He's looking for location (location, location), size, amenities, and, of course, price.

For you to score your ideal second home, consider working with an agent to negotiate pricing and terms on the home of your choice. Or you may choose to handle the hands-on dickering yourself. Check out Chapter 5, if that's the case. Like the seller, you won't settle until you feel like you're getting exactly what you want and for the price you want to pay.

There are also *motivated buyers.* These buyers *need* to purchase something and, thus, sometimes agree to a higher price than they're happy with in order to get the house they want, with what they want in it, in a location they're excited about. There may be lots of reasons for the urgency, but it boils down to an opportunity for the seller who holds the house the buyer is interested in.

The agent's game

The real estate agent's place is somewhere in between the buyer and the seller. His job is to shepherd the sale to the closing table . . . no matter what it takes to do so, all within the ethical guidelines, of course. (Real estate agents are obliged to follow their national real estate organization's Code of Ethics.)

Agents typically represent either the buyer or the seller and always work closely with the co-broker representing the other side of the deal. If there's no co-broker, then your agent deals directly with the seller. Everyone's goal? To come to terms on the second-home sale.

Because the agent works on commission, and also because he doesn't get paid until the deal closes, it's in his best interest to see that the deal reaches the closing table and that all parties are satisfied and cooperating by doing their part in creating a happy experience for all. (Chapter 6 has all the details of the agent's role and how you can work with him.)

If you're not using an agent, the process is still very much the same: Negotiate the price and conditions, sign the contract, get the necessary inspections and appraisals done, get the financing in order, and get the transaction to the closing table.

After You Purchase: Putting Together a Support Team

Second-home ownership is on the rise, so how hard can it be? You put your money down and voilà, it's your home, right? Depending on how you plan to use the home, you move some stuff in and plan for your next vacation, or you find some renters. Well, it's not quite as simple as that.

Buying and owning a second home adds a level of complexity to all aspects of your life, especially when your second home is several hundred miles away from your primary residence. If something happens, you can't exactly drop everything and stop by to check on the place. This section explains how you can deal with crises when they pop up.

If you don't have a support team, you'll be largely left to your own devices when any type of emergency or issue comes up. If you live 20 minutes down the interstate, then you can probably handle it on your own. But if your home is more than an hour or so away, then follow the advice in Chapter 13 and form a solid support team for yourself and your home.

For the day-to-day responsibilities

By forming strong, friendly bonds with property managers, real estate agents, and your neighbors, as well as with any friends or family who live close to your second home, you'll have a much easier time managing your abode from afar with all the day-to-day issues and responsibilities. Without this network, you're on your own.

Your support team can help maintain the home and handle any issues, regardless of how far you are from your second home. Your team's responsibilities may include cutting the grass, trimming the hedges, cleaning the gutters, and handling any other regular maintenance and upkeep.

If you're planning on renting your place, you can hire someone to help you with all the paperwork and upkeep. For example, a property manager can handle the marketing of the property to potential renters, keep an eye on the place when you're not in town, and hire subcontractors to handle odd jobs like plumbing problems and routine care like lawn maintenance. (Check out Chapters 11 and 13 for more on working with a property manager.)

Dealing with the late-night emergency call

Phones don't generally ring in the middle of the night for no good reason. When you live eight hours away from your second home and you get a call in the dead of night from someone living in or near your home, you can bet dollars to doughnuts something serious has taken place. This is when your support team can swing into action (it can also come to your rescue for emergencies during daylight hours, too).

Laying down the ground rules for people who use your home

If after you purchase your second home you decide to let friends and family use it, you want to ensure that you protect your investment.

A friend of mine owns a few vacation homes, none of which are rented out but all of which are used on a regular basis by his friends and family members. Like many of the owners I have rented from, he leaves a sheet of rules, instructions, and info on the refrigerator in the home. This list cuts down on the number of frantic calls he receives (telling him, for example, that the televisions won't turn on) and the amount of cleanup that he has to do after they depart.

The following set of House Rules — shamelessly pulled off my friend's second home's refrigerator and reprinted almost verbatim — paints a clear picture as to how guests should be instructed to treat a home like it's their own. (This list was developed after several infractions took place, and it's mostly directed at the owner's children and friends.) You'll want to do the same thing at your second home. Feel free to photocopy the rules or draft similar rules for your own guests.

House Rules

Note: This stuff is listed in no particular order of importance. I hope you enjoy your stay at my vacation home. In return for my generosity, I expect visitors to treat my home like they treat their own (better, if they're homes aren't clean and neat), report any damage or problems as soon as possible, and leave the place as clean (preferably CLEANER) as it was when they arrived.

1. Park your car _____

2. Questions that may come up while you are here can be directed to me. Home phone number is _____ and my cell phone is _____

3. Feel free to use the telephone for local and near-zone calls or to call me if you have questions. Please don't make other long-distance calls from my telephone. Note: The local telephone book is stored _____

4. Cleaning supplies (vacuum cleaner, dusting rags, glass cleaner, and so on) are located in _____

5. Feel free to watch TV and note that we have all the movie channels. Enjoy those channels if you wish, but don't order Pay-Per-View movies because they are billed separately.

6. I have wireless broadband available if you care to access the Internet wirelessly on your own notebook computer (not sure you have the hardware to do it, but it's available if you do). The wireless signal is very strong throughout the entire condo.

7. Don't open the garage door. It's locked, and I prefer to keep it locked.

8. If you find any mail in the mailbox, please leave it on the counter when you leave.

9. Upon leaving, check that all windows are properly closed and that all doors are closed and locked. Also, please remove any perishable food stored in the refrigerator.

10. Take any trash out.

11. In case you get locked out, don't panic. The next door neighbor has a spare key to our unit. Her phone number is _____

12. Leave me a note on the dining room table and tell me which beds were used. I will change the sheets at a later date. But, please do make the beds so that the rooms look neat and orderly upon my arrival.

13. Regarding towels, you have two choices: bring your own or use mine. If you use mine, that is okay, but drape the wet ones over the sliding tub enclosure and pile up the used dry ones on the counter by the sink, so I will know which ones are dirty. Same holds true for the three kitchen towels. There are more clean towels in the bedroom dressers, and more kitchen towels in one of the drawers to the right of the kitchen sink. There are more sheets in the bedside tables.

You may receive a late-night call for any number of reasons:

✔ **Maintenance issues:** A pipe broke, or the air conditioning won't kick on.

✔ **Security concerns:** The alarm company received a break-in signal.

✔ **Personal injuries on your property:** Some guy fell on your lawn and broke his arm.

✔ **Weather-related disasters:** A tree crashed through your roof, or your basement has 3 feet of water in it.

✔ **Unforeseen calamities:** A car jumped your lawn and is now in your living room.

✔ **Major property damage:** A fire seriously damaged your garage.

Having someone you can trust living near your second home is especially important if your primary home is a great distance away. A good way to deal with these issues is to think about them in advance and determine what steps you'll take when an emergency happens. If you plan to rely on a neighbor, friend, or relative to help you handle crises, give them a heads-up that if you get a late-night call, you may be waking them up, too. Chapter 13 can help you figure out whom to call and how to handle emergencies.

Retiring to (And Protecting) Your Second Home

When the time comes to retire to your second home, you want to take a few steps to shore it up and make sure that it's ready for full-time living. (Check out Chapter 16 for more advice and info on moving into your second home.) Here are some things that you can do:

✔ Have a security system installed and turned on to protect yourself and your belongings.

✔ Inspect all windows and door locks to make sure they're operable and can be properly secured.

✔ Check outdoor facilities (such as screen doors) for their ability to close and lock properly.

✔ Get adequate insurance coverage for the home (if you don't have it already) and its contents (particularly if you're going to fill up the home with all of your earthly belongings).

By protecting your home, you can feel more secure. Enjoy retirement and your home. You deserved it.

Chapter 2

Figuring Out Whether You Can Afford a Second Home

*O*ne of the first things you should do when considering a major purchase, whether it's a second home, third boat, or fourth car, is to make sure that you can afford it. When you're thinking about buying another home, you don't want to end up having two pieces of property draining your checkbook to an alarming level every month. In order to prevent you from biting off more than you can chew, this chapter helps you assess your financial situation, get a breakdown of the basic expenses associated with second-home ownership, and figure out how to pay for a second house and its upkeep.

Evaluating Your Financial Situation: Can You Afford a Second House Now?

Owning a second home gives you great bragging rights and probably some comfort when you think about your future. Because many people consider property ownership an important part of the American dream, owning two homes can translate into financial security: It's the type of investment that rarely loses its value. Plus, knowing where you'll be spending your retirement years provides reassurance about that phase of your life. But a second home isn't worth the commitment if you can't afford the upfront cost, monthly payments, and maintenance and upkeep involved in owning one.

Before you make the huge decision to buy a second home, this section helps you look at your finances to determine whether you have enough money for such a large investment.

Looking at your assets and liabilities

Before you take on the responsibility of a second home, you need to thoroughly and honestly evaluate your financial situation. An easy way to do this evaluation is to list your *assets* (how much money you have on hand) and then your *liabilities* (how much money you owe in the form of mortgages, personal loans, credit card balances, and so forth).

Your list of assets may include

- ✔ **Liquid cash:** Money you have ready access to in your savings, checking, or money market accounts.

- ✔ **Value of your investments:** How much money you have invested in 401(k)s, retirement funds, mutual funds, and other accounts, whether or not such funds are liquid.

- ✔ **Equity in your primary home:** *Equity* is the value of your primary home minus the total amount that you currently owe on your mortgage.

- ✔ **Personal property:** Valuable collections, such as stamps, art, guns, collectibles, jewelry, vehicles, and so on, are assets.

Your list of liabilities may include

- ✔ Mortgage balance (including home equity amounts) for your current home

- ✔ Balances on car loans and student loans

- ✔ Revolving credit card balances

- ✔ Personal loan balances (including *unwritten* loans you're paying off to friends or family)

Evaluating your net worth

After you know your assets and liabilities, you can figure out your *net worth,* which is the value of all assets, including cash, less your total liabilities. Knowing your net worth is important for second-home buyers because you can see exactly what you have to work with for a down payment. This amount can also be a source for closing costs and, perhaps, a new monthly mortgage payment (which will eventually be mitigated if you rent the place).

To figure out your net worth, subtract your liabilities from your assets. Here's an illustration:

Assets ($214,000) – Liabilities ($26,000) = Net worth ($188,000)

When looking at your net worth (what you're worth on paper) and your *monthly income* and *outgo* (what comes in and goes out every month), you need to ask yourself two important questions:

- ✔ **How much of your net worth are you able (and willing) to spend on a down payment for a second home?** This money will come from your savings, investments, a home equity loan, or a combination of these.

- ✔ **How much are you able (and willing) to spend each month on paying for your second home?** To answer this question, figure out your *current* monthly expenses: expenses that absolutely must be paid without fail. Then determine what's left over to pay for a second mortgage (see the next section). Of course, if you plan to rent your second home, you'll have a source of income to help pay the mortgage. (Check out Chapter 11 for more info on garnering rental income from your second home.)

When figuring your monthly income and outgo, make sure you factor in any additional income, such as alimony, child support, or other regular sources of funding you receive, as well as extra expenses, like alimony or child support. This cold appraisal of everything you bring in and spend allows you to determine the total amount of monthly income that is available to invest in a second home.

Figuring your monthly surplus

After you know what your current monthly income and expenses are, plug the numbers into Figure 2-1 to calculate your *monthly surplus* (the money you have left at the end of the month after you pay your expenses) available to pay for a second home.

The basic rule: The costs for your primary home should be a third of your gross income. So for example, if you earn $7,000 a month in gross income, your housing costs are $2,000 (including mortgage, taxes, and homeowners' insurance) and your monthly living expenses are $3,000, then you have $2,000 left in monthly surplus for a second home. You have to decide whether $2,000 per month is enough to comfortably afford a second home. It very well may be, depending on what your secondary mortgage will be. For example, if you buy a $200,000 property, put down $50,000, and get a fixed 30-year mortgage at 5.9 percent, your monthly payment without taxes will be $889.70. That would leave you with about $1,100 for property taxes and other expenses. Is that enough? You need to make that decision based on your own circumstances. If it's not, you may need to buy something cheaper, find a way to put down a larger deposit, or hold off on buying a second home right now.

1. Enter your gross monthly income (how much you earn before taxes and other expenses are withheld). _____

2. Enter your total monthly housing costs, such as mortgage payments, private mortgage insurance, taxes, and homeowners' insurance paid on your primary home. _____

Figure 2-1:
Use this worksheet to help you calculate your monthly surplus.

3. Subtract line 2 from line 1. _____

4. Enter your other monthly expenses, such as credit card debt, student loans, car loans, medical bills, and so forth. _____

5. Subtract line 4 from line 3. _____

6. This amount is your total monthly surplus available. _____

Mortgage bankers use gross income to determine worth and borrowing power. But in real life, calculating *net income* (what's left of your paycheck after taxes and benefit deductions) less outgo provides a clearer picture of your monthly financial situation.

Be honest with yourself about every penny that goes out, lest you wind up in the red after purchasing your new second home. Sometimes unexpected situations affect your financial picture. If a loved one is ill, for example, and you're helping to pay for medical care, you'll want to factor that expense in as a liability. If your daughter just went off to college and is burning through $800 a month in spending money, be sure to take that into account.

This bottom-line number can tell you where you stand financially and provide you with a glimpse of reality regarding your second-home purchase. Can you do it? Should you do it? Knowing how much more you will spend each month can help you answer those questions.

Knowing and staying within your limits

If you had a dollar for every time someone warned you not to overextend yourself financially, you'd probably be able to pay cash for a second (and third, and maybe fourth) home right now. (And after you read this section, I'm going to owe you a dollar, too.) I can't stress enough how important it is for you to realize that second-home ownership is a major undertaking.

If you don't understand your financial limitations before you move ahead with choosing and financing a second home, you risk losing at least your second home to foreclosure, and possibly your first house, too. *Foreclosure* is when the lender sells the home to cover the debt that you owe. And yes, it's as horrible an experience as it sounds. And adding insult to injury, not only do you lose the second home, but you also lose everything you put down on the place when you bought it. So think carefully before making the plunge.

Use the following fun short quiz to help you get a handle on your financial limits. Answer yes or no. Be brutally honest.

1. **Do I save money on a monthly basis?** _____

2. **Do I live paycheck to paycheck?** _____

3. **Am I in the red at the end of the month on a fairly regular basis?** _____

   (If you said "Yes" to questions 2 and 3, you may want to reconsider an outright purchase of a second home.)

4. **Can I afford the mortgage payment, insurance, property taxes, and upkeep on another home at this time?** _____

5. **If I answered "No" to question 4, is there an active rental market in my second-home location of choice right now?** _____

   (If so, then rent coming in on my second home every month may cover some or all the expenses associated with second-home ownership.)

6. **Considering my own financial situation and the current real estate market conditions, is real estate a good investment right now?** _____

   (For example, if it's a hot *seller's market* — a market where housing inventory is low, appreciation is high, negotiating room is limited, and housing prices are through the roof — but your job situation is iffy, you may want to think twice about buying a second home right now.)

7. **Do options like timesharing or leasing sound more feasible to me right now?** _____

   (These options are viable for individuals who want a vacation home, but who don't want to take on the expense of owning one outright. Check out Chapter 3 for how you can take advantage of a timeshare and the "Trying leasing before buying" section later in this chapter for more info.)

Only you and any cosigners will be responsible for the payments on your second home, so be honest with yourself when figuring out whether you can afford a second home. You may be counting on the rent of the home to cover its *monthly nut* (the total monthly expenses to keep and maintain the house), but tenants move out, and sometimes rentals stay vacant for a while. So always be sure you'll be able to pay for the home, even when it's empty. (Unless, of course, you're a gambler at heart and are willing to let the chips fall where they may! Not a recommended strategy, by the way!)

If, after reading this section and completing the quiz, you're now confident that second-home ownership is right for you and your long-term financial picture, then good for you. If, however, after these exercises you're still having doubts about your ability to afford a second home, retrace your steps, look again at the numbers, and weigh the pros and cons one more time before making a final decision.

Considering timing

Location means a lot in real estate, but timing is also very important. Life events — both expected and unexpected — can play a significant role in your ability to buy a second home.

That's not to say that everything needs to be perfect for it to be the right time to invest in real estate. It doesn't. But you should carefully consider job security, life events, and health issues before you jump into the second-home market feet first. You improve your chances of second-home success if you work through the timing issues now, in advance of signing on the dotted line.

For instance, if you're in the middle of a two-year divorce battle, now is probably not the best time to buy that $500,000 condo in Myrtle Beach, South Carolina. Think carefully before you plunk down a $10,000 deposit on that bungalow on the French Riviera (no matter how badly you may need a vacation there right now!).

Trying leasing before buying

What if your financial analysis *didn't* make you smile and you still want a second home? Just because your numbers aren't perfect doesn't mean you still can't have your own little slice of heaven nestled on a shoreline or situated a mile away from the Las Vegas Strip. If you enjoy visiting the same area on a regular basis, you may want to consider leasing first before buying.

You can rent a place from owners who, if asked nicely (and monetarily compensated, of course), will often hold certain weeks each year for their best customers. This arrangement can work well for you if you're not quite ready to buy a second home but want to know how it feels to vacation at the same place every year.

If you lease a home in a popular vacation area, you can also use your time to get to know other owners and suss out how they like their properties, whether maintenance and upkeep are affordable (you'll find that many will be almost too eager to tell you what you'd like to know, especially when it comes to what they're not happy about), plus their take on the experience of owning a second home. Use this time to your advantage, and factor all this knowledge into your final second-home buying decision, whether that happens now or in the future.

You can also check out "for lease/rent by owner" Web sites, such as www. vrbo.com and www.vacationrentals.com, where you can view properties and rates without any sales pressure.

Figuring Out How Much (Second) House You Can Afford

Assuming you already own your primary residence, you know what it took to get you there: You know what it's like to apply and be approved for a mortgage and to pay the closing costs on your purchase. You also know what it takes to pay that mortgage every month, while also covering the taxes, homeowners' insurance, home repairs, and routine maintenance.

However, owning a second home does have its differences. This section gives you a more detailed look at the financial commitments of second-home ownership, which can help you decide whether your budget allows for the added expenses.

Keep that calculator handy: Adding it up

Even though the real estate transaction process is, of course, similar for primary and second homes, buying a second home can be more challenging when it's time to get a mortgage. Just remember: Buying a second home is a numbers game. As with most real estate purchases, you want to look at not only how much money you have to spend on the property, but also how much money you can make on the investment from appreciation and rental income (if you choose to rent the property).

Using some nifty online mortgage calculators

Second-home buyers can use all sorts of free, online calculators to determine everything from basic monthly mortgage payments and tax advantages of second-home ownership to loan amortization schedules. Check these out for starters:

✔ **The Mortgage Calculator,** www. smartmoney.com/home: Smart Money's mortgage calculator figures the monthly payment, calculates the effects of prepaying the mortgage, and analyzes the composition of future monthly payments.

✔ **GMAC Mortgage Calculators,** www. gmacmortgage.com/Purchase/ Buy_a_Vacation_or_Investment_ Home/What_You_Should_Know/ benefits.html: GMAC's site offers biweekly and monthly payment, mortgage loan, ARM versus fixed rate, and annual percentage rate (APR) calculators.

✔ **Mortgage-Calc,** www.mortgage-calc. com: This site boasts a variety of mortgage calculators that help buyers compare different loan offerings, determine whether it's better to rent or buy, and figure out how much they can borrow.

When buying a second home, you'll likely pay higher interest rates and down payments than you did for your first home because lenders know that during tough financial times a borrower is more likely to pay for his primary home and leave the second-home mortgage to languish.

To calculate how much home you can afford, use the same reasoning that you used when you purchased your primary residence. A simple online search for a "mortgage calculator" can provide you with many tools.

To the do-it-yourselfers: There is no simple, by-hand formula for calculating a monthly mortgage payment. (That's why God made banks and computers.) However, there is a "down-and-dirty" trick you can use to at least give you a sense of what kind of monthly payment you're looking at:

1 **Simply divide the *loan amount* by the *term of the loan in months*.**

    For example, a $180,000 loan divided by 360 (the number of months in a 30-year mortgage) comes out to $500 a month.

2. **Multiply that amount by 1.5 (for a 3 percent interest rate) to 3 or more (for a 10 percent rate and up).**

    Doing so can give you a fairly good estimate as to what you'll pay just on the loan, without escrow.

    And this trick works: At a 3 percent rate, multiplying that $500 by 1.5 gives you $750. And what do the amortization calculators come up with? $758.89. And with the 10 percent rate? Multiplying $500 by 3 gives you $1,500. The amortization calculators come up with $1,579.63.

The mathematically astute readers can easily work this formula to come up with a rough estimate for all the rates in between 3 and 10 percent. For the math-challenged, I suggest you pick up the phone or go online to use a mortgage calculator.

After you have your final monthly payment calculated, you need to add on a few more costs: insurance and tax payments, as well as any recurring monthly fees associated with the home, which normally include maintenance and the amount you expect to pay a property manager to maintain and rent out the home while you're not using it (if you opt for this route). Of course, you need to also be prepared for unexpected repair bills. Whether you're renting out the house or not, a kaput water heater needs to be replaced *now*.

If, for whatever reason, the numbers don't work for you, the next step is to revise your target home's sales price down. If, for example, that $750,000 single-family home in the golf course community is obviously out of reach, then you set your sights on the $500,000 condo in the same 'hood.

Considering the expenses

Before you make the final decision to jump into the second-home market-place, you need to have a complete grasp of the various costs associated with owning a second home. These expenses go beyond your monthly mort-gage payment, and keeping current with them is every bit as important as meeting that monthly commitment.

Homeowners' association fees

The Community Association Institute (CAI) has estimated that about 1 in 6 Americans lives in a community managed by a homeowners' association. If you've never owned a home that was part of a development or a complex, you may be surprised at the additional monthly expenses that come with owning a condo or home that's managed by an association. Depending on where you buy, you may have to pay monthly, quarterly, or biannual associa-tion fees that cover such expenses as general neighborhood upkeep, lawn maintenance, snow removal, water and sewer expenses, electricity (for park-ing lot lights, tennis court lights, and so on), and cable.

Be sure to ask about the types of fees you'll be expected to pay in your com-munity and factor these costs into the budget for your second home. Condos have particularly high fees that usually cover several expenses that you'd otherwise have to pay on your own (such as water and sewer or exterior maintenance). Single-family homes and townhouses command lower fees, with much of the maintenance responsibility falling on the owner's shoulders.

Maintenance: Inside and out

No matter where your second home is located, you'll have to maintain the property inside and outside. Your grass will certainly grow, filth will find your windows, and loose trash may occasionally blow into your front yard. Maintaining your second home is an ongoing task, and you need to factor all these types of maintenance issues into your budget.

For example, owning a house by the shore may be hip, but the reality is that maintaining such a dwelling can be tough on your checkbook. All it takes is one active hurricane season with its delightful driving rain and 75 miles per hour winds to take a toll on what was once a beautiful little home by the sea. The interiors of homes in close proximity to saltwater also need TLC. Even if your home isn't located near the shore, it still has regular maintenance requirements. Lawns, yards, and swimming pools all need regular upkeep and repair, with breakdowns often occurring at the most inopportune times.

Keep these realities in mind as you preview properties, and don't be afraid to ask the current owners about their maintenance routines. (They probably won't tell you about the negatives, but asking doesn't hurt.) Be sure to set aside funds every year for maintenance and repairs. You can do some of the maintenance and minor repairs yourself (for example, mowing the yard), and some things won't be necessary at all depending on where you buy (you don't need to shovel snow in Miami, right?). And even if you buy a condo in Vegas where you have condo fees to pay, you'll still deal with regular, permanent maintenance expenses one way or another.

Damages and repair costs

You keep your primary home looking good and running like a well-oiled machine, right? You need to take care of your second home with the same diligence and attention to detail. It needs to be kept in tiptop shape, free of damage, and in the best condition possible. This ensures that your investment is protected, and it also assures that your home is aesthetically pleasing to neighbors, guests, and renters. Always be prepared for those bills for necessary repairs that rear their heads unexpectedly.

Many homeowners' associations have a year's income in the bank as a reserve for . . . well, for whatever must be paid on behalf of the complex. As an individual homeowner, you likewise should have an emergency fund to pay for repair or replacement of appliances and heating and cooling systems. The fund should be equal to the cost of the worst possible immediate problem you may face. For example, what if your stove, washer, or refrigerator dies? What would it cost to replace them immediately? Estimating high is a smart move. What if your furnace, central air conditioning unit, or water heater self-destructs? You need to know what it's going to cost to get these necessities repaired, so have a fund to tap as needed.

To be sure that you're not caught unprepared, you may want to keep $500 to $3,000 in reserve for unexpected expenses. Of course, you can always put these expenses on a credit card, but if at all possible, you don't want to add to your credit card debt by paying for necessary repairs.

You can delegate just about all the maintenance duties on your second home to a property manager, but you're going to pay for her time, in addition to the actual costs of the services. Is your time worth more than the costs of these services? You need to decide that and act accordingly. (Check out Chapter 13 for more on hiring a property manager and the related fees.)

Homeowners' insurance

Homeowners' insurance comes in many different forms, depending on where you live and the type of home you buy. Furthermore, as the owner of a second home, you'll probably have to shell out more than you're used to paying for your primary home. More things can go wrong when the owner isn't present, and insurers factor this reality into their rates for second homes.

Location also plays a key role in insurance rates. For example, you can expect to spend more money on homeowners' insurance in higher-risk states, such as Florida, where hurricanes have created a rough market for current insurers. Along with the additional cost, you can expect to spend extra time finding insurance for homes in high-risk areas.

If you're buying a condo, your condo association fees will cover your homeowners' insurance, which includes liability and hazard coverage. But you must also take out your own *contents insurance* to cover your possessions and furniture. For more info on homeowners' insurance, check out Chapter 8. For now, just be aware of the need for and cost of this coverage and be sure to factor it into your buying decision.

Taxes of all kinds

Benjamin Franklin said the only things guaranteed in life are death and taxes, and the latter certainly holds true for owners of second homes. Taxes come in many forms. (Chapter 14 discusses in detail how second-home ownership can affect your tax situation.)

- ✔ **Property taxes:** You may not be living in the home full time, and you may not have kids attending the local school district, but you still have to help fill the municipality's coffers for the coming year, *every* year.

  Property taxes are based on a fixed proportion of the value of the property being taxed. The property owner pays these taxes; she is liable regardless of whether the home is used and whether it generates income. The good news is that these property taxes are almost always deductible on your federal income taxes.

- ✔ **Income taxes:** If you rent out your second home, remember that rental income is taxable income.

  Renting out your second home can impact your right to deduct property taxes on your tax return. Talk to your accountant.

- ✔ **Automobile registration taxes:** If you decide to register a vehicle at your second home's address, you should first determine what the vehicle taxes will be and compare that figure with what you're paying now. You may be better off keeping your cars registered at your primary address.

  Also, check your state statutes: Some states require a certain period of residency for automobile registration (and resulting taxation). Registering a car in a second home's state to save on taxes when you spend 50 weeks a year at your primary home may not be legal.

Traveling to and fro your new home

A final expense to consider when purchasing a second home is the transportation expense that you'll incur getting there on a regular basis. With fuel costs fluctuating wildly, think about the gas your vehicle requires to make the trek. Sure, gas may be (relatively) cheap one day, but one global crisis can send prices skyrocketing, and you can't avoid this expense.

You may face other travel expenses if your second home is far from your first home. If it's more than a day's drive, you need to factor lodging, meal costs, and the myriad expenses that always crop up when traveling. Are you flying to your second home? Consider the airline ticket, any parking fees, and ground transportation costs to get to and from the property.

How Are You Going to Pay for It?

You can pay for your second home in a variety of ways, although most second-home buyers stick with one of three strategies:

- ✔ They take out a mortgage for the second home.
- ✔ They pay with cash.
- ✔ They rent the home and use the rental money to pay a mortgage.

If your primary home is already paid off, then the challenge of juggling two mortgages isn't on your radar screen. Thoroughly review your finances, though, to be sure you're ready for a new mortgage, property taxes, homeowners' insurance, and repair/maintenance costs.

This section covers the pros and cons of paying cash for your second home, addresses the realities of having two mortgages at once, and suggests that renting the property can offset some of the associated expenses.

Twice isn't always nice: Two mortgage payments

If you get stressed every month when you receive that three- or four-figure mortgage statement in the mail, and your other house-related bills (for property taxes, homeowners' insurance, and so on) add to your mental strain, then you may want to think twice about taking out an additional mortgage.

Two mortgage payments can stretch a budget thin pretty quickly, so enter into a second-home mortgage with a full knowledge of your monthly budget and available financial resources.

The good news is that more and more people are buying second homes these days, and mortgage lenders are responding by offering a wide range of products and services to meet those needs. Still, you should expect to search a little longer for your second-home mortgage to find a good deal.

Don't leap at the first loan that comes your way. Take your time and find the right lender for your situation. A little extra legwork can save you money.

Laying down cold, hard cash

Another option you have when buying a second home is to lay down your hard-earned cash. Where can you come up with such a large sum of dinero? The following are your main options along with the concerns you must think about if you choose that option:

- ✔ **You can cash in your 401(k) or other retirement plan.** But before you do, check out the rules associated with cashing in early. Most plans charge a 10 percent penalty.

- ✔ **You can borrow from friends and family.** These folks can be great sources of funds if they're financially well situated and inclined to help. In exchange, maybe you can offer them annual use of your new pad. However, borrowing from a close relative or pal can create problems that you can avoid by relying on a third party that you're not so close to.

- ✔ **You can drain your savings and investment accounts.** Approach this option cautiously. Consider using only a portion of your savings and investment accounts for the new home, and saving the rest.

- ✔ **You can win the lottery or strike it big in Vegas.** Sorry, but I don't have a strategy for this option, but hey, if you strike it big, you may be able to buy a second, third, and even fourth home. (Can you dream Bora Bora or someplace exotic and serene?)

Paying your mortgage with rental income

If you don't have a lump sum of cash to purchase your second home and you don't have surplus income each month to pay the home's mortgage, you may decide to rent out your second home and use the rent payment to pay your second-home mortgage. With careful planning, your second home can be a lucrative investment that not only appreciates in value over time, but also creates a revenue stream as soon as you begin renting it out. (Chapter 11 discusses in more depth what you need to know if you decide to rent out your second home.)

If, for example, you have a $2,000 a month mortgage on a property in Denver, Colorado, you may well be able to charge $2,000 a month in rent (depending on the time of year and what the market will bear), which will completely cover the monthly mortgage payment. Understand, however, that insurance and taxes will also come due, and that repairs and maintenance may also be in order. Of course, if the area market rental prices are higher, the rental income may be able to cover these expenses. (Which, truth be told, is a very nice set of circumstances!)

Although a long-term rental offers you a sense of security that someone is living in and taking care of your second home (and the lease guarantees income for a specific amount of time), short-term rentals in vacation spots can be particularly lucrative. The downside is that these units fetch the best rates (and are in most demand) mostly during certain seasons, and their pricing depends on their location and size. A two-bedroom, two-bath condo in Honolulu, Hawaii, for example, rents for $2,500 a week during the high season, while a three-bedroom, two-bath townhouse in Clearwater, Florida, rents for that much per month during the area's high season.

With proper planning, smart research, and a keen awareness of what appeal your second home has for renters, donning a landlord's hat can help ease the financial burden of paying for your second home.

Chapter 3

Considering Your Second-Home Options

*F*or a second-home buyer, the world is a cornucopia of home choices. You can choose from scores of different home styles, from detached single-family homes and townhouses, to condominiums and mobile homes. You can buy undeveloped land on which to build a new home, and if none of those options suit you, you can consider alternative ownership options.

This chapter covers the many different varieties of second homes and the pluses and minuses of each. With everything from basic structural elements to lifestyle preferences playing important roles in your ultimate selection, this chapter is where you can really nail down exactly what you are — and aren't — looking for in a second home.

Narrowing Your Options: What Do You Want?

Buying a second home can be a lot like buying a new car: Either you look around the lot and take what's available, or you dig a little deeper and ferret out a style, color, and model that you *really* want. You go through the same process when you're looking for a second home. If you're not too picky, you may be happy in a home that's already available. Sometimes getting what you want means you may have to wait several months for the home of your dreams to be built. Other times, you may have to be patient until a home with the right features in the right area hits the market. But whether you decide to select from what's available or wait, the point is the same: To get what you want, you need to *know* what you want.

To help you clearly spell out exactly what you're looking for in a second home, complete the following worksheet. Then use your criteria to review the various options available in your market and find the perfect second home. If you need more info about any of the different types of second homes, see the corresponding section in this chapter. Feel free to write in this book or make a copy of this questionnaire. Answer the questions and use your answers as a checklist or give the worksheet to your real estate agent for use during your home search.

Narrowing Your Options Worksheet

1. **What type of second home would you like to purchase? (Check the ones that apply.)**

   ❑ Single-family detached

   ❑ Townhouse

   ❑ Condominium

   ❑ Co-op

   ❑ Manufactured house

   ❑ Mobile home

   ❑ Undeveloped land to build on

   ❑ Timeshare

   ❑ Fractional ownership

   ❑ Rent before buy

   ❑ Other

2. **What features are you looking for?**

   • Minimum number of bedrooms: _____

   • Minimum number of bathrooms: _____

   • Total living area: _____ square feet

   • Total outside living area (decks, patios, and so on): _____ square feet

   • Basement: _____ square feet

   • Lot size: _____

   • Handicapped accessible? _____

   • Size of garage (how many cars): _____

3. **How old would you like your second home to be? (Check one.)**

   ❑ Brand spankin' new

   ❑ Less than 5 years old

   ❑ Less than 10 years old

   ❑ Less than 20 years old

   ❑ Less than 50 years old

   ❑ Less than 100 years old

   ❑ More than 100 years old

4. **Taking accessibility into account, would you like a home with multiple floors or a single floor? _____**

5. **What is your desired price range?**

   ❑ Under $150,000

   ❑ $151,000 to $250,000

   ❑ $251,000 to $350,000

   ❑ More than $351,000

6. **How often do you plan to use your second home each year?**

   ❑ Every weekend

   ❑ Once a month

   ❑ Once a quarter

   ❑ Once a year

   ❑ Other _____

7. **What do you see yourself using this second home for (skiing, seaside vacations, golfing, and so on)?**

   _____

8. **Which of the following amenities *must* your second home have? (Check all that apply.)**

   ❑ Central air

   ❑ Close proximity to arts/cultural venues

   ❑ Composite countertops in the kitchen

   ❑ Deck

   ❑ High ceilings

   ❑ Hot tub

❑ Laundry facilities

❑ Private pool

❑ Security system

❑ Waterfront or lakefront location

9. **Do you plan to rent out your second home? If yes, what other amenities or features do you believe will improve the home's chance of fetching the highest rent possible?**

_____

10. **What other elements or features not previously cited are important to you as you begin your home search?**

_____

Single-Family Homes: The Most Popular Option

Most people, whether buying a primary or secondary residence, buy a single-family home. Detached from any other residential structures, _single-family homes_ are usually landscaped with grass, trees, and flowers, and often include a garage and an attic. In many states, they may also have basements. In this section, I go over your basic options when purchasing single-family homes for use as vacation pads.

You as the one-and-only, original owner

As I write this, there's no time like the present to purchase a new second home. The real estate boom of the early 2000s resulted in an overabundance of new homes — particularly in areas where home values appreciate quickly, such as vacation spots. The good news for you is that builders have a surplus of new homes — many of which are competing with existing properties — that they need to unload. And because the market is more stable than it was a few years ago, you now have more choices and negotiating room when it comes to buying a new home.

If you buy a newly constructed home, you'll pay more for your second home than if you were to buy an existing home because of rising construction costs and the expensive modern elements that new homes often feature. Nonetheless, if gorgeous granite countertops, energy-efficient stainless steel appliances with all the bells and whistles, and stunning floors made of Italian tile are on your must-have list, then a new home may be your best fit and right choice.

Remember that even though new homes usually include many exciting features and modern conveniences, they're not perfect. Chapter 7 discusses the inspection process and what to look for, and look out for, when purchasing a new home.

The age factor: Modern, older, or historic

When buying a second home, do you need to consider when it was built and how old it is? It really depends. The age of a second home matters less than the owner's personal preferences and ability to maintain the structure. Comfort is king, and even if a home has every convenience and feature imaginable, it won't matter one whit if you don't look forward to going there and don't love being there. For example, to some individuals, a 150-year-old, historic home in downtown Philadelphia is the perfect getaway. For others, a 2-year-old, single-family abode with modern appliances and delightful amenities in West Palm Beach, Florida, is old enough for their liking.

An older home may ooze charm and warmth, and perhaps even nostalgia for bygone days if you buy something in the 100-year-old category (either you love or hate those separate bathroom sink faucets, right?), but the house may require too much upkeep for the out-of-state owner who uses it twice a year. Be sure to consider the maintenance factor before you fall in love with that quaint seaside abode that constantly gets buffeted by ocean spray, or the 19th-century Victorian that needs a new roof and exterior painting, and maybe a furnace one of these days. (Check out Chapter 13 for more on maintenance and upkeep issues.)

Don't dismiss older homes that need work if you're handy enough to do the repairs and improvements and you have the required time to do them. Being able to handle tasks like plumbing and carpentry jobs on your own opens the field of second homes. If you have a toolbox that could be on display at your favorite home improvement store, then by all means have at it!

Sizing up your square-feet needs

A 1,200-square-foot single-family home may be plenty of room to live in for some people, but that "smallish" home can get pretty crowded pretty quickly for others. Before you buy, think about the typical number of people who will use the home at one time, and consider their personal space needs. Here are some scenarios to think about concerning size:

✔ If you, your spouse, and two children are, for the most part, comfortable and happy in a 1,500-square-foot primary home, then a smaller vacation place will probably suffice.

- ✔ If your family loves its sprawling 6,000-square-foot, multifloor home in the country, then a beach house with plenty of room (2,500 square feet or more) would be a good choice.

- ✔ If your family often brings extended family and friends on vacation, then size matters — *a lot*. For the sake of everyone's nerves and the desire to avoid family feuds, opt for a larger home where everyone can be comfortable and not squished together like sardines.

Depending on your square footage needs, you want to make sure everyone who visits and uses your second home is comfortable and relaxed. Keep the two following points in mind when thinking about square footage:

- ✔ **Consider issues like kitchen and family room space when checking out homes.** Guests tend to congregate in these areas the most while on vacation. You don't want to buy a home that has a tiny kitchen and family room if you have a large family or group of friends who won't have anywhere to sit. Although if the trade-off is larger bedrooms, then it may be worth considering.

- ✔ **Make sure you have enough bathrooms and bedrooms.** You can never have too many bathrooms. Let me repeat that. *You can never have too many bathrooms.* (Make a pit stop at the next section.)

Counting up the all-important bathrooms and bedrooms

Does the number of bathrooms and bedrooms really matter for your second home? When thinking about these rooms, think in terms of the *minimum* number of bathrooms and bedrooms you find acceptable, as opposed to an exact number. This way, you won't risk missing out on a great house because it has one too *many* rooms.

A good rule for bathrooms: Start with one full and one half bath. No matter what the size of your family, this arrangement allows you to play the odds that more than two people won't need the bathroom *at the exact same time.* It may happen, of course, but that extra half bath really takes the pressure off.

When considering how many bedrooms and bathrooms your second home needs, remember the following before making your decision:

- ✔ **Choose the number of bedrooms and bathrooms in your second home based on the size and needs of your family.** Can two younger brothers share a room? Does your teenage daughter insist on her own bathroom or she'll "just die!?" A good rule: You need one bathroom for every three individuals in the home. So if six people live there, have at least two bathrooms.

Your own situation dictates how many bedrooms and bathrooms you need in your second home. If you, your spouse, your three children, and your two dogs (no insult intended to cats, of course, but they tend to be much lower maintenance animals) are comfortable back home in a four-bedroom, two-bath casa, then something along those lines should be just fine for your second home.

✔ **Factor in the needs of any guests whom you plan on bringing along on a regular basis.** Will it be a problem when Grandma, who's bunking on the first floor, needs to climb the stairs to use the bathroom in the middle of the night? If so, look for a home with first-floor facilities.

✔ **Consider the features that are likely to appeal to potential renters.** If you're going to use your second home as an investment property and rent it (check out Chapter 11), convenience, privacy, and comfort should be your watchwords when looking at a second home.

✔ **Look to the future.** Your second home's resale value will probably be higher if the number of bedrooms is equal to — or close to — the total number of bathrooms in the home. The convenience of having one bathroom per bedroom is perceived as a plus to buyers.

These days, a single-family home with at least three bedrooms and two bathrooms is highly desirable. Those homes with fewer of each tend to fetch lower prices or take longer to sell. If you plan to retire to your second home and not sell it in the foreseeable future, these issues won't matter as much as the comfort of you and your family does. If cleaning just one bathroom is more than enough, thank you very much, and you and your family have functioned with one loo just fine (the occasional door pounding and "I can't hold it!" and "You've been in there all day!" incidents notwithstanding), then feel free to buy that three-bedroom, one-bath unit being offered at a great price.

If you need to double up in certain rooms while you're on vacation, bunk beds, rollaway beds, air mattresses, and even sleeping bags are always an option for the younger kids (who may be at that age when sleeping on the floor is still considered an adventure and not something that will result in the need for a chiropractor!). In other words, even if you don't buy that four-bedroom home, with some creative accommodations you can still use your two-bedroom condo to its fullest potential when guests come over!

Time to level: One story versus multiple stories

If you want to buy a single-family home, you need to consider how many stories you want. Single-story and multiple-story homes both have their advantages. Keep these points in mind while compiling your criteria list for your second home:

✔ **Single-story homes** are conveniently designed and very accessible for those owners and guests who may need special assistance going up and down flights of stairs, or who just hate climbing stairs.

Retirees, especially, find these homes to be very attractive. Families with young children may also feel more comfortable in a single-level home, where mishaps like falling down the stairs are easily avoided. (But keep that door to the basement closed!) (Check out the next section for issues to consider between homes with basements and homes with slabs.) If you have a single-story home in mind, then you should have no problem finding a home that fits your budget.

✔ **Multiple-story homes** are attractive from the outside and afford enhanced privacy, especially if the living spaces and some of the bedrooms are separated from an upstairs master suite.

Multi-story homes are great fun to own on the water, overlooking golf courses, and tucked into the sides of ski slopes — pretty much anywhere there's a view. In these areas, you'll find high demand for homes where you can sit or stand on a deck and take in the sights. Expect to pay more for these single-family homes, which is understandable, considering their allure.

Guess what? They come back

Your kids may be "officially" out of the house, but there's "officially" and then there's *really* "officially."

Just because their rooms are empty *right now* doesn't mean you should immediately move into that cute — but small — studio apartment in New York City. Know this well, my friends: Just because the kids have left does *not* mean they won't come back. It could be for a visit, or it could be (dare I say it) permanent. And this homecoming is always because of their life circumstances: They graduated but can't get a job; they're married but have separated; their new business ain't makin' it and they can't afford to pay rent. And so forth. I'm sure you can come up with your own "circumstances."

So, instead of downsizing your lifestyle to the point where only you and your spouse can fit in the new place, consider a second home that can accommodate another individual or couple comfortably for a week (or more, if necessary).

This way, when daughter Joan graduates from college and needs to stay somewhere for the summer, you won't get the guilties when she has to stay at a friend's house — or in a short-term rental you know she can't afford.

The advice is simple: Live for yourself and enjoy your retirement years in your second home, but try to always leave a little room for loved ones who may need you down the road.

Basement or slab? Is one better?

In some areas of the country, you won't have much of a choice between homes with basements and homes with slabs. Homes in Florida, for example, are nearly always built on slabs, while those in the mountains of Pennsylvania almost assuredly will have basements.

If you do have a choice in the matter, opt for the one that gives you the most benefits. If you need the extra storage or living space, for example, then a basement home will work best. But if you're looking for a low-maintenance home with plenty of aboveground space, then a slab will do the trick.

Condos: Fun in the Sun (Or Snow) without the Yard Work

If you want a low-maintenance lifestyle — where someone else cuts the grass, cleans the pool, removes the snow, and maybe even pays the water bill — a condominium just may be your perfect pad.

What exactly is a condo? In a *condo,* you live wall-to-wall with your neighbors. You don't actually own the land under the condo, but rather share it with other owners. Legally speaking, you own one unit in a multiunit building. You and the other condo unit owners jointly own portions of the common elements, which include the roof, hallways, swimming pool, fitness center, parking lot, and so on. Put simply, a condo is like owning an apartment rather than renting it. Condos have their limitations, though. This section discusses the pros and cons of purchasing a condo as a second home.

The advantages of condo living

Not surprisingly, a large percentage of condo owners are seasonal residents, especially in vacation areas. Instead of letting their single-family second homes sit empty most of the year, hoping that the landscaper shows up and something major doesn't break, people who choose condos as their second home can rest a bit easier. They know that their condos (many of which have controlled access to the grounds) are taken care of under the watchful eye of their neighbors and property managers.

A condo may be good choice if you're

- ✔ Only able to get away to your second home a few times a year, for short periods.

- ✔ Interested in having a pool, tennis court, and fitness center — but aren't interested in maintaining them.

- ✔ Not at all interested in managing the upkeep of a second home.

- ✔ Unconcerned about the possibility of hearing other people's comings, goings, music, and noises.

- ✔ Keen on living on a high floor in a stack of condos.

- ✔ Enthused at the thought of having neighbors close by with whom you can socialize and rely on for safety and security reasons.

The low-maintenance and usually more affordable condo lifestyle can serve as a perfect stepping stone for a second-home buyer who isn't ready to purchase a single-family home.

The drawbacks to condo living

Owning a condo does have its drawbacks, as many owners will tell you. For starters, you're going to share at least one wall, probably two, and maybe even a ceiling and/or a floor, with other residents. Sounds that wouldn't make it from one single-family home to another, for example, can carry quite well from unit to unit in a condo. If your neighbors on the right have a brawl, you'll know it. If your neighbors on the left have a particularly powerful sound system, you'll hear it. If they're moving out upstairs, you'll feel it. You get the picture.

Think twice about that condo if you

- ✔ Don't like the idea of using an elevator to get to your home.

- ✔ Have a green thumb and/or love having a backyard to hang out in.

- ✔ Want your own pool or hot tub.

- ✔ Desire a large amount of square footage and the ability to expand the home's size in the future.

- ✔ Want to barbecue on your own deck, lanai, or patio. Some condos have strict rules on this issue. (See the section, "For the good of all: Rules for condo owners," in this chapter for more on condo rules and regulations.)

✔ Don't want to pay for community-wide repairs and upgrades through unexpected assessments. (See the next section for more info on fees.)

✔ Plan to resell your condo in the near future. (Condos can take longer to sell than single-family homes.)

✔ Are the upgrading type and like to modify your home. Commonly, condo bylaws restrict what you can and can't do to your unit. Adding a bathroom, removing or shortening a wall, or doing anything else that may affect the building's structural integrity is usually prohibited. (You can bring proposed modification before the condo association board, of course, but if an architect's evaluation is required before they'll approve a remodeling, you'll be the one paying the architect's bill.)

Pay up: Condo fees and taxes

As a condo owner, you must pay monthly or quarterly *condo fees* that cover the cost of general repairs and routine maintenance expenses for the complex's common areas. The money collected from each owner goes into a fund and is used to pay the monthly bills and to build a reserve for other uses, including immediate and emergency repairs, and capital improvements, like painting, parking lot resurfacing, and roof repairs. Fees vary widely from complex to complex depending on each development's situation, so be sure to talk to the current owner or your real estate agent about exactly what you will be expected to pay each month.

So condo fees are a double-edged sword. On one hand, your lawn maintenance, snow removal, and sometimes even your cable bill is taken care of. On the other hand, condo owners incur a fixed cost that stays in place until they sell their unit. It's convenience versus control: Things are taken care of, but you have no real control over the costs.

A board of directors, which you as a condo owner elect, oversees the fees and spending. Condo owners also pay property taxes on their individual units, and the municipality's tax collector assesses their unit individually. (See Chapter 14 for more on property taxes.)

Condo fees are "must pay" obligations. Legally, they carry the weight of a mortgage payment or a tax bill, and a condo association can, in most states, foreclose on a unit owner who is six months or more in arrears on his condo fees. And some condo bylaws allow only *three* months of nonpayment before foreclosure kicks in.

What happens when major work is needed?

When you own a condo, you share the ownership of the land with the other condo owners. So what happens if the property needs a new concrete sidewalk, tile roof, or parking lot resurfacing that isn't covered by the reserve fund? Or what if the board decides not to drain the reserve fund for one capital project? Guess what? You and the other condo owners will be *assessed* for the costs. The project's total cost is divided equally between the condo owners. If the condo building needs a new roof that will cost $50,000, for example, and if there are 100 owners, then each owner will have to pay $500 on top of any other regular fees that are due.

To ease the financial strain, condo owners often are allowed to make monthly payments toward the assessment. If an individual owner's share is $500, the board can decide to allow six months to collect the money, which would only add $85 or so to your monthly condo fee. This is possible, though, only if the reserve fund is adequate to pay the repair bill in a timely fashion, or if the contractor gives the association extended payment terms.

All interior repairs and upgrades are the condo owner's responsibility and aren't covered by the condo association fees.

For the good of all: Rules for condo owners

Because condo units are so close to one another, owners must follow rules and regulations that make for peaceful cohabitation. You receive a copy of these rules (known as the *bylaws*) before you close on your condo so you can review them. You must follow them or risk getting warnings, fines, and other ugly stuff in your mailbox if you don't. (Not to mention you'll tick off your neighbors.) So although you have to obey some rules, you and your neighbors benefit from regulations that are meant to keep any one owner from interfering with another owner's peaceful enjoyment of his home. And, in a sense, condo bylaws are a comfort. How? No single owner is alone. An owner can always go to the board with problems and questions. And the board always has access to professionals like lawyers, accountants, and inspectors if they're needed.

Some of the most common condo rules include

- ✔ Abiding by the hours of operation for certain community amenities. Pools may be open from 9 a.m. to 9 p.m., for instance, which means midnight skinny dips are not only not encouraged, but forbidden (no matter how much fun they are!).

- ✔ Restricting barbecues and other fire-related activities to community areas where common equipment is sometimes provided for your use. (You may want to bring some grill cleaner with you!)

✔ Keeping the noise level down during *quiet times,* which is commonly defined as the hours between midnight and 8 a.m. This ensures that your party-gal neighbor doesn't blast heavy metal through the hallways at 2 a.m. after a night of clubbing.

✔ Not renting out your condo to a third party for less than a specific period of time. This can range from one week to as much as six months, depending on the bylaws.

✔ Making sure that all renters abide by the condo bylaws. You, the owner, are responsible for assuring that they do.

✔ Maintaining a specified speed limit in the parking lot and driving areas. Also, the number of vehicles a unit owner may have on the grounds is often spelled out in the bylaws.

The list goes on, and many of the bylaws are just basic common sense. If, however, you have a problem with one more of the rules, you may want to reconsider your choice of location. Condo bylaws are determined and enforced by the board and can be difficult to change unless you have a high percentage of residents in your corner, ready to fight for the cause. And the odds are against that, because condo bylaws are designed for the good of everyone, and a single unit owner who wants something changed for his benefit is likely to get a chilly response from the neighbors.

Townhouses: Your Own Home and Land (Really) Close to Neighbors

If you want a little grass around your new place, but aren't interested in a single-family home, then you should consider a townhouse for your second home. This section covers the legal and physical characteristics of townhouses and discusses some of the issues associated with this property.

What exactly is a townhouse?

A *townhouse* is one of a series of single- or multi-story units attached to one another by common walls. Yes, townhouses look a lot like condominiums. Some townhouse communities, on the other hand, are designed to look like single-family homes. These types feature just two or three units in their own building. Other types of townhouse complexes consist of many units that are linked in a long row. A townhouse can be a great choice for the second-home buyer who isn't interested in a condo, but who doesn't want the responsibility of owning a single-family home.

Townhouses differ from condos and mimic single-family homes in their ownership structure. Townhouse owners hold title to their individual units *plus* the land that lies beneath them. Unlike condos, townhouses can't be stacked on top of one another, so you'll never have anyone living above or below you.

Townhouse owners pay property taxes on their individual units, which are managed by a property or homeowners' association that collects monthly or quarterly fees used to maintain the common areas (such as the grass, pools, and fitness centers). In this way — and in the fact that maintenance fees cover exterior maintenance and major repairs — townhouses are similar to condominium complexes. And like owning a condo, you definitely have to pay a plumber if your toilet clogs, but you don't have to pay a roofer if you end up with a leak in the master bedroom.

Owning a townhouse: Issues and benefits to consider

As do all things in life, townhouses come with their own pros and cons. Many of the same downsides to condo ownership (refer to the section, "The drawbacks to condo living," earlier in this chapter) apply to townhouses. Unlike condos, townhouses typically have small backyard retreats and other outside spaces where you can entertain and relax. These features make townhouses especially attractive for second-home buyers who are looking for the comforts of home without the responsibility of owning a detached dwelling.

Like condos, townhouses generally have less interior space than single-family homes. ***Note:*** The "bigger and bigger homes" trend is changing this notion because more townhouses are now being built in the 2,000- to 3,000-square-foot range. Also, townhouses don't allow for future expansion. And another point to remember is that reselling them can take longer than it would to sell a single-family home, because certain buyers steer clear of such options.

Mobile Homes: More Than a Trailer

If having an affordable, low-maintenance second home is at the top of your shopping list, you may want to consider a mobile home. A mobile home has no permanent foundations and can be moved from one mobile home park to another. They've come a long way from the days when the world knew them as nothing but boxy, single-wide trailers traversing the nation's highways. Today, the newer versions of mobile homes are fully updated and built from top-quality materials. Many models include the latest amenities like floor-to-ceiling windows and screened-in porches.

Today's mobile homes are also wider than their predecessors, and many are undeniably attractive inside and out. As has been the case for homes without wheels, aluminum siding has given way to more attractive vinyl siding for mobile homes, and some units feature carports and long driveways.

This section points out what's good and what's not so good about owning a mobile home and offers some valuable tips and warnings about purchasing this style of home.

Where to look: Your main options

If you think a mobile home is your ideal second home, you want to know where to look, right? This section helps. Most mobile homes are situated in mobile home parks, where multiple owners use the land in one of two ways:

- **They own the land under and around the home outright.** This option is the optimal one: It solidifies the mobile home owner's place in the park and in the municipality where the park is located.

- **They lease land from the park's owner.** In some areas, leasing a spot in a mobile home park may be the only option, but you should understand that it's not the *best* option. Why? Because the park owners can raise lease fees at any time, and the owners may sell the park, which also often results in higher lease fees. (See the "Potential problems with a mobile home" section for more details on the downsides.)

If you have your eye on a mobile home in a rural area, then chances are good that the unit won't be situated in a park, but on a plot of land. Because you own the land plus the home, this option provides great flexibility if you're considering eventually removing the mobile home to make way for a new single-family dwelling.

Before buying a mobile home, thoroughly investigate the park where your mobile home is located by talking both to residents and to the park owner. (Don't expect the seller to reveal too much, though.) High land costs have created a hot market for land used for mobile home parks, and many park owners are leaving their mobile home lessees high and dry by selling out to commercial buyers who want to build condos and other structures on the land. Then what? Check out the area and the scuttlebutt about the possible changes in the park's future before committing.

If you're buying an existing mobile home in Florida, whether in a mobile home park or not, look for one that was built after 1992, the year of Hurricane Andrew. That storm inflicted substantial damage on mobile homes in the southeastern portion of the state, and since then, building codes have been upgraded to reflect the need for more-robust mobile home construction.

Pros of owning a mobile home

When you first think of a mobile home, images of small, dingy trailers along a county road or in an overcrowded trailer park with loud kids running around may pop into your mind. However, in the right setting, mobile homes can make the perfect vacation or seasonal getaway and can be a good choice for the right buyer. Owning a mobile home does have three significant advantages:

- ✔ **Lower cost:** Mobile homes cost less and have lower property taxes and insurance rates.

- ✔ **Convenience:** They're always one story, which is great for people with mobility issues.

- ✔ **Total control:** As the name implies, you can move your mobile home to another location. If you tire of visiting California and decide you'd rather have a second home in Las Vegas, you can find a mobile home park or piece of land in Sin City, secure your home and its contents, and find a mover to transport house and all to your new address.

Potential problems with a mobile home

As affordable and convenient as they are, mobile homes come with their share of challenges and, yes, drawbacks. Here are a few to consider:

- ✔ **Structural integrity:** The structural integrity isn't equal to that of a single-family or attached home, although newer mobile homes are said to last longer and withstand the elements much better than their predecessors. However, if the mobile home is located in a hurricane-prone area, you'll be the first to evacuate, and you may not have much to come home to after the storm has passed.

- ✔ **Expensive to move:** Moving a mobile home to a new park or location isn't cheap.

- ✔ **Different interest rates:** Because mobile homes are classified as *personal* and not *real* property, they are often financed by using loans with interest rates that are higher than mortgage interest rates.

- ✔ **Quick loss in value:** A mobile home can lose a significant portion of its value within just a few years of being built, making long-term loans burdensome on owners who can't recoup their investment.

- ✔ **Stricter local zoning regulations:** Certain cities and counties may prohibit mobile homes within their jurisdiction, thus leading owners to put their homes in inferior or undesirable locations.

- ✔ **More difficult to sell:** Selling a mobile home may take time because the number of buyers looking to purchase this style of home may be limited.

Buying Land and Building a New Home

Building a home from scratch is generally considered to be the most expensive, time-intensive, and, some say, frustrating way to buy a second home. You acquire the *undeveloped land* (with or without sewers, gas, electricity, and such), potentially hire an architect, and build the house from scratch.

In this section, I walk you through the basics of this time-honored American tradition, discuss buying a prefabricated home, and help you understand what really goes into building a second home from the ground up. (Sorry. I meant from *below* the ground up, because you'll also have to take care of pouring a foundation!) If you're really serious about building your own home after reading this section, check out *Building Your Own Home For Dummies* by Kevin Daum, Janice Brewster, and Peter Economy (Wiley).

Going the contractor route

If money is no object and a new, custom-designed home is what you absolutely must have, then a new second home built on a piece of purchased land is the way to go. After selecting your location (for more about finding the right location, see Chapter 4), you'll then scout around for the best new-home builder you can find — the contractor who will help you bring your dream to fruition.

Finding a reputable contractor

Before you break ground on that new home, you'll want to put some time into finding the right company to handle the job. Here are a few ways to find a contractor:

- Ask for referrals from family, friends, colleagues, and business associates who have had personal experiences with specific builders in the area.
- Check out your local newspapers and business journals for published feedback on the company and its performance.
- Call the local Better Business Bureau and ask if any complaints have been filed against the particular builder.
- Drive around and look at homes that the contractor has already built.
- Talk to homeowners who have recently worked with the builder. The builder should be able to supply you with a list of referrals you can contact.

Asking the right questions

After you develop a short list of potential contractors, take the time to interview each one extensively. By asking the contractors the following types of questions, you can find out a lot about their experience and which one is right for you.

- ✔ **How many houses have you built?** The more the merrier. The contractor who has successfully built dozens of houses is a wiser pick than someone just starting out.

- ✔ **How many years have you been building homes?** Experience counts. So you can truly feel a level of confidence if the contractor you're considering tells you he just celebrated his 25th year in the business.

- ✔ **How realistic are your time estimates?** This one may be a toughie in terms of getting a straight answer, but it's worth asking anyway. If the contractor tells you his track record is excellent and that he more often completes jobs on time rather than late, then seriously consider him.

After you choose: Working with and negotiating

After you decide which contractor to use, you'll likely have several phone and in-person meetings with him (and possibly members of the contractor's team) during which you'll discuss floor plans (stock, customized, or hybrids of the two), timetables, the construction process, and what specific amenities and features are — and aren't — included in the price.

With the homebuilding industry coming off a multiyear boom, now is the time to negotiate hard for the extra features and amenities that you want in your new home. If you want a specific upgrade (such as granite countertops rather than laminate), don't be afraid to ask. If you do have to pay for them, haggle with the builder until you get to a price that you're comfortable paying. Get these negotiations taken care of upfront, not after the home is built.

When actually negotiating, my best advice is to do your homework and try to get a sense of what the feature you want generally costs. This exercise is worthwhile. Prices can be all over the place. A friend of mine once needed a foundation crack sealed and was quoted prices ranging from $50 to $600. Sure, that's for a repair, but the principle is the same and applies to new builds: materials and labor. So ask around, go online, and then throw out a figure you feel is fair and reasonable and make it clear that you won't pay higher.

Putting up a prefab

You can considerably trim the cost of putting up a new second home by going *prefab,* a nifty abbreviation that stands for *prefabricated home.* The pieces for these homes are built at a factory. Then the pieces, called panels or *modules* (which is why these homes often are referred to as *modular homes*), are delivered to your property where they're assembled to form your home. Prefab homes are considered single-family homes, but unlike a traditional home, they require far less onsite construction time because the components of the house are premade.

Prefab homes are generally less expensive than traditional single-family homes, but you get as much bang for your buck. When it comes to the home's design, you usually select one of the home designer's standard available floor plans, although custom variations are usually also possible. Many of today's models have been carefully and beautifully designed by architects who engineer them in such a way that the typical passerby can't even tell that your second home is a modular.

The bottom line? For the second-home buyer who owns land and isn't interested in a mobile home or in building from scratch, prefabs can be the perfect solution. One important caution, though: Be sure to check upfront about the feasibility of connecting to utilities like water, storm sewers, electrical lines, and sanitary sewers before you buy the parcel (if you think one day you'll probably build on it), or before you visit your prefab dealer so you can answer these questions when they come up.

Considering costs

Not sure yet if you want to build from scratch or put up a prefab? If cost is an issue, then prefab may be just the ticket, because these homes generally cost 20 to 30 percent less than custom-built homes. And because time is money, consider that a prefab home can be ready for move-in up to six months sooner than a custom-built home.

When erected and maintained properly, prefab homes hold their value and appreciate at the same rate as the traditionally constructed homes around them. And if you're purchasing a home and land together — or if you already own the land and place the home on it — you should have no problem finding a lender who will offer you a traditional mortgage at the market rate. If money isn't your primary concern and you want a lot of custom features, then building a new house will come much closer to fulfilling your dreams. Just be sure to get regular updates from your contractor on costs that are being incurred as those extras are added.

No matter if you choose to build a custom home from scratch or put up a prefab, you need to be aware of the following costs.

Buying the land

Before you actually start on the house, you need to buy the land. But how does one buy land? By the parcel. And my advice is to start with a pro. Talk to a real estate agent and have handy the following info:

- ✔ The cities or towns where you want the lot located
- ✔ How much you want to spend
- ✔ How big a lot you're looking for
- ✔ What your future plans are for the lot (for example, build and sell what you build, build and live there, sell later at a profit)
- ✔ How "developed" (trees cleared, sewers nearby, for example) the parcel needs to be

With this info, the agent can scour the Multiple Listing Service (MLS) land listings and come up with parcels for you to consider. Then when you find that acre you like, it's back to basics: financing, building, and everything else that goes with committing to a second home.

Getting the building fees and permits

After you buy the land and before you can build, your builder needs to secure the necessary permits and comply with any zoning or building regulations set forth by your city and/or county. If your builder isn't handling this aspect of the process, be sure to check with your local building and zoning department for specific requirements and guidelines.

Landscaping your grounds

Plopping a home down in the middle of piece of land just isn't enough these days. (Not to mention the danger of structural damage from indiscriminate plopping. Never a good idea.) Homeowners today strive to create a pleasing environment outside their homes, and that costs money.

Consider the following issues when landscaping your second home, and determine how much you really want to spend:

- ✔ **How often are you going to be there?** If you're not going to be at your second home at least once a month to mow, weed, and garden, then select low-maintenance ground cover and trees.

- ✔ **What do the neighbors have in their yards?** Odds are they've learned what works by trial and error, saving you the time. If your second home will be near other homes, you'll want to create a landscape that blends well with and complements the rest of the neighborhood, while still maintaining a unique look for your own yard.

- ✔ **What grows well in the area?** You don't want to plant palm trees in Colorado or gigantic oaks in coastal Florida. Can you grow hibiscus in Hawaii? Do some research in books or check online to figure out what species of plants and trees are native to the area and grow well in the various seasons. (And yes, you can grow hibiscus in Hawaii. It's the state flower!)

✔ **Do you want to maintain your grounds yourself?** For $60 to $200 a month (depending on the size of your lot and the complexity of the landscaping), you can hire a crew to take care of the grounds maintenance for you. (Check out Chapter 13 for more info.)

Understanding the time investment

When you buy an existing second home, you can usually start using it the day of closing, or in some cases, 60 to 90 days after you sign a contract. New homes don't work that way. Even prefab homes can take longer than expected to complete. Custom, onsite homes can be held up for months because of bad weather, material shortages, and other issues beyond your control.

You should expect a new home that you're building from scratch to take about a year or longer to construct. Expect a prefab home to take at least six months from concept to completion. Be sure to add a few months of cushion into your own schedule to avoid last-minute stress (and other problems) when the original finish date passes and construction continues. Because you're not buying a primary home, you may want to put off those furniture purchases and family gatherings until you know for sure when you'll have the keys in hand.

Contemplating Other Options If You Don't Want to Buy Outright

If, after reading this chapter, you decide not to purchase a second home after all, that doesn't mean that you're completely out of the game. In fact, you're in luck because you have several other options available. In this section, you can find out more about partnerships, timeshares, fractional ownership opportunities, and rent-before-you-buy options.

Partnership

Also known as *co-ownership,* a *partnership* consists of several individuals or families who purchase a second home together and share the costs and use of the property. Each of the partners owns a specific percentage of the property, and everyone's names are included on the title and deed as owners. If the property is financed, they each act as a co-borrower on the mortgage.

Even if your "partner" is a family member, a handshake just won't cut it. To protect yourself, use a written, detailed co-ownership agreement that covers costs, usage rights, and responsibilities — including default and dissolution — among the various partners.

When you want to cooperate

If New York City's Broadway plays, Central Park, and its other cultural attractions (not to mention its restaurants!) make the Big Apple your favorite getaway, then you need to know about cooperatives or *co-ops*. Concentrated in New York and a few other large cities, these properties look like condos or apartments, but are set up quite differently when it comes to legal ownership.

In a cooperative, the title to all associated real estate is held by a corporation, rather than its individual shareholders (that is, the property owners). To buy a co-op, you purchase stock in that corporation (much like you do when buying stock in a company) and become a shareholder.

Each shareholder holds a lease to the unit for the life of the corporation and can sell this interest at any time. The corporation pays the property taxes and mortgages, and the shareholders pay a monthly fee to cover these expenses, plus the costs required for unit maintenance and operation. An administrative board elected by the shareholders is called upon to approve new co-op shareholders before they can buy into the complex.

For more about cooperatives, check out the National Association of Housing Cooperatives' Web site (www.coophousing.org), which includes resources for those looking to buy into a housing co-op.

Timeshare

When full ownership of a second home isn't feasible, a *timeshare* (or *interval ownership*) can be a viable option, especially for those who truly enjoy visiting the same area every year for a set amount of time. When you own a timeshare, you pay for only the time you use it each year, and you become the exclusive owner of those *intervals.* You're the outright owner of the unit, for which you hold the deed that allows you to rent, sell, exchange, bequeath, or give away the weeks just as you can do as the outright owner of a piece of property. (If you want more info about timeshares, check out *Timeshare Vacations For Dummies,* 1st Edition, by Lisa Ann Schreier [Wiley].)

Some organizations offer timeshare owners the opportunity to trade their weeks with owners in other locations. The general rule: Select your weeks in an area that you want to visit on a regular basis, and expect to use those weeks each year. If you can swap weeks one year, fine, but you shouldn't enter into a timeshare expecting to visit a different place every year.

Timeshares do have their disadvantages. They aren't always easy to sell. Their audience of potential buyers is limited by the number of people who are interested in buying these nontraditional vacation home options. You need to make sure the place is right for you before you buy. Also remember that if you're looking toward retirement, a timeshare won't fill the bill. You can't convert it to a permanent residence, nor buy 100 percent ownership.

Inside the United States

Timeshare opportunities are available in most vacation spots nationwide. Offered at a fraction of the cost of owning outright a second home, timeshares command annual fees that cover the maintenance and upkeep of the property's common areas. The fee also covers some or all of the following: home and grounds care, taxes, insurance, and utilities.

As to what you'll pay for a timeshare, prices are really across the board. When you start looking, you'll likely find a wide range of prices with, of course, the most popular spots costing the most. As for finding the perfect timeshare unit, I heartily recommend hitting the Web first, specifically www.timesharetravel.com and www.timesharelink.com. These sites list timeshares available both in and outside the United States and most timeshares offer three-day/two-night deals during which you can try them on for size. You'll stay there, see the presentation, and then you'll be able to decide.

Outside the United States

If you've decided that your second home will be outside the United States, and you know you plan to visit the area once a year for only a few weeks or a month, then a timeshare may be just the thing for you. Your first stop should be the Web, where international timeshare opportunities are listed on the sites mentioned in the previous section.

Check out the descriptions and photos, and then contact the owners directly to find out exactly how the sale can be handled from afar. Fax machines and overnight mail services are efficient tools for getting the paperwork into everyone's hands. Also check out the local real estate market and compare prices among the various properties that are available. (Make sure you check out Chapter 9 for more info about buying overseas.)

If you own a timeshare in the United States, you can make good use of the services of a company like Interval International (www.intervalworld.com). They'll help you exchange your weeks at locations that are based overseas.

Fractional ownership

Fractional ownership offers individuals the opportunity to buy partial ownership of a luxury-type home in a desirable area. The properties are generally concentrated in coastal areas, on islands, or near ski resorts.

Through this option, the buyer purchases only a fraction of the property rather than the whole property. Options vary by development and/or property. *Quarter shares,* in which a buyer can use one week out of every month, are the most popular choice among buyers, who agree to share the property with three other purchasers. Under this unique form of *strata title ownership* (secure ownership), an owner has a registered title to one-quarter interest in the condominium, estate, or townhouse.

With fractional ownership, a third party or a homeowners' association handles property management. One of the biggest attractions for buyers (many of whom could afford the entire purchase, if they so desired) is the reduced expense and responsibility of ownership. Some fractional developments also participate in global vacation exchange clubs, offering buyers the ability to travel to different properties while maintaining the fractional ownership of their original home.

The difference between fractional ownership and a timeshare lies in the prices, the financing, and fees. Timeshares are cheaper. Fractional ownership costs can run six figures or more. For a look at some fractional ownership opportunities, check out www.partialowner.com.

Rent before you buy

If you have your eye on a specific unit and/or location, and if the seller isn't in a hurry to sell the property, then you can look into renting the place before you buy it outright. This is a good way to test-drive the home, townhouse, or condo and determine if it's in the right location, is the right size, and, ultimately, is the right choice for you and your family.

LLC ownership

LLC ownership stands for *limited liability corporation.* It's not necessary for every second-home owner, because most don't have partners as co-owners, but just in case you *do* have partners and have real estate investing on your mind, I include this short section. Basically, if you buy a second home with a partner or partners, and you rent it out for profit, you can form an LLC if you want to reduce your individual liability. With an LLC, you gain the advantage of being a corporate entity — a business situation in which shareholder liability is reduced or eliminated.

If you have more than one partner, and you want this added layer of protection, talk to an accountant and real estate lawyer about setting up an LLC for the "business" of your second home. (If you want more information about LLC ownership, check out *Real Estate Investing For Dummies* by Eric Tyson and Robert S. Griswold [Wiley].)

Chapter 4

A Second Home Is All about Location

Y ou've probably heard the saying "Location, location, location." It originated sometime in the 1950s when a Midwestern real estate columnist wrote that the three most important features of a home are first, its location; second, its location; and third, its location. Although it has become something of cliché these days, the adage's validity is still solid. And the truth of it doesn't change just because you're buying a second home rather than a primary dwelling. The fact is, the right location combined with the right amenities and a few added niceties can make up for any compromises that you may have to make when it comes to home size, interior features, and/or price.

The avid reader who purchases a condo on the beach will love strolling out onto the sand a few times a year with a book under one arm and an umbrella under the other. She will be thrilled time after time with her second-home choice — even though the condo is situated two floors higher than she would have originally liked it to be. And the family of five that loves to ski together won't mind the somewhat cramped quarters of their mountain bungalow after a long, thrilling day on the slopes.

In this chapter, I walk you through the basics of finding the right location for your second home. (In Chapter 3, I talk about finding the right second home.) This chapter helps you review your main options and drills down to some of the finer points about a community that you should keep in mind when you make your final decision.

Asking Yourself Where You Want to Retire

Admit it: For some of you, retirement is the farthest thing from your mind right now, right? You're busy with work and kids and just the general craziness of life. (Not to mention keeping up with all those shows and movies you TiVo'ed!) For you, your second home is for vacations, and maybe some rental income.

But even if you are 15 or more years away from retiring, this doesn't mean you shouldn't at least factor your golden years into the equation when selecting a location for your second home. That means choosing somewhere that you actually *like* and where you can see yourself living on a full-time basis at some point. Because one day, you might.

Those of you who are within a few years (or months) of retiring should check out Chapter 15, where I discuss in further detail how to move into a second home for retirement.

Three factors are usually involved when purchasing a second home:

- ✔ Your ability to use this home as a vacation getaway for the next few years or even decades
- ✔ The opportunity (if so desired, and allowed by the community rules) to rent the unit out to others when you're not using it
- ✔ The idea that, upon retirement, you'll move into your second home and live there full time

If you haven't considered the possibility of your second home eventually being your retirement nesting place, you should. If, however, you have already decided that you will retire to your second home, you want to choose a location that fits your idealized future lifestyle — a place that's all that you want it to be as both a long-term investment and a place where you want to live.

Because many of you certainly do plan on using your second home one day as your retirement refuge, I start this chapter with a look at where you want to retire so you know where to begin scouting for your second home. If you don't plan on retiring in your second home, feel free to skip this section. However, if there is the slightest possibility that you will retire to your second home, check out this important info that can help you select the right location.

Choosing a location that fits your future lifestyle

The fact that your second home will at some point become your primary dwelling can make a big difference when it comes to choosing a location. Whatever your preferences, the key is to find an abode that will not only accommodate you now, but will also be a place you'll later be happy to call home on a full-time basis.

If you're not convinced of this, try taking this short quiz. Feel free to write in this book:

1. **What is your current age?** _____

2. **What is your expected retirement age?** _____

3. **In how many years do you expect to retire?** _____

4. **List the top five or so vacation activities that you enjoy right now:**

   _____

5. **Picture yourself X number of years down the road and think about whether your favorite activities will likely change.**

   Be realistic. Do you now enjoy strenuous activities such as hiking, mountain climbing, surfing, long-distance running, or vigorous competitive outdoor sports? Can you see yourself continuing these activities in 10 years? 15 years? 20 years? The tolls of time and aging may steer you to less strenuous sports such as golf, swimming, fishing, or nature walks. Jot down a few activities that you would like to be doing in your retirement years, and compare them to the favorites you listed in No. 4.

   _____

If you plan on retiring in five years or less, then the types of activities and amusements that fill your vacation days now may very well be perfect for your golden years. If, however, retirement is ten or more years away, put your thinking cap on and come up with a practical, down-to-earth picture of what you expect you'll be doing, and where you want to do it, when you retire.

After you develop a realistic picture of your retirement lifestyle, consider those elements when you embark on your second-home search. If, for example, you've always wanted to be able to play tennis like a pro, then select a home that's in a community that has tennis courts, or that's situated near city or country club courts. If fishing is your passion, then find a home within a few miles of a lake or ocean where you can spend your days happily casting that reel.

Avoiding places that sound good on paper, but may not be a good match

When searching for your second home, especially if you're looking in a location far from where you currently live, you may rely heavily on real estate ads, brochures, and the Internet.

However, don't fall prey to the gorgeous brochures, expensive Web site marketing, and the sleek ads. Even though the Web and mail are great ways to get your hands on information about a specific area, neighborhood, or even a particular unit, you need to use your own two eyes (or at least the eyes of a trusted family member or friend) to check out the place firsthand before you buy. When all else fails, use the following logic: If it sounds too good to be true, it probably is. To avoid any problems in this area, take a short vacation to the prospective areas (after you've narrowed your location choices) to visit the homes you found on the Internet or the one your in-laws are "just positive" you'll love. You'll thank yourself later.

Real estate ads can be very enticing, right? They have pretty pictures and often seem to promise every amenity possible. Chamber of commerce and relocation bureau advertisements can be equally alluring, and understandably so, considering that these organizations spend oodles of dollars to attract visitors and residents and pump up their regions' tax bases.

Furthermore, developers' brochures often feature the homes themselves, but leave out pictures of or details about the surrounding area. With land prices in vacation spots soaring, homes are being built on odd pieces of property that may or may not ultimately be favorable to vacationers (or to the miserable homeowner who will have to look out his windows day in and day out at a not-so-pretty picture). A unit may look great inside and out, yet the area on the other side of the gate or out the back door may not be as attractive.

Where to Look for Your Second Home

Finding the perfect place for a weekend getaway, a monthly retreat, or an annual family vacation may be a cinch for some, but a challenge for others. If you already have a place that you love and visit regularly, then your selection process for finding your dream second home may not be too difficult.

But if you like a number of locations and really can't narrow them down to one place, or if you're a bit indecisive, maybe you can use some help. This section provides some great advice on how to check out your main options, boil them down, and come up with one that meets your needs.

Surveying your main options

You can buy a second home near a lake. You can buy one on the slopes of your favorite ski resort. You can buy one in a different country. You can buy one on an island. You can also buy one just down the street from your primary home. (Okay, I know you may not want to do that one, but it's still an option.) The world is your oyster, and that can make the selection process fun, exciting, and, yes, more confusing and difficult.

If you're hung up on where to buy, try whittling down your choices by crossing off those places where you absolutely *don't* want to buy. You may be surprised at how short your list is after you've wielded your merciless editor's pencil! Do as much research as possible, using online and real-life resources on your top locations. Other homeowners, visitors' centers, and real estate agents can be great sources for details on the local market conditions and availability of homes.

You can also talk to people about the day-to-day issues that come with living in the area. You might ask residents about traffic congestion issues, grocery store lines, how quickly potholes are fixed — even how noisy the weekly trash pickup is! — and other issues. Don't be afraid to ask a fellow exasperated patron in a local restaurant, "Is this a usual wait time here?" These "quality of life" issues can often make or break a place.

When considering your main options and narrowing your list, keep the following questions in mind:

- ✓ **What are you going to use your home for?** Is it for family vacations? A long-term retirement plan? For rental income? Purely for investment? A combination of these? (If you're considering using it as a rental property, check out Part III.)

- ✓ **What type of climate are you most interested in for your second home?** For instance, if you're a skier, Denver, Colorado, or Lake Tahoe, California, are your best bets. If you like to sunbathe during your downtime, then Naples, Florida, or the French Riviera are better choices.

- ✓ **How far away do you want your second home to be?** If you want to avoid air travel, then pick somewhere that's far enough away for a vacation, but close enough to drive to; three to four hours by car is ideal. If you don't mind negotiating airports, you automatically expand your options.

- ✓ **How close do you want your home to be to family and friends?** If you plan a lot of gatherings with those near and dear, then pick an "in the middle" location that everyone can get to easily. Pick a hideaway if you don't want a lot of visitors.

- ✓ **What types of properties are available?** If you're dead set against a townhouse and that's all that's available in the area, look somewhere else.

✔ **What is the cost of living?** If you're on a budget, you must consider the cost of food, taxes, transportation, and other necessities in the area.

✔ **What ages and types of neighbors do you want to be surrounded by?** If you absolutely do not want to be surrounded by neighbors, regardless of their ages and types, then you should definitely consider a "hide-away"-type location. Also, if the home is located in a "retirement" area, and you're 30 years old, you may not be as happy as you would be in a neighborhood where most of the homeowners — your new neighbors, remember — are younger professionals. (Although here's something to keep in mind: With all the "50 is the new 30" stuff making the rounds in our culture, don't be too quick to dismiss an area simply because you notice more 50-plus people living there. I personally know people in their 50s who live in close proximity to singles and couples in their 20s and 30s, and they are all close friends and really get along well. So eschew stereotypes and see for yourself.)

✔ **How long are you willing to wait for a home to become available in a high-demand area?** The real estate market is cyclical, so check into "days on market" statistics (with a real estate agent) to see exactly how long the best homes are available for the picking.

After you narrow your list, visit one or more of the areas that you're interested in. Eat in the restaurants, shop in the stores, and meet some of the locals and visitors to get a real flavor for the area before you buy there.

The following sections cover seven second-home locations for your consideration.

Near oceans, lakes, and rivers

Mention the word "vacation home" to someone and they'll likely conjure up images of beachfront property with umbrella-lined sundecks. There is enormous appeal to being near or on the water, and homes built near oceans, lakes, and rivers rank high in popularity for second-home buyers.

If your idea of a great vacation (and eventually, a fulfilling retirement) involves fishing on a river, water-skiing on a lake, swimming in the ocean, or tanning on golden sands, then you'll want to focus your home search on places such as Florida, the Carolinas, California, Hawaii, Mexico, and the Caribbean, plus other areas where single-family homes, townhouses, and condos dot the shoreline.

Price can be an obstacle when buying on or near the water, and these areas are also prone to weather such as hurricanes and extreme heat in the summer months, so be sure to factor that into your buying decision.

The best of both worlds

What better place than the banks of Narragansett Bay to own a condominium where you can vacation for as many or as few weeks as you want and not have to worry about maintenance and upkeep? That's exactly the logic that Mitch and Robin Pozez used when they purchased a condo at a Newport, Rhode Island, golf course community a few years ago.

Looking for a place to escape Arizona's summer heat, the Pozezes had previously vacationed in California, but they never really felt it was the place where they wanted to purchase a second home. During a trip to Cape Cod, Massachusetts, Mitch wandered into a real estate office and picked up a brochure for a nearby golf course community. After noticing the community's waterfront location — a key criteria for Robin — they decided to see it for themselves.

"I drove down there, played the golf course, and loved it," says Mitch, who at the time resisted buying a home that he'd have to close up, leave, and worry about for nine or ten months out of the year. Instead, the couple opted for a condo-style property with three bedrooms, three baths, and 1,900 square feet of living space.

Their new second home comfortably accommodates the Pozezes and their three children, who range in age from 17 to 23. The family typically spends seven to eight weeks at their second home each summer, during which time they enjoy golfing, boating, and working out in the fitness center.

Mitch says he immediately fell in love with the community's golf course, which was designed by British architect Donald Steel. "The more I play it, the more I like it," says Mitch, who also likes having a boat dock and is looking forward to a new marina that will be built there.

The low-maintenance aspect of condo living has been especially appealing to the Pozezes who, for years, have reveled in being able to close up their unit and know that it will be taken care of while they're gone.

Mountains

If the mountains are your thing, then check out areas of Tennessee, Georgia, and the Carolinas as possible second-home locations. The Northeast also offers its own share of mountain getaways, as do states like Montana and Colorado. There, you can enjoy the fresh mountain air, along with all the hiking, horseback riding, skiing, and relaxation that these alpine retreats have to offer.

Friends of mine get away to Gatlinburg, Tennessee, every year with their families and come back refreshed and revived. They now own a few weeks of timeshare there, after they rented places for years and eventually discovered that they could save money by taking the plunge into ownership.

If you're leaning toward the mountains, keep in mind that homes won't always be near the amenities (malls, stores, movie theatres, and cultural amenities) that you're accustomed to. Plus, it will almost always take you longer to get there. (All those long and winding roads, y'know?)

Resort and golfing communities

If you're a golfer, there's nothing quite like teeing off in your own "backyard" and playing 18 holes on a course designed especially for your and your neighbors' use. This appealing lifestyle can be found in golf course and resort communities nationwide. Packed with amenities such as swimming pools, tennis courts, fitness centers, and oftentimes a full social calendar, these environments are designed for fun, relaxation, and an atmosphere of exclusivity that comes from being a member of a private community.

Like the waterfront homes, these abodes tend to be more costly than those that aren't on the links. They're also somewhat "microcosmic" in nature because they're usually gated, which means your social circle (and activities) will be somewhat limited to what the community has to offer.

Small towns

America's small towns can make great vacation getaways if what you have in mind is resting, relaxing, and getting away from the daily grind. Sprinkled with historical sites, antique shops, and people who still enjoy the simple things in life, such as evening strolls and afternoon tea, these oases of calm can be found in nearly every state. They are often best discovered in your own state by simply hopping into a car and driving around for several hours, getting off the highways, and visiting the small towns the country roads lead you to.

If that strategy doesn't work or is too hit-or-miss for you, think back to your childhood and the places that you and your family visited or drove through on a weekend afternoon. Was there a farm town nearby where you went on a Sunday afternoon to buy fresh vegetables or sample freshly churned ice cream? How about a small theater that you visited for the occasional play or 99-cent movie? Or perhaps you vacationed in a tiny beach town once in a while or visited a relative who owned a cottage there? You can also pull out a U.S. map and find places with fun or famous names to check out, like Gas City, Indiana, or Rome, Ohio! (Or Hygiene, Colorado, or Santa Claus, Indiana!? And let's not forget Frostproof, Florida! Imagine telling your friends your new address!) Think about it — you may be surprised at what you come up with.

However, you should also realize that the places you loved as a kid may not be as alluring to you as an adult. Keep that in mind as you make your way back to those little towns where you grew up.

Cities

If Broadway plays, an active nightlife, and an endless list of cultural attractions are on your second-home "must have" list, a big city may be your best choice. You should expect to pay more for a home there than in a smaller locale, but cities do offer advantages that other areas don't. For example, most are within close proximity of international airports, making transportation to and from your second home that much easier. And the convenience factor is unbeatable in a big city, whether it's restaurants, shopping, or office space you're interested in — and many of your destinations could very well be within walking distance.

If you're interested in buying an older home that needs a little extra TLC, you may find a real gem (and possibly even a bargain) in a big city. Many of America's cities are in the midst of an organized, ongoing *re-urbanization trend:* Cities are actively trying to lure more residents back within their limits. And it's working. The resultant higher demand for city homes, however, has elevated their sales prices, making them unaffordable for some second-home buyers.

Owning a second home in the city may be especially attractive to country dwellers in search of more excitement than their hometowns provide. What might be called the *hustle-and-bustle option* can also work for someone looking to rent out their second home year-round in anticipation of eventual retirement. Demand for living quarters in cities is usually high, particularly in areas with positive job growth, and the second-home owner with an apartment in the middle of or close to lots of action won't go wanting for renters.

However, cities can be busy, dirty places where unsavory individuals hang out and where simple things such as parking are a real pain in the butt. Make sure you're really in love with the city of your choice before you invest in real estate there.

College towns

You may think that "college town" and "peaceful retirement" are mutually exclusive and, in many cases, you'd be right. (Although not every college town is manic. Some smaller towns like Franklin, Indiana, and its 1,000-student Franklin College would better be described as "quaint.") But owning a second home in a bustling college town can certainly be a lucrative endeavor. Parents of college students will often shell out big bucks during the school year to house their children. They're eager to get their kids out of the house and into a semblance of independent living, and in many cases, the kids love the idea of living in a rented house rather than the dorm. Because the rent is usually split between several families (depending on the size of the home, of course), landlords (you!) can command big bucks in college towns (not all of which are crazy, party-oriented places).

This option may be best for someone who is looking for second-home income for the majority of the year, but who still wants to use the home during the summer months — when most of the students have gone home and the residents happily reclaim their streets, restaurants, and malls.

However, this choice may not be so good for those of you who would rather archive your college memories after reaching adulthood, and don't enjoy the sight (or the sound) of partied-out coeds wandering the streets at 2 a.m. on Saturday mornings.

Foreign countries

Ready for a Greek villa on the water, a cottage in the Tuscan countryside, or a beach house on Grand Cayman? So am I. Regrettably, these options are out of reach for me and for many others because of cost and distance. But these spots may be the perfect second-home choice for someone who enjoys overseas travel to the same place, and who has the financial resources needed to pay for and maintain a dwelling overseas.

Being able to get away to another country on a regular basis, experience the cultural differences, master a new language, and mingle with a more diverse group of people are just a few of the terrific benefits of owning a second home overseas. (See Chapter 9 for more details on buying internationally.) If you can swing it, you should try it. You may like it.

Going the distance: How far is too far away for a second home?

Are you a natural-born driver, flyer, or mass-transit type? Is "traveler" your middle name? (Mine's Mary.) If how you get there doesn't matter to you, then the distance to your second home probably won't matter, either. If, however, you hate to fly, and you detest driving more than two hours to get to your destination, and you think choo-choos are for basements, then you'll need to carefully consider distance when purchasing your second home.

Here are some key points to consider:

- ✔ **How much time will you usually have to get to and from your second home?** If you're working 70 hours a week and only have Saturday and Sunday to enjoy your getaway, then you'll want it to be relatively close by, say within three hours by car — or even closer if you find the thought of a routine three-hour drive on a Friday night loathsome. On the other hand, retired or semiretired individuals who have more free time than they know what to do with can travel across the country — or halfway around the world for that matter — because they follow their own schedules rather than an employer's. So be sure to factor all this into your decision on where to buy.

- ✔ **How often are you going to use the second home?** If you're planning monthly trips to your new home, and you just know that your budget won't withstand buying 48 plane tickets (based on a family of four) a year, be sure your second home is somewhere within driving distance. If you plan to use your home once or twice a year, you can comfortably opt for somewhere a bit farther away, such as five to eight hours' driving or flying time. A long trip a couple of times a year won't grate on your nerves or budget, and you'll have a larger area to choose from.

✔ **How close do you live to the airport?** It can take three hours to park a car and go through the security lines at an airport these days. Be sure to factor in this time — plus the time it takes to get to the airport (on both sides of the trip) — when selecting a location.

✔ **How reliable is your car?** Is your primary car more than a few years old? Do you use it to commute? Realistically, can it handle the additional several hundred miles to get to and from your second home on a regular basis? These factors are important if you're planning on driving to your second home. What's that? You have a second car you'll use to get to your second home? Great! But keep in mind that the added wear and tear on an older vehicle may make long, monthly trips a problem. If you have no plans to buy a newer car in the near future, then you may want to look at a closer location.

✔ **Who else will be using the home?** If you're the welcoming, "open door" type and you foresee a crop of family and friends at your vacation house every month, pick a location that's central to as many of them as possible. If it's just you and your significant other (and Max or Marcy the dog), you can guiltlessly pick something completely off the beaten path if that's what you want.

Ultimately, you want to find a location that is easy to get to but far enough away that it truly feels like you've escaped the day-to-day grind. (It's a little more difficult to unwind and recharge when you're only a few minutes away from home. "Did I leave the stove on? I'll run home and check." "You forgot your hair dryer? Let me run home and get it." This scenario is not all that conducive to relaxation, y'know?) For some, this means a beach house 30 minutes away; for others, it translates into a cottage in the Australian Outback. It's your choice.

What to Look for in Your Second Home's Area, Now and Later

We all like to "live in the moment" once in a while, but that's not the wisest tack if you're buying a second home. For a big move like that, you need to consider both the present and the future before making your decision. By factoring in things such as the local weather, an area's cost of living, and the availability of health-care facilities before you say "I'll take it," you have a much better chance of buying somewhere where you truly want to be now *and* in the future.

This section takes a more detailed approach to your location search by looking at 13 areas of interest for second-home buyers. In this section, I discuss everything from the cost of living and the weather, to property taxes and nosy neighbors. Because financial concerns are a top priority, I begin with cost of living, and then look at other factors in descending order of importance.

Cost of living

If you plan on retiring in your second home, you must consider the area's cost of living. After all, you don't want to live full time in a place where your retirement income can't even cover your basic living expenses. Take Hawaii, for example. It's a beautiful place (and I grew up there, incidentally), but even back in the 1980s a carton of milk and loaf of bread were three times the price of what you could buy them for on the mainland. So if budget is an issue, you may want to cross this state off your favorites list.

If you currently live in an expensive locale, like New York City or San Diego, and are buying in an area with a significantly lower cost of living, like Fayetteville, North Carolina, to be near your grandkids, for example, consider the money that you'll save and factor those savings into your decision.

To check out an area's cost of living, a number of Web sites offer cost-of-living calculators that can be used to compare different locales. A great one is BankRate's cost-of-living calculator at `www.bankrate.com/brm/movecalc. asp`. There, I compared the cost of living in Honolulu versus Tampa, Florida, and found that even though home prices are about $500,000 higher and energy bills about $60 more expensive in Hawaii, I can bowl a game in the Aloha State for about 68 cents cheaper than I can here, and it would cost me seven bucks less to pay a visit to the vet with the kitty.

You can also talk to real estate agents in your target city to find out more about the cost of living there, but let's face it: These professionals' job is to sell homes, not spread negative news about their local economies, prices, and costs of living. Your best source of objective advice are people who live there, or who have lived there in the past. (Try a "Hi, potential neighbor!" chat while you're out looking at homes.) And be sure to check out the afore-mentioned BankRate Web site for specifics on cost differences between where you live and where you're considering moving to.

Good weather

Weather is, for the most part, pretty easy to figure out: January in Fargo, North Dakota: 10 degrees. January in Miami, Florida: 80 degrees. But there's much more than temps to think about when selecting a locale for your second home. You also need to consider rainfall, fog, snow, floods, humidity, wind, hurricanes, tornadoes, droughts, brushfires, and other climactic concerns. What type of climate do you prefer? Would you like something in the middle like Myrtle Beach, South Carolina, where summers are hot and winters are bearable? Or are you a "snow bunny" and the colder and blusterier the better?

Your own tolerance for extreme heat or bitter cold will dictate where you should begin your search on the map. If, for example, getting frostbite on your nose while whipping down a ski slope on a snowboard is your idea of fun, then by all means select a home in the area of the country where the cold starts to roll in as early as October. If you're like many of the rest of us, zero in on somewhere warm.

It's also important to consider the time of year that you'll be using the home. If you want to spend winters in South Florida, for example, then the expected (bet on it) 90-degree-or-higher days and exquisitely "drippy" humidity of the summer won't bother you.

Safety and security

Safety is a critical issue that's often overlooked when a buyer finds a dwelling that he absolutely *must* have. Hailing from out of town and completely enamored with the property, the second-home buyer often jumps into the deal without ever checking out the area's crime statistics or talking to other residents about things such as break-ins, muggings, and police patrols.

For example, what if it's widely known locally that a particular resort area has a high number of break-ins. Or one particular shopping center experiences lots of purse snatches. Or that there's a certain neighborhood in a quaint town where anything left outside vanishes almost immediately. This is the kind of information you should try to ferret out from locals, real estate agents, and even the cops. It will help you make the right decision as to where to buy.

To familiarize yourself with an area's crime status and safety statistics, check out the Relocation Crime Lab's crime indexes for U.S. states online at www. homefair.com/homefair/calc/crime.html. The U.S. Census also offers "quick facts" about specific cities on its site at http://quickfacts.census. gov/qfd. Finally, Sperling's Best Places also offers crime reports at www. bestplaces.net/crime. If your area isn't listed on one of these sites, a call to the local police station should produce the information, or at least get you headed in the right direction. Also, a Google search for your prospective town's name will provide you with a slew of info, often including links to local newspapers and other resources that can serve as a window into the area.

Healthcare

With the nation's population aging and baby boomers retiring in droves, access to healthcare is becoming a hot-button issue for second-home buyers. Because illnesses, accidents, and medical emergencies are unpredictable, you want to make sure that there are a fair number of hospitals, doctors, dentists, medical specialists, and clinics in the area where you plan to retire.

To find out what health-care facilities are available in a specific area and what medical services they offer, talk to a real estate agent in the area, browse through the local newspaper (many are available online these days) to read health-related articles, or do your research the old-fashioned way and pick up the phone book to see what's out there. Also, the American Hospital Directory offers a free search on its site (www.ahd.com/freesearch.php3) for hospitals by city, state, zip code, name, and telephone area code. Search results provide a list of all hospitals within the criteria with clickable links.

Outdoor activities

Are you and your family outdoorsy people? Do you enjoy taking nature walks, picnicking by a lake, and swimming all afternoon? If you want to be close to the outdoor activities that you love, consider the following questions when looking for a second home:

- **Are your favorite outdoor activities available?** For example, do you like swimming and boating? If so, is there safe water access? Do you enjoy birding and hiking? If so, are there wooded areas nearby?

- **Are the activities in quality locations?** You want to enjoy your favorite activities at nice facilities, right? For example, do you want to play at a golf course with brown greens, or do you want to take your grandkids swimming at a polluted lake? Of course not. So check out the quality of the recreational areas if you plan to spend a lot of time there.

- **Are the activities close (or too close) to your new home?** You need to consider how long it takes you to drive to and from an activity. For example, if you have to drive an hour just to play nine holes of golf and you absolutely can't live without golf, then is this home right for you? If golf balls landing in your front yard and bouncing off of your windows (or, heaven forfend, your noggin) doesn't sound very appealing, be sure to select a home that's far enough away from the links (or other recreational hot spot) so you'll be left alone.

Active social life

If an active social life is important to you, then you want to buy a home in an area where homes are clustered together. This kind of proximity often creates a sense of community and togetherness, virtually guaranteeing that you'll form social bonds. Chatting with your neighbors over the back fence is much less likely in single-family home neighborhoods where houses are on large lots and are often situated an acre or more apart.

An active social life also includes having relatively easy access to amenities, such as good restaurants, entertainment, and shopping. If you're used to running out to the store to quickly pick something up, or deciding at the last minute to go out for dinner, an hour drive to accomplish these things can rapidly become a drag.

Good restaurants and entertainment

Some people like to cook at home and watch movies on DVD. (You know who you are. Chinese food and *The Devil Wears Prada*? I am so there!) Others like to eat out a lot and go to movie theaters. (And you know who *you* are.) Most of us fall somewhere in between: We like to do both, and insist on proximity to great eateries and entertainment venues. Look around your new environs and be sure that there are enough of these amenities around to keep you occupied (and well fed!).

Shopping

I'm convinced that there's a little shopper in all of us — yes, even those of us who don't want to admit it. Look around at the malls, strip centers, downtown shopping districts, and even the small boutique stores in your prospective new area. Do they compare with what you're used to and can they meet your needs (perhaps, with the help of some Internet shopping as well)? If not, you may want to consider an alternative location.

If you're used to and enjoy having these types of amenities nearby, be sure to pick a second-home location that provides a similar quality *and* quantity of places and activities. If, for example, you're the city type who likes grocery stores to be a mile or less away, then you'll want to steer clear of those attractive, inexpensive cabins in the backwoods.

Active cultural life

If museums, art galleries, plays, and concerts are your passion, then check in with the convention and visitors' bureau or chamber of commerce in your targeted city. They will be happy to offer you a colorful brochure (or point you to a Web site) that lists all the entertainment, cultural amenities, and sporting events that a city or town has to offer. They're proud of their home, and their literature will usually highlight the most exciting cultural offerings in the area.

Property tax levels

Every municipality sets it own property tax (or *millage*) rates. These rates are used to calculate how much a property owner must shell out annually to cover the costs of public schools, libraries, and government services. These rates vary greatly from state to state (and from city to city within the same state) and are something you should consider before deciding to buy. Your real estate agent can help you figure out how much you'll owe in annual taxes and also clue you in to the rate at which those taxes have increased (or decreased — hey, it's possible!) over the last few years.

Many county and city *tax assessors' offices* (they levy the taxes) post millage rates and those for specific properties online. A great site for locating this information is www.taxsites.com/state.html. Just click on the state where your prospective home is located, and the link will take you to the state's main tax site where you can check out all manner of state tax info. *Note:* Some states' revenue/tax Web sites refer you to the individual town's Web site for tax info specific to the town (like millage rates), but starting with the state's main tax site makes it very easy for you to get to the site you need.

Zoning

Unless you're planning on leveling the structure that you're purchasing and building another home in its place, zoning issues probably won't be of much concern to you as a second-home buyer. If, however, your home is located in an area where commercial land is located right next door and a large big-box store is slated to move in, you may want to think about zoning issues. (*Zoning* is the process by which municipalities decide what type of real estate development goes where within the county and/or city. And zoning can often be appealed by means of requesting a *variance,* which allows types of development in an area not previously zoned for it.)

The individual owner can't do a whole lot regarding such zoning issues, but it's a good idea to keep an eye out for any activity that can adversely affect your property's value and influence your enjoyment of your second home. In some cases, you and your neighbors may be able to join forces and fight an unwelcome proposal. If you see something unsavory coming down the pike (like a massive big-box store eyeing what has long been a pristine forested area), it may be time to rally the troops to oppose it. Just as residents can request variances to allow zoning changes, there are also legal means to protest against such changes.

Covenants

Now for the rules and regulations, often called *covenants.* Most neighborhoods and all condos have them, and you have to abide by them if you want to remain in good standing with the association that created them. The covenants are handed over to new buyers at the closing table, but can usually be obtained in advance from your real estate agent and/or the condo or neighborhood board.

Here are a few covenants you can expect to find in your bylaws:

- ✔ Grass and landscaping must be maintained, and grass may be no higher than (xx) inches at any given time.

- ✔ Trash cans can't be placed on the curb before 5 p.m. on the night before trash day and must be removed from the curb by 10 p.m. on trash day.

- ✔ Property owners cannot add permanent structures (such as decks and fences) to their units without written approval from the association.

- ✔ Pets are limited to (xx) per household.

  Sometimes bylaws restrict pet ownership to cats; some contain weight and height limits for dogs.

- ✔ Properties cannot be leased on a short-term basis (the time varies by community) by any owner, at any time.

  This restriction is especially important for owners planning on renting out their homes to generate income.

If you don't play by the rules, you can receive a warning or a fine, depending on the language in the bylaws. If, after reading through the community's bylaws, you feel that you won't be able to abide by one or more of them, you may want to cross that neighborhood off your list.

Neighbors

Neighbors are a lot like family: You really can't pick 'em, and in the end, you're stuck with 'em. If you're only planning on using your second home once a year, then you probably don't need to worry much about the neighbor issue right now. But if you're going to be there every month — and if the couple next door lives there year-round — then you'll almost certainly wind up forming a relationship with them.

Before you buy, it's hard to get a handle on who your neighbors are and how it will be to live close to them. However, sometimes opportunities arise when you're shopping for homes.

If your prospective next-door neighbor is watering his lawn when you pull up with your real estate agent, or his wife is unloading groceries from the car as you're touring the grounds, it's easy as pie to introduce yourself and mention that you're considering buying next to them. Most of us can get a pretty good sense of people whom we meet for the first time. Although this shouldn't be the deciding factor, having a warm and friendly chat with someone with whom you may be sharing a property line can certainly add to the "pluses" column for a particular property.

Demographically speaking

Demographics are the common characteristics of a population in specific areas. Factors covered include age, sex, family size, level of education, occupation, gender, postal code, location of residence, and income.

These numbers can help you determine whether you're looking in the right place for your second home, and are usually available through your real estate agent or local chamber of commerce. You can also find them by typing words like "demographics" and the name of your town into a search engine on the Internet.

In doing so, you'll probably come up with information that looks like this:

✔ **Average income for families with children:** $107,208

✔ **Average age:** 36.9

✔ **Percent married:** 56.1

✔ **Percent with children:** 35.6

✔ **Percent high school graduates:** 95.6

✔ **Percent college graduates:** 66.4

✔ **Average SAT scores:** 1077

✔ **Education expenditures per student:** $10,726

✔ **Land area:** 495.5 square miles

✔ **County population:** 873,341

✔ **Population density per square mile:** 1,763

✔ **Population growth rate (5 years):** 1.5%

✔ **Favorite takeout food:** Pizza (Only kidding about this one!)

This stuff is all great to know when considering buying in a specific location.

Also, an agent may voluntarily offer details on who the people close by are and what they do. "That house belongs to the Smiths. He's a chemist, and she's a kindergarten teacher." Or, "Over there are the Browns. They're retired. They've lived here forever. They both volunteer at the hospital now."

When you're a second-home owner, your neighbors serve a key purpose that goes beyond friendship: They can watch your place when you're not there. You don't want to turn them into property managers, but having neighbors available during emergencies can be a godsend. You'll want to swap cell-phone numbers and home addresses with these folks. Most neighbors are happy to alert their fellow residents to any problems at their property when they're away. Some really close neighbors even swap keys.

Home value and appreciation

Every home has two important numbers associated with it. *Home value* is the price that a real estate agent, appraiser, or other authority states that a home is worth. *Home appreciation* is the amount of money (usually expressed in a percentage) that a home increases in value on a year-over-year basis.

Home values is an area where your real estate agent can really help out, because home appreciation is one of those hard-to-pin-down, all-over-the-place concepts. Because agents are in the trenches with home sellers daily (and those trenches can be kinda dusty, lemme tell ya), they can usually rattle off home value information off the top of their head, telling you how this $200,000 home sold in 1999 for just $140,000, and how this $750,000 penthouse condo hasn't sold because it's overpriced.

Your state Board of Realtors may also have reports on its Web site, and these reports will often be jampacked with details about specific areas where values are going up or down. The Florida Association of Realtors, for instance, lists monthly housing reports on its site at `http://media.living.net/releases/archive.htm`.

Home appreciation can be a double-edged sword for the second-home buyer: You want a good deal on the property you're interested in, but you also want to see that property increase in value. To strike that balance, seek out areas where appreciation has remained steady over the past few years, and steer clear of pockets where property values have risen or fallen wildly, a sure sign of an uncertain market.

Communities for people older than 55

There's a place just around the corner from my house where snowbirds make their annual pilgrimage, descending on the community with glee, eagerly looking forward to their winter in the Sunshine State. Known as The Top of the World, the sprawling village is reserved only for buyers who are 55 or older. Bridge, chess, poker, and shuffleboard bring the *joie de vivre* to the community's residents — those cold-state exiles who merrily spend their days blissfully oblivious to children or teenagers (and snow and ice).

These communities dot the landscape in many resort and vacation towns and are particularly appealing to adults who aren't interested in navigating skateboarding teenagers in the parking lot or in getting loaded by the swimming pool. Because their target buyer falls into a specific age group, these properties cost less than other second homes, but they can take longer to resell. The narrower the potential market, the greater the obstacles (or at least, the delays) in selling.

An over-55 community can be particularly attractive for someone looking to retire to a second home within a few years. But keep in mind that these complexes have set rules for who can own and live in the homes — with a special emphasis on residents' ages. If you're thinking your 30-year-old son may want to move back in with you after you're settled into an over-55 community, do some homework: You may or may not be in violation of the rules if he stakes a claim in one of your bedrooms. Be sure to read and understand the restrictions carefully before moving forward. As always, your individual situation should influence your decision.

Part II
Searching for Your New Home and Sealing the Deal

The 5th Wave   By Rich Tennant

"I'm entering all the bank's requirements for a mortgage, and I either have to buy a computer with more memory, or start looking for a smaller house."

In this part . . .

Are you actively searching for a second home but not quite sure where to look? Are you wondering if you need the help of a real estate agent? And what happens after you find the property and are ready to make an offer? Well, as they say down under, no worries, mate. Just read the chapters in this part, and you'll be on your way.

In this important part, I get into the nitty-gritty of finding your second home, working with reliable professionals, inspecting the property, securing financing, and purchasing a second home, whether it's located in the United States or overseas.

Chapter 5

In Search of the Perfect Second Home: What You Can Do

In This Chapter

▶ Tackling the second-home search on your own

▶ Beginning the search for your new home

▶ Using available (and free!) resources to your advantage

▶ Making an offer they can't refuse

*I*f you've dreamed of a second home for several years (or even just for a few days) and you've finally decided that now is the time to take the plunge, you may be a bit hesitant on where to start the actual search. You basically have two choices: You can hit the streets in search of your second home, or you can hire a real estate agent or other professional to help you. (If you want to rely on a professional, check out Chapter 6).

However, if you consider finding your second home an adventure, want to locate your second home on your own, and plan on negotiating and closing the deal on your own, then what are you waiting for? Your perfect second home may already be out there, and this chapter provides the necessary tools and tips you need to make your search (and purchase) successful, starting with looking for your second home; using resources, such as the Internet and newspaper, to locate properties; uncovering deals; and finally negotiating and closing the transaction.

The Do-It-Yourself Approach: Finding Your Second Home on Your Own

Some people like to do things on their own, while others like a little help. Some people work best with the support and guidance of a professional or other knowledgeable individual, and there's nothing wrong with that. But in this section, I address all of you who refuse to ask for directions or hire a plumber to fix a leaky pipe — the do-it-yourselfer. You know who you are.

Deciding whether to be your own real estate agent

I've bought homes by using a real estate agent, I've purchased for sale by owner (FSBO) homes on my own (with no agency representation on either side, except for a transaction broker who handled the paperwork), and I've acquired properties without any agency representation whatsoever, making good use of the help of the seller's agent.

In each case, there were pros and cons to my decision. In each aspect of a real estate transaction, buying a second home compares to buying a primary home in that your choice of using an agent or not depends largely on your level of comfort with handling the details of a real estate transaction on your own. (See Chapter 6 for more in-depth coverage of the types of agents, their duties, and responsibilities.)

If your second-home purchase looks to be relatively cut and dried with few challenges or issues to resolve (perhaps you're buying a home from a friend or family member and know what you're getting into with this particular home), then you may seriously want to consider the do-it-yourself approach. If, however, you think you'll have to tackle complex legalities and an extensive negotiation, then you should seriously consider working with a real estate agent (who is usually paid from the seller's profits) and an attorney. (And it never hurts to talk to an accountant, too.)

The pros to being your own agent

Probably the most appealing element of representing yourself is that you're the one in charge, so you have total control and all the decision-making authority. If you feel you're up to being your own agent, and you have the time for it, then more power to you.

If you've handled real estate transactions by yourself in the past, then buying a second home on your own is certainly a plausible notion. A huge help in this endeavor is that most Multiple Listing Services (MLS) are online through national sites such as Realtor.com and Yahoo! Real Estate, as well as on local real estate agent sites. Thus, you can access the majority of the information that an agent would have right from your desktop or laptop.

Doing it yourself also means

- ✔ Negotiating on your own
- ✔ Determining your own spending thresholds

✔ Dealing with *contingencies,* such as a mortgage contingency (which allows a buyer to "get out" of the deal within a certain number of days if the financing doesn't come through) or a home inspection contingency (which allows a buyer the same privileges if an inspection turns up major problems that the seller isn't willing to repair)

✔ Handling the more intricate parts of the transaction, such as setting up inspections and appraisals

You can also save some money when you represent yourself. See the "How much you'll save and is it worth it?" section in this chapter for more information about how being your own agent can save you dough.

The cons to being your own agent

When you're your own agent, you'll encounter a few downsides. For starters, if you're purchasing a second home a fair distance from your own community, or you're buying in a vacation spot that you're not familiar with, you'll lack important market and trend information that the typical real estate agent can rattle off without hesitation. Without doing some intensive research, you may not know the following:

✔ **Basic market conditions:** This sort of data includes the number of days it's taking to sell homes, and how the prices compare to, say, homes sold one year earlier.

✔ **Current home values:** Have they gone up, down, or stayed level over the past few months?

✔ **The most current property listings available:** National Web sites aren't always current.

✔ **Communities to consider and those to avoid:** Will you know which neighborhoods are in high demand? How about the one that's always in the news for levying large assessments on its owners?

✔ **Community makeup:** After you know which type of property you want to buy (see Chapter 3), you need to know where those types of homes are located.

✔ **Sellers' reactions to offers:** If it's a hot market, for example, some sellers may be turning down decent offers hoping for higher ones.

Never forget that doing it yourself means you *do it yourself.* No one else will set up appointments, shuttle you around to houses, steer you to those listings that meet your criteria, shuffle the paper stack (which is usually, let's call it, "abundant"), point you to lenders, and sit next to you at the closing table. It's all you.

If, after taking all this into consideration, doing it yourself still sounds like a good choice, then it's time to begin your home search.

How much you'll save and is it worth it?

There's no doubt that you'll save money by being your own agent, particularly if your buyer's agent commands a fee from your pocket for her services (many don't, but some do). In this section, I give you some valuable money-related information about using an agent versus not using one.

No agent fee

If you decide to search for and buy your second home on your own, you can save significant money in terms of agent fees. By doing your own legwork, you don't have to pay for the services of a *buyer's agent*. (Buyer's agents usually represent only the buyer and help her find a home, negotiate the terms, and get to the closing table on time. They charge for their services in addition to receiving a commission check, which customarily comes from the seller. Check out Chapter 6 for more about buyer's agents.)

You may not be completely off the hook from some of the agent fees. If you're representing yourself and you find a great FSBO (for sale by owner) property owned by someone who refuses to pay a real estate agent's commission, then you won't have to cover a real estate agent's fee out of your own pocket. But, in the event you do use a buyer's agent and because someone has to pay the agent for his time, you'll undoubtedly have to cover his commission (usually half of the going rate, unless otherwise negotiated in advance) if you purchase the FSBO with an agent's help.

What's your time worth?

Ah, time. Benjamin Franklin was right when he said, "Remember: Time is money." And time is something none of us ever seem to have enough of these days. If your time is tight, and you feel like I do about wanting to spend it wisely, then you may want to reconsider being your own real estate agent. (You may want to consider using a buyer's agent to help you.)

For example, say your time is worth $100 per hour, and you include in the umbrella term of "my time" the time you spend at work, with your family, and on your own — including sleeping and pursuing leisure activities. All of this time will be affected (and reduced) by the time you spend searching for a second home. If it takes you six months at about 10 hours a week to find the right place, that's 240 hours, or $24,000, based on your hourly rate.

If that seems like money well "spent" to you, then by all means, forge ahead on your own. If, however, it makes you think twice about giving up all that time, then you should reconsider just what a buyer's agent can do for you.

Tackling the task list

If you have the do-it-yourself gene in you (it's right next to the "Of course I know where I'm going" gene), kick off your second-home-buying journey with this simple to-do list.

✔ **Nail down the details of what you're looking for in your second home.** You need to know how much you can afford for your second home (see Chapter 2); the type and size of home you want (see Chapter 3); the features that are important to you (see Chapter 3); and where you want to look for your home (see Chapter 4). If you're unclear about any of these specifics, review the appropriate chapter.

✔ **Visit a Web site for a national aggregator and look for homes that fit your criteria.** Realtor.com (www.realtor.com), HomeGain (www.homegain.com), HouseHunt.com (www.househunt.com), and Google Real Estate (www.googlerealestate.com) are good places to start. Enter as many of your parameters as possible into the search page. (See "Taking Advantage of Nearby Resources" in this chapter for more information on Internet searches.) The results will give you a good feel for what's available in the locations you're interested in, and if your price range and other parameters are in line with what's for sale right now.

A *virtual tour* is a 360-degree Flash or QuickTime tour of one or more rooms and the exterior areas of a home. Not all listings have them, but those that do give prospective buyers a detailed look at the property's size and floor plan that still photos can't provide.

✔ **Make an appointment to see the property.** After you've found a few properties that interest you, and you've checked out their online pictures and information and taken their virtual tours (if available), you can contact the *listing agent* — the agent representing the seller and whose name and contact info accompanies the listing — or the owner (in the case of a FSBO home) to set up a showing so you can do a walk-through of the home.

When to Start Looking for a Second Home

"For everything there is a season, and a time for every matter under heaven," right? There is, in fact, a right time for everything, and that includes second-home buying. In this section, I help you determine the best possible time to start your new-home search and give you an idea of how long it will take to find your new place.

Are you ready to start looking?

Of course, it's ultimately up to you as to when you want to start poring over MLS listings, talking to real estate agents, and making offers. The following scenarios may help you decide if now is the time.

Now is probably the right time if

- ✔ Your financial house is in order, and you know that you can afford the additional responsibility of another home.

- ✔ You've been vacationing in the same place for the last ten years, you love it there, and you know you'd love to own a home there.

- ✔ The housing market in your area of interest has either leveled off or is working in favor of the buyer with lower housing appreciation and a glut of listings on the market.

- ✔ You've been saving for the last ten years to make the down payment and the monthly mortgage payment on a second home.

- ✔ You already have a home picked out, you know you can afford it, and it's available.

Now is probably *not* the right time if

- ✔ You're going through a divorce or some other life-altering event that will impact your finances over the next 6 to 12 months.

- ✔ You enjoy traveling the world and haven't been able to decide on one place where you'd like to own a second home.

- ✔ You're just not ready to be a landlord right now — a particularly important point for those looking to rent out their second homes while not using them.

- ✔ You plan to retire where you live now, and you don't need a second home to move into at some point.

- ✔ The housing market in your area of interest is off the charts, with very few listings, high housing appreciation rates, and sellers who are tough negotiators who stick to their price.

There are variations on each of these themes, of course, but I'm sure you get the overall picture: Make sure that your finances, your wants and desires, and the relevant market activity are all in order before you begin your home search.

How long will it take?

Finding your second home doesn't happen overnight. In fact, it can take quite a long time, so if you're wondering what kind of time commitment you're in for, take a deep breath and accept that your patience will likely be tested. In fact, according to the National Association of Realtors' most recent second-home buyer survey, the typical buyer searched seven weeks to find her second home and looked at six properties along the way. But this is all relative, and ultimately, the time you spend will depend on you and your own situation.

Different situations can affect whether you find your second home after a few days or after a few months. For example, if your brother is selling his home on the beach and you want it and are ready to buy it, then the journey from home search to closing table may be much shorter and only take a few weeks.

If you have no idea where you want to buy your second home, and you are searching several areas of the country for potential sites, you may spend six months to a year (or longer) looking for exactly the right second home to meet your needs.

Taking Advantage of Nearby Resources

When it comes time to find the right second home, you have scads of resources at your disposal. If you have a computer and Internet access, then the Web should be your first stop. The local newspaper can also be a great source of for-sale homes. And of course, never overlook what may be one of the most effective search tools: word of mouth.

This section helps you begin your search on your own and use the multitude of free resources that are yours for the taking.

Use the Internet to your advantage

The Internet has changed the home-search process like nothing before. In the primeval, pre-Internet and Web days, real estate agents compiled and hoarded thick, bound books of MLS listings and doled out the information in these tomes to clients very carefully. Today? That information is all over the Web. The trick is to find what you want to know without becoming utterly overloaded with useless information.

Surfing for a house: The how-to

The Internet can quickly become a vast, frustrating abyss for the second-home buyer who is looking for information about specific listings, neighborhoods, and regions. To start your Internet search

- ✔ Begin by using authoritative national Web sites (see the "Starting with the best sites" section in this chapter) to get a good overview of what's for sale in the areas that you're interested in.
- ✔ Check out informational sites like EscapeHomes.com and ReloHomeSearch.com for state-by-state information, listings, and articles on second-home buying.

If you're looking for a newly constructed home or one that's currently being built, you probably won't find it on the major MLS sites. A local real estate agent working in the area can often be a big help, or you may need to contact the builder directly (perhaps by visiting or calling the sales office) to get information on pricing and availability. To find a good builder, check with your local builders' association, which will provide you with a listing of members who are working in the region.

After you know what types of homes are available in your chosen area and the features you want in your second home (see Chapters 2, 3, and 4 for more specifics), follow these steps to search the Internet for your perfect second pad:

1. **Enter the number of bedrooms, bathrooms, price range, and so on into the search fields on the site's home page.**

2. **Hit "Search" and check out the homes in the area that meet your requirements.**

3. **View any or all still photos, virtual tours, and basic information about the home to get a feel for it, its surroundings, and its size.**

The Internet is a great place to preview homes, but nothing replaces an actual, in-person showing. Real estate agents aren't usually photographers, so if you think a home has a good shot at being "the one," but you're turned off by a poorly taken photo or bad video footage, you may want to consider seeing it in person before crossing it off your list.

If you do find a house online that interests you, but you want to see more of it, call or e-mail the real estate agent who has listed the home to set up a showing or to find out what else is available in the area. Often, the agent may have an inside track on other listings that aren't yet in the MLS, such as brand-new construction. If you only want information on a single home — and if you're not interested in working with that particular agent — let him know your intentions. That will save both of you time, because the agent who thinks he has a "hot one" on the hook will likely continue to follow up with you repeatedly.

Protecting yourself online

As a potential home buyer, you walk a fine line when it comes to accessing the information you need and protecting yourself from online fraud. Online identity theft and fraud are very real problems in today's technological, information-based society. Defined as the act of deliberately assuming another person's identity, *identity theft* is a crime that finds crooks rummaging through garbage cans (*dumpster diving*) to find old bank and credit card statements, and hacking into and stealing personal information from computer databases of organizations that store large quantities of this type of data.

To protect yourself, you can keep in mind these two helpful hints:

- ✔ **Only deal with companies that you trust.** If you're in the market for a second home, you may have to give personal information to Web sites such as online lenders or homeowners' insurance companies to get quotes and tap opportunities. Make sure the companies you deal with are reputable. Check with your local Better Business Bureau to see if complaints have been lodged against the company.

  You can also figure out if a company is trustworthy by googling the name of the company and add keywords like "complaints," or "problems." The results will often be illuminating.

- ✔ **Use caution when revealing more than your e-mail address and name on a Web site.** On the Internet, identity theft often begins with an e-mail scheme known as *phishing.* Criminals target consumers' personal identity data and financial account credentials through *spoofed* e-mails — e-mails that look like they're from a legitimate company or bank and that lead unknowing users to counterfeit Web sites of "hijacked" brands. After they're on the site, victims are tricked into divulging financial data, including credit card numbers, account user names, passwords, and Social Security numbers. An unsuspecting person voluntarily gives out sensitive information to a party that looks like a legitimate firm, such as a bank or government agency, but which, in fact, is a criminal endeavor to rob them blind.

If you get an uncomfortable feeling about what's being asked, go with your gut and pick up the phone to call the company, instead of just doling out the information that the Web site requests. If you call a company you have questions for, you'll be talking to a legitimate rep from that firm. Credit card companies, PayPal, eBay, the IRS, and banks do *not* e-mail people and ask them to visit their site and confirm their personal info and login details. Correspondence from these financial entities comes in the U.S. mail or in a personal phone call.

It's also a good idea to have a "public" e-mail address that you can use for Web pages that ask for one — an address that can always be deleted without affecting your normal correspondences if you start getting blasted with spam and phony phishing e-mails at that address.

Starting with the best sites

Many Web sites offer real estate information, but not all of them are reputable, current, or regularly updated. But fear not. Over the past few years, several sources have established themselves as good places to go online to find a second home.

Here are a few I personally recommend and that you'll want to check out:

- **The Real Estate Book,** www.livingchoices.com: This is the online version of those little, full-color magazines that you find in racks on street corners and in grocery stores.

- **Realtor.com,** www.realtor.com: The granddaddy of all real estate sites, the bulk of the nation's MLSs post their listings here.

- **Coldwell Banker,** www.coldwellbanker.com: This large real estate franchise offers a simple property search online.

- **HomeGain,** www.homegain.com: You can find listings for existing homes, foreclosures, and new construction on this site.

- **Private Islands,** www.privateislandsonline.com: Okay, I had to include this one, in the event that price is no object (congrats!) and you've always wanted a second home on your own island.

For homes that owners are selling themselves, try:

- Help U Sell, www.helpusell.com

- Assist 2 Sell, www.assist2sell.com

- For Sale By Owner, www.forsalebyowner.com

Here are some other popular sites to check out:

- **Foreclosurenet.net,** www.foreclosurenet.net: This site lists (for a fee) *foreclosed properties.* (Foreclosed properties are those that owners have stopped paying for, and that lenders have taken back and are selling via foreclosure.) For more about them, see the "Keep an eye out for second-home deals" section later in this chapter.

- **HUD Homes & Communities,** www.hud.gov: This U.S. Housing and Urban Development Web site offers a free search of all properties HUD has foreclosed on and is selling. Click on "HUD Homes" on the left-hand rail, and then click on the state where you're looking for your second home. You can search by zip code or price, and the site provides details on all properties offered, including location.

- **EscapeHomes,** www.escapehomes.com: You can search this site by location, interest (in wine country, along the beach, near golf courses), or by property type.

✔ **Vacation Rentals By Owner,** www.vrbo.com: Before you plunk down thousands of dollars for a second home in an area you're not very familiar with, check out this site that lists rental units. You can visit the area first to see whether it suits you. This site can also help you figure out how much rent to charge if you plan on renting your second home when you're not using it.

Read the newspaper (Not the funnies)

In days of yore, the only way people knew a home was on the selling block was through the newspaper. Sometimes yard signs and word of mouth spread the news, but the local paper's classifieds section was the only surefire place to find out what was for sale. The Internet has definitely stolen some of the old black-and-white's glory, but real estate agents and owners continue to list their properties for sale in the paper, particularly on Sundays.

Starting with the Sunday extravaganza

The Sunday paper is thick for a good reason: It's jampacked with ads. One thing you can be sure of finding in the Sunday paper is a plentiful supply of full-page, color ads placed by real estate agents and offices proudly displaying their latest listings, as well as a slew of smaller ads from agents and owners in the plain ol' classified columns.

To make your life even easier, many larger newspapers in the United States place their classified ads online. So even if you're considering buying a home outside your geographical region, you can always search that city's newspaper's classifieds on the Web. If the newspaper that serves your desired location doesn't place its real estate classifieds online, you'll want to subscribe to that paper. Remember, however, it may take a few days for the paper to land in your mailbox, and any hot listings may be sold by the time you get the paper and pore through it.

In the Sunday paper, you'll also find listings of open houses, many of which will likely be happening on the very weekend that you're reading through the ads. Open houses are a great way to get out and look at homes without having to deal with any high-pressure sales tactics that a listing agent may try on you when you're dealing with them one on one.

If you do come across a for-sale ad that strikes your fancy, be sure to act fast. You can probably get your hands on more information about the property on the Internet. Many ads include Web addresses for the agent's office and/or the individual property, as well as phone numbers that will provide info via an automated system. Don't waste any time. You can bet dollars to donuts that you're not the only one poring over the real estate ads on a Sunday morning.

Monitoring the classifieds

Don't assume that one stroll through the Sunday paper will hand you the second home of your dreams on a silver platter. It takes seven weeks, on average, for buyers to find a second home, which means that you'll need at least that many go-rounds (if not more) with the classified section. In addition to the Sunday paper, you can also check out the daily classifieds in case a new listing pops up.

Put time into your second-home search, and combine your newspaper perusals with Internet searches and yard sign spotting (see next section for more information on lawn signs) for the best results.

Take a road trip

When you're looking for a second home and the area where you're buying is within driving distance, there is simply no substitute for hitting the road and looking around for both existing and new properties. You can discover a lot about available real estate simply by taking an afternoon drive. Look for open house signs, and use these events to take quick tours of homes that you might be interested in. You may also find FSBO properties on your wanderings.

Hit the road, drive around a little, and check out what's sticking up out of people's lawns. Many signs offer detailed information sheets on the home, as well as flyers that list prices and even comparable properties that are available in the area. Some signs provide phone numbers you can call to obtain automated information (known as *talking houses*), and all will include the agent or owner's contact information.

Keep a pen, paper, and cellphone handy at all times during these jaunts, and be prepared to jot down the info from the sign. Grab any info sheets housed in those plastic tubes or boxes hanging from the sign, read them thoroughly, and then, if you like what you see, make the necessary calls to the owner or agent to set up a showing.

No matter how great that two-story beach house looks, don't approach the owner directly about a showing (unless, of course, he's selling it on his own). Most sellers list their properties with agents for a reason, and that's because the agent acts as a buffer and handles all the contacts, showings, and negotiations for the property.

Some developments restrict or outright prohibit the use of "for sale" signs by property owners. If you're very interested in a specific complex or neighborhood, you'll almost certainly do better using an MLS search (versus driving around looking for yard signs) to determine what's on the market.

Rely on the MLS

The Multiple Listing Service (MLS) is to real estate what the Kelly Blue Book is to cars: a gold standard for the industry and a source that everyone in the business has used and relied on for decades. The definitive resource for many different types of home listings, MLSs serve a purpose by aggregating all the listing data in one place where buyers can efficiently browse through their second-home choices.

Defining an MLS

An *MLS* collects and displays real estate listing data for Boards of Realtors and real estate associations nationwide. An *MLS area* is an area of a county that has been designated a name and number, which allows the potential buyer to specify the geographic area where she wants to concentrate her second home search. (For example, if you're looking for a second home in downtown Chicago, you tap the Northern Illinois MLS, which lists all homes available in and around the city). To find the MLS that includes listings in your area of choice, type "MLS" and the county name and state into a search engine, or ask a local real estate agent for the information.

Many real estate Web sites run by individual real estate agents and/or offices have MLS data posted on them. National aggregators like Realtor.com actually purchase the data from the national MLSs, and then display the information in a consumer-friendly format online.

Working like a Realtor

The MLS was once a thick, somewhat overwhelming book that was delivered on a weekly basis to every real estate agent's desk. Later, the info was put into an electronic format that was accessible by computer, but it was still only viewable by agents who were members of the specific MLS or Realtor board.

Times have changed. Today if you're searching for a second home on your own, you can rely on a consumer-friendly version of that info now available on the Web from various sources (see "Use the Internet to your advantage" in this chapter). And although it's not the same exact information that agents have access to (specific street addresses, for example, are sometimes omitted from what are known as "public" sites), this Web info still gives second-home buyers a good look at what's on the market and at what price.

So don your real estate agent hat (You don't have one? That's okay. You can hunt for houses chapeau-less!) and peruse some of these sites. Enter your parameters and criteria, and the MLS will find one or more homes that fit your wants and needs. Agents routinely check the MLS in the morning and afternoon to pick up any new listings that have come on the market during the day. If something catches your eye, do as the agents do and jump on it!

Keep an eye out for second-home deals

Perhaps you're in the market for a second home, but you want to try and score a hidden deal. A few nontraditional ways to score a great second home include foreclosures, auctions, and bargains that come about because of divorce, death of a family member, or last-minute relocations. Here's how to navigate the bargain-basement terrain.

Foreclosures

If you're up for rooting around for information and don't mind a bit of leg-work, then you may have a shot at getting a second home via the foreclosure process. Basically, these homes are in the process of being *foreclosed* upon — that is, taken back — by lenders who haven't been paid. (Because the house or real property always secures a mortgage loan, if you don't pay, the lender takes the house.)

Foreclosures could take up an entire chapter, or even a book, so I'll wrap things up here with this: Although they can present good opportunities for those who are willing to do the extra work involved, buying foreclosed homes can be risky business for the uninitiated. If you're seriously considering buying a foreclosed home, don't do it alone. Be sure that you have good professionals (attorneys, real estate agents, accountants, and so forth) on your side before getting into it.

Web-based services like RealtyTrac (www.realtytrac.com) provide info on foreclosures that are taking place or are about to take place nationally. Second-home buyers can search through the listings (available via paid sub-scription) by state or many other criteria for properties that meet their needs and budgets.

Auctions

You probably already know about homes being sold to the highest bidder on eBay, so it's quite possible that you as a second-home buyer can find your perfect vacation and retirement home at a traditional auction. If going to for-sale auction events attended by other potential buyers is something you'd consider, you may want to think about purchasing your second home at auction.

Real estate auctions come in three varieties:

- ✔ **Absolute sale:** At this type of auction, the house goes to the highest bidder, with no minimums or reserves.

- ✔ **Minimum bid:** At this auction, sellers agree to sell at the highest bid above an established sales price.

> ✔ **Reserve:** These auctions allow sellers to set a *reserve price* that is above the minimum starting bid and not revealed to bidders until it has been met. Should the bidding not exceed that reserve, the seller doesn't have sell the property. (Yes, just like they do on eBay for ordinary everyday auctions.)

Check with a real estate agent or call an auction house in the area where you want to purchase your second home to find out where auctions are taking place. Another good resource is the local newspaper's classified section, which often lists current and upcoming home auctions, along with the home's basic information and starting bid price.

Bargains

Bargain is an umbrella term I use to describe any house or piece of property that can be purchased at a price below market value. These homes don't always become available through foreclosures or auctions. Sometimes an owner will *have* to sell, and price becomes secondary to unloading the property. Possible scenarios include

> ✔ **The quick sell:** Your cousin just got a new job 3,000 miles away at double the salary and has to sell his house and move like, oh, yesterday. You happen to know that his mother (your aunt) left him the house and that it has no mortgage. (Lucky him, right?) It isn't far-fetched to imagine him selling it to you, his beloved cousin, for much less than he could get if he had more time and was willing to wait. Make a (low-ball) offer and you may be pleasantly surprised.
>
> ✔ **The "just-get-rid-of-it" sell:** The couple down the block is getting divorced and rancor abounds. They now not only loathe each other, but they also each loathe the house they lived in. Make a discrete inquiry about buying, and they may be happy to get rid of it and give you a rock-bottom price.
>
> ✔ **The regretful sell:** The elderly widow who lives on the water and whom you know through your mother has decided to move into a retirement community. She just can't maintain her house on her own anymore. A conversation with her about you possibly taking it off her hands may result in you scoring a lovely beach house for a great price.

Keeping your ears open can lead to a wonderful second home at a terrific price.

Making an Offer and Negotiating

After you've found the perfect second home — the one that meets all your criteria, including location, features, and price — you can make an offer to the seller. In this section, I give you a brief look at how this process works, and some advice on how to handle it on your own.

Knowing what the listed price really means

In today's traditional real estate market, you'll rarely find a home that's underpriced, so be prepared to make a reasonable offer based on market conditions, the home itself, and recent and comparable sales (*comps*), and not so much on what the seller *thinks* she can get for the home.

As a buyer, you need to follow one rule: Make darned sure that the price you're offering to pay is based on professional knowledge and data, and not on someone's opinion of what her home might be worth. Make sure that the person who advises you on what to offer knows what they're talking about.

Bargains are out there, of course, but in the majority of cases, you'll likely be paying a market value based on informed advice. And you won't pay higher than the "right" price if you do your homework.

Using an appraiser to help you determine a good offer

An *appraiser* evaluates the property's condition and size and determines how much it's worth. He reviews several aspects of the home, including

- Comparable, recent sales in the area
- The property's location
- The home's square footage
- Replacement costs
- The structure's construction quality
- The age of the property
- The property's amenities (such as pools and patios)

You can get an appraisal before you make an offer on a home, as long as you don't mind shelling out $250 to $500. This can be a particularly good strategy in a situation where you know that the house is overpriced, but can't otherwise prove it. Appraisers usually come on the scene after a purchase contract has been written and an appraised value is necessary to obtain financing.

An appraiser doesn't necessarily need access to the property's interior, but keep in mind that if you don't get the seller's permission to conduct an appraisal, you risk upsetting her to the point where she won't entertain or accept your offer. Be careful about making an end run that could alienate the seller.

Sooner or later, you have to have an appraisal done on the home you plan to buy if you're taking out a mortgage. A lender will always require an independent appraisal of the market value of your second home before closing. Why? Because the loan amount generally cannot exceed 95 percent of the appraised value or purchase price, whichever is lower. But check your financing options carefully. Some lenders loan 100 percent to well-qualified buyers.

Mastering the art of the offer

When you're ready to make an offer, here's a rundown of what needs to be done:

1. **Decide on the amount you're prepared to offer on the home.**

   A good rule of thumb is about 10 percent lower than the asking price, unless there are extenuating circumstances (such as a hot seller's market where ten buyers are bidding on a home at the same time, or a home that you know needs major repairs and is not worth anywhere near the asking price). So for a $300,000 townhouse, you might start at $270,000.

2. **Prepare a written offer on a Purchase Agreement.**

   You can get a complete, inexpensive "Offer To Purchase Real Estate" kit at an office supply store. Include information such as the offer price, proposed closing date, any conditional issues (such as a financing contingency that says your deposit will be refunded if you can't obtain financing), and the amount of *earnest money* (essentially your "deposit," which typically ranges from $500 to $2,000) you plan to fork over with the offer. Be sure to include a time frame during which the offer will be valid and a stop date.

3. **Present the offer to the seller.**

4. **Allow the seller a specific amount of time to think about the offer and make a counteroffer.**

   Give the seller three or four days. (An example of a *counteroffer:* The listing price is $300,000, you offer $270,000, and he comes back with $285,000.)

5. **Mull over the counteroffer and decide if you're willing to accept it.**

   If you don't want to accept the counteroffer, evaluate whether you want to continue the process until no more negotiating is feasible and it's all over, ending either successfully (you and the seller agree on a purchase price) or unsuccessfully (you walk away from the home and continue your search).

6. **After the seller accepts the final, written offer, you and the seller sign the document.**

   At this time, the document becomes legally binding. Be sure that you *read and understand* everything on the contract before signing. When you're handling the purchase of your second home yourself, comprehending what you're signing is absolutely critical.

Chapter 6

Relying on the Experts When Buying Your Second Home

. . . .

. . . .

*R*eal estate agents serve a purpose in the world of second-home buying, but some of you may want to steer clear of these professionals altogether. Perhaps you've bought and sold dozens of properties in the past, or maybe you know the home seller and the property well enough to not need an intermediary to help the transaction along. (If you plan to take the do-it-yourself route, check out Chapter 5.) Either way, how you purchase your second home is a highly individualized choice that rests largely with you, the home buyer.

You already own a primary residence, so you know how stressful the entire home-buying experience can be. Furthermore, buying a home is a huge time and financial commitment. Now that you want to buy a second home, you may know that you don't have the time, energy, or motivation to devote yourself (almost) full time to such an important process.

You needn't worry though, because plenty of professionals — everyone from real estate agents to buyer's agents and transaction brokers — can help make your home-buying process go smoothly. These professionals make a living out of helping people just like you get from the initial offer to the closing table in the most seamless way possible.

This chapter explains the roles a real estate agent plays in the home-buying game in the United States and how you can rely on buyer's agents, transaction brokers, and other professionals to purchase your dream second home. (If you're considering purchasing a second home outside the United States, check out Chapter 9 for more info.)

How the Real Estate Game Is Played (And Possibly Has Changed)

In days past, around the time your parents bought *their* first home, they dealt with a real estate agent who operated as a *listing agent.* This agent probably represented sellers, while occasionally helping a buyer navigate through the home-buying maze, albeit without any binding obligation to the buyer. Those days are gone. As real estate transactions became more complex, and baby boomers began buying homes in record numbers beginning in the '60s and '70s (in a sense, foretelling their later interest in second homes), the market and the professionals involved in it needed to change and adapt. Today, many of the professionals' services now overlap.

Today's real estate agents are different, and they fall into two general categories (and one subcategory):

- **Listing agents:** These agents, also called *real estate agents* or *Realtors,* list homes for sale, advertise and market them, show them to interested parties, and put them on the Multiple Listing Service (MLS).

    Realtor is a trade name and copyrighted — not all real estate agents are Realtors. Only members of the National Association of Realtors can be called Realtors, and they are bound to a strict Code of Ethics.

- **Buyer's agents:** These agents work mainly (or solely, depending on the agent) with buyers, hooking them up with properties, negotiating for them, and remaining by their side until the property closes. For more about these folks, see "Making a Buyer's Agent Your Right-Hand Man (Or Woman)" later in this chapter.

- **Transaction brokers:** These professionals typically fall into one of the above categories, but also handle deals on a "piecemeal" basis. For instance, they take care of the paperwork for a for sale by owner (FSBO) deal where no listing or selling agent commission is being paid. Transaction brokers can work out a deal with the buyer, the seller, or both, and they are paid at closing for the work performed. To better understand how these pros can help you, skip ahead to the "Using a Transaction Broker" section in this chapter.

Every real estate transaction is different. Just because the last transaction you wrapped up went like a well-oiled machine doesn't mean that you'll be able to buy a second home without at least a few challenges.

The next two sections look more closely at what real estate pros can do to help you find your ideal second home.

Making a Buyer's Agent Your Right-Hand Man (Or Woman)

If setting up showing appointments and calling title companies isn't your bag, then you want a buyer's agent on your side during your second-home purchase. For most people, it makes sense to have a knowledgeable, hardworking individual in their corner, making sure that all the steps have been covered before the two of you converge on the closing table.

Some states allow a practice called *dual agency* (also known as *designated agency*). This is when one agent represents both the buyer and the seller. The intent of dual agency is to streamline the transaction. And many people in states where it's allowed — on both sides of the transaction — have been pleased with a dual agency arrangement when they bought or sold a house.

However, because of the potential for ethical and conflict of interest issues, full disclosure of a dual agency is required, and both parties must agree to it. A dual agent is forbidden to reveal to the seller what the buyer is willing to spend, and likewise forbidden to reveal to the buyer what the seller is willing to take, meaning you're on your own regarding coming up with an offer if you're buying. Many people don't feel comfortable negotiating such a huge financial transaction without the advice of a trusted pro working solely for them. That's why, if at all possible, I recommend you avoid dual agency and go with a buyer's agent or transaction broker (see later in this chapter for more details on these two types of real estate pros).

Normally, in return for shepherding a client through the real estate transaction, the buyer's agent earns a commission when the deal closes. That commission is paid by the seller at the closing, and the amount is split fifty-fifty between the two agents who are co-brokering the transaction. That's good news for you, as the buyer, because you don't have to pay any out-of-pocket fees for the benefits of agent representation.

If you decide to use a buyer's agent, be sure to ask her about possible situations in which you would be asked to pay her commission. Any agreement you reach with a buyer's agent should be in writing. For example, if you decide on a for sale by owner (FSBO) home, the seller may not be willing to shell out a commission, and you, as the buyer, may have to compensate your real estate agent for her services.

This section delves into the roles of a buyer's agent and how she can help you find your second home. This section also helps you find a buyer's agent who is right for you and discusses what you need to know when signing an agreement with a buyer's agent.

Defining a buyer's agent's responsibilities

Unlike selling agents, who work harder at representing sellers and marketing their listings, buyer's agents put their time into working with people just like you.

A buyer's agent's duties include, but aren't limited to

✔ Getting the best possible price and contract terms for you.

✔ Disclosing all material facts (problems with the roof, plumbing issues, and so forth) about the property (that they have knowledge of) that you're interested in buying.

✔ Sharing with you any relevant, personal facts about the seller that could affect your negotiating power, such as an impending divorce, foreclosure, or the fact that the condo has been on the market for two years without so much as a nibble.

More specifically, buyer's agents perform myriad tasks for second-home buyers, including (but, again, not limited to):

✔ **Pointing you in the direction of financing:** Your agent arranges a meeting with at least three lenders, who can prequalify you for a second-home loan, thus putting you in a strong negotiating position when you're ready to make an offer on a home.

✔ **Figuring out what you want:** Expect to sit down or chat on the phone with your agent for a few minutes to provide some key information that she can use to find the right second home for you. Your agent may ask you about the number of bedrooms, baths, and total square footage you want, as well as information on the minimum lot size, and what amenities and other features you're looking for. (See Chapter 3 for more details on defining what you want in your second home.)

And because you get more than just a building when you buy a home, you and your agent can easily access info online about neighborhoods, schools, shopping, taxes, and other important factors to consider. (See Chapter 4 for info about the location of your second home.)

✔ **Searching for eligible properties:** With your wish list in hand, your agent hits the streets (well, not literally anymore) to find out what's on the market. She may use the following resources:

• **The local Multiple Listing Service (MLS):** She can look at the MLS where all homes listed by real estate agents are posted.

- **Other real estate offices:** She can call real estate offices in areas where you're looking to buy (if they're outside of the agent's typical area). She can also contact local new developments and talk with area builders.

- **The Internet:** She can look online at Web sites, such as www.realtor.com (a national hot spot for real estate listings).

✔ **Previewing properties:** With a printout in hand (either from your own Internet research or from the material provided by your agent from the local MLS), your buyer's agent will likely preview several potential properties to avoid wasting your time. She can do this in person or online via virtual tours, which give potential buyers a pretty good idea of what a home looks like without having to visit it.

✔ **Taking you to see properties:** Your agent will tell you when it's time to pile in the car and check out the inventory of possible homes. The Internet has made this process much easier and less time consuming because it allows you and your agent to look at properties and eliminate those that don't match your criteria before you spend hours driving all over the city.

✔ **Negotiating on your behalf:** When the right property comes along, a buyer's agent will refer to the MLS to come up with a stack of recent sales on comparable properties, and then work with you to come up with a feasible starting offer that includes price, terms, and conditions. After you and your agent determine a solid starting offer, your agent presents the written offer to the seller through the seller's agent. Both professionals then negotiate in concert with their clients over the offer until there is an acceptable contract, or the buyer moves on to another property. When the buyer and seller are both satisfied with the outcome of the negotiating process, the deal can move forward.

✔ **Standing by at the closing table:** Yes, your buyer's agent may even attend the closing if round-table closings are the norm in your area. If not, an escrow agent will handle all the paperwork, and you won't have to be present.

Your buyer's agent can be ready to answer your questions and help with last-minute issues that crop up. She'll serve as your go-between with the selling agent and other professionals who are on hand to see the deal through to closing. Because your agent represents *you,* you can feel confident that your interests will be protected. The closing is also when the real estate brokerage collects a check for a job well done.

Finding the right professional

You want to use a buyer's agent to help you find and purchase your second home, but you don't know where to find this illustrious individual, right? The following are great ways to find the right buyer's agent:

- ✔ **Talk to the agent who sold you your first house**. This is a good place to start because you already have a relationship with this professional. And even if he can't help (perhaps he doesn't work in the new area where you're moving to), he can certainly point you in the direction of someone who can, and perhaps receive a referral fee (from the agent you do work with) in the process.

- ✔ **Ask for referrals from friends, family, and colleagues.** Referrals are always the best way to get a good, reputable agent. Talk to people you know who have purchased second homes in the last few years and find out who they worked with, but understand that if they bought a vacation home on Maui — and if you're looking in New England — that the person may not be able to help. Ask them what the experience was like, what the person's good and bad points were, and how it all worked out in the end.

  If you don't like what you hear, talk to the next person until you hear about a buyer's agent who sounds like a good fit. If, for example, your best friend tells you that her agent called her ten times a day over a four-week period to introduce properties that weren't at all up to par with what she was looking for, then you've found an agent to avoid.

  If, however, the guy in the office next to you bragged up an agent who negotiated a great price on a beachfront condo, and then pointed him in the direction of a great local furniture store that helped him save a ton of money outfitting the place, then you just may have yourself a keeper.

- ✔ **Go online.** Conduct a Web search for agents in your geographic area who bill themselves as agents who work only with buyers. You can find an agent who works only for or primarily with buyers through the Real Estate Buyer's Agent Council (REBAC) at www.rebac.net. Click on "home buyers" on the bottom of the page and then "Find a Buyer's Rep." Enter the area where you plan to purchase your second home, and you'll get a directory of accredited buyer's representatives who serve that area.

A simple REBAC search by state may return an overwhelming number of agents (sometimes in the thousands). Enter the zip code (use the closest big city's zip) to narrow the list of agents to a more manageable number.

There are a lot of good agents working in the market, so don't get discouraged if the first few you talk to don't pan out. Just keep looking, keep asking for referrals, and sooner or later you'll find a great match.

Choosing your agent

So you've found an agent you think can help you. He listens when you speak, seems knowledgeable, and has a pleasant, nongrating personality. So how do you know if your instincts are accurate? Easy. You ask questions. When you find a buyer's agent whom you think you'd like to work with, here are a few key questions you should ask:

- ✔ **How long have you worked in this area?** Someone who moved into the area just last week, or who hasn't sold anything in the vicinity you're considering for a year or more, may not be very helpful.

- ✔ **How many clients do you typically work with at one time?** You want someone who's busy, but not overly busy. If the agent is handling 40 (or more) different clients at once (yes, there are agents who do this), he is probably not going to have the time to do a thorough search for you (particularly if what you want is going to take a few months to find).

- ✔ **Are you familiar with the type of home I want to purchase?** If you're looking for a condo and the agent works only with high-end, single-family homes, then choose another agent. Likewise, if the agent specializes, say, in condos and commercial properties, he may not be knowledgeable enough about single-family homes.

- ✔ **Are you comfortable searching for homes in my price range?** Again, if this person is working in the $100,000 to $200,000 range and you're looking for a $1.5 million waterfront mansion (or vice versa), continue to look and find someone who specializes in what you're in the market for. (For example, you can take a drive down by the water to see which agents have signs out in the yards of the large homes that are for sale).

- ✔ **Are you an effective negotiator?** Odds are the agent's response to this question will be a resounding "Yes!" so expect it. But the reality is that you can't tell for sure if this is true until you see him in action. In the meantime, it doesn't hurt to ask questions like:

  - How much money do you typically save your clients over the asking price?

  - What other terms do you typically negotiate for (a quick move-in date, for example)?

The *real* house-buying process *begins* when you find a place you love, so you want an agent who knows how to finesse the transaction to save you as much money as possible and get you the best deal.

When you've found someone who's a good fit, it's time to formalize the relationship (see the next section).

Signing an agreement with a buyer's agent

Because real estate agents earn their keep by helping buyers and sellers through to the end of the transaction, they don't receive a dime for their services until closing day. Buyer's agents use legal contracts called *buyer agency agreements* to outline the business terms between you and your buyer's agent. These agreements can be exclusive or nonexclusive, and they answer questions like:

✓ Will the buyer's agent be paid from the commission the seller pays at closing? Are there situations where this may not happen? If yes, what are they?

✓ Is this an exclusive agreement with one agent, or is it a nonexclusive contract that frees you up to work with other buyer's agents?

✓ What's the duration of the agreement? How long will you work with this agent?

✓ How will the buyer's agent represent you if you decide to make an offer on a home that she has listed or on a property that another agent in her office has listed?

✓ Is the agreement valid only in a certain geographic region, or does it cover real estate that you purchase anywhere?

✓ Is the contract renewable? Can it be canceled without penalty? If not, what are the consequences if I cancel it?

Every contract comes with its own terms, so be sure to go over these points carefully before signing.

Read the fine print before signing the buyer agency agreement, because most of them generally specify that the *seller* will pay the buyer's agent's commission, but this occurs only if the seller has *agreed* to pay. If the seller isn't willing to pay, however, the buyer — *you* — may have to pick up the tab if it's stated in the buyer agency agreement. Look for specific language that says something like "buyer hereby agrees to pay to the agent a commission of X percent or $0000." This commonly means that the seller has already refused to pay and the agent's fee is coming out of your pocket. If you can't live with this, don't sign, and then renegotiate the terms.

The buyer agency agreement is negotiable, which means that if something stands out as being "not right" about the contract, you don't have to sign it. Ask the agent to modify the contract until both of you are satisfied with the end result. Consider asking one of the professionals I talk about in the "Depending on Other Professionals during the Purchasing Process" section to review the contract.

Using a Transaction Broker

What is a transaction broker? A *transaction broker* is a real estate pro who represents both the buyer and the seller, but has no binding financial responsibility to either person and does not act in the capacity of a full-service real estate agent. A transaction broker facilitates the deal — and helps the parties reach an agreement. He handles the paperwork for the transaction for a fee when you're *not* working with a buyer's agent. He must abide by all laws, as well as all professional codes of conduct and ethical standards.

You don't need a transaction broker if you're working with a buyer's agent or other real estate agent who is representing the deal and handling the paperwork.

This section highlights what a transaction broker can do for you and what you need to know before you decide to use one.

Do you really need a transaction broker?

Should you use a transaction broker? The following questions may help you determine if a transaction broker is right for you and your second-home purchase.

- ✔ **What are the benefits of using a transaction broker?** A transaction broker is a neutral party. He looks out for the accuracy of the process, the correctness of the paperwork, and the professional execution of the sale. And he'll charge less than an agent.

- ✔ **Is a transaction broker an agent?** A transaction broker is not acting in the capacity of a real estate agent — although he may, in fact, be a licensed real estate agent. The transaction broker is simply an intermediary seeing the transaction to its successful completion. If you don't need the services of a real estate agent and just need someone to handle the paperwork, then a transaction broker can help, but he's not acting as a real estate agent on your behalf.

✔ **What services won't a transaction broker perform?** He won't negotiate price, he won't shop for houses, he won't find you financing. A transaction broker is simply someone to handle the paperwork and serve as a go-between when you don't need a full-service real estate agent.

✔ **What will a transaction broker cost me?** As the buyer, it won't cost you anything. The transaction broker receives a flat fee, which the seller pays.

✔ **Will a transaction broker negotiate the best price for me?** A transaction broker will not negotiate price in your favor — or the seller's favor — but does act as an intermediary in discussions of price, offering advice and information. Remember that the transaction broker has no financial responsibility to either party — a transaction broker is a "non-agent" (even if he has a real estate license) but can be a valuable asset in seeing the deal to a happy conclusion.

Finding a reputable transaction broker

Many listing and buyer's agents will perform the limited services of a transaction broker for those buyers who do not want (or need) to work with a full-service agent working at a full commission rate (ranging from 5 to 7 percent of the sales price, depending on the area where the home is located).

When you sign a buyer agency agreement, you can forget about wondering whether to hire a transaction broker. Your agent will take care of everything.

Depending on Other Professionals during the Purchasing Process

Financing, real estate, the law, and taxes are complex fields, strewn with all kinds of land mines, and dangerous to naively stride through unassisted and unprotected. That's where professionals of every stripe come in, and during the process of buying your second home, you may need help from one or all of these experts.

Also, if you're using a transaction broker (or tackling the home-buying process alone — and if you are, make sure to read Chapter 5) to buy your second home, these pros can be key to not only assuring the professional execution of the transaction, but also to letting you sleep nights.

The following list focuses on other important people you may need to hire when buying a second home. These people can guide you in making wise decisions and protect you and your new investment.

If you're using a buyer's agent, you may not need to use some of these people because a buyer's agent can take care of many, if not all, of the important details.

✔ **Lawyers:** A popular billboard says, "Buying a House? Call a lawyer first." Because a group of attorneys sponsored the billboard, it's easy to understand the sentiment, but perhaps it isn't necessary to call a lawyer first. Granted, it can't hurt to call one at some point, but it's your decision whether to retain a private attorney to represent you in your second-home purchase. And it's perfectly okay if you do. But in many cases, your attorney will be duplicating the work of the other professionals handling your deal — meaning you're paying twice for the same services — not a smart move. Some states do require an attorney to handle real estate closings, so depending on where you live, you may have no choice. But check out the requirements before retaining your own lawyer at your own expense. Both listing and buyer's agents can answer questions about the legal requirements and, if necessary, possibly even recommend a local attorney experienced in representing home buyers.

✔ **Accountants:** If you have an accountant prepare your taxes, have a chat with Ms. CPA before you begin looking for your second home. Your accountant can discuss your current tax situation with you and what will change if you take on additional financing, begin receiving rental income, and need to spend money to maintain an income-earning property. An accountant can also help with long-term planning for your future and retirement, as well as advise you on the tax consequences when you decide to sell your primary home and move into your second home. (Refer to Chapter 14 for more info on the tax implications of owning a second home.)

If you don't have an accountant, your buyer's agent can probably recommend someone who will offer a free consultation and help you determine whether you need professional accounting services at the moment.

✔ **Appraisers:** Home appraisers are knowledgeable about comparable home values in the neighborhoods where you're thinking of buying. They figure out a property's value by looking at factors such as the property's age, size, and condition. Establishing a relationship with an appraiser can help when you need an appraisal of the property you're considering buying and don't want to use the seller's appraiser or the ones recommended by the agent. Appraisers are especially important in areas where vacation homes are skyrocketing in value. See Chapter 5 for more information on appraisals.

Your lender will also appraise the property you're considering buying, and that appraisal alone may be enough to qualify you for financing. Then you won't need a "second opinion."

✔ **Loan officers:** The loan officer at your bank can fill you in on financing opportunities for your second home. The mortgage field constantly changes, and banks are always creating new programs for borrowers (see Chapter 8). A chat with a loan officer can prepare you for that time when all the price and fee negotiating is over and you have to decide how to pay for your second home.

It's a wise idea to get preapproved for a mortgage and request a preapproval letter from a potential lender. This way, you know you can secure a loan when the time comes to make an offer on your second home, and it will give the seller a better idea of you as a buyer. If a seller knows you're preapproved for a mortgage, she'll take you seriously and possibly negotiate a better price with you.

✔ **Mortgage brokers:** Like a loan officer at a bank, a private mortgage broker can fill you in on a slew of borrowing programs, from hundreds of companies offering financing. You may want to stick with the bank where you have your first mortgage, but it can't hurt to talk to an independent broker. Also, having a bank and a mortgage company competing for your business can only help you.

✔ **Insurance agents:** You'll need homeowners' insurance on your second home. Talk with your insurance agent before you start looking for your second home. Sometimes insurance companies offer discounts when existing clients add coverage to their policies. (Check out Chapter 8 for more on insuring a second home.)

✔ **Home inspectors:** You'll want to have the home you're thinking of buying inspected, and you'll want it inspected by someone working for you, not the seller. (Check out Chapter 7 for more about finding the right home inspector for your second-home purchase.)

✔ **Title company reps:** I have been to closings involving nothing but a title company representative, who handles the research to determine whether the seller has *clear title* (ownership of land that is without competing claims or other defects so it can be sold without complications) on the property she is trying to sell you. You need to know earlier, rather than later, if there are liens on the property, and a title company can provide peace of mind for a reasonable fee.

Chapter 7

Inspecting Your Second Home before You Sign on the Dotted Line

In This Chapter

▶ Finding a great home inspector

▶ Identifying what inspectors usually miss, and why

▶ Getting the details of the inspection in writing

▶ Handling problems that rear their ugly heads

▶ Making decisions based on the inspection

*O*nce upon a time, real estate agents considered home inspectors to be the ultimate "deal breakers." If there was any one person who could come in and quickly make a purchase unravel, it was the home inspector. Times have changed, though, and as society became more litigious, and agents found themselves tied up in lawsuits brought by home buyers who felt duped into purchasing unsound properties, home inspectors have become the agents' best friends.

In today's real estate market, inspectors can also be your best friend as you navigate your way through the final days of your second-home purchase, but they can also be the bearers of bad news. They typically charge anywhere from $250 to $500 (depending on geographic location and the size and complexity of the home) to scour a home's physical structure and major systems *looking* for problems. If your inspector finds problems during the inspection, you can save a significant amount of money and hassle by first, knowing about them, and then either resolving them or saying "no thanks" to the deal.

In this chapter, I discuss the importance of a second-home inspection, help you find a good inspector, advise you on the right questions to ask, and explain how to spot areas of a home that an inspector may overlook. And when inspections turn up problems, I show you how to either resolve them or walk away.

Recognizing the Importance of Your Second Home's Inspection

No matter how many homes you've closed on in the past, and no matter how savvy you are about housing construction and the ins and outs of home heating systems and plumbing, it always pays to have a second set of eyes give the home a thorough once-over before signing on the dotted line. Home inspectors can point out common problems with homes in the area. For example, if the region is known for having *sinkholes* (those large pockets of land that open up and swallow everything sitting on top of them), the inspector can clue you in to this issue. Inspectors can also point out home-specific issues, such as how mold can cause big problems for second-home owners whose abodes are in humid, damp climates.

An inspection typically takes place within ten days or so of the buyer and seller executing a purchase agreement. It's a good idea to include an inspection contingency in your offer, stating that if serious problems are uncovered, you can either renegotiate the purchase price or back out of the deal completely without losing your earnest deposit money.

An inspector won't tell you if you're getting a good value for your money, nor will he establish a "home value" for you, so avoid asking these questions. Instead of putting the inspector on the spot, take the solid information the inspector provides and use it to form your own opinions.

This section explains why the home inspection on your second home is important, pointing out what gets inspected, what often gets overlooked, and what your rights are as a prospective owner.

Knowing your rights and options

When buying a second home, you have every right to have that home inspected by a professional (check out the section about finding and hiring a reputable inspector). For a fee, your inspector will give the place a good once-over, scouting out any problems and issues that could turn into real headaches down the road. Even if you're looking at a brand-new home, you should still arrange an inspection. Let's face it, they don't make 'em like they used to!

Your goal is to protect your investment and avoid problems that could crop up later. The last thing you want is for your central air conditioning unit to suddenly fail at your housewarming party on a hot July afternoon in Texas. Trust me. It won't be a pretty picture. The builder assuring you, "It's a brand-new unit! Trust me!" is not enough these days. Understand what warranties the builder is offering and get it in writing. If you're buying a preowned property, consider purchasing a Home Warranty insurance policy (or ask the seller to pay for one) to cover most of the components for the first year or so.

If the seller refuses to allow a home inspection (which is, for the most part, a rarity, but still . . .), politely ask her if she needs any help raising that red flag up the flag pole in front of her home. Refusing an inspection means she's probably trying to conceal a problem — major or minor — and is not disclosing whatever is wrong on the mandatory seller disclosure — which she's required to do by law in most states. (See "Understanding Disclosure Statements" later in this chapter for more information.)

The problem could be as simple as a couple of (or eight) leaky faucets, or as major as an entire mold colony growing in the basement. Regardless of the suspected seriousness of the problems, if the seller won't give you the opportunity to discover what they are, say, "thanks, but no thanks," and walk away from the property.

What gets inspected

As they search for defects or other issues that can turn into significant problems down the road, home inspectors focus on the safety and construction of

- ❑ **Electrical wiring:** Homes can have insufficient electrical service, makeshift wiring connections, poor overload protection, and safety issues.

- ❑ **Heating and air conditioning systems:** Broken controls, unsafe or inadequate venting and exhaust removal systems, cracked heating exchanges, faulty thermostats. HVAC equipment tends to be the Achilles' heel in many homes.

- ❑ **Roofs:** Usually the most expensive component of a home to replace, roofs that leak cause consistent problems that range from water penetration and rotted joists, to mold and ruined sheetrock — and everything in between. And the problems only get worse with time.

- ❑ **Plumbing:** Defects in this category can range from minor stuff like a faucet needing a washer, to more involved problems like old and incompatible pipes, cracked toilets, faulty fixtures, leaky pipes, and major clogs.

- ❑ **Structural issues:** Foundation walls, attic rafters, windows, doors, ceilings, and floor joists are all vulnerable areas where home inspections may turn up problems.

- ❑ **Surface grading and drainage:** Water can penetrate into a basement or crawl space very quickly when the area around the home doesn't drain properly. I once knew a man whose backyard became a pond when it rained. Needless to say, his basement always had water.

- ❑ **Maintenance problems:** This category includes cracked and peeling paint, broken appliances, cracked floor tiles, broken doorknobs, torn carpeting, and other costly annoyances.

You can also have the home inspected for termites (often it's a requirement) and radon at an additional charge and, in most cases, you'll need an expert if you want absolute assurance the house has neither. A standard inspection may include a visual check for termites and a meter reading for radon, but a specialist will always go the extra mile and really make sure the structure is clear of both.

Using a checklist-style procedure, the inspector will slowly work his way through the entire home, front to back, top to bottom, and room by room, using a critical eye to uncover any and all defects and problems that are immediately apparent or waiting in the wings to descend upon the owner later. He'll make notes on his findings and transfer them to a final report after he completes the inspection. A typical inspection takes two to three hours and sometimes more, depending on the size of the home and how many problems turn up.

What inspectors often miss

Inspectors aren't infallible, and inspections aren't the final word about a home. Even the most experienced professionals often can't uncover everything that's wrong with a home during their inspection.

They can't, for example, see behind walls. And they can't lift up the entire length of carpeting in a hallway to look for problems (most will peel back a corner or two to check it out). Hidden damage inflicted by insects, mold, rot, and unwanted water are among the biggest "misses" to look out for. Other issues include roof-related problems (hire a roofing contractor to inspect the roof more thoroughly if you suspect problems), and problems with major components (like central air conditioner units) that may look and sound okay during the inspection, but that may unexpectedly die on you within a year of buying the home.

Four years ago, I bought a home in Florida "as is," but had an inspection anyway, just to be sure the house didn't have any major problems. The inspector (who did a very thorough job) told me at the time that the home's tile roof had at least "another good 15 years on it." Two years later, though, the roof was leaking like a sieve and in need of replacement. Turns out the previous owners (obviously do-it-yourselfers) had taken it upon themselves to replace about 50 tiles, and they tore the underlying tar paper in the process. This created hidden holes that the inspector's eye didn't catch. You can't do anything about eventualities like this, but you can at least be aware that — as I discovered — inspections are not the final word about a home.

Don't look at the inspection as the end-all statement about your second home. If you see black mold growing up the side of that gorgeous little cottage on Long Beach Island, take a closer look, point it out to your inspector, and get a second opinion on its presence and possible danger, if necessary. When you're at the home for showings and meetings, make a list of the things you're concerned about and discuss them all with the inspector. Are there curling shingles that don't look right? Bring it up. A long crack in the driveway? Bring it up. A large chunk of cement missing from the corner of the foundation? Bring it up. You'll be glad you did.

Finding and Hiring a Reputable Inspector

Hundreds of home inspectors in your area are ready to spring into action and uncover any and all problems with your second home, from leaky faucets to worn-out roofs.

And their fee is a bargain, considering the value of the information. For just a few hundred bucks, they'll go through the place with a fine-toothed comb (it's a pretty big comb, though) and tell you what you need to know before you decide whether to go through with your purchase. An inspection is a great service for the money, considering that it may save you $15,000 for a new roof or $2,500 for a new air conditioning unit in six months.

In this section, I help you sift through the slew of home inspectors to find one who will work as your advocate, and tell you exactly what's wrong (and right, by the way) with the dwelling you hope will become your second home. And, because some states don't require home inspectors to undergo any special training or licensing, I explain how to make sure your inspector is on the up-and-up, even if your second home is in one of those states.

Uncovering potential leads

Home inspectors have reputations that they need to protect, uphold, and even enhance to stay in business.

To keep their companies afloat, they rely heavily on referrals from "happy home buyers" whom they have serviced. This means that your first stop on your home inspector shopping trip should be friends, family members, and colleagues who may have had positive experiences while working with an inspector and would be happy to tell you all about it.

If at all possible, try to hire an inspector who is a licensed contractor or structural engineer. These professionals typically have more in-depth knowledge of residential structures and can provide straightforward, informed advice and information on the expected longevity and operability of major systems and structural components in your prospective home. Ask the inspector if he's a licensed contractor and/or engineer, and if the answer sounds shaky, ask to see a copy of his license for proof.

If your second home is in an area where you don't have friends or family, then your best bet is to ask for referrals from your real estate agent, go online, and check professional directories to find a good one. The following sections give you some more in-depth info. After you've found a couple of inspectors you think you can work with, use the questions listed in the "Knowing what to ask a potential inspector" section later in this chapter to find one whom you like and who is reputable and experienced.

Getting referrals from your agent

Your agent probably won't refer you to just one home inspector, but almost certainly will provide you with a list of several reputable inspectors from which you can choose the one you want to work with. Why? Because recommending one inspector could be construed as a conflict of interest if a problem should arise. By offering several names of inspectors, agents avoid a conflict of interest that could be alleged if a buyer were sent to the agent's "inspector of choice" to receive a clean bill of health for the home in order to ensure a smooth closing.

Checking real estate guides

Home inspectors regularly advertise in those full-color, real estate magazines that line the street corners and grocery store entrances in nearly every town across the country. You've seen them, right? And until you started looking for your second home, you ignored them, right?

Well, they're a gold mine of information, and you should make a point of picking one up on a regular basis. Flip through them, get some names, make some calls, ask some questions, and choose your inspector.

Going online

The Internet is another good place to find a quality home inspection firm to check out your second home. To acquire lots of names with very little effort, type the words "home inspection," the name of the town where your potential home is located, and your state into a search engine, such as Google. Don't be surprised if the results include thousands of names and firms. See the upcoming "Contacting professional inspector organizations" section for more details on using professional organizations' directories to find a qualified inspector you'll want to work with.

An attractive Web site with lots of bells and whistles does not necessarily mean its owner is a qualified, reputable home inspector. Keep this in mind as you peruse the Web for good candidates, and always ask questions.

Asking other experts for advice

Your attorney, accountant, or even your insurance agent may know of a great home inspector in your area, so don't be afraid to ask around. If these professionals have worked directly with an inspector — or if they have clients who have — then they can surely point you in the direction of a good one.

Unlike asking a real estate agent to recommend an inspector, it's not a conflict of interest for a professional whom you depend on for good advice in non–real estate transactions to provide a name or two. Because their commissions aren't hinging on the closing of the sale (they get paid anyway), these pros can usually point you in the direction of the best possible source of services and/or information.

Contacting professional inspector organizations

Professional inspector organizations are great ways to find good inspectors who follow their organizations' codes of ethics and performance. Two national home inspector organizations allow second-home buyers to locate home inspectors in their area.

- ✔ **American Society of Home Inspectors (ASHI),** www.ashi.org: I punched my zip code into the "find a home inspector" link and came up with the names of 25 home inspectors in my area. (To have a similar list mailed to you, call ASHI at 800-743-2744.)

- ✔ **National Association of Certified Home Inspectors (NACHI),** www.findaninspector.us: This site gave me a very long list of inspectors within a 20-mile radius of my zip code.

Looking into licensing requirements

Unfortunately, home inspectors operate in what I like to describe as "a highly unregulated environment." That's right, folks. Home inspectors are entrusted with uncovering problems that can impact one of the largest financial transactions you'll make in your lifetime, but in many states, they don't even need a license.

The following states do *not* require any type of licensure and/or criteria for home inspectors: California, Colorado, Delaware, Georgia, Hawaii, Idaho, Iowa, Kansas, Kentucky, Maine, Michigan, Minnesota, Missouri, Montana, Nebraska, New Hampshire, New Mexico, North Dakota, Ohio, Tennessee, Utah, Vermont, Washington, West Virginia, and Wyoming.

Please be aware that new laws are being enacted all the time, so check with your state department of business regulation if you're unsure of whether inspectors are licensed in your state.

If you live in one of these states, you can protect yourself and ensure that your inspection is on the up and up by working with ASHI or NACHI members (see the previous section) who have to follow a code of ethics and take continuing education classes to maintain membership.

Those states that do require home inspectors to be licensed have strict parameters for their licensees. In Illinois, for example, all home inspectors must be at least 21 years old and have a high school diploma or equivalent course of study (GED). All candidates for licensing must successfully complete 60 hours of prelicense education and pass the Illinois Home Inspector License Exam. The states that require inspectors to be licensed have similar guidelines.

States with home inspector licensing requirements have a supervisory board or department that handles anything to do with the licensing process. (In Massachusetts, for example, it's called the Board of Registration of Home Inspectors; in North Carolina, it's the Home Inspector Licensure Board.) If you have a problem with a particular inspector or have any questions regarding home inspection, you should call the department in the state where your second home is located.

Knowing what to ask a potential inspector

When hiring an inspector, be sure to ask questions and not just select the one with the most impressive Yellow Pages ad, or the toughest-sounding name. Just because a guy calls himself The Inspectinator doesn't mean he's got inspection superpowers. When checking the experience and knowledge of a home inspector, remember that rule No. 1 is "the more, the better." The "Finding and Hiring a Reputable Inspector" section can help you compile a list of potential inspectors.

After you have your list, call those inspectors and ask them the following questions, which will help you determine who's the best of your inspector candidates:

- ✔ **How much do you charge for a typical inspection?** It should range from $200 to $300.

- ✔ **What is your education, training, and experience?** Look for someone who has been in the business for five or more years. If someone just started in the business last week, don't walk away: Run.

✔ **What are your professional certifications or credentials?** Ask to see a state license and proof of membership in a group like ASHI or NACHI. This is particularly important in states where inspectors aren't licensed, and where almost anyone can claim to be a home inspector. (See the preceding section for more on licensing.)

✔ **How many other homes like mine have you inspected in the past 12 months?** You don't want someone who specializes almost exclusively on condos to inspect your new, 15-room castle on the beach.

✔ **What is your availability?** Make sure the inspector can meet your timeline.

✔ **Do you have any conditions or stipulations, such as me having to be present when conducting an inspection?** This will cut down on surprises on inspection day.

✔ **When you perform a home inspection, who are you working for?** The answer should be the same every time: the home buyer.

✔ **Can I tag along during the home inspection?** You don't want to get underfoot, but being there can make a big difference, especially if problems turn up.

✔ **Can I ask you questions during the inspection?** The inspector should be more than willing to explain everything, answer questions, and address any and all of your concerns. After all, he's working for you, and you're paying his fee.

✔ **Will you provide a written report?** This is pretty standard, but ask anyway. You'll want a written record of what went on during the inspection, details on all problems that were uncovered, and the inspector's written opinion on issues like roof age and status of major systems.

✔ **Can you provide an approximate written estimate of repair costs?** This can come in handy when negotiating with the seller over necessary repairs.

✔ **Can I call you at a later date for information and advice?** You may want to chat about that furnace that the inspector red-flagged as being "old and outdated," so you need to know if he's willing to keep those lines of communication open as part of his service.

From inspectors' answers to these questions, you should be able to whittle the list down to one inspector whose experience and credentials match what you're looking for, and whom you trust and have confidence in for something as important as an inspection.

Using the Inspection Report

A top-of-the-line home inspector will give you a written report that details exactly what is wrong (and some of what is right) with the second home that you plan to purchase. The reports can range from just a few pages to 20 or more, are usually organized by area or room of the home (kitchen, bathroom, and so forth), and may even include digital photos.

If your inspector is tech-savvy and online (which, truth be told, probably describes 99 percent of real estate professionals today), he may also, upon request, e-mail you a digital version of the report as a PDF or other file.

When you receive the inspector's written report, don't just file it away without reviewing it. First, slowly read through the opening pages of the report. Doing so gives you an overview of the home's major components (roof, foundation, and so on), systems (plumbing, electrical), and condition.

Next, go through the report and check out the negative findings, or areas the inspector identified as needing attention. The following list gives examples of the types of comments an inspector is likely to make. These are the concerns that you and the seller will need to hash out before closing day.

- ✔ The wood deck is showing signs of wear and tear. Maintenance and protection (painting or staining) is needed in the near future to preserve the wood and extend its life.

- ✔ A buildup of soot and creosote exists in the chimney. This is a dangerous situation and should be evaluated by a qualified professional and cleaned out as soon as possible.

- ✔ The central vacuum unit in the basement is nonoperational.

- ✔ The stopper in the tub in the main bathroom is missing.

- ✔ There is a water stain on the first-floor bathroom ceiling, which is directly below the master bath. My best guess is a toilet leak, probably from a worn-out wax seal. A plumber is needed to correct this problem.

But just because the inspector finds problems doesn't mean you should grab your *earnest money* (the deposit you put down when you signed the contract) and run. The seller may not even know that her air conditioning unit is on the blink or that all her living room windows are in sore need of replacement.

After you've reviewed the report, you need to think about the problems the inspector identified and make some decisions:

✔ **Which items need to be addressed?** Prioritize the problems the inspector identified. Which issues do you want to bring up with the seller, and which ones are minor enough that you can take care of yourself at a later time?

✔ **Who will be responsible for fixing the most-pressing items?** You can ask the seller to take care of the repairs (including paying for them), or you can plan to have them done after you own the home.

✔ **If you plan on taking care of the repairs, do you want to ask the seller for a reduction in the purchase price?** This may come in the form of a check from the seller to you at closing.

✔ **Should you still go through with the purchase?** If any of the problems are too costly for you to repair or call into question the integrity of the structure, rethink whether you want to invest so much money into this home.

The next section covers in more detail your options for handling problems.

What to Do When the Inspection Turns Up Problems

No home is perfect. And the problems in a home can range from the trivial — missing electrical faceplates on the outlets in the living room or a bathroom sink stopper that needs to be replaced — to the major — a pool that leaks an inch of water each day or an air conditioning condenser that needs a good swift kick to get it going every morning. It's a given that your second home will come with a few relatively minor, let's call them, "idiosyncrasies."

In some unfortunate cases, your second home will have major defects. You'll want to get these ironed out before you buy, or you'll need to accept a few persistent problems and their subsequent aggravation as part of the ownership process. If you and the seller can't agree on solutions to major problems, you may want to walk away from the home. In this section, I help you work through these issues.

Getting the seller to fix problems

In some states, sellers are required by law to disclose any known defects with a property as soon as they put it on the market (see the "Understanding Disclosure Statements" section). If the home inspection turns up more problems than those that are listed on the disclosure statement, then the seller is normally the first in line to take care of the repairs.

Threatening to walk away from the deal is one way to get the seller to sit up and take notice. You can also ask the seller for *concessions* (you fix this major issue, I'll take care of the smaller problems) that will help both of you get to the closing table in a satisfied state.

If the problems are small, the seller will usually deal with them to keep the sale moving forward. If the repairs are large (and, thus, costly), then the process outlined in the next section will commonly kick into action. Everyone jumps into the fray — the seller, the buyer, the real estate agent — with a single, common goal: Get the deal to the closing table.

Instead of fixing the problems herself, the seller may be flexible with the purchase price or contract terms if major problems are found. If you're willing to accept a price reduction and then take care of the repairs yourself (or not, if you don't care about some of them — not everyone wants a central vac, for instance), then this option may work in your favor.

Otherwise, it's up to you and the seller to negotiate a solution to the repairs that you can both agree to, or accept that the transaction will likely fall through. If you take a more flexible approach and decide that a few loose roof shingles, a broken dishwasher, and a leaky faucet in the guest bathroom are "minor," then by all means close on the home and have them fixed yourself.

Negotiating over major repairs

Sometimes a home inspection will turn up problems that you and/or the owner simply don't want to deal with. For example, say that gorgeous Myrtle Beach pool home that you've had your eye on for two years is actually a money pit in disguise. According to the home inspector's report, the pool needs an $8,000 resurfacing job (and is now leaking as a result), the heating and A/C unit doesn't run well and may soon fail altogether, and the steps leading up to the front door are rotted and need to be replaced.

How can you handle these issues? Keep the following potential steps in mind when dealing with inspection problems:

1. **The process starts with the seller, who — as long as the home isn't selling "as is" — must shoulder the responsibility of doing whatever is necessary to bring the home up to "selling shape."**

   As the prospective buyer, you don't have to deal with these issues. (Check out the earlier "Getting the seller to fix problems" section.)

2. **If the seller doesn't want to shell out the money it's going to cost to resolve the potential problems, then negotiate.**

   If you want the home badly, and the price is right, perhaps you can split the cost of the repairs.

3. **The listing real estate agent may kick in some of her commission to make the transaction work.**

   (Hey, don't laugh. This is an entirely feasible scenario if the agent wants to sell the house badly enough.)

4. **If none of these strategies work, however, then you're faced with a tough decision, which boils down to precisely two choices:**

   - Pull the plug on the transaction.

   - Pay for the repairs yourself.

Because no two real estate transactions are alike, you'll have to look carefully at your own situation to help you decide whether it's worth closing on this second home. You need to understand that every home (yes, even brand-new ones) will have at least a short "to fix" list after a home inspector makes his way through it. It's up to you to decide whether that list is short enough and determine if the seller is willing to do the necessary repairs or maybe compensate you (by cutting the price) for the cost of fixing them.

You may walk away from this property, but the next buyer will also want a home inspection, and that one will turn up the identical problems that yours uncovered. Make sure that your agent explains this to the seller before you back out. It may give you some bargaining power in getting those critical items fixed — or scoring a significant enough reduction in the price to pay for the repairs yourself.

This Is It! Deciding Whether to Buy the Home

A home inspector can go through the second home you have under contract in a thorough, professional manner. He can point out problems, suggest improvements, and probably give you an idea of repair costs. He can send you a voluminous report detailing nearly every inch of your potential domicile, and he can back up his evaluations based on past experience and industry knowledge.

What he can't do, however, is make the final decision on your home purchase. You have to do that yourself, based on the information he's provided you, what you already know, and what you know you want out of your second home. Before buying, carefully consider the questions in the following sections that look at basics of the home, the inspection report, and your own needs.

Accepting the home's basic features

Some factors you just can't change about a home, as much as you may want to. If you can't live with these features today, you can be certain you won't want to live with them every few months during visits, or a few years down the road, if you plan to retire to your second home. Think about these questions:

✔ **How old is the home that you want to buy?** It's no big secret that older structures need more TLC and upkeep — all of which costs money. And takes time. And causes headaches. Older homes can, in some cases, also be harder to finance. Banks may not want to lend on a very old home, and insurance may be more difficult and/or expensive to obtain.

Also keep in mind that there's a difference between a house's effective age and its chronological age. (Yes, just like people and their health profiles! You've heard of situations where 50-year-olds are said to have the "blood pressure of an 18-year-old." Same thing.) A house's *effective age* reflects how old a home is based on its condition and improvements, whereas *chronological age* is the actual age from time of construction. For example, if a house is 75 years old, but it has a brand-new 30-year roof, then obviously that's what you take into account when calculating the longevity of the roof.

✔ **What is the home made of?** Wood is good, but concrete slab and block construction is safer when it comes to a fire risk. Insurance companies take into consideration what homes are built of and rates will vary — up and down — based on a home's construction. You may even see a difference in mortgage rates if you buy a brick house. You don't like brick houses, you say? Fine, but just be aware of the differences in construction when looking at second homes and know what these differences mean.

✔ **Is the home's "great outdoors" not so great?** Take a good look at the grounds, the condition of any trees on the property, the state of the lawn and bushes, and any other external elements. Huge patchy spots on the lawn, obviously sick trees, yellowing or dead bushes, huge puddles of standing water, and any other blatantly "not right" exterior basics are worrisome and can cost you big bucks down the line.

Envisioning yourself in the home

Whether you spend only a few weeks of the year in your second home or nearly every weekend there, you need to know that you're going to be happy in it. If you're buying this property as the place you'll live in after retirement, it's doubly important to make sure that you've found a homey dwelling. Consider these factors:

✔ **How many levels is the home?** If you had your heart set on a single-level ranch, but that gorgeous bi-level called out to you during a showing, think twice and be sure that you end up buying something that suits your lifestyle. If, for example, an extra floor — and its extra set of stairs — will make visits from an elder relative difficult, you may want to reconsider your choice. Multilevel homes are spacious and afford more privacy, but they also bring with them stairs. A rhyming reminder: Stairs can be a bear for those for whom we care. (And I'm a real estate expert, not a poet, by the way — and you can probably tell why.)

✔ **What are the individual spaces like?** Take a good look at all the rooms in the house and try to picture your family using them. Is one of the bedrooms big enough for your daughter and her doll collection? Is the master suite large enough for your liking? And for your furniture's liking? Is there plenty of closet space? Are there enough bathrooms? Will everyone be cramped and in the ideal situation to annoy each other? Or will they be comfortable enough to enjoy themselves? The features of a home that affect our day-to-day lives often become the most important. Take all these things into consideration before buying.

✔ **Is the kitchen big enough?** If you're not really into cooking, dining, and socializing in and around your kitchen, then skip ahead. A good-sized kitchen probably won't matter that much to you. However, if you're like a lot of us, you tend to gravitate toward this room more than once during the course of a day. (If "How long are you going to stand there with the refrigerator door open?" sounds familiar to you, take an extra-good look at the kitchen.) Make sure the kitchen is big enough for your lifestyle, and that the appliances are on par (or replaceable) for how you expect to live in your second home.

Taking the inspection report into account

You didn't spend a couple of hundred dollars on a home inspection and a good chunk of time with the inspector to just disregard his findings. It's critical to think about the following questions:

✔ **What does the roof look like?** Here's where an inspector *can* help — big time — by telling you the age of the roof and giving you his assessment of its condition. He'll most likely say something like, "There are X number of years left on this roof." *You should pay attention to him when he says this.* A roof can be one of the most expensive elements of a home to replace, so think about this information carefully. "X" years will be here before you know it, y'know?

✔ **How old and how efficient are the major systems?** Water heaters, air conditioning units, heating systems, and plumbing are all expensive to repair or replace, so check the estimated age of each system and be sure that your inspector gives you his opinion of how much life is left in each of them. If the homeowner is present, you can also ask her if she's had any problems with any of those systems and if she's made any repairs to them in the last few years, or if she's replaced anything big (or ask your real estate agent to get this information for you). For example, a central A/C unit that's only a couple of years old is a plus. Likewise a relatively new water heater. Also talk about her utility bills with her: electric, gas, water, heating oil. You can determine how efficient these systems are when you have an idea of what these expenses run each year.

✔ **What else could go wrong with this home?** Pools, hot tubs, and fireplaces are all great, fun amenities in any second home, but they can also be nightmares if they're not operating properly. As you give the home in question a good hard look, ask yourself: What *could* go wrong with these various "toys"? Pools and hot tubs leak. Fireplaces stop venting properly. Built-in intercoms stop working. And on a personal note, *every one* of these things happened to me in my Florida home, despite the fact that I had a thorough home inspection before I bought. Keep these issues in mind as you ooh and ahh over the delightful extras that come with the home, and as images of romantic nights before the fireplace and glorious summer days by the pool cloud your thoughts. As Cher said to Nicolas Cage in *Moonstruck,* "Snap out of it!"

Handling Long-Distance Inspections: How to Protect Yourself

Don't fret if you're buying a home that's outside of your geographic area and you simply can't be present for the inspection.

Just be sure to select a reputable inspector (use the guidelines from the "Finding and Hiring a Reputable Inspector" earlier in this chapter to make sure you do precisely that) and, if possible, have your real estate agent (or another trustworthy person) attend the inspection and report back to you any problems or issues that come up. (You may want to make attending the inspection a condition of your agent's representation. Why not? It's one more house call for them, and you've got peace of mind.)

If you can't attend the inspection, schedule a follow-up phone call with the inspector as soon as possible after the inspection. Ask for his thoughts on the overall condition of the home, and question him about details of the report that require more explanation.

Remember that home inspectors rely heavily on their reputations to score new and repeat business. This means that a high percentage of them are careful to prepare accurate, helpful reports that can help second-home buyers make the right purchase choices. The fact that you're not watching him like a hawk as he moves around the home has nothing to do with his ability to conduct his inspection and prepare a report that you can put to good use when purchasing your second home and negotiating any repairs with the seller.

Home inspectors put their reputations on the line with each report they write. This should bolster your confidence in the process and assure you that you'll be properly taken care of. As long as you hire a pro, you'll be in good shape.

Understanding Disclosure Statements

Sellers must disclose facts about the home that can negatively affect the purchase price or a buyer's interest in the property. If the seller knows something about his house that he is almost *certain* would turn off a buyer, as much as he hates to do it, he has to spill the beans and disclose it.

The seller's real estate agent will have him fill out a disclosure statement. *Disclosure statements* were created to protect consumers from making uneducated home-buying decisions. These statements give you, as the home's prospective buyer, an idea of what defects the home has, or at least the defects the seller knows about. That's why you need to get the home inspected — to reveal problems that may not show up on the disclosure statement.

Some disclosures are straightforward, such as admitting that a pool leaks 1 inch per week during the dry season. Others are a little more, well, curious. Like whether a death occurred in the home within the last three years. (Believe it or not, this is required in California and some other states. Apparently enough people don't want to buy homes in which someone has died that disclosing it needed to be codified into law.)

Some states require disclosures about whether the home is in an earthquake zone; what natural disasters have occurred in the area; whether those lovely trees up on the ridge pose a fire hazard; and the fact that the noise from incoming jets is so loud you won't be able to have a conversation with your mother in your backyard when a 747 is coming in for a landing. Your real estate agent will help you navigate these waters by pointing out which disclosures are required in your state. For example, the lead-based paint disclosure is an example of a fairly clear-cut disclosure. The seller of a home built before 1978 must disclose whether he knows if any lead-based paint was used in the home. This only applies to homes built before 1978 because, after that, lead-based paint was outlawed. (Unfortunately, you can still buy it in some places.) If this is an issue with your second home — either the seller is certain the paint was used, or simply doesn't know — then you'll have ten days to conduct an inspection for the problematic substance. After you know, then you can decide how to proceed.

Take disclosure statements with a grain of salt. It's nice to think that everything "bad" about a property will be listed on them, but it's unrealistic to assume that every homeowner is going to be 100 percent honest when filling them out. That's why God made home inspectors.

Use the disclosure statements to support your home-buying effort. If the statements turn up something disturbing that you can't afford to manage, negotiate your way out of, or that you simply don't want to deal with, then move on. There are lots of homes out there for sale.

If, however, the statements are clean enough to keep you moving forward and counting the days toward that closing date, then forge ahead and proceed with the purchase.

Chapter 8

Financing Your Second Home and Closing the Deal

*H*ave you found the second home you want to buy? Have you signed a contract and are you ready for the "fun stuff," also known as the financing? No need to be scared. Although negotiating all the financing for your second home may at first be intimidating, I'm not going to leave you treading water.

This chapter explains the major aspects of financing, including discussions on the differences between a primary mortgage and a secondary mortgage, credit scores, taxes, and homeowners' insurance, all of which will at some point be blips on your second-home-buying radar screen. Big green blips — *important* blips — that should not be ignored or treated lightly.

For you cash-rich buyers (you know who you are), I include a section on how to make the right choices when you have the luxury of avoiding the traditional mortgage system and forking over cash for your second home instead. There are pros and cons to this strategy. I go over both so you can make the right decision if you're sitting on a pile of cash that keeps nagging you to spend it on a second home. Understand that this chapter isn't really a "how-to" on financing your home, but instead a look at the different options you can choose from. For the heavy stuff, you'll want to talk to a pro. But this chapter will give you a solid foundation of info you need to know before you get too deep into the financing process.

Starting the Financing Process

When you buy a second home, you'll pay cash for the home, take out a mortgage for it, or — as most people do — use a combination of these two payment options. In this section, I explain why a second-home mortgage is different than a primary-home mortgage (at least to the lender), how your credit score factors in (and how to improve it), and how to be sure that your own financial house is in order so you're ready to purchase a new property.

Understanding how second-home loans differ from primary-home loans

Second-home loans are different than primary-home loans. And you need to know how they're different when you embark on the second-home safari.

For starters, when you buy a second home, you're promising a lender that on top of the basic expenses associated with owning your primary home, you can also take on the responsibility and added expenses of another property. For some, this is just not possible, considering that a good portion of the average American's paycheck goes for mortgage payments, property taxes, insurance, repairs, and maintenance. (And we still have to eat, too!)

With a second-home mortgage, consider the following differences:

✔ **Higher down payment:** At closing, you'll probably have to come up with 20 percent or more of the purchase price as a down payment, because lenders know that in the event of a financial emergency, the second-home mortgage payment will be a lower priority. Because of this reality, lenders like to see a substantial down payment, which signifies a genuine commitment to the purchase and the debt.

✔ **Slightly higher interest rate:** Mortgages on second homes historically have higher interest rates and closing costs than those on primary residences. It isn't uncommon for second-home mortgage interest rates to run a quarter to a half point higher than a first mortgage.

✔ **Higher mortgage payments:** Your second-home mortgage itself may be more expensive because of the higher interest rate. Also, the homes themselves are more expensive, probably because so many are located in highly desirable areas — places vacationers flock to on a regular basis. The same two-bedroom, two-bathroom townhouse in Indianapolis, Indiana, for example, would certainly cost more if purchased in Myrtle Beach, South Carolina.

A lender may offer a variety of mortgages that require that you pay *points*. A point is 1 percent of the mortgage amount, usually paid in cash at the time of the closing. Why pay points? To get a lower interest rate on your mortgage. Points are essentially interest you're paying early to reduce the amount of total interest paid. Lenders offer a wide array of products both with and without points, so shop around and see which plan works best for you, factoring in the amount upfront as a down payment and then the monthly payments until you find the one you're most comfortable with.

Lenders also want to know if your home will be owner occupied or empty, or rented out for any period of time during the year. If you're planning on renting it (see Chapter 11 for more info), then lenders will view your second home as an investment property, and use a different set of rules to determine whether they should loan you money for the purchase. Your mortgage interest rate, for example, will likely be higher than it would be if you were using your second home as a traditional vacation home. Some lenders may not even be willing to get involved in financing a second home that will be used as a rental property. This is because selling these loans on the *secondary market* (that's where lenders sell the loans in packages to other lenders) can be difficult.

But you can get around those rental issues. You'll have an easier time of getting a loan if you can prove that the property will, indeed, generate cash flow on an annual basis. You'll probably be asked for a *cash-flow statement* showing the income you can expect from the property.

The good news is that, like the primary mortgage market, second-home lenders have become more lenient over the last few years, and now offer a variety of options for second-home buyers. Don't be discouraged, and do be prepared to put some extra elbow grease into finding the right lender, and your efforts are sure to pay off.

Fe, FICO, fo, fum: A look at credit scores

You may be earning big bucks — say, $500,000 a year — and paying for your expensive cars, big-screen TVs, elaborate vacations, and luxury goods in cash, but if your *FICO credit score* is considered poor by mortgage industry standards, you won't get a good interest rate on financing for your second home. (FICO stands for *Fair, Isaac & Co. Inc.,* the company that first evaluated individuals' credit histories.)

If your credit score is *really* subpar, you may not even be able to get financing at all. That's because lenders look at your past payment history before they look at anything else. All of your financial activity — both positive and negative — is wrapped up into that one neat little number.

Understanding what your FICO score really means

The numerical FICO score range is 375 to 900 points. The lowest numbers are the worst and the highest numbers are the best. To come up with a FICO number for you, the three credit-reporting bureaus analyze your credit history, factoring in the following issues:

- Late payments on revolving debt (such as credit cards and other mortgages)
- How long ago you established credit
- How much credit is used versus how much is available
- How long you've lived in your current home
- How long you've worked at your job and other employment history
- The presence of negative marks against your credit, such as bankruptcies and collections

These factors are in order of importance. Thus, the bureaus consider late payments the most serious problem when evaluating potential borrowers.

Historically, anyone with a 700 score was considered an "A" credit risk, while anyone with 720 or higher was "AA" credit. This changed in 2006 when the three credit bureaus, Equifax, Experian, and TransUnion, devised the following simplified scale:

A = 901–990

B = 801–900

C = 701–800

D = 601–700

F = 375–600

If you're unsure of your own grade, request an updated credit score for yourself and any other borrowers to find out exactly where you all stand before you apply for a mortgage.

To request a free credit report, visit `www.annualcreditreport.com`. A *credit report* shows how long you've held employment, how much of your available credit you're using, and how long you've lived at specific addresses, thus creating a complete financial history. Check all these details carefully. Errors are common on credit reports and you should correct any that you find as soon as possible. Contact the reporting agency and ask about the specific procedure to correct mistakes.

You can request a free report once every 12 months from each of the credit-reporting companies: Equifax, Experian, and TransUnion. Make sure to check all three credit reporting companies because the credit score for each will be different because each one uses its own criteria and the lender will always look at all three before approving a loan. But keep in mind that free credit reports don't include your credit score. You can check it over for mistakes and make sure everything is accurate, but you'll have to buy your credit score from one of the agencies if you want to know what it is.

If after you receive your report, you don't like what you see, read on.

Improving your FICO score

You can improve your credit score in several ways, but most of them take some time to implement. Knowing your score before you start applying for a mortgage gives you time to start correcting any problems. Here are some basic steps you can take:

- **Pay your bills on time.** Late payments and collections can have a significant negative impact on your credit score.

- **Avoid filling out every credit application that comes your way.** Applying for too many credit cards makes it look like you're trying to get credit from a number of sources — not a good sign to a lender. This, too, can negatively impact your overall score.

- **Don't max out your credit cards.** The higher your balance relative to the total credit line, the worse off you'll be, so reduce your credit card balances as much as possible.

- **If you don't have credit, get some.** It's important that your credit record shows *paid as agreed.* You need this paper trail.

- **Get more credit if you need it.** Not having enough available credit — which proves that you're capable of paying on a revolving basis — can negatively impact your score. If you need to boost your levels of credit, apply for one or two credit cards and use them monthly (and, if possible, pay them off in full every month).

It can take months for "positive" marks (made possible by creditors who report your payments or payoffs) to find their way onto your credit report and improve your credit score. It doesn't happen overnight. If your credit score is in need of an upgrade, start working on it now.

Getting your financial house in order

Before you fill out any second-home mortgage applications, cash out your IRA, or hit up your family and friends for cashola, make sure your own financial house is in order. (Maybe you already did this in Chapter 2, but you can't be too cautious.) Take a close look at the following areas, taking into consideration exactly how much you're spending each month, how much money is coming in the door, and how much "extra" you have left at the end of the month.

- ✔ Your monthly income

- ✔ Your total liquid assets (cash, along with investments that can be easily turned into cash)

- ✔ Your monthly expenses (bills, repairs, maintenance, your kid's room and board at college, money you send your parents, and so forth)

- ✔ How much extra money you need to keep in reserve as a *life cushion* (money that shouldn't be allocated to a down payment or monthly payments on a new loan)

- ✔ How much money you have left over to pay the mortgage payment, taxes, insurance, and other expenses of your second home

If everything's working, you're ready to proceed with your second-home purchase. If your review reveals problems — for example, you discover you're spending way too much on luxuries that you can easily cut back on — shows, restaurants, shopping splurges — then make some adjustments so the ins and outs better line up.

Get your financial house in order three to six months before you plan to buy a second home. With enough advance planning, any issues that come up can be resolved well in advance of the home's financing and ultimate purchase.

Okay, you've checked the numbers and you're ready to take the plunge. Now's the time to start making copies of the pertinent paperwork that you'll be required to show to a lender, beginning with the following basics (you'll also need copies of the same documents for all cosigners):

- ✔ Pay stubs

- ✔ Tax returns and copies of W-2s (for the last three years)

- ✔ Checking and savings account statements (for the last 12 months)

- ✔ Additional documents that can prove your income (such as copies of alimony checks, child-support payments, and so forth)

- ✔ Any other paperwork that would support any income that you're claiming, such as rental income on other properties

- ✔ Your driver's license and Social Security card

While you're tuning up your financial house, you can start putting together a file of these papers. It's often easier to do it well in advance of when you'll actually need all this stuff.

You can expect your lender to ask for more documents, but having these handy will expedite the process and make it easier when the time comes to fill out a mortgage application and turn over the supporting documents.

How not to end up house poor

House poor is a phrase that's thrown around a lot in real estate circles. It basically defines a situation in which the homeowner pays out nearly all of his monthly income in housing payments, maintenance, utilities, and repairs. The outgo is so great that there's not much left for dining, entertainment, movies, concerts, or any other fun stuff. The thought of having two significant drains on a budget can be scary, but if you plan it out carefully and correctly (using the self-assessment information covered in Chapter 2), you can conquer the challenge.

To avoid ending up house poor, keep the following pointers in mind:

- ✔ **Don't stretch yourself too thin.** If you know that $5,000 comes into your bank account every month, and $4,500 of it is spoken for, then don't take out a mortgage that sets you back another $1,500 a month.

- ✔ **If your current financial situation puts you out of the running for the chance at a second home, check into some alternative options.** You can consider timesharing or *fractional ownership,* whereby several owners go in together to purchase a second home. (See Chapter 3 for more on these options.)

Getting preapproved for a mortgage before you find your home

Getting a preapproval letter from a lender before you start looking for a home can help you gain an edge on the competition — those other buyers who may be eyeballing the very home you've decided you absolutely must have. Being *preapproved* means, in a nutshell, that a lender has committed, in writing, to lend you the money for your second home.

A preapproval letter is an especially valuable tool in a hot market where homes are selling fast and sellers don't want to bother with buyers who can't afford to buy. (No seller wants to lose a sale they've committed to because the buyer's financing "fell through.") Preapproval gives you peace of mind, knowing that you can afford what you're looking at — and being able to state this with certainty to the seller.

Keep in mind that there is a difference between being prequalified and preapproved. The *prequalification process* isn't nearly as thorough as being preapproved and boils downs to nothing but an "estimate" of what you can afford. Yet, you go through the same motions during the process — credit approval, income verification, and so on — that you do when you apply for a loan. My advice is to avoid prequalification and shoot for the preapproval process.

Knowing Your Financing Options

The good news is that you have many lending options available to you as a second-home buyer. You can use traditional mortgages to finance your purchase, or you can investigate innovative loans. You can put lots of money down upfront or just a little bit. You can ask friends, family, or even the seller for funds. The bad news is that sorting through all these choices to find the one that's right for you is no easy task. This section gives you a brief overview of the basic financing options and some tips on how to tap into them.

Relying on traditional mortgages

Cash is always king when it comes to buying a second home — if you've got that kind of cash at your disposal — but many buyers take on a mortgage to finance the property. In this section, I show you the most common loans that buyers use.

The two most popular types of mortgages are *adjustable-rate mortgages* (ARMs) and *fixed-rate mortgages.* The main difference between these mortgages is in the interest rates; the interest rate fluctuates (or adjusts) over the life of an ARM, while the interest rate remains exactly the same (or fixed) for the life of a fixed-rate mortgage. (Now you know how they got those creative names.)

Adjustable-rate mortgages (ARMs)

An adjustable-rate mortgage (ARM) uses an interest rate that is linked to an economic index. The lender periodically raises or lowers the loan's interest rate and your monthly payments as the index fluctuates. The lowering of the rate and payments is the ARM's advantage; the disadvantage is when your rate and payments go up.

Using a retirement savings account for your down payment

You can tap your Individual Retirement Account (IRA) for your second-home purchase, but carefully investigate all the advantages and disadvantages before making such a move. Your IRA is your retirement nest egg, after all, and you don't want to leave yourself short later, or scramble to make up for what you cashed in. For those of you have larger 401(k)s (compared to your IRAs), you may consider tapping that resource first because the same rules apply.

You can tap your IRA for a down payment without paying penalties, if you're a first-time home buyer. The IRS defines *first-time home buyer* as someone who hasn't purchased a home within the last two years. So if you purchased your primary home 15 years ago and are still paying the mortgage, you qualify as a first-time home buyer to the IRS and can make use of the benefits regarding using your IRA as a down payment.

You can withdraw a maximum of $10,000 from your IRA to put toward your down payment. That's the limit the IRS allows each person. If both you and your spouse have IRAs to tap, the total you can use is $20,000. The money has to be used within 120 days of receiving it.

There are different types of ARMs, such as those loans that start out adjustable (for two, three, five, or more years, usually) and then transform into fixed-rate mortgages for the remaining number of years. Or an ARM may always be variable: For as long as you carry the loan, the interest and payments will fluctuate based on the index.

The most common index used for calculating ARM interest rates is the one-year U.S. Treasury note. The interest rate is recalculated weekly, although ARMs adjust according to the terms of the loan. The lender will add a *margin* (the fixed portion of your loan rate which, when added to the index rate, equals your full interest rate) to the rate of the most recent one-year note at your adjustment date, and voilà, that's your new interest rate. Talk to your lender for the specific details and rates.

Be sure to check out the current mortgage and real estate market before taking out an ARM. The historically low interest rate environment of the early 2000s made ARMs extremely desirable. Why? Because their rates reflected the industry's steadily falling rates. But this period passed, and as rates began to climb, ARMs fell out of favor as many buyers scrambled to "lock in" low rates with fixed-rate mortgages.

Fixed-rate mortgages

The interest rates on fixed-rate mortgages are locked in for the life of the loan, typically 15, 20, or 30 years. Monthly payments are steady and predictable, but if interest rates happen to bottom out when you've owned your second home for ten years, you'll have to refinance to take advantage of them.

Considering financing your home through the seller

Depending on market conditions, some builders and owners may be willing to personally finance the sales of their homes in order to unload them — meaning that you, the buyer, pay the builder or seller directly instead of a bank or mortgage company. When you finance through the seller, expect to make monthly payments and a down payment on the loan.

This arrangement is particularly useful when you can't obtain any other kind of financing, or when you're purchasing the home from a friend or relative whom you know and trust. Trust is the key here. Anytime you enter into a financial relationship with an individual rather than a company, you take a risk.

Even if you have every reason to trust the person with whom you're dealing, follow the first rule of business: Put the deal in writing. An attorney is an absolute *must* for such deals, and you should consult one before you sign anything or hand over any cash to the seller. And it should be *your* attorney who drafts the paperwork.

If you explore this financing option, remember that you don't always have to rely on the seller for all the financing. You can get part of the financing through a lender, with the seller providing the balance of the funding you need.

Adding a second mortgage on your primary home

One way to pay for your second home is by taking out a *second mortgage* on your *primary* home. You borrow money against the existing *equity* (the sales price of your primary home, less the amount of money owed on the mortgage) in your primary home and use the money to pay for your second home.

The two main types of second mortgage loans include

- **Home equity loans:** You borrow a lump sum amount against the total amount of your home's value. A homeowner with a $500,000 house that she only owes $200,000 on (in the form of a mortgage) can theoretically borrow up to $300,000 in equity from the home (based on the individual lender's requirements and approval).

  Many home equity lenders cap the amount they're willing to loan against equity at 75 or 80 percent. Some will go to 100 percent of the equity, but a reduced percentage is more common.

- **Home equity lines of credit (HELOC):** A lender gives you a revolving credit line that works like a credit card and only incurs interest on the amount of money that is *borrowed* — meaning the amount you actually spend from the credit line amount.

  You can use a line of credit to pay for some or all the home's sales price and closing costs. But the lender will want something as *collateral* to secure the credit line. That can be a business you own, another property, that gold coin collection hiding in your closet, or that comic book collection you've had for decades and were just offered 50 grand for.

Second-mortgage lenders take on significant risk when they make these loans. The first mortgage always gets paid, well, *first* in the case of foreclosure, and there may be little or nothing left over for the second guy to collect. Thus, the interest rates are higher for second-mortgage loans than they are for primary mortgages.

Using a home equity loan to buy a second home can create problems if you default on your first mortgage and your primary home goes into foreclosure. Speak to your financial experts and advisers about what could happen to your second home if you lose your first home so you go into the situation with your eyes open. Also check out *Personal Bankruptcy Laws For Dummies* by James P. Caher and John M. Caher (Wiley).

Using a reverse mortgage to buy a second home

If you're not 62 or older, you can skip this section. However, if you're nearing 62, like the many baby boomers who are purchasing second homes today, or if you're the child of a baby boomer who has purchased a second home, then make sure you read this section.

Most seniors commonly have a large amount of equity in their homes. A *reverse mortgage* provides a means for tapping home equity without creating monthly payments for the homeowner. A reverse mortgage isn't like a

Finding mortgages on the Net

The Internet has become *the* place to go for prospective home buyers who are looking for information on how to buy and finance a house. You can get reams of facts with nothing but an e-mail address and a zip code.

Granted, many of us are reluctant to give out personal and financial information via the Web (and for darned good reason), but as with all financial matters, if you deal with established, trusted institutions that protect customers' information from fraud, theft, and misuse, you shouldn't have a problem. It's done every day, and security breaches are rare enough that they make the news when they do happen. If you're questioning the legitimacy of a company, pick up the phone and call the company. If it sounds shady, it probably is.

A good place to start when searching for mortgage info on the Internet is at a site like LendingTree (www.lendingtree.com), which aggregates consumer information, shares it with lenders, and sifts through the information to come up with multiple options for the buyer.

National mortgage lenders like Wells Fargo (www.wellsfargo.com), GMAC Mortgage (www.gmacfs.com), or CountrywideFinancial (http://my.countrywide.com) are also aces in my book. From these sites, you can check current interest rates, read and find out about the various programs offered, apply for loans, and take myriad other steps toward second-home ownership.

Also, be aware of Online Transaction Management (OTM) if your second home is some distance away from your primary home. OTM companies can provide both sides of a transaction with secure access to a Web site where all the transaction's pertinent documents are stored and can be modified by either party before the signing. When all the terms are agreed upon and the forms completed, hard copies of the documents are then sent to the parties (*mail-away transactions*, they're called) for physical signing. OTM is fast and accurate and may be right for you.

conventional mortgage in which you make a monthly payment to a lender. Instead, you receive monthly payments or a lump sum of cash from the bank in return for a mortgage on your home. You can use this money to pay off an existing second-home mortgage, make a down payment on a second home, pay off debt, or simply have money to live on.

The property is used as security against the loan, which is paid off when you pass away or when you sell the property and move to another home (perhaps your second home). To be eligible, you must be 62 years old, and you must own and live in the home you want to mortgage. When you take out a reverse mortgage, you pay no monthly mortgage payments, but you're still responsible for property taxes, homeowners' insurance, and maintenance expenses. For more on reverse mortgages, check out Chapter 17.

Borrowing money from family and friends

Got a well-off relative? A wealthy friend? And do these people like you? A lot? If yes, then these folks may be great sources of money for a second home. Your first challenge will be finding someone with the money to lend. But you probably already have a short list of "People with Money" whom you know. You then need to convince one of these people that you are not only set on buying that second home, but that you can also afford to pay them back for the amount borrowed.

 If you borrow from a family member or friend, make sure it's a personal loan that is *unsecured*. This means that nothing you own, or will own, will be used as collateral to secure the loan. Document the amount borrowed and how you'll pay it back. The lender will want to know.

If all goes well and your benefactor forks over the dough, this money can be used to reduce the amount you need to borrow from a lender for a mortgage.

 But know this well, my friends: Borrowing from family or friends comes with more than the simple financial obligation of paying these people back; such moves come with *baggage*. If all goes well, and you meet your repayment obligations on time, then nary a peep will be heard. But the first time you miss or are late with a payment, then expect static. "You couldn't pay me this month, but you could go to Atlantic City for the weekend?" Bear this in mind when deciding to borrow from people with whom you are personally involved.

Above all, these types of arrangements need to be *done right,* and that means *in writing*, with everything — amount, payments, interest — spelled out in detail. Have a legal contract drawn up and have everyone involved sign. "I have to have a contract with my own mother?" you may be asking. The answer is an unequivocal "yes." Why? Because if something should happen to your mother and she has property, then the borrowed amount becomes part of the estate. When everything is in writing, then everything is clear. If all these factors don't spook you, then such loans can provide a solid foundation for your second-home purchase.

Considering interest-only loans

Interest-only loans allow the second-home buyer to purchase a home with no principal payments. You make payments only for the amount of interest that accrues on the loan over a specified term. The loan terms are usually one to ten years, at which point the principal is due. You then have two choices:

- ✔ **Refinance to a more traditional loan option.** This entails taking out an entirely new loan for the balance owed (with closing costs and associated lender fees) under new terms.

> ✔ **Pay off the balance entirely.** This equates to the original purchase price plus any other closing costs that are wrapped into the mortgage, such as prepayment penalties. (You can request a *payoff amount* at any time from your lender.)

These loans have come under fire recently because many borrowers are getting hurt when the loan's term expires. They need to refinance, and they get hit with much higher monthly payments that they can't affordably pay.

Interest-only loans can be useful for several types of buyers. If, for example, you're expecting a big payoff sometime in the foreseeable future — maybe an inheritance, a large raise, a big commission payment, a significant bonus, a lottery settlement, an insurance settlement, or a stock sale — using this type of loan now and then paying off the total loan amount when it comes due could be a good move.

Managing the Cash Deal

If you're fortunate enough to be sitting on a pile of cash that you're not currently using, then you may want to use some or all of it for your new second home. When you pay cash for a home, you walk out of the closing with 100 percent equity. In this section, I look at the pros and cons of this strategy and help you decide if paying cash is the best move for your situation.

The advantages of paying cash

If you're bent on owning your second home outright, paying cash may be a smart alternative for you if you have a nice-sized stash that isn't already spoken for. If you're seriously considering paying cash, the following are a few advantages to doing so:

> ✔ **You don't have any liens or encumbrances hampering your enjoyment of your place.** You begin reaping the rewards of housing appreciation right out of the gate because you don't have a mortgage or interest to pay off.

> ✔ **You don't have to worry about the interest costs and other administrative fees that are typically associated with a mortgage.** Closing costs can be steep, but you don't have to pay lender fees or credit check fees.

> But just because a bank won't be breathing down your neck about appraisals (required when you get a mortgage) and pest inspections (mandatory by some lenders), you'll still want to have one of each before you purchase. In fact, because you'll become the immediate owner of

your new place, you need to have peace of mind that, first, you're paying the right price for the second home, and, second, that it isn't infested with wood-destroying insects such as termites. You should also have the home inspected (see Chapter 7 for more info on inspections).

✔ **You could "flip" your house and make a nice profit.** If the real estate market really heats up shortly after you buy your second home and your place appreciates enormously in value, you can sell it quickly and make a nice profit. You may not want to do this if you love your new place and are more interested in enjoying it than profiting from it, but this is a nice option to have when you pay cash. Anything over your purchase price is pure profit! (For more on flipping houses, check out *Flipping Houses For Dummies* by Ralph R. Roberts and Joe Kraynak [Wiley]).

When you pay cash for a second home, in addition to the full selling price of the home, you also have to come up with the transaction's closing costs out of pocket.

The disadvantages of paying cash

When considering paying cash for your second home, you need to think about more than just whether you have the money to cover all the related costs. You also need to keep in mind long-term tax strategies and the economy of the area where your second home will be located. Second-home buyers sometimes view these factors as disadvantages to a cash deal:

✔ **When you file your federal income taxes, you don't get to deduct the mortgage interest that you paid.** You lose out on this key benefit of homeownership. You need to figure out exactly how much money you would save on taxes by taking out a mortgage, and compare that with how much money you would save by not paying monthly principal and interest payments. If calculating this is out of your realm, talk to an accountant or financial advisor who is knowledgeable about the tax benefits of homeownership. She can set you straight as to which is the smarter financial move. (Check out Chapter 14 for more info on the tax-related benefits of mortgage interest.)

✔ **The value of your new place may depreciate before it appreciates if the home is in an area where home appreciation is stalled or heading downward.** If you're paying cash, make sure your intended home is in an area where appreciation is on the upswing. You'd also be smart to buy where homes are priced below market value and ripe for an increase in value. Talk to a real estate agent to determine which way the market is headed. If he tells you that homes are losing value, consider saving your money and taking out a mortgage.

When is a mortgage the smart move?

When you pay cash for a house, you avoid the entire mortgage process: choosing a lender, filling out never-ending piles of paperwork, figuring out what sort of mortgage is best for your financial situation, and all the rest. But sometimes the application process is worth the hassle. A mortgage can be useful if:

- ✔ Mortgage interest rates are extremely low and outpace any investment return that you can score by putting your money elsewhere. (We saw this exact scenario during the real estate boom years of 1999–2005). If the expected appreciation in your second home will result in a higher return than putting your money into a CD paying almost nothing, then you're better off taking out a mortgage for your real estate investment.

- ✔ You want to keep your cash available to make other investments, instead of pouring some or all of it into a second home.

- ✔ You don't want to risk your entire cash investment should the home be foreclosed upon. (Hey, it can happen. If, for example, you take out a home equity loan at a later date and default on it, the second home would be taken.)

- ✔ You want to take advantage of the generous mortgage interest deduction offered by the IRS. (See the preceding section for more on this.)

Who does the transaction?

When you pay cash for a home, you and the seller have a couple of choices as to how to close the transaction:

- ✔ **Work with a real estate agent:** If either or both of you are working with a real estate agent, she will typically handle all the paperwork for you, set up the closing, and tend to all the other required steps.

- ✔ **Hire a professional who is familiar with real estate transactions:** If you're buying an FSBO (for sale by owner) home and aren't working with an agent, you can hire a transaction broker (see Chapter 6 for more on how to work with these professionals) for a flat fee to handle the paperwork involved with the deal. You may also want to hire a real estate attorney to review the paperwork and provide feedback.

Check out the statutes in the state where your second home is located to find out whether a real estate lawyer is required for cash home-purchase transactions. Some states require an attorney to oversee the paperwork.

As for the closing itself, it can take place at a title company or attorney's office. The seller may choose the location. A title company or escrow officer can handle it. In this case, you and the seller don't need to be present. (See "Knowing What to Expect when Closing on a Second Home" for more details about this process.)

As far as the buyer's (your!) role in all this, it's pretty simple and boils down to two steps:

1. **Have a cashier's check made for the final amount (as calculated and prepared by the pros you're using).**

2. **Hand it over.**

Knowing What to Expect when Closing on a Second Home

When it comes to real estate transactions, all roads lead to the closing table. On that momentous day, the various parties convene at the closing table to sign the documents, turn over cashier's checks, and walk away richer in terms of money or —in the case of the second-home buyer — with a new set of keys in hand.

But you just can't walk in, sign a few papers, and walk out. You're getting ready to close on a significant investment, so you want to make sure that you come prepared, including bringing the right people and paperwork and knowing what questions to ask. On the other hand, an escrow agent may handle the closing, and all you have to do is pick up your keys. There are two types of closings, a *round-table closing*, which is when all parties involved are present, and an *escrow agent closing* when just key people attend. This section helps you get ready for that day and explains how to ensure that nothing prevents you from walking out with the keys to your new castle.

Pulling all the paperwork together

The world revolves around numbers on paper. At least in financial matters it does. And nowhere is this more evident than in real estate transactions where every amount is calculated to the penny, and every element of the deal is spelled out in precise detail.

As you know from buying your primary home, lots of papers are created when you buy a house. The settlement statement, the inspection report, the proof of insurance, the sales contract, mortgage papers, and so on, and while your agent will take care of requesting and compiling much of this stuff, by the time closing day arrives, you will be in possession of most of them and will be required to bring them with you.

You need to bring these papers to a round-table closing, where you, the seller, your agent and/or attorney, and the closing agent will be present to sign the closing documents and close the deal:

- Your good faith estimate, given to you by your lender just after you applied for your loan.

- A homeowners' insurance policy or binder. (Check out "Buying the Appropriate Homeowners Insurance on Your Second Home" later in this chapter for the lowdown.)

- The HUD-1 settlement statement that you received 24 hours (sometimes earlier) before closing. (See the "'Sign and date' ad infinitum" section for more details.)

- Your closing funds in the form of a cashier's check.

- A driver's license or picture ID.

Being prepared: Who to bring with you

At your closing day for your second home, you should have the following people attend your round table closing:

- All your cosigners
- Your real estate agent (if you're using one)
- Your real estate attorney (if you're using one)

The title company or other closing agent will be on hand to orchestrate the event. The seller typically chooses the closing location, which can be the title company's office or the seller's attorney's office.

If you want to bring your parents, kids, or supportive friends, by all means do so, but understand that you'll be conducting an important business transaction in a professional environment. There will be no toys to occupy your kiddies, nor will questions by curious friends be entertained. So think twice about whom you ask to accompany you to your closing.

"Sign and date" ad infinitum

At an escrow closing, which is what's used in some states, neither party is present. Because you're likely more interested in the round-table closing — and for good reason, because that's the one you attend — the following information applies to that type of closing only.

Because you've purchased real estate before, you know that closing day equals carpal tunnel syndrome, right? You go home on closing day with a sore writing hand because you sign a ton of paperwork. You or your lawyer should read all the documents. The closing agent will also explain some of the wording in simpler terms. If your lawyer has read the ten-page homeowners' insurance declaration, you can probably skip reading every word of it if it essentially boils down to "I have homeowners' insurance in effect."

Also, if you have questions about anything at anytime, don't be afraid to pipe up and ask. And *do not* sign forms with blank lines or spaces. If something makes the hair on the back of your neck stand up, ask your real estate agent, attorney, or closing agent for further explanation before signing. And sign only after that hair has settled back into place.

You may have seen most of these documents when you closed on your first home, but I want to give a quick overview of the major documents you'll be seeing (again):

✔ **Your HUD-1 settlement statement:** This is a detailed list of all costs related to the home's sale. Similar to the *good faith estimate* that you received from your lender (the rough estimate of the numbers that were refined to the penny for the closing), the HUD-1 reflects the actual settlement costs that both you and the seller must pay (and both of you must sign this document).

Settlement charges listed on the HUD-1 include, but aren't limited to:

- Loan origination fees
- Appraisal fee
- Credit report fee
- Mortgage insurance application fee
- Mortgage insurance premium
- Hazard insurance premium
- Title examination fee
- Recording fees

Before you break out your pen for this one, though, check the statement carefully against the good faith estimate to ensure that the costs don't differ greatly. Some minor adjustments are okay because there were bound to be small changes made between the signing of the purchase contract and the closing.

When you compare the two forms, question any amounts that are

- Higher than what was originally quoted

- Added to the form where previously no charge was listed

If you aren't satisfied with the answers you receive, don't sign anything! Speak up immediately to the closing agent about the discrepancy, and let the professionals hash it out among themselves until the mistake is corrected, or a legitimate explanation is presented — and accepted by *you*. You can, of course, defer to your experts' advice, but make sure you're satisfied that *they're* sure it's been corrected or explained. (Also see the "What questions to ask" section later in this chapter.)

By law, you have the right to review the HUD-1 statement 24 hours before closing. Avoid surprises by taking advantage of your legal right to review this document.

✔ **Final Truth in Lending Act statement:** You get the first copy of this statement when you apply for a mortgage and the final version of it on closing day. The TILA statement includes the cost of the loan and the annual percentage rate, as well as any interest rate or point changes that were made between the time you applied for the loan and closing day.

✔ **Mortgage note:** This is the biggie. When you put your John Hancock on this one, you promise to repay the mortgage on your second home. This document includes the amount of the loan and the loan terms, as well as a gloriously specific summary of the bad stuff the lender can do to you or your home if you fail to make your payments.

✔ **Mortgage (or deed of trust):** This document secures the mortgage note and provides the lender with the power to take your home if you fail to comply with the terms of that note — like, y'know, not paying it, for starters. The mortgage is, essentially, the written pledge stating that your house is the collateral for the loan you're taking out to pay for it.

✔ **Certificate of occupancy:** This is only applicable for newly constructed homes. Buyers of new-built homes must sign this document to take occupancy of their new domiciles. Some communities in some states have a Point-of-Sale inspection ordinance before the title can transfer to the new buyer. Be sure to check this out before you get started.

What questions to ask

By the time you finally sit down at the closing table, you'll have hopefully asked — and had satisfactorily answered — any and all questions relating to your second-home purchase. The closing table is not the place to "spring" things on any of the parties. Seriously. Surprises are not looked on favorably at these events, and unexpected major issues can delay the closing and jeopardize the deal.

But that doesn't mean you should not speak up about concerns you may have. You should question documents you find confusing and ask whatever other questions come to mind. You may, for example, want to know when your first payment is due, or whether you will need to take care of any other tax or legal issues after closing.

What if something's different on paper than what you were told?

While carefully reading the paperwork that you're signing, you notice a discrepancy, what do you do? For example, if your $200,000 loan has magically transformed itself into a $225,000 loan overnight, bring it to your real estate agent's or attorney's attention immediately.

As soon as you notice any discrepancies in any numbers or terms, alert your real estate agent or attorney immediately. They will then address these issues with the lender or whoever drew up the paperwork (the problem may be a clerical error). If the problem can't be immediately resolved, and you're sure the problem is valid, then the closing should be delayed or postponed until the issue is resolved. Don't just sign something for expediency's sake that you'll later regret. And don't worry about inconveniencing the agents, lawyers, and lender. This is their job and they're not there out of the goodness of their heart. To them, your deal is another day's work. But this is a major financial event for you, so if you're concerned, reschedule.

Buying the Appropriate Homeowners' Insurance on Your Second Home

All second-home owners have to purchase insurance coverage for their abodes. Some may be required to by their lenders; those paying cash must simply protect their valuable investments on their own. If you're buying property in an area that's particularly prone to natural disasters, you need to be even more diligent about getting the right kinds and amounts of insurance.

For example, in 2004, four hurricanes ripped through Florida — a popular state in which to buy a second home — leaving behind a swath of destroyed and damaged homes in need of repair and replacement. Homeowners reached for their phones, and insurance providers reached for their checkbooks. By 2006, the hubbub of settling claims had mostly subsided, but the state of insurance affairs was very tenuous in one of the nation's hottest spots for vacation homes. It didn't take a genius to recognize the value of — and elusiveness of — good homeowners' insurance for Florida residents.

In this section, I guide you through the basics of obtaining coverage — a step that must be taken before closing on your home.

How much homeowners' insurance do you need for a second home?

You're getting ready to purchase a large investment. You want to protect that investment, don't you? To ensure that you get the appropriate coverage for your second home, when you approach an insurance agent or other provider for homeowners' insurance, ask for a quote on the following:

- ✔ **The home's structure:** You need enough insurance to cover the cost of rebuilding your home at current construction rates. That means that your $150,000 single-family vacation home may require $250,000 in structural coverage to build it from scratch today.

- ✔ **Your personal possessions:** Most policies cover your personal possessions at the equivalent of 50 to 70 percent of the total structural insurance you've taken out on your home. Talk to your insurance agent about the limitations in this coverage area. Jewelry, for example, may be limited to $1,000 to $2,000. If you plan to keep a $20,000 diamond necklace at your second home, talk to your agent about additional coverage. You may want to leave your expensive stuff at your first home because insuring high value items at both homes can get costly.

- ✔ **Additional living expenses:** If your second home is damaged and you're forced to live elsewhere while it's being repaired, the policy generally covers your living expenses for a set period of time while your home is rebuilt or repaired. This coverage is definitely necessary after you've moved into your second home full time (see Chapter 16 for more on moving into your second home). The amount offered varies from company to company.

- ✔ **Liability coverage:** Most homeowners' insurance policies provide $100,000 of liability insurance (which covers you in case someone is hurt on your property), although more coverage is available. Because of our increasingly litigious society, more homeowners are buying $300,000 to $500,000 in liability coverage.

Talk to your insurance agent about how much insurance to buy for your second home. You need to decide on a comfortable self-insurance figure you can live with, and your agent can help you figure that out. Being *self-insured* simply means that you'll foot the bill for whatever costs come up that are not covered by your insurance in the event of a major loss. It's a balancing act: Total replacement coverage for absolutely everything in the house is expensive, but maybe you want that type of protection and can afford it. If not, then a lesser dollar amount that you feel will protect you in most circumstances may be fine. Talk to your agent.

Considering flood insurance

If you're buying a home that's in a flood plain, then you definitely need to buy flood insurance. No ifs, ands, or buts, unless you want to come home one day to a foot of water throughout your house with no insurance to cover the damage. Most standard homeowners' policies *do not* cover flood damage (read that part again, okay?), and also keep in mind that some lenders won't talk to you if you're in a risk area and you decline to buy flood insurance.

Flood insurance covers losses to your property caused by flooding. So if a hurricane hits your second home and causes major water damage from flooding, your primary insurance probably won't cover the flood damage, but your flood insurance will. (Your homeowners' insurance will cover damage caused by wind or flying debris from the hurricane.)

A standard flood policy covers

- Structural damage inflicted by the flood (including damage done to furnaces, water heaters, and air conditioners)

- Cleanup of flood debris

- Repair or replacement of floor surfaces

- Damage from sewer backup if it's caused by flooding (Damage from sewer backup caused by a blockage or a broken pipe isn't covered under standard flood policies, but may be covered by your standard homeowners' policy.)

- Contents that have been damaged by the flood (if you've purchased contents insurance)

How can you determine if your new home is near a flood plain and if you need flood insurance? (I hope you did that research before your closing day.) You can check out the National Flood Insurance Program's Web site at www.floodsmart.gov. Review the "What's Your Flood Risk" determiner. The site also offers a premium estimator tool that homeowners can use to figure out how much insurance they need on their second homes. On its Quick Quote Residential page, for example, the NFIP cites a premium of $2,053 per year for a building (and its contents) located in Zone A, which is considered a high-risk flood area with a 1 percent annual chance of flooding.

Finding the best insurance deal

In the past few years, the insurance industry has been hit by high losses from a large number of devastating storms (such as hurricanes and tornadoes) and massive catastrophes (such as the terror attacks of September 11, 2001). As a result, "deals" on property insurance have been harder and harder to come by.

Your second home's location plays a large role in just how much you pay for the insurance, as does the fact that it's a *second* home. Because you're not there all the time to keep an eye on the place and maintain it, insurance often runs higher for these properties.

Going with an agent for help

When shopping around for homeowners' insurance, first check with any insurance agent or broker whom you've worked with in the past. If he can't help you, he likely knows someone who can. Check with consumer guides, online insurance quote services (mentioned in the next section), and organizations like the Independent Insurance Agents & Brokers of America (www.iiaa.org), whose "Find an Agent" link allows consumers to search its membership directory by location.

Some insurance companies offer discounts (usually around 10 percent) if you have multiple policies with them. For instance, if you insure your cars and your home with the same company, you may be able to save some money. And some companies even offer renewal discounts if you stick with them year after year. Talk to your agent. Every little bit helps, right?

Looking online

A good place to look for insurance rates is online. Check out the following sites:

✔ Esurance.com (www.esurance.com) or Insurance.com (www.insurance.com), both of which offer quotes to consumers on a variety of insurance packages, including homeowners'

✔ Major individual insurance companies, such as State Farm (www.statefarm.com) and Liberty Mutual (www.libertymutual.com), for rate quotes and information about coverage

What about contents insurance when you don't live there?

If you don't live in your second home, and you want to protect its contents, you need to carry *contents insurance*. Most standard homeowners' policies include contents coverage. If, for some reason, you don't have contents coverage as part of your policy, you'll want to take it out separately. Also, keep in mind valuable items that you may leave at the second home from time to time. (For example, if you have your grandmother's $20,000 diamond necklace, you probably need contents coverage.) If your second home is in an area where you'll be hitting nightclubs and fancy restaurants, and you routinely keep your best jewelry there rather than in your primary home, then that's the home where your contents coverage should include these items.

To make sure you're getting the best deal, be sure to shop around and compare quotes from different companies before purchasing a policy. Be sure to compare apples to apples by looking at exactly what *is* and *isn't* covered by each policy, and then compare the premiums you'll have to pay.

You can check up on the financial stability of insurance companies by visiting the Web sites of rating companies such as A.M. Best (www.ambest.com) and Standard & Poor's (www.standardandpoors.com).

If you're buying a second home in Florida, make sure you allow adequate time to find an insurance provider, and expect to pay a hefty annual sum for the coverage. Hurricanes Andrew, Jeanne, Frances, and Ivan — among others — all took their toll on the state's insurance industry. Consumers now have fewer carrier choices and must pay high annual premiums.

What Happens After Closing Day? All the Paperwork and Such

The keys are in your hand, the papers are signed, and the stress of closing day is behind you. But before you toss that thick file of paperwork you hope you never have to look at again (yes, I know the feeling) into the spare bedroom closet and start enjoying your second home, read this section to help you get organized and plan for the future as a second-home owner.

After the closing: A checklist

You've signed all the important paperwork and walked out with your new set of keys. However, the hard work has just begun because you're responsible for two homes now. After you leave the closing table or receive a call that the title has transferred into your name, make sure you do the following:

- ✔ Call the municipal office for garbage pickup and recycling removal.

- ✔ Get the power and phone activated, and establish a turn-on date for the next time you're ready to use the home.

- ✔ Replace or rekey all exterior locks.

- ✔ Have a home security system installed or upgraded.

- ✔ Change all the batteries in smoke detectors and carbon monoxide monitors (and record the dates that the batteries were changed).

- ✔ Change all the air filters in the home.

- ✔ Set up a maintenance schedule for the furnace, pool, air conditioner, and other major systems (and record the dates for this schedule).

- ✔ Take any home inspector recommendations to heart and set a completion schedule for them.

- ✔ Check the lawn, garden, and other equipment needed to keep the place maintained.

File everything on time

After you leave the closing table, a number of documents will need to be filed with local government offices. The *closing agent* (the title company employee, attorney, or other professional who is handling the closing) should handle most of this for you, but you'll need to do a few things yourself. For example, the lender will probably give you a first-payment coupon to use if your first mortgage statement doesn't come in time to make that initial payment. Keep this in a conspicuous place — or set it up for automatic bill pay — so you don't forget about it.

You will also want to file an application for a homestead allowance, if your state offers this perk. A *homestead allowance* exempts a certain percentage of your home's value from property tax assessment. Check with your local city or county assessor's office to find out if your second-home state offers this. (And remember, if a homestead allowance is offered, most states have cutoff dates for filing for it.) Make a quick call to the closing agent a week after the closing and make sure the deed and any other forms were filed with the appropriate parties.

Storing important papers

You can expect the closing agent to hand you one neat (and thick!) file of signed documents and other important papers related to your home purchase.

Keep this file in a safe place — preferably in a safe with the rest of your important papers. You need this file when it comes time to pay your taxes (see "Pay those taxes," later in this chapter), when you want to look at your property lines (on your property survey), or if you have momentary brain lapse and forget how much you paid for the home, or how many points you paid for your mortgage, or even what your new zip code is.

Knowing what to do if you lose important papers

In today's digital environment, losing important papers simply isn't as catastrophic as it once was. Because real estate sales involve so many parties — all of which have their own paperwork and pertinent documents — misplacing that mortgage coupon or property contract isn't the end of the world. You can almost certainly request another copy from the relevant entities for a fee. So don't panic when you realize you've lost, misplaced, or thrown out something important.

If something is missing, start with your real estate agent or closing agent, both of whom are required to retain a year's worth of files associated with their work. If you need a deed or other legal document showing your owner-ship rights, the city or county clerk's office in your community should be able to point you in the right direction.

Transfer the deed

A *deed* is the document that transfers ownership of real estate. The deed contains the names of the previous and new owners, as well as a legal description of the property. At a round-table closing, the person transferring the property signs the deed, and a notary must notarize the deed before it's accepted for recording. This transfer will happen at the closing table, and the closing agent will have it *recorded* (or filed) at the Register of Deeds (usually located in the courthouse) in the county where the property is located. At an escrow closing, the escrow agent handles the deed transfer.

Pay those taxes

Depending on the time of year you close on your second home, you'll have either paid for or been reimbursed in advance for property tax payments. This is known as *prorating* or sharing, and the amount you pay becomes a deductible expense on the current year's tax return.

These tax prorations are calculated by dividing the taxes between buyer and seller, based on the date that those taxes are due in your state. (This varies from state to state.) In some states, there is a difference between the assessed period and the collection period for real estate taxes.

If the seller paid taxes to cover a period that extends beyond closing, the seller will be credited for this expense. If the taxes weren't paid yet, the total amount will be charged to the buyer and added to her closing costs. If there is any doubt in your mind as to how — or how much of — the property taxes are to be paid, make sure your attorney and agent look into the specifics for your state, and that you pay everything according to the law.

When the next tax hit comes, it will be all yours to take care of. The county tax collector will first send you a TRIM (truth rate in millage) notice, announcing the amount you owe and when it's due. Shortly thereafter, you'll receive a final tax bill that will either be paid from your escrow account (if you have taxes and insurance folded into your loan) or out of your own pocket.

If your second-home mortgage payment includes principal, insurance, and taxes, then your monthly payment will cover any tax bills and the lender will pay it. If this is the case, be sure that the tax bill is sent to the lender. If it comes to you by mistake, forward it immediately to your lender. (And if you do receive a bill and your lender is paying the taxes, be sure to read it carefully; sometimes tax offices send a duplicate bill to the homeowner for her records, even if the tab is being paid by the lender.)

Chapter 9

Thinking Like a Global Home Buyer

So you have your eye on that little cottage in Tuscany or that lovely chalet you stayed in last time you went skiing in Switzerland (and were excited to find that it was for sale). Admit it: You're even surprising yourself, right? You're seriously considering buying property in a foreign country!

Although the concept of owning a second home outside the United States may seem far-fetched for many people, the practice is becoming more popular for U.S. buyers who want to go beyond that beach house on Jersey Shore or that mountainside cabin in Tennessee.

Why the growing popularity, you ask? Well, this chapter explains why more and more people are looking outside the United States for a second home. This chapter also helps you through the basics of buying overseas and even points out a few "hot spots" to consider during your home search. Although this chapter could be a book in and of itself, consider it just the need-to-know info of how to break into the international home-buying market. You can then take it from there.

Contemplating Whether an Overseas Home Is Right for You

Purchasing a second home is a big deal, period. Purchasing a home overseas is an even bigger deal. After you're outside the United States, many home-buying processes are done differently, and you need to be familiar with the details to make your ownership of property in a foreign country go smoothly. For example, getting there for emergencies won't be as easy, and following the rules of the road may be more complex. (Check out "Considering Key Issues When Buying a Home Overseas" later in this chapter for some differences and how to deal with them.)

People purchase second homes, including ones overseas, for a wide variety of reasons. As you try to figure out whether buying a second home overseas is right for you, consider the following reasons to buy outside the U.S. of A:

- ✔ **You frequently travel and visit far-off locations.** You travel overseas extensively, dropping a bundle on hotel rooms and meals in the process, and you're the type to spend six weeks (or more) a year in your favorite international spot.

- ✔ **You have friends or family in a foreign country and need a nice place to stay while you're visiting them.** You've reached the point where hotels just don't cut it, and you can't (or won't) stay with your family, yet you fly to your homeland a few times a year to see your aunts and uncles, grandparents, and cousins, no matter what.

- ✔ **You have the time required to tend to and take full advantage of a property that's located thousands of miles away from your primary home.** Homes require maintenance and TLC, neither of which you'll be able to provide personally if you don't have the time to get to the home.

- ✔ **You have plenty of money to spare.** Owning and maintaining a second home overseas isn't cheap. In addition to the routine costs of financing and upkeep, you'll likely have much higher travel costs, overseas phone calls, and other expenses. If you're thinking these costs might be an issue in your current financial situation, buy domestic.

- ✔ **You like the idea of being able to say you own a home overseas.** Owning a home overseas comes with some bragging rights. Although being able to brag shouldn't be your sole motivating factor, you can still have some pride when telling others you own a home in a foreign land.

If you find yourself nodding your head in agreement with one or more of these points, then an overseas second-home purchase may be right for you.

But not everyone is a jet-setter flying all over the world. The following are some reasons that you probably should stay away from an overseas second-home purchase:

- ✔ **You can't afford buying overseas and you know it.** Owning and maintaining a second home isn't cheap. Owning overseas when dealing with different currencies, exchange rates, property values, and such can be even more difficult. (Check out "Understanding how financing differs abroad" for more info on pricing and financing.) I also suggest you check out Chapter 2, which can help you determine whether you can afford a second home.

✔ **You want to own a home overseas almost solely for the bragging rights.** You have one annoying friend in mind to whom you would do the most bragging. As I've mentioned, bragging rights should *not* be your primary motivator. Buy a home for you, not to show off to others.

✔ **You have too many responsibilities.** You know that no matter how much you twist and turn, you absolutely can't get away from the grind of your daily life often enough to justify the travel associated with owning an international second home.

✔ **You just saw the movie *Under the Tuscan Sun.*** After the movie, you realized that you absolutely must *own* a home on the Italian countryside before you die. You simply *must!* (Okay, probably not the smartest rationale for buying overseas.) Stay rational about this significant decision, and steer clear of far-fetched ideas that might turn into debacles down the road. Rash, emotion-based decisions almost always end up being a problem because they're not thought through carefully.

After considering the factors that apply to you, you should be able to come up with a reasonable justification for or against purchasing an international second home. Buying is an emotional decision, so the ultimate decision, after determining whether you *can* buy the house, boils down to one question: Do you *want* to buy the house? These guidelines are practical info. And even if all the factors are in your favor and you really don't want the particular house you're considering — for whatever reason — then you're not going to buy it. (See Chapters 3 and 4 for more info on how to choose the right home to purchase and where to look for the best options.)

And if your conclusion is "Am I crazy!?" (or something of that ilk), don't forget that many places in the United States can serve as a pleasing substitute for the conditions you found so appealing in Italy, France, or wherever. A chateau in California's wine country, for example, can be your own little place in the Tuscan wine region, or a condo on Myrtle Beach can be surprisingly similar to a place on the shore of France. And don't forget you don't need a passport to fly to California!

Considering Key Issues When Buying a Home Overseas

If you've decided that you want to pursue an international second home or just want a tad more info about the whole process, you're in the right place. (If you haven't decided, check out the previous section, which can help you make your decision.) You're about to undergo an exciting, yet complicated, undertaking, but there's no need to worry.

Yes, you'll face different issues when you buy a second home overseas than if you were to buy a second home in the United States. However, this section helps you through some of the key issues you may encounter as you make your way through the transaction.

Relying on a pro to help with the purchase

Purchasing a second home in an international market can be daunting. You have to navigate different rules and regulations. You need to make sure you get all the correct paperwork signed and so on. How can you guarantee that you've dotted all your i's and crossed all your t's? A real estate agent, local to that specific market, can make all the difference. In fact, unless you're a seasoned, foreign real estate investor with a slew of in-country contacts, you probably won't be able to get through the real estate transaction without some assistance from a real estate agent working in your country of choice.

If you don't know any real estate agents in your country of choice, don't fret. To find a real estate agent in the country where you want to buy a home, go to the International Consortium of Real Estate Associations (ICREA) Web site at www.icrea.org and search through the group's member listings. Furthermore, most of the large, U.S. brokerages (Coldwell Banker, RE/MAX, Century 21, and so forth) have their own overseas offices, so you may want to ask your local agent for a referral within his own organization. Trust me, he will be happy to help. Your favorite agent will get a small commission on the transaction at closing (through the referral network), and you'll get an agent who comes highly recommended.

And don't dismiss the possibility of a referral even if you're using a small, two-person agency. One certainty in my business: Real estate agents know other real estate agents. Ask. You may be pleasantly surprised at who your agent refers you to.

Hook up with a real estate agent in your target country *before* putting too much time into your search. You have to consider foreign currencies and exchange rates, different taxation systems, and various other issues that have to be handled carefully, and your agent can help.

Just as you would if you were buying a home in the States, you want to interview real estate agents before deciding which one to work with for your overseas or outside-the-U.S. purchase. In addition to the basic questions in Chapter 6, here are a few additional questions to ask prospective agents:

> ✔ How often do you work with American home buyers looking for second homes in your country?
>
> ✔ What challenges do American buyers typically face?
>
> ✔ How do you help Americans work through any problems they face?
>
> ✔ How many deals have you *lost* that involved U.S. buyers purchasing in your country?
>
> ✔ What do you need to do to get the financing on the transaction worked out? (Check out the next section for more details.)
>
> ✔ How much will you charge me for your services? (In the United States, the seller pays, but that's not always the case in other countries, so be sure to ask.)

From the agent's answers, you can determine if this agent will be a good match for your situation. If, for example, she's only handled two deals for Americans — and lost them both (and actually admits that to you!) — then you probably want to look elsewhere for representation.

Understanding how financing differs abroad

Overseas transactions are complicated, especially for those buyers who have never dealt with the intricacies of foreign trade. You'll probably get a little anxious when documents start getting faxed and overnighted from another country to you, but it's done all the time. Just be sure to have someone in your corner and you'll be fine.

Don't be surprised if you hear that cash is king in your country of choice. In fact, it very well may be your *only* financing option. The truth is, the mortgage systems in foreign countries aren't always as sophisticated as those of the United States where dozens of lenders stand by ready, willing, and able to lend out hundreds of thousands of dollars to individuals looking to purchase homes. As a result, you have two main choices:

> ✔ Pay cash from personal savings if you can afford it (or borrow it from friends and family).
>
> ✔ Take out a domestic mortgage and use the cash proceeds to pay for your foreign house.

The United States has a very sophisticated financial system in place, and often, there's a shorthand when dealing with bankers and closing attorneys and agents. Our system makes it easy to buy — but to buy *here*. It may take a little more effort to find the deal you want, with terms you're comfortable with, when you're buying overseas.

If you do find a U.S. lender for a foreign home, be prepared to put down 40 percent or more as a down payment. Because of the transient nature of the foreign-home buyer, and the fact that the property securing the loan is outside U.S. borders, this is a customary practice. Lenders ask for higher down payments to reduce the risk they're assuming by making a loan for a foreign purchase. Also, if the documents come through in the language of the foreign country, you have to pay translation costs.

Comparing property values

Evaluating property values on a potential second-home purchase in the United States isn't that difficult. You ask a real estate agent to pull up some comps, and voilà, you're presented with a few recent sales on comparable homes that you can use as a baseline for your own home purchase.

However, in a foreign market, comparing property values isn't so cut and dried. When you compare property values in an overseas market, go into the adventure with open eyes. Gather the pertinent information that can help you better understand your country of choice's real estate market. Doing so ensures that you get the best value for your dollar.

The following guidelines can give you an overall sense of the real estate situation in the area of the foreign country in which you're considering buying. These guidelines are similar to what you do domestically, but the info is somewhat more difficult to acquire. That's why having a real estate agent is so important. (Check out the section "Relying on a pro to help with the purchase" earlier in this chapter for more info.) I recommend that you not tackle this list as a do-it-yourself effort.

- **Look carefully at recently sold properties in the region.** Your agent can help you with this. Look closely at what similar homes are being sold for in the country you have in mind.

- **Consider market trends in the area.** Is it a buyer's market? A seller's market? A balanced market? (Check out Chapter 1 for more info on these types of markets.)

- **Compare estimated property values to the asking price.** This info is available through a real estate agent who has access to the area's MLS.

- **Ask ahead of time (when you write the offer to purchase) about the closing process.** Don't assume a foreign country has the same safeguards as the United States. Ask about title searches, title guarantees, deed restrictions, escrow procedures, and so on. A good real estate agent can be very helpful at this stage of your buying experience.

Don't get bogged down comparing overseas prices to U.S. asking prices for homes. Make sure you're comparing like to like. You may find yourself automatically doing it: "They want how much for that small one-family in Germany? Didn't so-and-so two blocks over pay such-and-such for almost the identical house just a couple of weeks ago?" This is distracting and self-defeating. You're not buying so-and-so's house two blocks over that he paid such-and-such for. You're interested in a similar house in Germany on the River Rhine.

Buying a place sight unseen

You may live halfway around the world from your second home's country, but you're still interested in purchasing a home. You may not be able to drop everything and fly 12 hours to see the place before you put an offer on it. In years past, if a client had asked me if he should buy a house sight unseen, I would have unequivocally said no. My advice would have been to go see it, no matter what it took to get there.

But times change. And so has my advice. And it all boils down to the Internet. The Internet has changed the rules — *drastically* — regarding buying homes. The Web has helped home buyers worldwide purchase abodes without ever setting foot in them. You now have several ways of knowing precisely what's for sale:

- ✔ **Real estate agent/MLS descriptions, as found in the local MLS:** You can access this info yourself (ask your agent for the Web addresses), or your agent can mail or e-mail it to you. This info tells you how many bedrooms and bathrooms and so forth.

- ✔ **Virtual tours:** You can take a video tour of the home's inside and outside.

- ✔ **Still photos:** You can view digital pics of the home's inside and outside posted on a Web site.

- ✔ **Your own knowledge of the area in which you're buying:** This comes from surfing the Web, reading about the area, and talking to people.

However, I recommend that you take this tack only if you have to. For instance, if the market is just so darned hot that four other buyers are interested in a property you've had your eye on, and you know that an extra week of travel arrangements and packing would probably cause you to lose the deal on the home that you just *have to have,* then go for it.

But if you have the luxury of time, and if you were planning on going to the area where you plan to buy your second home within the next month or so, then take your time and go see one or more properties before buying.

If you do decide to buy a home sight unseen, be sure to hire a qualified inspector to go through the home before you sign on the dotted line (see Chapter 7).

Pinning down property taxes

Property taxes vary from country to country, so be sure to go over your obligations in this regard long before you get to the closing table.

Get the answers to these questions before you sign so you don't have any surprises when (property) tax time comes around. You need to know the following from your real estate agent or a local government source:

- ✔ How the property tax on your property is calculated.

- ✔ How often the tax can change.

- ✔ How often you will be billed.

- ✔ How you will pay it. For example, can the tax be included in your mortgage and your domestic bank can pay it? Or will you receive a bill from the foreign tax assessor? Will the bill be mailed to your U.S. address or the foreign property? And so on.

Dealing with problems after you've bought your home

Handling problems at overseas properties — locations that you can't get to within a few hours by car — can be tough. For example, what happens if high winds break a window, a pipe bursts, or something else bad happens and no one is nearby to take care of the problem?

If you take a few precautionary measures, you can protect your investment when problems, both small and large, happen. (And they will.) To handle problems with your property as they arise, do the following:

- ✔ **Establish your own network of friends and neighbors who can help out while you're not there.** You can have peace of mind knowing that your overseas friends and/or neighbors can be at your overseas place within minutes if something happens. Seek out and meet people living close by your place. After you're friendly, you can broach the subject of keeping an eye out and helping out when necessary. If you have relatives living nearby (and you may if that's one of the reasons you bought where you did), then they should be first on your network list.

✔ **Consider hiring a professional property manager.** You pay a property manager to regularly check on your property and handle any issues that arise.

See Chapter 13 for more info on how you can rely on a reputable property manager to maintain your home and for details on how to set up a safety net of real estate agents, repair companies, and neighbors to keep an eye on things while you're away.

In addition, to protect your investment when something happens, make sure you insure your property. The best place to start is with the insurance agent who handles your U.S. home. If such policies aren't something your agent's company handles, she can do the research and provide you with some info and the names of some people to talk to.

Marketing your international home and finding renters

If you own a second home overseas and want to snag some rental income from your place, you need to do many of the same things that a domestic homeowner does, only on a larger, more geographically dispersed scale. However, some things will be a tad different. For starters, assume that you'll be using your foreign home less frequently than would the New York City folks who buy a home on the Jersey Shore.

Because you'll have to fly to get there, and because weekend drop-ins are probably not very feasible, your place will probably be available for rent for a good portion of the year. (And that's only an assumption. If you *will* be in your Swiss chalet or house on Italy's Lake Como for two weeks out of every month, more power to you!)

Keep the following initial steps in mind when marketing your overseas digs and searching for renters:

1. **Figure out when you want to use your home and when it will be available for rental.**

   Think about what seasons or times of the year you do or don't want to use your home, and what times of the year renters will be interested in using your home.

2. **Identify your sphere of interest.**

   Much like the owner whose second home is in the United States, a sphere of influence provides a great network to use to spread the word about your fabulous home. Ask yourself:

- Who do I know who would like to go to [insert the country here] for a week or more this year or next year?

- What type of business or social events will I be attending soon, and can I brag up the property a bit?

- Which of my friends, family, and close acquaintances really need a vacation to a place like [insert the country here] right now?

The answers to these questions can help you come up with a list of potential prospects for your international vacation home.

3. **Get the word out to your contacts.**

Not everyone knows someone who owns property overseas, so you want to tell your own network of friends, family, neighbors, and colleagues about your vacation getaway. Many of these acquaintances may make good customers for your foreign rental. Talk to these folks about the home, e-mail them photos and updates, and take other measures to help spread the word about your new place.

4. **Hit the Web.**

Go to the Internet, where sites like iVacation (www.ivacation.com), Holiday-Rentals (www.holiday-rentals.com), and VacationVillas (www.vacationvillas.net) cater to a largely international audience. By spending the $150 to $200 a year that it takes to get the word out about your place on these popular sites, you can start racking up a fan club of past and future renters for your property.

If this prospect sounds scary to you, you should consider hiring a property manager in the country where your home is located. Someone who can speak the language, who knows the terrain, and who understands the local real estate market may be well worth their salt. This approach is similar to American companies that do business overseas hiring local operators. Being in the zone can be an enormous help to you when you're thousands of miles away from your property and hoping for all to go well.

Ultimately, your goal is to find good renters who are willing to pay the fees you're asking, follow house rules, and treat your property with care while staying there. These kinds of people are in every country all over the world, so don't limit yourself in terms of who stays at your place while you're not there. Even a local may be interested in your place and, with the proper support from area pros, you could end up with a very nice — and lucrative — rental agreement.

Reporting rental income to Uncle Sam

You must claim any money you earn from an investment that is located out of the country as income. The IRS taxes *you* and whatever you *earn;* it doesn't matter where the money comes from. (This may be a "duh!" moment for many of you, but you wouldn't believe how many people wonder if what they earn from outside sources is taxable as U.S. income.)

You'll absolutely be required to pay income tax on the rental income, claiming it on Schedule E, Supplemental Income and Loss, of your IRS Form 1040. (Check out Chapter 14 for more specific tax-related issues when renting a second home.)

Some of the common questions involving overseas earnings include

- ✔ **What about the exchange rate? If I'm paid in euros, do I claim the euros or convert them to dollars?** On your Schedule E, include the income at the exchange rate that was current when you received the rent. If you receive 1,000 euros a month as rent, you claim as income around $1,300 (based on, for example, today's exchange rate).

- ✔ **If I have to pay fees to have the funds converted, are those deductible?** Yes. The fees are an expense of doing business. And, exactly as you do with a domestic rental property, you can deduct all the expenses related to the rental, such as repairs, depreciation, insurance, property taxes, and maintenance. And as with all business matters, be sure to keep all supporting documents and paperwork.

  If you own a home overseas that you're renting, you can also deduct expenses like long-distance phone calls to check on the property, the cost of Internet advertising to find tenants, and the travel costs associated with managing the property.

- ✔ **If I get stiffed on the rent from my tenant, can I claim it as a loss?** If your tenant doesn't pay, you probably won't be able to deduct it as a loss, even if a lease is in place. However, if the tenant damages the place and moves out, and you can't rent it to someone else, ask your accountant if you apply for any loss of income provisions.

Avoiding Pitfalls When Buying Abroad

After you begin the process of buying your overseas second home, you may run into a few roadblocks along the way. So before you can bask on the beach in Rio de Janeiro, or sit gazing at the vineyards while sipping espresso on the little balcony off the master bedroom of your Tuscany cottage, read on.

This section discusses some potential pitfalls you may encounter when buying a second home overseas, including knowing what to do if you hired the wrong real estate agent, and dealing with the unavoidable geopolitical issues that may hamper your ability to do business (in this case, transact real estate) in certain countries.

Grappling with ownership issues overseas

When you purchase a home in the United States, you receive a warranty title stating that you're the property owner. Sometimes the bank holds this title (if you have a mortgage, for example), but the basic point is that the owner holds the title, plain and simple.

Getting the title to your property isn't quite so plain and simple overseas, however, and you'll want to talk to your real estate agent, attorney, or other knowledgeable professional about the ramifications in your specific country well before you buy.

What can happen if you don't do this important piece of homework? A lot. Because the land transfer procedures and physical boundaries in foreign countries are different than those in the United States, you may well find yourself going head to head with the great-great-great-grand-son of the land's original owner, who has decided to make a claim on the land. It happens.

The good news is that the burden of proof lies on the person who is making the claim. By working with a notary who can help read the land's title history to ensure that it's "free and clear" and able to be purchased, you'll know whether the title has any problems that need to be cleared up before you buy.

Using the wrong real estate agent

Sometimes in life, after you've worked a while with a business associate, you unfortunately realize that you're not a good fit. This definitely can happen when working with a real estate agent. Perhaps she's not finding the types of properties that you want. Perhaps she's not staying within your budget. Perhaps she's not submitting the required paperwork on time.

If you discover at any time during your overseas second-home search that you've hired the wrong agent, don't fret. Thank her for her services. You may need to go back, find another real estate agent, and start your search over. You may not have to completely restart your search, but now is the time to take action. You don't want to wait until it's too late and you find yourself stuck in a situation over your head without an agent's help. Don't waste any time. See Chapter 6 for details on how to find the right agent.

Considering a country's troubles

Geopolitical issues and problems are a fact of life in today's world. In fact, economic, political, cultural, religious, military, criminal, terrorism, environmental, and transportation troubles can break out anywhere these days. (Sometimes makes you want to stay locked in the house, doesn't it?)

Any of these upheavals — many of which can happen in an instant — can affect an entire country's economy, housing market, residents, health and welfare, and everything in between. Unfortunately you can't guarantee the future of any country. But the odds are that the more stable and the more free a country is, the better the chance you'll enjoy your second home abroad in peace and comfort for years to come.

Before you buy in a particular country or region, do yourself a favor and check with the U.S. State Department about the stability and safety of the countries where you're interested in purchasing a home. The agency's Web site is `www.travel.state.gov`. Armed with this info, you can make the right decision for your own situation. For example, if you know that the country's grape farmers have been striking for the past three months, causing all ground transportation to slow down, you may want to reconsider that country. Watch carefully, and as you decide whether or not to buy a home, take into consideration anything that happens that you suspect could impact your peaceful enjoyment of your place.

Where to Look for Your Foreign Home

If you're serious about owning your own slice of heaven outside the United States, you have unlimited choices in nearly every country in the world. So where exactly do you start? This section looks at a few favorite places where second-home buyers buy consistently. Also check out Chapter 18 for a more extensive list of areas to consider.

When choosing a location, keep in mind travel costs. The multitude of new budget airlines has made foreign travel more affordable than ever for Americans. If your travel budget is a key factor in your buying decision, first do a little research on a site like `www.orbitz.com` or `www.expedia.com` to figure out how much it will cost you to go to and fro on a regular basis. Also, prices vary by season, so if when you travel isn't critical, you may get a better rate at a different time of the year. And sometimes choosing a different airport that's still close to home can also save you some cash. For example, sometimes flying out of Hartford, Connecticut, instead of New York City can make a big difference and score you a terrific cost-saving fare.

The neighbor to the north: Canada

So close, yet so far away, Canada offers buyers an international location that's fairly accessible, as well as being super-friendly to Americans and, in some aspects, quite similar to the United States. In fact, traveling to your Canadian second home will be fairly easy, unless, of course, you opt for a place far from civilization, way out in the cold wilderness. Then you may need a kayak or two.

TIP

If you're into outdoor activities like hunting, fishing, water skiing, and skiing, consider shopping for your second home in Canada. Lots of Americans have discovered that Canada is a great place for a vacation getaway and a second home. Calgary (in Alberta) and Ontario are especially popular areas for second homes.

The neighbor to the south: Mexico

In close proximity to the U.S. mainland, Mexico boasts myriad options for second-home buyers in search of

- ✔ Warmer weather
- ✔ Varied cultures
- ✔ Proximity to home
- ✔ Affordable real estate
- ✔ Mexican food!

Mexico offers an enormous number of resorts, condos, and cottage-type buying options. And people know it, too. The latest reports show that 1 million Americans now live both full time and part time in Mexico. This is up from only 200,000 in 1996. The major areas where Mexico lovers have settled down include Southern Baja (including Cabo San Lucas and La Paz), Puerto Vallarta, Sonora (on the Sea of Cortez), and the ever-popular Cancun region.

Take advantage of the exchange rate

Exchange rates can make a big difference in how much you ultimately have to pay for your overseas home. At press time, for example, the exchange rate for the euro wasn't working in your favor. The American dollar was worth about 78 cents compared to the euro at the end of 2006, which isn't the best news for buyers looking to purchase homes there. But when you look at the amount of home you can get, it can still be a great opportunity to fulfill your dream.

At the end of 2006, the euro was trading for less than $1.32, down from $1.35 in January 2005. So,

a property that in 2005 cost $300,000 euros was actually $405,000 American dollars, while one selling for the same price in 2006 would only go for $396,000 — a savings worth considering.

And for currency conversions online, I recommend www.x-rates.com/calculator.html. It's super-simple and free. Also, Translatum — www.translatum.gr/converter/currency.htm — is very good.

Something for everyone: South America

Okay, now I'm stepping a bit further outside the box (and the States!), but that shouldn't deter you from considering South America for your second-home hideaway.

People today are looking at countries like Peru, Uruguay, Argentina, Brazil, and Chile as potential second-home spots. With the glorious South Pacific on one side and the Atlantic on the other, this vast continent offers a wide variety of environments, from rain forests to beaches, and everything in between. If you've been to South America and loved it, or you have family there that you want to visit more regularly and for longer periods of time (say for a month or more), then a second home there may make sense for you.

The economies of the various South American countries fluctuate, sometimes drastically, and many of them are greatly affected by geopolitical issues. Before you buy in South America, be sure to talk to a knowledgeable real estate agent in the area. You should also do your own homework to make sure you're getting the best return for your money. Look at housing prices, days on the market, appreciation, and other issues that can affect your investment. Also, try to uncover a little about the political goings-on of the country where you're interested in buying. Hey, coups happen.

Where has everyone gone? Europe

Foreign ownership of European properties has been on the rise for years, so if you're considering buying a home there, now is probably a good time to start making some moves to make it happen. The "big three" are France, Italy, and Spain. They're the most popular choices, but the less touristy countries, such as Portugal and Ireland, have their own allure and are also lately attracting Americans who truly want to "get away from it all" while on vacation.

Property prices in certain European countries (such as France) may be particularly attractive for Americans. You may be used to shelling out an arm and a leg for even the smallest abode, so you may be surprised at how much house you can buy in a European country for what you want to spend. In fact, a decent place just outside Paris may cost half of what you would pay for a New York City apartment. That's right. *Half.* So shop around and do your homework before you buy. Like I said, you may be pleasantly surprised.

Tropical paradise: Island homes

I have traveled extensively through the South Pacific and the Caribbean. I can tell you unhesitatingly that the islands would be my first choice for a second-home location.

Also consider Puerto Rico, Caribbean locales like Grand Cayman, and South American options like Aruba. (Plus, don't forget Hawaii! It's still a tropical paradise, so add it to your list if you want to stay local.)

Visit a few of these places first for a vacation, and be sure that they can provide all the wonderful amenities — beaches, pools, scuba diving, windsurfing, and so on — that beach bunnies just can't live without.

You'll almost certainly pay a premium for an overseas island home. Anything that's waterfront with a view tends to command a high price these days. Shop around, work with a real estate agent, and do your homework before buying.

Part III
Making Your Second Home a Smart Investment

The 5th Wave   By Rich Tennant

Yeah, but as an investment in a second home, we're well ahead of the trend.

In this part . . .

A second home can be a great investment for someone looking to diversify his or her portfolio by adding a nice healthy dose of real estate to it. And because everyone wants to make smart investments, and because real estate has long been an investment winner, in this part, I show you how to do precisely that as it pertains to your second home.

From furnishing and renovating it, to advertising it, to renting it out for the short or long term, I help you with everything you need to know about turning your second home into a profit center — if you want to. You get a good look at how professionals such as property managers can — for a fee — take on certain responsibilities that you'd rather steer clear of.

I also include an important chapter on the financial implications of renting out your second home and the different tax situations that may crop up. After all, you definitely want to keep Uncle Sam happy, right?

Chapter 10

Setting Up Your New Digs

· ·

In This Chapter

▶ Outfitting your second home

▶ Buying furniture

▶ Settling into the neighborhood

· ·

*Y*ou found the perfect second home, you had it inspected, you secured financing on it, and— *Ta Da!* — you closed on it. Now it's time to create a real feeling of home in your new abode. For many people, doing so is the fun part. For others, it will be an unpleasant chore — but no matter how you look at it, getting settled is definitely a task that is worth the effort.

After you have your second home just the way you want it, you can then move on to experiencing other facets of living in your new place. You'll want to get out and explore your new environment. You'll also want to meet your neighbors and make new friends. Both of these endeavors can sometimes be a challenge, but in the long run, they're more than worth the effort.

In this chapter, I take you through some of the basic considerations involved in making your new place livable, and I help you set up your new home according to your budget, wants, and needs. I also show you how to make the most out of the people, places, and things in the area.

Furnishing Your New Home

A second home is great to have, but if it's nothing but an empty space with some futons thrown on the floor, you're not going to be happy or comfortable there. The good news: You don't have to spend an arm and a leg to furnish your new abode in a way that's both pleasing to the eye (and other body parts) and also functional. Domestic accoutrements can range in price from free to "Are you kidding me!?" expensive, and everything in between.

If you plan on retiring to your second home within the next three to five years, consider buying furnishings that will serve a dual purpose: They'll be comfy for vacations and, later, suitable for permanent residence. For example, if the queen-sized bed is only $50 more than the double, go for the larger one, knowing that it will be more practical down the road for year-round use — not to mention it'll give you and your significant other lots more room!

When furnishing your second home, take as much time as you need to pick out just the right sofas, tables, chairs, and so on. Don't hastily spend thousands of dollars on items that you may not need. You have the luxury of time when outfitting your second home, especially if you're not spending much time there during the first few weeks or months that you own it.

In this section, I help you sort through your various options and help you budget for those options so you can create a living space that you, your family, and your friends (and potentially your renters) can enjoy for years.

Knowing how to budget

If you're on a budget, you've come to the right place. Before you purchased your second home, you probably thought about what items you would need in the new place, and allocated a guesstimated amount of money for furniture, appliances, drapes, decorations, and other home accessories. The budget covered how much you could spend and afford, balanced against what you wanted. You'll want to do the same thing for all the furnishings. Write out a budget — and then stick to this budget — even if it means shopping around more for stuff than you typically do for your primary home.

To create your all-important budget, you need to know two things:

✔ How much you *want* to spend on the extras for your home

✔ How much you *can* spend on those goodies

With your daunting house-buying search-and-borrow mission successfully completed, you can now turn your attention to the fun part of owning a second home: dressing it up!

Here's a simple, fairly cut-and-dried method of coming up with some numbers: If you dole out $3,000 a month in second-home related expenses, and if your extra pre-second-home income was $6,000, then you have roughly $3,000 a month to work with. Cut that number in half, and set funds aside for maintenance and upkeep; you'll have a workable amount of discretionary income. So, if you have $1,500 set aside per month, a typical scenario would have you using that money to buy a $650 loveseat, a $250 ottoman, a $200 rug, and a $400 end table one month. The next month, you may use your $1,500 set aside for a $1,500 air handler. Be sure to factor in any extra savings or resources that you may have already stashed away for setting up your new home. (Check out the next section for actually budgeting for different furniture items.)

You may want to spring for more dinero on your second home by purchasing it completely or partially furnished or decorated. For example, say that during the showing, you see one or more items that you'd not only like to own, but you immediately know are the perfect thing in the perfect place, and that it would save you time if the items were there when you moved in (like that top-of-the-line toaster oven in the kitchen, or that mahogany shelving unit in the family room). Mention these items to the seller and ask if you can work out an arrangement to buy them (and be sure to get that agreement in writing, for your own protection). If the answer is yes, you'll save time and money — and get some things you already know that you'll enjoy.

Budgeting for couches, curtains, and other homey touches

The amount you budget for home furnishings and decorations for your new place will rely, of course, heavily on your own personal resources. As a guideline, the National Association of Homebuilders reports that owners of new homes spend an average of $8,900 to furnish, decorate, and improve their homes. About 77 percent of that money (about $6,800) goes toward furnishings and changes and improvements to the property, while the remainder is typically spent on appliances.

So what particular items should you furnish your second home with and how much should you spend? You may want to include the items in Figure 10-1 in your new second home. All these items cost money, ranging from peanuts for a bath mat or artificial plant, to thousands of dollars for living room furniture or a new computer. Feel free to photocopy this worksheet and carry it with you. After you create a budget for furnishing and decorating your second home, use this worksheet to help you stay on budget. Figure out how much money you want to spend per category and per item and write that amount in the allotted space. After you buy a piece of furniture or other goods, record the amount that you spent to keep track of how much you've spent per category.

Furniture Type	Budgeted Amount	Amount Spent
Indoor furniture	_____	_____
Living room	_____	_____
Family room	_____	_____
Kitchen	_____	_____
Dining room	_____	_____
Office	_____	_____
Bedrooms	_____	_____
Outdoor furniture & accessories	_____	_____
Patio	_____	_____
Lanai	_____	_____
Porch	_____	_____
Poolside	_____	_____
Deck	_____	_____
Barbeque grill	_____	_____
Electronics	_____	_____
Televisions	_____	_____
Stereos	_____	_____
Computers	_____	_____
VCRs/DVD players/digital recording devices	_____	_____
Gaming equipment	_____	_____
Phones	_____	_____
Floor coverings	_____	_____
Carpets	_____	_____
Tile	_____	_____
Hardwood	_____	_____
Vinyl or linoleum floor coverings	_____	_____
Throw rugs	_____	_____
Welcome mats	_____	_____
Bath mats	_____	_____

Figure 10-1:
Keep track of your budget and what you spend for furniture and other items for your second home.

Don't feel like you have to spend thousands of dollars to outfit your second home. If you have the time, you can surf the Internet or spend hours roaming around furniture wholesalers, consignment stores, flea markets, and local shops and markets to find the best possible bargains. The key is to stick to your budget and to only purchase those items that contribute to the result you want: a tasteful, comfortable living space where you can enjoy your time away from the rat race of everyday life.

Furniture Type	Budgeted Amount	Amount Spent
Wall coverings & decorative hangings		
Wallpaper		
Pictures		
Murals		
Mirrors		
Shelves for knick-knacks		
Bookshelves		
Window coverings		
Draperies		
Curtains		
Blinds		
Appliances		
Microwave		
Coffeemaker		
Refrigerator		
Stove		
Toaster		
Toaster oven		
Blender		
Washer		
Dryer		
Decorative touches		
Lamps		
Fake plants		
Real plants		
Decorations		
Candy dishes		
Ashtrays (yes, some people still smoke)		

Figure 10-1:
Continued

Considering new or used furniture

If you're contemplating how to furnish your home, your first thought may be that you have to spend thousands on brand new furniture for your new second home. However, you've already spent a boatload on the home. Even if you've decided that your second home needs everything from a couch and desk to a hutch and bedroom furniture, you have many options that range from gleaming new items to those plucked from curbs, and everything in between.

Choosing your style

Just as you did with your primary home, you'll want to choose a style for your vacation home that fits its personality. If your new place is near the beach, for example, you can consider light-colored furnishings, seaside landscape pictures, seashell decorations, and a light oak kitchen table and chairs. Perhaps a few wicker pieces for the porch would be nice.

If you bought a log home in the country, you can opt for a more rustic theme that includes burgundy or hunter green couches and chairs, a picnic-table-style dining table made of pine that's been stained a dark color, and rough-cut wooden bunk beds in the kids' room.

By deciding on a theme before you start shopping, you avoid accumulating a hodgepodge of different furniture styles and a mishmash of decorations in your new home. Instead, you can create a warm, welcoming environment — on any budget — that you can truly call your own.

The furniture and decorations should have an identity. Just like you do!

If you're strapped for time, if the prices meet your budget, and if the styles match what you're looking for, then buying new from a major retailer is often the easiest and fastest way to completely outfit your new second home.

Most national and some local furniture stores offer terrific "same as cash" offers to customers who sign up for their credit cards. You've probably seen TV commercials (they generally air around major holidays) for furniture retailers in which they advertise extended credit for up to a year or more with no payments for 12 months and no interest charged if the balance is paid off by a certain date. If your home-buying experience has left the coffers a bit low, the big boys can be good furniture-buying options for you to check out.

If you're feeling a bit adventurous, however, and you want unique or unusual pieces to add to your home, then think outside of the (furniture) box and scope out these resources for slightly used furniture with tons of character:

✔ **Online furniture wholesalers:** Search online for "furniture wholesalers" for furniture resources, including comprehensive directories of suppliers.

✔ **Local consignment shops:** People who want to sell stuff bring it to one of these shops that then take it on *consignment,* meaning the shop gets a percentage of the selling price, but only if the item sells. People often put unusual things on consignment, and you may just find that perfect table or mirror you've been looking for.

✔ **Area thrift shops:** People have donated the items in these shops, and the original owner has nothing to do with the goods anymore. You may be able to negotiate a rock-bottom price for that rocker or chest of drawers. And often, part of your purchase supports a local nonprofit agency, so not only do you get a bargain, but you also give back to the community.

✓ **Auctions:** They can be hit or miss, but are definitely worth a shot if you have the time and wherewithal to get out there and bid on stuff that you'd probably never find in a modern furniture shop (or even a pawn shop, for that matter).

✓ **Garage sales:** Garage sales are usually hit-or-miss in terms of finding what you're looking for, and you may have to visit a lot of them on a weekend. However, when you do find something you like, the price is often incredibly low. Make sure you have access to a truck to bring home your purchases.

✓ **Flea markets:** Flea markets are more organized than garage sales, although their offerings are similar. Flea markets, also called *swap meets,* are where people pay a fee to rent a space and sell whatever it is they want to sell. The smaller flea markets commonly offer household goods and a wide range of other objects, often at low prices. The larger flea markets often have established retailers offering their goods in an outdoor venue. The plus of browsing a flea market is that you're, in a sense, hitting dozens of garage sales at one time and in one place.

✓ **Classifieds:** Either in the paper or online (at a site like `www.craigslist.com` — check out your local area first to avoid shipping issues), these advertising vehicles can be great sources of furniture and odds and ends for a second home. And don't overlook those weekly "flyers" that come in your mailbox, where sellers post ads (usually for free) for affordable, used items.

✓ **Your neighbor's curb:** That's right. Your neighbor's curb can be a great source of furniture for your new vacation home. You know what they say: One man's trash is another man's treasure. This definitely holds true when it comes to used furniture. That nightstand sitting next door on the curb may have lost its appeal to your neighbor for a variety of reasons — it's scratched, the hinge is broken, one of the drawers needs a new bottom, whatever. But if you're handy and you know that the defects can be easily remedied, then you may be able to score a lovely piece for your second home for zero money down, and zero money due later! So give a peek out the window when it's bulk pickup time and see whether anything out there catches your eye. Plus, if you do rescue a bookcase because you know you can refinish it and make it a lovely addition to your den, that's one less contribution to the landfill!

If your new second home is more than a few hours away by car or plane, you should seek out new and used furniture resources in the town where the house is located, or relatively close by. Otherwise, you'll spend an undue (and aggravating) amount of time and money trying to coordinate the purchase and delivery of goods to your across-the-miles abode.

The pros and cons of used furniture

When furnishing a home, the vast majority of buyers buy new furniture. Many people would never even consider buying used furniture. But this is a little shortsighted, especially if you're on a budget and want the most for your dollar. You buy used cars, right? And used musical instruments, used window air conditioners, used books, used bicycles, used TVs, and, of course, "vintage" clothes. So why not the occasional "preowned" piece of furniture? If you're completely against the idea, I may not immediately persuade you to change your mind, but indulge me, okay? Read through these pros and cons of used furniture. You may discover something.

Pros

✔ You can find older, more unusual styles not available in modern furniture stores.

✔ You can haggle with the seller for a better deal. (You'll be amazed at the offers people will accept!)

✔ You'll spend less than you would on new furniture (unless, of course, you plan to outfit the home with one-of-a-kind antique furniture — then you're venturing into a whole 'nuther world!)

✔ You may be able to talk to the owner about the piece and discover any flaws or problems with it. (Often, flaws in older pieces are perceived to add to its character. Also, don't expect a furniture salesman to reveal this kind of information!)

✔ Hunting for used furniture will be right up your alley if you're the type who likes to pick through flea markets and consignment shops for undiscovered gems.

Cons

✔ You may not be able to find "complete" sets, or create a uniform look in your second home.

✔ The items may be dirty or damaged and need cleaning or repairs, or both.

✔ You won't get a warranty for the goods, which will be sold "as is." As is means as is: If a cabinet has a missing shelf and you didn't notice the holes for it until you got home, you're on your own. Sure, you can call the seller and ask if they forgot to give you the shelf, but if it's gone, you either live with the cabinet as is, or try to replace the missing shelf.

✔ You never know who used the furniture, or what they used it for. And if this notion grosses you out, used furniture may not be for you. Also, here's a friendly Biohazard Alert: Stay away from used mattresses and toilet seats — even if they're free. Seriously.

Putting the right amount of personal touches in your home

You probably won't use your second home in the same way or with the same frequency that you use your primary home (although if you plan on retiring to your second home, you may later use it similarly to how you currently use your primary home). So you need to decide what you really *do* need in your new second home, and what you really *don't* need. Needs and wants: They're often at odds, but these questions will help you differentiate between the two.

To figure this out, you have to know how you're going to use your new place. Ask yourself the following questions, and answer realistically based on your work and lifestyle:

- ✔ How often am I going to use this home?

- ✔ How long will the home be rented out to others?

- ✔ Will my family and friends be using the home?

- ✔ Will I rent the home on a full-time basis until I plan to retire there in five (or however many) years?

- ✔ Am I going to use the home a few times a year and rent it for the rest of the time on a seasonal basis?

The following examples are three different scenarios pertaining to your second home. In each one, consider what to include when you outfit your place, as well as what not to include:

- ✔ **You plan to use your second home only for your own vacation purposes.** If this scenario rings true for you, feel free to fill your second home with as many or as few personal touches as you want. If you envision blue carpeting, avocado appliances, and that Hawaiian hula girl lamp that everybody but your husband hates, then decorate to your heart's content because you'll be the only ones who have to navigate it.

- ✔ **You plan to use your second home a few times a year, and rent it the rest of the time.** Here's where you want to create a cross between a comfortable "homey" home and a hotel room. Doing so means bringing in the basics (and making sure that they're both tasteful and functional), as well as throwing in a few personal touches that say, "Yes, you're using this home now, but it belongs to someone else."

- ✔ **You'll rent the home on a full-time basis until you retire there at some point.** Stick with the basics and avoid the personal touches if this scenario applies to you. Go with some tasteful living room and dining room furniture, basic bedroom sets, and enough bathroom accoutrements to keep a renter comfortable. Eschew the "you," and the pic of your daughter's ballet debut, and let them bring their own shampoo.

Ultimately, your goal is to create an enjoyable living space without exceeding your budget. Because this won't be your primary home (at least not yet), my suggestion is to adopt an "out of sight, out of mind" philosophy. In other words, forgoing that $5,000 grandfather clock that you know would look great in the foyer probably isn't a bad idea. You won't get to see it every day anyway, and why spend that kind of money for an unoccupied house or to make guests or renters happy? Use common sense when spending, create a sense of style that you like, and stick with it for the best results.

Shoot for simplicity

That gorgeous plush velvet couch may be screaming your name from the consignment shop window, but if buying it means you'll spend half of your vacation with a lint roller in hand, removing Fido or Fluffy's hair from its folds, then you may want to steer clear of it.

Instead, aim for a low-maintenance furnishing approach. Think about the daily maintenance required of the pieces you're buying, and shoot for items that need little or no hands-on attention beyond regular, routine cleanings.

A good general rule when outfitting a second home is "less is more." After all, you can always add more at a later date if you're feeling deprived — or if you simply can't stand that empty foyer one second longer!

Clothing Matters: Packing It or Keeping It in Your Home

Packing is a drag. You know it, I know it, and yet it's one of those things that must be done. But you *can* avoid packing suitcases and lugging luggage every time you visit your second home, which brings me to an important question: Do you need to pack your clothing every time you visit your second home or can you leave some there?

To ease your packing woes, consider leaving at least some of your clothing and toiletries in your second home. It's not absolutely necessary, of course, but doing so is a wise move if you plan to use the place on a regular basis. And, as you figure out which clothing and belongings you want to keep permanently at your second home, my advice is to stick to the basics and avoid going overboard.

Avoid leaving valuables (such as jewelry and collectibles) at your second home if other people rent it, stay there, and/or use it for day trips. I'm not suggesting that your renters are thieves. But you're courting trouble when you leave valuables lying around when you're not there. Better safe than sorry.

This section helps you decide what to pack and what to leave at your second home so you aren't lugging extra suitcases each time you visit. This section also looks at how much you plan to use your second home so you know how much to leave there and how much you need to pack each time you visit.

Beginning with the basics

Keeping outfits and other necessities in your second home doesn't have to break the bank. You can have the basics without spending a fortune. Start with the essentials and avoid overdoing it right out of the gate, lest you find yourself up to your ears in too many boxes and outfits. Keep in mind that you can always bring more stuff later.

Here's a list of the things you'll likely need to live comfortably for a week or more. Season to taste as needed.

- ✔ 5–7 casual, everyday outfits

- ✔ 2–3 dressy outfits (if you plan to socialize and eat dinners in fancy restaurants)

- ✔ 3–4 pairs of shoes (including casual, athletic, and dress)

- ✔ Enough sleepwear and undergarments for a week to 10 days

- ✔ Bathing suits, ski outfits, workout clothing, and/or other items you'll need to enjoy recreational activities

- ✔ Duplicate sets of toiletries, makeup, and hair accessories

- ✔ A first-aid kit and over-the-counter medicines that you have at your primary home and use on a daily or semiregular basis

- ✔ Soap, towels, washcloths, toilet tissue, paper towels, bed linens, blankets

- ✔ Laundry and kitchen essentials like soap, bleach, softener, dish washing detergent, scouring pads, cleanser, window cleaner, and all that necessary "stuff" for cleaning

- ✔ A small clock, a few tools, a flashlight, pencil, and paper pads

- ✔ Games, novels, puzzles, playing cards, and such

- ✔ Any gadgets or other items that you simply can't live without (like that high-end espresso maker, your favorite lighted makeup mirror, or a copy of whatever emergency repair programs you use when your computer crashes — computer woes seem to never take vacations, right?)

Don't forget your prescription medications. Explain the situation to your doctor, and be sure to get extra refills on those medications that you take on a regular basis. You don't want to have to run to the nearest drugstore the day after you move in.

Having an enormous selection only means more to rummage through when you're looking for that perfect outfit . . . and more laundry to do! As long as your home is equipped with a washer and dryer — and as long as you're not planning to stay more than a month or two at a time — you should be able to get away with a week's worth of clothing and goods.

Stashing the right stuff for your stays

You truly don't need to bring everything but the kitchen sink to your second home. Instead, use a more calculated approach to stocking the place with exactly what you (and any of your renters) will need. You wouldn't schlep your entire household with you if you went on a week's vacation, right? Just because you own the place you're vacationing at shouldn't change your thinking as to what you should bring.

Just how much you bring to — and leave — in your second home depends on a few factors:

- **How much time you plan to spend in your second home:** If you'll only be visiting your place for two weeks out of the year, then lugging your belongings on each trip probably isn't that big of a deal. However, if you're fairly certain that weekend trips to the home are in the cards, keeping the basics on hands instead of dragging them with you every single time will be much easier (see the preceding section about what to keep at your house). If you return home on Sunday night and have to work the next day, those suitcases may not get unpacked before Thursday or Friday rolls around and it's time to pack again.

- **Whether other people will be staying in the home:** If you plan to rent your villa during the times that you're not using it, you don't want your underwear drawer with all its exotic sundries to come under the scrutiny of others. Use your private *owner's closet* for storage of private stuff and keep the dressers and closets empty for your guests to use.

I've stayed in dozens of privately owned condos over the years and have found that most owners reserve one locked closet in which they keep their own personal items (like wine, pictures, books, and things they don't want used by others) out of sight, secure, and untouched. Commonly called *the owner's closet,* it provides a place to stow things when renters, family, or friends are using your second home.

- **How much space is available to store the goods:** Space won't be an issue if

  - You've purchased storage furniture such as dressers or closet organizers.

  - No one else is going to use the home while you're not there.

If you fall into these categories, then you can, of course, spread your stuff all over the house any way you want to. However, if space is limited, or if others will be prowling around, you'll want to keep your clothing and personal effects in a safe place.

Adjusting to Your New Environment

Moving is never easy. And, yes, purchasing a second home and establishing a new life in a new place — even if it's only part time in the beginning — counts as moving. Although you aren't leaving your primary residence behind (at first), you do have to adjust to your new home's surroundings so you can truly enjoy your new dwelling.

This section provides some pointers for getting acclimated to your new surroundings. By exploring the neighborhood and meeting your new neighbors, your second home can start to feel like home, sweet home.

Get to know your new community

Ultimately, you'll leave your primary home and live in your second home full time. You'll leave behind dear friends, familiar routines, and favorite places. Then you'll need to make new friends and uncover new favorite places in your second hometown. This sounds daunting, but it need not be.

Instead of hiding behind those four walls, though, get out and explore your new environment. If in the past you've spent significant time in the area that's home to your second home, you may already be familiar with some or all the attractions, parks, restaurants, entertainment venues, shops, and shopping malls. If not, familiarize yourself with the activities and amenities available — both in the immediate neighborhood and in the city or town where you've touched down. If the area is all new to you, however, start at the area's convention and visitor's bureau or the chamber of commerce. You can find them online or in the phone book.

By spending a few minutes at these places, you can get your hands on

- ✔ The most recent, magazine-style publication touting the area and its attractions, eating establishments, and stores
- ✔ Brochures advertising individual attractions and entertainment venues
- ✔ Maps of all kinds
- ✔ Info for new residents (directions to the post office, how to get your water hooked up, and so on)
- ✔ Tips from the locals; you can uncover some amazing tidbits during a friendly conversation with the woman at the visitor's bureau or the man at the chamber of commerce

Expensive advertising can lure diners in, but one of the best ways to find the top restaurants in the area is by asking neighbors or acquaintances where they like to eat. Because everyone's perception of a "good restaurant" is different, be sure to specify whether you want "value" (big portions at good prices), "high-end" options (higher prices and impeccable service), or just the best tasting food available. Also, be sure to specify what types of food you're really into. If you love Italian, and want to know the best Italian restaurants and pizza places in the area, say so. After all, a sushi restaurant just won't satisfy your pizza craving, so ask about your faves.

Now comes the fun part. Armed with this info, you can explore the area and try different places without getting lost. As you make your way around, be sure to note which places and restaurants are worth one or more repeat visits and which aren't. You can do this right on the guides that you're using to find the places or in a separate notebook.

Keeping a visitor's notebook in your second home is a great idea if you plan on renting it. The notebook doesn't have to be fancy. Just use a plain spiral-bound notebook with one page for restaurants, one for shopping venues, one for theaters, and so forth. And be sure to include your comments about each place. For example, be sure to inform your renters about that little strip mall that has a dollar store, or the takeout place that offers free delivery. The renters will appreciate your thoughtfulness. Figure 10-2 shows a sample index card. You may want to keep track of this info on index cards or in a file on your computer. You can then transfer the most relevant stuff to your visitor's notebook when you get a chance.

Figure 10-2:
Keep track of local restaurants and other amenities so you know whether to recommend them to your guests and renters.

> Name of the venue: _____
>
> Location (travel time to get there) (approximately): _____
>
> Date visited: _____
>
> What we did there: _____
>
> What we liked about it: _____
>
> What we didn't like about it: _____
>
> Should we go back? _____ yes _____ no

Because you'll be living in your new community on a part-time basis — and not immersed in it year-round — having this info handy is useful for future visits and can help you avoid those places that simply aren't worth returning to.

Meet your new neighbors

Back home you probably have a network of friends and family with whom you socialize, eat meals, gossip, play games, travel, barbecue, and otherwise enjoy spending time. Depending on your personality and socialization skills, you'll probably start forming similar bonds in your new environment.

One of the best times to get out and meet your neighbors is in the first few weeks after you buy your second home. During this period, neighbors are usually very interested in knowing

- ✔ Who you are and where you're from?
- ✔ Why you moved into the area or purchased a second home there?
- ✔ How long you plan to stay?
- ✔ How often you'll be there?
- ✔ What are your hobbies? (If you're into fishing, for example, and the guy across the street has a boat and likes to fish, you're in luck.)
- ✔ What they can do to help you move in and get comfortable?

Being neighborly is especially important for second-home owners who aren't around to watch their properties throughout the year. By making friends with the families next door, across the street, or across the hall, you can make arrangements to watch each other's places while you're away. You can establish your own little security team, and you'll sleep better knowing that a trusted friend is keeping an eye on things.

If you've purchased a home in a 55-plus community, a country club environment, or other socially oriented development, then chances are good that at least one event will be held annually to get the owners together to meet and mingle. Whether you play bingo, enjoy cocktail hour, or participate in a neighborhood garage sale, these events provide a great way for new homeowners to get to know everyone and form bonds with those who share similar interests.

If it turns out that one or more of your neighbors are unfriendly or downright unsavory, don't let it ruin your weekend getaways or family vacations. Just chalk it up to the fact that it takes all kinds, and go about your business without worrying about whether the guy next door likes you.

Chapter 11

Renting Out Your Second Home to Pay for Itself

*O*ne of the nicest aspects of second-home ownership is that, if you want to, you can rent out your abode for cashola. That's right, folks: If you plan on using your second home for only a few weeks or months out of the year, you can turn the place into a moneymaking machine by renting it out to visitors or vacationers. And it's your call as to how long to rent it for; from a few summer weeks to vacationers, to six-month or longer stretches to someone who needs a retreat for a few months.

Renting your second home doesn't necessarily mean you'll be dealing with a long line of strangers who want to use the place for a week at a time. You can choose who to rent to and when to allow them access to your new digs, although if you have property in a prime location, such as the beach, you may end up renting it to people you don't know during peak summer months when you aren't using the home. If you'd rather not deal with strangers, you can rent your second home to friends and relatives. Your second home can provide a versatile, lucrative revenue stream, depending on your preferences.

In this chapter, I show you how to rent your home by using a property manager or by managing the property yourself. I also review the basics of advertising your second home to the eager-to-rent masses and discuss how to price your rental and screen renters who will be staying there.

How to Turn Your Second Home into a Cash Cow

Put on your entrepreneurial cap for a minute. (Even if you've never worn it before, I'll betcha it fits just fine!) Now take a good long look at your second home — but not through your rose-colored glasses (you removed them before you put the cap on, right?). Don't look at your second home as only a place where you and your loved ones can gather around a cozy fire with a cup of cocoa and sing holiday carols, but rather as a component of your investment portfolio and as a potential moneymaker.

This section helps you cash in by explaining a few key points you need to understand before you actually rent your second home. I help you tackle concerns about location and whether the community where the home is located allows rentals, how much to charge, and most important, making sure you spend some time in your home away from home.

Will you have to follow someone else's rules when renting your home?

Before you start filling out the deposit slips for your rental profits, be sure to check the neighborhood covenants of the community in which you're considering buying. Community bylaws vary from development to development, but many prohibit anything other than owner-occupied units. Be sure you're allowed to rent your home before you start looking for renters.

This issue is important for those of you who are considering renting out your place on a short-term (couple of weeks) or super-short-term (weekends to a week at a time) basis. Full-time residents in many areas of the country have been crying foul over the loud partying and raucousness sometimes associated with those who come in, vacation for a week, and then leave. As a result, many communities have instituted "minimum stay" rules for vacation homes.

 Make sure that the place you're purchasing meets your needs when it comes to rentals. If renting out your second home is important to you, "Can I rent out my unit?" should be the first question you ask an agent when he suggests looking at a condo in a prime vacation spot. If renting is unequivocally *not* allowed, then you need to consider a different location. Check the rules — and then double-check them — if you're thinking seriously about renting out your second home.

Often, even if a community does allow rentals, many boilerplate condo bylaws these days forbid rentals of less than six months. This won't work for you if you're thinking about renting your place out for a week at a time from

June to September every year. And in many cases, the bylaws also require that the association's executive board approve the tenant. This gives the board veto power over your potential tenant. You need to know all of this before you sign your purchase agreement.

If you can't get your hands on a copy of the neighborhood or community rules, speak with a real estate agent or attorney in the area about the issue. They should be able to answer your questions and give you some free advice before you buy.

This concern is, of course, irrelevant if you're purchasing a log home situated on 20 acres in rural New York, and you have no one to account to but *you*. But if you have your eye on a condo in Fort Lauderdale from which a vacationer can gaze out onto the glorious Atlantic Ocean, you need to do some serious investigation into whether the condo rules allow you to rent your unit to a third party.

Location is key

Location is everything in real estate, particularly for those of you who are looking to rent out your second homes to willing customers. Buy or build a mansion smack in the middle of the Mojave Desert, for example, and your pool of potential renters will be pretty limited, no matter how great it is. But snag a place by the seashore in just about any state and you'll probably find yourself turning down potential customers during the high season. See Chapter 4 for more information on selecting the right second-home location.

Think about the following factors — all of which are relevant to renting out your place:

- ✔ **The location of your second home:** Is it in an area where seasonal or year-round visitors like to go on a regular basis?

- ✔ **The style and size of your home:** Do the features of your place lend themselves to short, frequent stays by other individuals or families?

- ✔ **The home's and/or community's amenities:** Just how enticing are they to other individuals or families?

If, for example, you own an oversized two-bedroom, two-bath condo on the beach in Naples, Florida, and it's in a complex where the community residents have access to a pool, tennis courts, fitness center, and private beach, then finding renters to pay a premium to spend a week in your home during the in-season should be a breeze.

If, however, you and yours are the rustic type and you own a log cabin in Tennessee where "roughing it" is the name of the game, then your pool of potential renters will be significantly smaller, as will the number of weeks that you'll be able to feasibly rent your home out during the year. It's a given that more people — especially vacationers — are "beachy" rather than "woodsy."

How much to charge

If you're seriously considering renting your second home, then you need to know how much to charge the renters. The price will depend on several factors, including the going rate in your second home's market, the demand for rentals, and your costs.

To determine a fair rent to charge for your second home, ask yourself the following questions:

✔ **How much are other owners charging for similar properties?** This question is likely the most accurate indicator of what you can get for your rental. That's because, all things being equal, price will almost always prevail when someone goes on the Internet or flips through the Sunday paper looking for a two-bedroom, two-bath home for rent on Long Beach Island, New Jersey. The one that's $5,000 a month may be beautiful and have great amenities and a spectacular view, but the similar, tad more "adequate" one that rents for $3,000 a month will probably get more attention because of its comparable affordability.

✔ **How much are people willing to pay for home rentals in the area?** What will the market bear? The more homes available for rent in a particular area, the lower the demand will be for yours, and the lower the rent you can charge. It's basic "supply and demand" Economics 101, and exactly the opposite is true in areas where supply is scarce.

Put yourself in a renter's shoes. Compile information on comparable properties as if you were looking to rent one. There's nothing like first-hand data to shine a light on areas of uncertainty and provide facts you can use. Get out and shop around the area where your second home is located with your renter's cap on. Surf the Internet, and check out area newspapers for current rental prices. You can even ask real estate agents who handle rentals to dig up this information for you. The agent who sold you your second home may also be able to help you with this info.

During this research, pay attention to the following:

• The condition of the homes you look at and how they compare with your house.

• The homes' sizes and the number of bedrooms and bathrooms.

• The differences in amenities between your home and the homes you look at. If you have a hot tub on your deck and the other ones don't, you may be able to fetch a little more for your house.

- How much the rent is and what it includes.

- Whether the season makes any difference in what's being charged. In some areas, you may be able to command higher prices — even on long-term rentals — during a peak season, like summer in beach areas, fall in foliage areas, and winter in ski areas.

- Any other selling points property owners are using to snag a higher price. You may be able to use comparable features in your home as justification for a higher rent. Consider high-speed Internet access, telephone, cable TV, and central air to justify a higher price.

✔ **How much cold cash do you need to bring in to break even or earn a profit on your second home?** After you figure out what to charge by using the previous questions in this section, whip out that calculator and plug in the total monthly cost of owning your second home (check out Chapter 2 for more info). If the numbers show you breaking even, or even better, earning a profit, then you're in business. If they don't, then you may want to reconsider your rental price, or completely rethink what to buy and where to buy it.

If you're rental minded, think of your second home— at least until you move into it full time — as a business. It must be competitive with other homes on the market to be attractive to renters and (ideally) turn a profit.

Vacationing in your second home

Even if you plan on regularly renting out your second home to others, be sure to carve out some time for you and yours to spend there during the year. The second-home owners from whom I've rented all do the same thing when it comes to their own vacations: They mark out *their* weeks first on a calendar, and then accommodate their guests and renters on the remaining weeks.

It's a simple exercise, but it ensures that your own desires and needs are satisfied before you invite the rest of the world into your home. Start by coming up with a few days, weeks, or months during the year that you think you'll be able to get away to your getaway. Grab a red marker and a calendar, and put a big X through all the days you want. This is your way of declaring, "These are *my* days to enjoy *my* second home!"

Thus, when the lure of rental income beckons, you can look at your calendar and work the renters in around your days, which — as a second-home owner — you deserve. And if a potential vacationer really needs a certain week, and it's no big deal to adjust your plans, you'll do it, right? But blocking out *your* time is a good way to start.

Considering Your Rental Options

If you're considering renting your second home, you have two basic ways to do so: short term and long term. However, you can also be a bit more creative to generate bucks from your abode.

This section takes you through the basic rental options and also discusses a few innovative methods for renting out a second home. I also explain how to resolve the inevitable "family" issue — y'know, when your family or best friend wants to stay in your second home for *free?* — and I show you how to do it in a way that doesn't upset Uncle Ted and Aunt Fran (and any other kin who may feel a sense of entitlement to *your* place).

Comparing long- and short-term rentals

When you decide to rent your home, you'll likely consider a variety of factors: how much time you'll allow the house to be rented, how much income you want the home to generate, and how often you want to deal with the turnover in tenants. Your decisions about these factors will influence whether you establish your second home as a long- or short-term rental.

✔ A *long-term rental* is exactly what it sounds like: A family or an individual lives in your second home on a year-round basis, usually with an annual or month-to-month lease.

This plan is terrific for someone who wants to purchase a second home now, but doesn't need to, or want to, live in it (or even visit it) immediately. If you're thinking about retiring and moving into the home ten years from now, for example, then you would be a good candidate to offer the place as a long-term rental. You'll own it, it'll appreciate in value (I hope), you'll know where you'll be retiring to, and, in the intervening years, the home can earn money for you.

✔ A *short-term rental* provides you with some "second-home time," yet still allows you to reap some of the financial benefits of renting out your place. Short-term rentals can range from weekend and single-week rentals to vacationers, friends, and family, to longer, one- to six-month stints for visiting executives, professors, and others who need a place for a short period and prefer to live in a home rather than a hotel.

Short-term rentals are particularly common if your second home is in a popular vacation spot. If you're buying a second home in a hot vacation spot, then there's a good chance that you'll be able to rent it out to vacationers on a fairly regular basis, particularly during the *in-season* periods of the year. In Florida, for example, in-season is between November and April, when the rest of the nation is shivering in its britches. In Colorado, the in-season is during ski season, when vacationers flock to the state for its powdery slopes.

Vacation rentals, especially during the right season, can be lucrative for owners. If you expect your home to be vacant during certain times of the year, you'll definitely want to consider offsetting some of your expenses with rental income.

The Internet has opened up the rental business to virtually anyone, making it much easier for renters and owners to find each other and pair up. By posting a description of your home and its location, a few photos, whether it's a long- or short-term rental, and a calendar on a site like www.vrbo.com or www.vacationrentals.com, owners can expose their vacation homes to the world and do business with renters from around the globe. If you'd rather focus on finding a long-term tenant, consider placing an ad on the Web site for the local newspaper in the area where your second home is located.

Look at your own situation and determine which option is best for you. If you're buying now to prepare for a retirement that's coming several years down the road, then a long-term rental is a good idea. If, however, you're planning on vacationing at your second home three or four times a year, then the short-term rental option may be your best bet.

Doing business with family and friends

Okay, you're a good person. You may have already planned on "giving away your house" to select friends and special family members from time to time throughout the year. And you would never think of charging cousins Ricky and Gladys rent, right? Think again.

Give some serious thought to actually charging your friends and family for the use of your home. If it makes you feel better, you can give them a discount, but collecting at least something in rent is a good way to recoup some of your monthly investment. Your family and friends would have to pay full price somewhere else, right? So why not charge them a reduced rent to make up for the wear and tear on your place? A modest fee (perhaps half your regular rental price?) is well worth the enjoyment they'll get out of using your place.

This is a good way to raise some additional cash to pay for your investment, while also instilling responsible practices in your own kin and acquaintances. Come up with a fair price based on what you would normally charge a stranger to rent the home, but factor in the related renter's budget and ability to pay. (And because we're talking about people you're close to, you'll probably have a pretty good sense of their financial particulars.)

Home exchanging can let you see the world

Bet you didn't know that other second-home owners are ready, willing, and able to "exchange" their homes with you for a week or two, did you? They are, and by connecting with them, you can travel the world and stay in other people's vacation homes. The practice is called *home exchanging,* and second-home owners do exactly what it sounds like they're doing: They exchange properties with one another on a short-term basis as way to see more of the world.

Done on a formal or informal basis, setting up a home exchange can be as easy as thumbing through the classifieds or browsing an online rent-by-owner site to find someone who is renting out a vacation home in an area that you'd like to visit. By offering your own home for a week or two in exchange for a couple of weeks in theirs, you're essentially setting up your own home exchange.

More formal arrangements can be made, too. Several reputable Web sites list homes available for exchange. Targeted at second-home owners, these sites include ExchangeHomes (www.exchangehomes.com), HomeExchange (www.homeexchange.com), and TradingHomes (www.tradinghomes.com).

Of course, nothing is free these days. Searching for area-specific listings is usually free, but expect to pay a membership fee to join these exchanges and get the contact info you need to set up the exchange. HomeExchange, for example, offers a $59.95 yearly membership, or lower rates for those who join for more than one year. The service also accepts rental listings (as opposed to straight exchanges), which are placed into their own category and accessible through the site's online search features.

The IRS looks carefully at rental properties that are being run (and deducted) as for-profit "businesses," but that aren't being rented out for anywhere near fair market prices. Keep that in mind when you slash prices for your friends and family. (Check Chapter 14 for more info.)

Using Property Managers to Handle the Rental Process

If you're toying with the idea of renting your second home, but you aren't all that thrilled with wearing the title of "landlord," you have an alternative.

Instead of dealing with phone calls from potential renters at 3 o'clock on a Sunday afternoon, you can unload the responsibility onto a *property manager* who — for a fee — will handle almost everything having to do with the rental and maintenance of your second home. Property management firms can be especially useful for off-site owners who need help finding renters and filling the rental calendar.

In this section, I discuss the property manager's role, how much you can expect to pay for one, and how to find one who can help you rent out your valuable vacation property.

The property manager's role

If you think you want to rent out your second home, but aren't sure about all the ins and outs of finding and keeping track of renters from afar, a property manager can be your best friend. *Property managers* serve as a liaison between you, as the home's owner, and your tenants. They provide a valuable service to those owners who can't physically be onsite, ensuring that their properties are rented, maintained, and safe. If you can't oversee the rental of your second home yourself, the peace of mind is certainly worth the money. (You can also use a property manager to maintain your second home, whether you're renting it out or not. Check out Chapter 13 for more info.)

If you have only one second home, and if your schedule (and your primary home's proximity to your second home) allows for frequent visits, you may not need a property manager. Weigh the manager's fees (check out the next section for more on fees) against what it would take to rent out, maintain, and inspect the property yourself. If doing it on your own is significantly less expensive than hiring help, nix the property manager. (But just be prepared to be on call whenever a renter is in the house.)

How much they charge

The fees charged by property managers can vary greatly. The factors that determine what a typical property manager charges include the following:

- **The location of the property:** If your home is in a hot vacation spot where there are a lot of second homes (and, thus, probably a lot of rental activity), expect to pay more than if your place is in a less popular area.

- **Demand for managers in the area:** If demand is high for property managers in the region, you'll pay more than you would in an area where there is a glut of managers and a scarcity of properties to represent.

- **The size and complexity of your home:** The owner of a one-bedroom condo will certainly pay less for management services than the owner of a five-bedroom, six-bath single-family home on two acres of land.

- **The services you need:** Property managers will be more than happy to provide an array of services not included in their flat fees — the fee they charge for the most common, routine services. Whether you want or need these extras is entirely up to you.

✔ **The number of individual units that the property manager is handling at a time (the size of the management company):** To help their business survive and grow, most property management firms oversee multiple properties. If you're dealing with a large firm with hundreds of properties, you may pay a little less than you would for one that handles just a dozen homes.

If you hire a property manager to manage your second home, you can expect to pay the following fees based on your situation:

✔ **One month's rent or 5 to 10 percent of the income for long-term rentals:** Most property managers charge a month's rent or 5 to 10 percent of the total rent collected on a property that's rented out long term. Expect to pay at least this much while you're renting out your home on a full-time basis and using a manager. When the time comes to retire to your second home, you probably won't need or want a property manager's rental services, although you still may want to retain one on a limited scale to handle grounds maintenance and other routine chores.

✔ **A flat fee:** Some property managers nix the commission route and instead cover their own expenses by charging owners a flat monthly fee. These fees vary greatly, so be sure to shop around before you choose a manager to handle your property.

The flat fee route may work if you're not using a management company for anything but the basics — maintaining the property. If you're having the rent sent directly to you, and you have a plumber cousin, and you have no problem doing a top-to-bottom cleaning when the tenant moves out, then talk to property managers about an *a la carte* deal in which you pick the services you want and pay a flat rate.

✔ **25 to 50 percent of the income for infrequent rentals:** If you're renting your home out on a less predictable basis (a few times a year, perhaps), you'll probably pay 25 to 50 percent of the rent in property management fees. The higher fees are because there is more involved with keeping such frequently unoccupied properties maintained, rented out, marketed to the masses, and in an appealing, safe condition.

Before you agree on any fees and before you hand over your home's keys to a property manager, put everything you discuss in writing, and make sure all significant parties sign on the dotted line (including you). You may also want to have an attorney review the agreement just to be sure that the language is clear and the deal is solid.

The agreement should clearly spell out the property manager's duties and state exactly how much you'll pay on a monthly, quarterly, or annual basis for those services. It should also list a termination (or renewal) date, all contact information for the owner(s) and property manager, and the terms for solving any breach of contract issues.

Finding a reputable property manager

If you've determined that a property manager is the way to go to keep an eye on your second home when you're not around, check with the following people in your search for a reputable property manager:

- ✔ **Other second-home owners who have used these professionals:** These folks can tell you the good, the bad, the ugly, and even the wonderful of working with specific managers. Some of your neighbors or friends may even be willing to recommend a good manager to handle your property.

- ✔ **The staff at the National Association of Residential Property Managers (NARPM):** If you don't know any other second-home owners in the area, contact the NARPM, which has local chapters around the country. Check out the group's Web site at www.narpm.org. Click on the "Search Property Managers" link, which allows you to fill out a search form and retrieve names of NARPM members based on your criteria. These members are required to follow a code of ethics and stay current on their educational requirements.

- ✔ **Anyone you know who owns or lives in a condo or apartment complex maintained by a property management company:** Property managers handle condo developments, senior housing complexes, and apartment buildings, as well as individual homes. You can ask a friend who owns a condo who manages her property, what services are included, and what she thinks of them.

After you find a property manager located near your second home, check out his credentials. You also can call your state's Division of Real Estate or Division of Business and Regulation for specific property management requirements for your area. In certain states (not all, though), property managers must be licensed and must meet initial and continuing education requirements. Property managers must also carry liability insurance, and many are associated with trade groups that set forth their own ethical guidelines and professional requirements.

Does that mean the property manager with the most designations after his name is the best one to work with? Not always, but it does mean that that person has put out the money and agreed to the time commitment involved with getting as much education as possible in the field.

Asking the right questions

As you narrow the list of prospective property managers to a few, call them and ask the following questions. You want to ensure that they're going to take care of your property.

✔ **How long have you and/or your firm been managing properties?** You want someone with experience, not someone who is new to the business.

✔ **How many second homes/vacation homes have you managed in the last five years? Have you worked in the community where my second home is located?** Steer clear of property managers and firms who work only with commercial properties (such as apartment buildings) and who don't know your neighborhood.

✔ **Is licensing required in this state and, if so, are you licensed and is your license current?** It's important to work with someone who has to abide by the rules of their licensing agency.

✔ **Do you belong to any trade groups, and/or do you have any other professional credentials?** This is a good indicator that the property manager cares about his reputation and about what's going on in the industry.

✔ **Do you carry liability insurance?** If the answer to this one is "No," move on.

✔ **What type of marketing program do you use to attract tenants?** Have them go over in detail the marketing programs they'll employ to get your rental calendar filled.

✔ **What specific services do you offer and at what cost? Are your costs negotiable?** Have a good idea of exactly what the manager will do and for how much money.

✔ **How often will you inspect the property?** You want inspections to take place after tenants vacate the home and on regular intervals (such as quarterly).

✔ **What types of security measures will you take in the event of a natural disaster or emergency?** This will be particularly important for out-of-state owners whose homes are in places prone to natural disasters, which include floods, blizzards, ice storms, brush/forest fires, earthquakes, and hurricanes. Also, as disconcerting as it is to consider, many regions today are prone to terrorist attacks, and this must also be taken into account when preparing for emergencies.

✔ **How available will you be to answer renter's questions? How quickly will you respond to maintenance calls?** You want someone who is available and responsive.

✔ **Will you provide me with the names and contact numbers of three second-home owners who you're currently representing?** Ask the references what their experiences, likes, and dislikes are as they relate to the property manager and his services.

Renting Out the Home on Your Own

If a property manager isn't in the cards for you, and you want to rent out your home on an annual or short-term basis, then you'll have to take it upon yourself to create a marketing campaign to get the word out about your rental.

Can you just throw a free ad online, sit back, and wait for the renters to e-mail or call you? Sure. If, for example, you only want to rent your place out for three months out of the year, and your luxurious, yet affordable condo is in a highly desirable location, then you may just get lucky with this no-frills strategy.

But if your home is swimming in a sea of equally great rental properties, you'll need a more aggressive and wide-ranging approach to score renters. You'll also need to screen renters, to ensure that the folks renting your home won't leave it in shambles. In this section, I help you figure out what will work best for you.

Getting the word out

To maximize profits and keep your home occupied during the weeks that you're not using it, you need to consider it less a home and more a business. That means doing what real estate agents do: They talk up their listings (in this case, your home and its amenities, price, and availability), they ask for referrals (from happy renters), and they spread the word about how wonderful the getaways are that they represent. This is by far the easiest and most economical way to fill those empty weeks.

The easiest place to start soliciting renters is in your own backyard. Neighbors, friends, co-workers, relatives, and old high school and college buddies are basically your own *sphere of influence* (a term real estate agents use to describe their individual networks of potential, future, and current clients). By tapping this network first, you get free, unlimited advertising for your second home. I say "unlimited" because when you tell four friends, and they tell four friends, and they tell four friends, and so on, you exponentially expand your pool of potential renters. Word of mouth can be very effective. And because you probably share similar interests with at least some of these people, there's a good chance that someone in this network will give your place a shot when it comes time to fill in those vacation weeks.

When these folks have a good time at your place, there's an equally good chance that they'll then spread the word to their own networks. This continues to increase your sphere of potential renters, a gold mine of potential leads you create by simply mentioning at a lunch event that your lovely place on Galveston Island is up for grabs for a few months this summer.

Identify your market

Your own network of potential renters should be easy to contact. You probably already have their phone numbers and/or e-mail addresses, and you should have no problem making each of them aware of your rental property. But if you want or need to reach out into the large World of People You Don't Know to find short-term or long-term renters for your home, then you need to identify exactly who you're trying to reach.

And how do you accomplish this seemingly overwhelming and daunting task? You do what good marketing pros do: You pinpoint your *target market* before going after it. To get started, ask yourself this key question: What kind of person, couple, family, or group would want to rent my second home?

Answer the following questions to get a pretty accurate profile of your ideal renter:

- ✔ **What type of person typically lives or vacations in the area where my second home is located?** Moms, dads, and kids? College students? Young professionals? Empty nesters?

- ✔ **What kind of amenities do these folks look for, and does my home (or the community where it's located) offer them?** If you're in a beach town, but the beach is miles away, then you may want to focus on one or more amenities closer to your home.

- ✔ **If I'm looking for a year-round renter, what type of person or family do I want to see renting it?** Remember that you can't discriminate based on race, color, creed, or religion, but you can choose young or old, kids or no kids, smokers or nonsmokers, singles or couples, and so on.

- ✔ **What age group does the typical renter fall into in my area or community?** If you purchased a second home in a 55-plus mobile home park, for example, then your target market will have to meet the age rules of the community.

- ✔ **Where would I typically find this type of renter? Is he surfing the job boards online? Is she leafing through the newspaper? Are they working with a real estate agent?** The answer to this question will clue you in to the best place to spend your hard-earned advertising dollars and most effectively implement your marketing strategies.

After asking yourself these questions, you can conjure up a pretty clear image of potential renters for your unit.

Set an advertising budget

Now you need to set an advertising budget to reach that now-defined target market. This is important because you don't want to discover later that the six print ads and three Web site promotions you invested in ate up all of your rental profits.

To get started, set your budget at a relatively low 10 percent of your estimated profits. Then adjust your ad expenditures from there based on how well the advertising and marketing is performing for you.

Be sure to track your expenses for tax purposes, because you'll be able to write off the cost of advertising at the end of the year.

How much money you allocate to advertising your rental depends on a few key factors, including:

- ✔ **The frequency at which you plan to rent out the home:** If your place is a year-round rental that someone will move into and not leave for a year or more, your budget will almost certainly be minimal. If, however, you plan to use the home yourself for two months and rent it out the other ten (probably to different individuals in week-long or month-long blocks), then your budget will be considerably larger.

- ✔ **How desirable the home's location is:** A great location can be a double-edged sword. Sure, you'll attract more renters to your lovely condo on the sands of Myrtle Beach, but your unit will also be up against hundreds of other rentals in the area. And this means you'll need to spend more, and spend more frequently, to stand out from the crowd.

   And if your second home is in a location that isn't as popular with tourists, you can't just sit back and wait for renters to inquire about your home. Granted, your log cabin in the West Virginia wilderness will likely have little competition for renters, but that means that getting the word out about it may take a little more elbow grease and more time and money to bring your place to the attention of potential renters.

- ✔ **How good you are at networking and spreading the word:** Your personal networking tools include face-to-face conversations at business meetings and chats at social gatherings during which you rave about your place, as well as talking it up in online blogs and forums. The more of this stuff that you can do on your own, the smaller your advertising budget can be.

- ✔ **Your own financial situation:** If you can afford to put half-page ads with photos in the local newspaper for your mountainside chalet, by all means go for it. But if you can't, be sure to create a realistic monthly or annual budget for your second-home marketing efforts.

Figure out your advertising strategy

An *advertising strategy* is basically a plan in which you determine how often to advertise, where to advertise, and how much to spend on advertising. I cover much of this in the previous sections, but an important point to remember is that *oversight is crucial*. You need to keep track of all the elements of your plan and note the response. For example, if you made a point of telling 15 friends and colleagues about your home for rent, and the response was one call that went nowhere, then obviously your existing circle of charming cohorts doesn't boast potential renters.

Or say you ran an ad in the small, local newspaper in the town where your second home is located and received 19 calls within a two-week period. Bingo! You have found a medium that the people you're looking for check out on a regular basis, and this is where you should target your ad budget.

Your advertising strategy is often a hit-or-miss situation that may seem in the beginning like you're just throwing money at newspapers, posting ads online, talking to people, and getting nowhere. That's why you need to be diligent in keeping track of your attempts, assigning a relative value to each one ("worthless," "not bad," "excellent"), and writing notes to yourself.

The following are a few advertising strategies. One of the most popular, using the Web, is so important that I give this topic its own section. Check out "Advertising your home online" later in this chapter.

Use real estate agents

Real estate agents who work with rentals can serve as great go-betweens for owners and potential renters. Find an agent who works frequently with rentals (not all do, so just ask) and who already has multiple rental listings to offer renters when they call the office looking for a place to stay. You may want to start with the agent who sold you your home, or ask him to refer to you an agent who specializes in rentals.

You'll find the most helpful (and willing) agents in areas where rentals are especially popular. The downtown Chicago market, for example, is one area where agents work regularly with condo owners looking to farm out the advertising, marketing, tenant screening, and rent collection duties to someone else. Beach and vacation areas also abound with agents who are accustomed to potential renters calling to ask, "What do you have for rent on the beach this summer?"

For annual rentals, expect to pay one month's rent or 5 to 10 percent of one year's total rent in commission to the real estate agent. For vacation rentals, the rates vary. Talk to your real estate agent about her fees, and negotiate accordingly.

Rely on the out-of-town newspaper

The local newspaper is still a good way to reach potential renters in the immediate area, although the fact that the paper is such a mass medium makes it hard to pinpoint specific audiences. Expect to pay anywhere from $150 to $300 for a few lines in the classified section. Larger display ads are more costly but do draw a reader's eye to them on the page.

You should understand that some of your potential customers probably *don't* live in the town where your second home is located, so if you're on a budget you may want to skip to the next strategy. However, many people like to vacation locally, and I personally know families who rent beach cottages for a couple of weeks in the summer only ten minutes from their home.

Measure your success

Unless you're on an unlimited budget (and congrats if you are!), the last thing you want to do is throw a bunch of money out there for dozens of different advertising methods and then sit back and wait for the renters to come.

Instead, stick to two to three advertising strategies and measure each one's success (preferably over 6 to 12 months) before nixing them or adding any new ones. This targeted approach will ensure that you're spending your advertising dollars wisely and aren't wasting them on strategies that simply aren't generating business for you. If you get zero responses in six months from newspaper classifieds, but ten calls from a Web site listing, then you'll know where to put your money. (Check out "Figure out your advertising strategy" earlier in this chapter for more info.)

When a new renter comes your way, immediately ask her how she found out about your place. This is very valuable info. Keep notes on this type of feedback and use the information to make smart advertising decisions in the future. If, for example, 50 percent of your renters come your way through ads placed in their local papers, then you'll want to keep using that strategy.

Advertising your home online

One of the more popular strategies to advertise your rental property is just a click away. The Internet is a godsend for second-home owners looking to rent their homes to those eager nomads who love vacations.

The Internet can also be a terrific resource for the owner who is looking for a long-term tenant. Web sites like Rent.com (www.rent.com) and Move.com (www.move.com) charge a fee for rental listings, which potential renters from all over the world then browse. In this section, I get into the basics of finding short-term renters online and tell you how to avoid chasing bogus inquiries.

Online rental sites for owners

Second-home owners are making good use of the Internet these days. Folks with homes to rent post their information on sites like Vacation Rental By Owner (www.vrbo.com) and Vacation Rentals (www.vacationrentals.com), and then travelers looking for homes to stay in (instead of hotels) hit those same sites to find great deals on condos, cottages, and houses.

The sites charge a membership fee for second-home owners, and they also offer enhanced listing features (such as *virtual tours* — 360-degree views of the home's interior) for additional fees. You can include descriptions, photos, contact information, availability calendars, and other features that help lure in potential renters.

Check out several sites before you choose the one (or ones) on which you want to list your property. Along with the two listed above, I also recommend CyberRentals (www.cyberrentals.com) and GreatRentals (www.great rentals.com) as potential online showcases for your listing.

Because they compete with one another to score your second-home listings, online sites charge a fairly standard rate for their services. Prices vary, ranging from $150 to $200 for a one-year membership that includes a listing and multiple photos.

Dealing with bogus leads

Bogus leads are a routine occurrence for anyone who does business on the Internet these days. Over time, you'll sense what to look for when determining the validity of a lead. In the meantime, make up a boilerplate "initial response" to send to people who express interest.

In that e-mail, introduce yourself as the property owner, and ask the potential renter for contact info (name, home address, phone number, hat size, and e-mail address) and when they want to rent the property.

After you receive this information, give the renter a quick call to check the phone number and make sure the person isn't a teenager pulling an online prank. If you hit a dead end upon dialing (she gave you a phony number or the number's not in service), there's a good chance that the person may not be as interested as you might hope.

But it can also mean that the person enjoys the anonymity of the Internet and just doesn't want to give out her phone number, so don't throw away the lead too quickly. And if her response to your introduction is, "We want to come June 1–30. Where do we send the deposit?", then you're in business.

Maximizing your online presence

You can increase the number of "hits" that your vacation home receives and maximize its exposure by using the following tactics:

- ✔ **Develop an individual Web site for the home.** Set up shop online for your home by establishing a Web site where potential renters can view pictures, get rates, check the availability calendar, and contact you directly. If you don't know how to set up a Web site, check out *Creating Web Pages For Dummies,* 8th Edition, by Bud E. Smith and Arthur Bebak (Wiley).

✔ **Use search engines, keyword searches, and other advertising strategies to increase the flow of visitors to that site.** The higher up on the search engine rankings your site is, the better the chances are that potential renters will see it. Maximize search engine results by adding relevant words to your page: "vacation home," "vacation rentals," "vacation getaway," and other keywords that search engines will find when people look for rentals online.

✔ **Choose and work with one or more of the online vacation home sites mentioned earlier in this chapter.** These sites aggregate listings of vacation rentals from all over the world and spend oodles of money on advertising to get renters to check out their listings.

✔ **Carefully hone the wording used on the site to describe the home and its amenities, and include information about the surrounding community.** Accentuate the positive, steer clear of the negative, and create a marketing pitch that will lure in potential renters.

✔ **Post only those photos that show the home in its best possible light.** Include photos of the living room, master bedroom, and any other rooms that look great in pictures. (Avoid photos of bathrooms, for example, no matter how pretty you think yours is.)

✔ **If your home is in a picturesque setting, include one or more photos of the view from a deck, lanai, or front porch.** This will give renters an idea of what they'll see when they get there.

✔ **Update the home's Web site, listing, or other posting regularly to reflect upgrades, remodels, or new amenities or community offerings that would help lure in a renter.** Seeing the words "recently upgraded kitchen and bathrooms" is music to a renter's ears. If you've invested in the home recently, be sure to mention it.

✔ **State your rates.** One of the first things someone browsing your site will want to know is "What's the rent?" (Remember the *Seinfeld* episode where that was the first question asked when anyone mentioned an available NYC apartment?) People will have in mind a price they're willing to pay, and by stating yours upfront, you'll weed out renters who are looking for a dirt-cheap deal and for whom even your reasonable price (it is reasonable, right?) is too much.

Protecting your investment

One of the best ways to keep tabs on your property and the people who are using it is by conducting regular, physical inspections of the property. This can be handled by a real estate agent or property management company, but you should also do some hands-on looking around (maybe "eyes-on" looking around is a better way to describe it?), because often you will pick up on problems much faster than someone who isn't as familiar with the property.

When an inspection turns up a problem, be sure to address it right away. It could be as simple as throwing out a $15 toaster with a plug that "gets too hot" or as serious as replacing a roof on a single-family home. Even though it's not your primary home, you'll want to keep your second home in good working order to protect the investment, reap the rewards of property appreciation, and create happy tenants.

Creating a home that's fit for the pages of *Better Homes & Gardens* is nice, but it's not a very practical way to decorate and furnish a second home that you're planning on renting out for a significant portion of the year. If your second home will be rented out regularly, stick to the basics and avoid scattering a lot of breakable, valuable items throughout the place.

Doing Business with Renters

If you market your home effectively, you may have dozens of people who want to spend a few days or a few weeks in your home (not all at the same time, I hope!). But you don't want to hand over the keys to your second home to just anyone. And you want to treat your renters right, because you want them back, same time, same place, next year. (And maybe for a bump in the rent?) So when it comes time to actually work with your tenants, you need to know who's living in your home, make the agreement official, and follow up with them after their stay.

Screening renters

As an individual renting out your own property, you need to be careful that you don't give the wrong people access to your home and belongings. You can safeguard yourself by *screening* your potential renters. You want to know a little bit about them, their rental background, and their credit rating and ability to pay for the rental period. You'll also want to ask for a *security deposit* upfront (about $200 to $300) to cover any damage they may inflict on your place or any additional cleaning that may be necessary after they vacate.

I've rented dozens of condos and townhouses directly from individual owners, and I've never been "screened" for anything. In the back of my mind, as I've spent time in the properties, amid the owners' possessions and furnishings, I've always thought to myself: "I can't believe no one asked any questions, or requested referrals from past condo owners I rented from."

So the moral of the story is this: By taking some time to screen potential renters, you'll be ahead of the game when it comes to intercepting people who may be problematic renters. However, you may also chase some tenants away, because, from my experience, it seems like very few owners are doing it themselves (although their real estate agents and property managers very well may be).

Finding out whom you're dealing with

You can screen potential renters without offending them by asking for some basic information during your first conversation or e-mail exchange with the renter. Here are a few good basic pieces of info to ask for:

- The prospective renter's name, and the names of all others who will be staying in your home

- The ages of any children who will be living at or visiting the place

- Home address (getting a business address isn't a bad idea, either)

- Home phone number

- Cellphone number

- E-mail address

During the exchange, you can also talk about other condos or homes that the person has rented, their experiences with those homes, why they're visiting the area, and their likes and dislikes. This casual, friendly type of conversation can help you informally screen renters without them even realizing it! To protect yourself further,

- **Keep an eye out for red flags such as fake names, addresses, and phone numbers.** Do a cross-check on a site like Switchboard.com (`www.switchboard.com`) — it offers reverse phone lookups — to find out if a phone number matches up with a name.

- **Do a background check on potential renters to make sure they're legitimate.** This involves contacting the person's local police or sheriff's department to see whether the applicant has been involved in any run-ins with the authorities.

- **Google applicants.** See if they show up in any articles that raise eyebrows.

- **Do a quick online search of their state's public records, including civil cases.** If you discover your potential tenant is being sued by a credit card company for lack of payment, or is involved in a lawsuit for hitting a pedestrian, you may want to think twice about that person.

Putting the agreement in writing

When you've found a renter you think you can trust with the keys to your second home, and their security deposit check didn't bounce (see the next section), you now need to make the agreement official by sending a *confirmation letter*. This letter should include

- The dates that the home will be rented
- The cost of the rental, including security deposits and other fees
- Check-in and check-out times
- Locations of keys (for getting into the place)
- Parking information

You're not a visitors' bureau, but when you send out the confirmation letter to your renters, it would be nice to include a few brochures for area attractions, dining and shopping suggestions, and a map of the area. (These materials are available from local visitors' centers and chamber of commerce offices.) This small gesture can make your renters feel like you really care about their stay and can lead to repeat business and referrals.

Taking security deposits and collecting the rent

Some owners take security deposits, others don't. A security deposit basically ensures that you're going to get your home back as it was when you rented it (within reason). If you don't, you can use the money to make any necessary repairs or take care of any cleaning that goes beyond the basics.

You decide on the security deposit amount you'd like to collect. This can range from $200 to $300, depending on the size of the home and length of the stay. Any higher and you'll almost certainly price yourself out of the market. Any less and you won't be able to cover minor damage inflicted by your renters.

You should collect the security deposit after you and the renter have made a verbal agreement that she can use your second home for a specific time and price. After you have deposited the security deposit, you should send the renter a confirmation letter (see the preceding section).

Getting what you're due: The rent

As a general rule, I recommend that you collect all the rent for a short-term rental in advance. If you're renting your beach cottage to a family for two weeks, the total rental amount should be in your hands before you hand over the keys. If you know the people and want to allow them to pay the second week's rent at the beginning of the second week, that's fine. It's your call. But as a general rule, get the money upfront.

If you're renting out the unit on a multiple-month basis, you can ask for one month's rent, plus a security deposit, upfront. The monthly rent would then be due on the first of every month, and you can also give the renter a five- or ten-day grace period to get the check to you.

Returning the security deposit

You should return the security deposit promptly after the tenants have left and you've inspected for damage. In the past, I've waited months for a paltry $200 deposit to be returned, which did not endear that particular landlord to me.

You need to realize that "normal wear and tear" is typical in any home, and that a place being used by multiple individuals and families during the course of a year is bound to show its age faster than an owner-occupied unit. Before you snag $100 or more from the security deposit and risk alienating a potential repeat client, though, be reasonable and ask yourself if the dings on the kitchen splashguard or the inoperable microwave were *really* her fault, or if they can realistically be attributed to normal wear and tear. This is especially important when it comes to appliances. When appliances break, they break. If it had been you, rather than your renter, who turned on the 10-year-old dishwasher when it broke, you would have chalked it up to "it's time to buy a new dishwasher." If, instead, the renter is unlucky enough to be the one to turn it on that one last time, she shouldn't be held responsible for replacing it.

Following up with renters

After your renters' stays are complete, take a few moments and follow up with them. You can send a quick e-mail or make a short phone call to see how the stay went. Doing so is a great way to do an informal inspection. By talking to the renters, you can find out about problems with the property without even being there.

So whether it's ants in the kitchen, a toilet that takes an hour to flush in the guest bathroom, a few "streaks" of water coming down the wall in the foyer, or "hot" water that ain't all that hot, you can probably find out a lot from the folks who recently lived with these issues for a week or more.

Being Aware of the Downtimes

Your vacation home can be a cash cow, but only part of the time because some factors are simply out of your control. For example, geopolitical issues, a faltering economy, high fuel costs, and catastrophic storms can all louse up people's vacation plans.

And even though these issues may not have affected you directly in the past, they will most certainly impact your bottom line as a second-home owner looking to rent out a unit to vacationers who are spending their discretionary income.

If you're renting your property out as a residence full time, you aren't exempt from market fluctuations. Even the best places on the Atlantic Ocean in Florida can be affected by events such as hurricanes, a bad economy, or insane gas prices, so adopt a practical approach to most efficiently manage the financial aspect of second-home ownership.

Realistically, no property that is also used occasionally as a residence can be rented out 100 percent of the time. Don't go into renting your second home thinking that you can rent it every day of the year. If that's what you want, then you should buy a rental investment property that you'll never stay in.

One of the best ways to estimate just how often you'll be able to rent out your place is to talk to other owners in the surrounding area. Ask them these questions:

✔ How many weeks out of the year is your place rented out to third parties?

✔ How long do your renters usually stay?

✔ What's the going rate around here? (They may not tell you the truth, but it's worth a shot!)

✔ Have you ever experienced a dip in demand for your place, and if so, when and why?

✔ Was your home ever empty when you didn't want it to be? Why?

✔ Where do you advertise/promote your rental?

If you can't find an owner to talk to, a local property manager or real estate agent should be able to help, although the latter tend to paint fairly rosy pictures (for obvious reasons!) of their markets even when things are less than great. Use whatever facts you can come up with through your own research to prepare for the inevitable lean times.

Chapter 12

Investing in Your Investment: Renovations That Pay Off

. . . .

In This Chapter

▶ Remodeling your second home: Yes or no?

▶ Choosing improvements for your home

▶ Creating a master plan for renovating

▶ Taking the DIY route or hiring a pro

. . . .

*W*ho doesn't want to buy an existing, state-of-the-art home that's completely upgraded, fully functional, and, well, just plain *perfect?* Nobody, that's who. That's right: No one wants anything less than the perfect house — but as the song goes, "You can't always get what you want." Unless you're buying a newly constructed home built exactly the way you want it, you almost certainly will want or need to upgrade areas of your second home — some more than others.

In this chapter, I help you decide which areas of your second home need the most attention and which improvements can produce the best possible returns on your investment. Whether you're looking to add a bathroom, remove wallpaper and throw on a coat of paint, or get rid of those antiquated thermostats and old-fashioned doorknobs, you've come to the right place.

Understanding the Value of Renovating Your Second Home

Renovating your second home is one of the best ways to increase the value of your investment, but don't think you have to start tearing down walls. Plenty of resources are available to help you tackle a multitude of projects, from the simple ones, such as painting a bedroom, to more complex ones, such as renovating a kitchen and adding a bedroom.

Even a small project or two can increase your home's value. In the last few years, American homeowners have seen significant increases in their homes' equity. High housing appreciation has spurred many homeowners to do extensive and elaborate renovations to their homes. This growth in equity, combined with the fact that some of the nation's homes are getting older, drives the upward trend in dollars spent on home remodeling.

The payoff from investing in remodeling projects is significant. According to *Remodeling* magazine's most recent survey comparing construction costs with resale values over the past four years, homeowners have gained the best returns on bathroom and kitchen remodelings.

However, before you jump into a project, keep this point in mind: Don't spend a lot of money on a project that won't yield a significant return if you want to get back what you put into it. The return on remodeling projects varies based on the area of the country and the state in which your second home is located. If recouping your outlay is important, be sure to talk to local real estate agents, property managers, and homeowners about specific projects — and their payoffs — before sinking any money into your second home.

Keep in mind that there's more than monetary value to remodeling a home. Ripping out that awful green-and-orange wallpaper or replacing those avocado-colored appliances can result in a great deal of satisfaction for second-home owners worried less about recouping their costs and more about creating a great place to live. (Unless, of course, you like avocado-colored appliances. Then you can leave things as is and you'll be a happy camper!)

In this section, I discuss the value of renovating specific areas of your second home, from the bathroom to the roof, and everything in between. This section explains which projects are worth undertaking and which aren't.

Adding and remodeling bathrooms

If your second home is cursed with outdated bathrooms, toilets that don't run right, drippy faucets, peeling floors, cracked tiles, and antique shower-heads, then the bathroom is probably where you should begin your remodeling. A bathroom *renovation* is the selective replacement of specific elements of a bathroom: sink, fixtures, lighting, toilet, and so forth. A bathroom *addition* is the construction of a brand-new bathroom in a spot where there wasn't one.

According to remodeling and real estate experts, owners recoup 102 percent of their investment for a typical bathroom renovation (new tub, toilet, tile, fixtures, vanity, medicine chest, flooring, and wall covering). That's all the money you put into the project *plus* some more. That means that on a $10,500 bathroom remodeling project (which would be a pretty big job), you'll get back $10,710 when (and if) you sell your place.

So if you're considering adding or remodeling a bathroom, keep the following do's and don'ts in mind.

Do:

- ✔ **Take a good look at every component of the bathroom in question and decide what needs to be changed (or eliminated).** Focus on flooring, lighting, cabinetry/vanity, fixtures, and accessories.

- ✔ **Decide on a budget ahead of time and get prices for the things you want done.** Always factor in both materials and labor so you won't have any surprises.

- ✔ **Determine what jobs you and your loved ones can do and what jobs you need professional help with.** Make a list of the tasks you and your loved ones feel comfortable tackling, such as installing stick-on floor tiling, mounting a new medicine cabinet, and painting. You also can make a list of the tasks that you'll need a pro for, such as plumbing, electrical, and major carpentry work.

- ✔ **Keep in mind the amazing difference the simplest of things can make.** New luxurious towels, for example, are very impressive and relatively inexpensive. A lovely wall hanging and a wrought iron shelving unit can also add a lot of eye appeal for not too much moolah.

Don't:

- ✔ **Rip stuff out and order supplies without keeping track of your spending.** Doing so is an easy way to overextend your budget. Plan what you want to do and keep track of every expense.

- ✔ **Decide to replace big, expensive fixtures like the tub/shower, toilet, or sink because you're excited about the remodeling project.** Be conservative. If the tub is a mess, though, and it needs to be replaced, then, of course, go for it. If the toilet's ancient and temperamental, then that can go, too. But don't replace things just for the sake of getting something new when it's unnecessary.

- ✔ **Be reckless to save money.** If you're not experienced with electrical wiring, hire an electrician to put in that beautiful new lighting fixture. Likewise with plumbing. If you've never even changed a washer on a faucet, don't start taking apart the bathroom sink and assume you'll figure it out as you go along.

If you're considering adding a bathroom and you have the space, make sure the plumbing work won't be prohibitive (for example, you have to cut a support wall — not the best decision). If you purchase a home that has, say, one or one-and-a-half bathrooms, and adding a bathroom in the master bedroom or even in the basement is feasible, do so. It's a great way to add not only comfort and convenience, but also value. For extensive info on how to remodel bathrooms, check out *Bathroom Remodeling For Dummies* by Gene and Katie Hamilton (Wiley).

Remodeling kitchens

A kitchen remodel can range from a simple $5,000 cabinet refacing job in a mid-size kitchen, all the way up to a $30,000, the-sky's-the-limit complete replacement of cabinets, sinks, fixtures, countertops, appliances, and flooring. If you're considering a remodeling job, it will probably fall somewhere in the middle of the range, and will almost certainly translate into a good return on your investment because the kitchen is often the room that "sells" the house. Show a prospective buyer a great kitchen, and help her visualize a houseful of friends gathered around the breakfast bar, and you've won half the battle. (You can discover more about kitchen remodeling in the book *Kitchen Remodeling For Dummies* by Donald R. Prestly [Wiley].)

Know that a little goes a long way when remodeling this all-important room. Keep the following do's and don'ts in mind.

Do:

- ✔ **Take steps to increase the functionality (a larger sink), durability (countertops that don't scratch), and eye appeal of the kitchen.** These moves will pay off big time for you.

- ✔ **Opt for less-expensive improvements, such as cabinet refacing.** A process like this uses existing cabinetry foundation and costs 40 to 50 percent less than the cost of new cabinets.

- ✔ **Add in a new, reasonably priced kitchen set and a pretty new paint job or some attractive wallpaper.** The change will be breathtaking.

Don't:

- ✔ **Assume that you have to completely gut the kitchen to add value.** Even the most outdated kitchen may not need an entire overhaul.

- ✔ **Forget to update the hardware (drawer knobs and handles) in the kitchen.** Doing so can give the room a fresh look without draining the budget.

Assuming the typical remodeling job costs about $15,000, *Remodeling* magazine reports that most homeowners recoup 98.5 percent of their total remodeling investment (or $14,775). That's an excellent return, considering that many improvements don't come close to recovering their costs. The actual numbers vary by geographic location, but it's clear that such projects definitely pay off when it comes time to assess the value of and/or sell your second home.

Renovating master suites

Master suite is a term used to describe the master bedroom, a private bathroom, and additional amenities, such as a walk-in closet, sitting room, a window seat, and other conveniences and luxuries within the same space. The master suite is often a home's showpiece. It's the space that commonly elicits the most oohs and aahs (also known as *sales appeal*), and if yours isn't up to snuff, you may want to think about an overhaul soon.

Unlike some other renovations that result in you recouping more money than your original investment when you sell (like bathrooms; see the "Adding and remodeling bathrooms" section), master suite remodels usually don't bring a 100 percent return. They do, however, add significant sales appeal to the property and, depending on the market at the time you sell, can warrant a higher price when selling.

When renovating your master suite, keep these do's and don'ts in mind.

Do:

- ✔ **Change the lighting and the wall coverings or paint.** These moves are relatively inexpensive and can make a dramatic difference in a room.

- ✔ **Consider small accessory touches.** They include items such as artificial plants, mirrors, throw rugs, *objets d'art*, and other touches that can freshen up a room without having to completely overhaul it. (Don't forget that you'll take most of these goodies with you when you sell, but they can nonetheless work their magic when they're on display in your home. You'll enjoy their aesthetic appeal, and if you do eventually sell, they'll show buyers how pretty the rooms can be.)

Don't:

- ✔ **Put in hardwood floors just for aesthetic reasons.** Sure, they're nice, but they're costly. If the carpeting is in good shape, and it's clean and attractive, leave it. If the color is bad, though, replace it. (And if that's the case, *that's* when you decide to go with costly hardwood — or not.)

- ✔ **Rip out bathtubs, showers, and toilets in the master suite unless you absolutely have to.** Replumbing homes is expensive, time consuming, and messy as all get-out.

Adding storage space

Newer homes, built in the last 20 years or so, usually have ample closet and storage space. However, older homes seem to have been built for people who had seven outfits, a coat, two towels, and a mop and bucket. Consumer goods — including clothes, appliances, books, DVDs, and more — now fill homes, and storage space is always a problem in closet-challenged residences.

Like other renovations, adding closet and storage space can increase the value of a second home. So if your second home falls into the closet-strapped category, you'll be eager to find ways to increase the amount of available storage space. Using a two-bedroom, two-bathroom townhouse as an example, here's what you should shoot for:

✔ Ample closet space in both bedrooms (walk-ins are nice!)

✔ Linen closets in or near one or both bathrooms (with lots of shelves for towels and stuff)

✔ A utility closet (if the home has a garage, a corner can double as a utility space)

✔ A pantry or other space for kitchen overflow (y'know . . . like those cafeteria-size cans of tuna and olives you bought at the warehouse store because you couldn't resist the price!)

Is your second home wanting for any of these areas? If so, consider what extra space exists in your home that can be converted into storage space. If, for example, the master bathroom includes a 2-foot-x-2-foot space that's just sitting there unused, consider making it into a linen closet.

The easiest way? Purchase a prebuilt linen closet from a home furnishings store like HomeGoods or Home Depot (which offers *lavatory valets,* which are furniture-like bathroom linen closets), or online at a site like www. homedecorators.com. Prices range from very inexpensive for cabinets needing assembly and painting or staining, to elaborate units with glass doors, drawers, and lots of shelves. Linen closets start around $100 and come in all shapes and sizes.

And if that one-car garage houses only a small sports car, you can take advantage of the excess space by building a utility closet and even a small pantry for your canned and packaged goods out there. You can also line an entire wall with inexpensive metal shelves that can store huge amounts of stuff. Get creative and make the best use of your unused spaces. You'll be pleasantly surprised at what you come up with.

If you prefer to go beyond do-it-yourself efforts and make major structural changes to your home to add more closet or pantry space, talk to a couple of residential remodeling contractors about the projects. Figure out how much you're willing to spend, and you should be able to find someone who can help design and build add-ons to make a more storage-friendly second home.

If you want to take advantage of the storage space you already have, check out some of the closet organizer kits available for $20 to $100 at national discount stores. And if your budget allows for a $500 to $1,000 investment, hire a professional organizer to install the hardware and organize your stuff.

Replacing the roof

"And the roof is brand new!" is a proud proclamation you'll often hear coming from the mouths of eager home sellers and their real estate agents. And you can easily understand why this fact is front and center in their sales presentation, because replacing a home's roof is expensive. It can run $15,000 to $35,000 and more, depending on the size of the home and style of the roof and its coverings.

However, putting a definitive return on investment on a roof replacement or major repair isn't easy because the item is a functional, critical part of the house. The roof is also the Achilles' heel of any home: When it goes bad, it can result in leaks, interior damage, mold, and myriad other problems. In other words, if it's seriously broke, fix it. Your decision to replace or not to replace what looks to be a still-viable roof depends on one thing: how many times a year you have to call the roofer to come and fix leaks. (And keep in mind that some leaks may be hidden from view.) When those repair visits become necessary more than a couple of times a year, replace the roof.

Before you start soliciting estimates for your second home's roof, ask an expert to tell you how many years are left on it. Most roofs these days use 15-, 30-, or 50-year shingles or coverings (such as tile), and if the one on your second home was replaced five years ago, then it's certainly not time to replace the whole thing. If the roof is leaking, a roof repair can often remedy the problem.

Improving the outside

When you pull up to a home, what's the first thing you notice? Do you notice its dingy color and flaking paint on the house's exterior and overgrown bushes and wild weeds overrunning the flowerbeds? *Curb appeal* — that initial (hopefully positive) reaction from people when they first see your house and grounds — adds a ton of value to a home. It's one of the most important elements of showing your home. Like the old adage goes, "You only get one chance to make a first impression."

Because of this critical first-impression factor, many homeowners work hard to keep their homes looking sharp and clean on the outside as well as the inside — all the time, not just when looking to sell. Think about how you feel when you drive up to a run-down property versus an attractive, clean one. To assure a smile rather than a frown when people see your place, take a walk around the perimeter of your home and look at it through a stranger's eyes. Lots of stuff you overlook every day when you live in a place is immediately noticeable by someone who is seeing the home and grounds for the first time.

Don't forget that exterior improvements can increase a home's value. By just how much depends on exactly what you've done to the home and how much the home is worth overall. But these types of improvements and enhancements are about as close to a sure thing as you'll find when trying to increase your home's value.

When looking at your home's exterior and grounds, ask yourself the following questions:

- **Are the lawn, hedges, flowerbeds, trees, and other natural elements trimmed, neat, and good looking?** If anything is rotted or overgrown, that's your starting place for making the outside look great.

- **Is the home painted a pleasing color, and is the paint job in good shape?** Is mold growing on the outside walls, or do peeling paint chips regularly dot the ground? If so, it's time for a good painting.

- **Is the roof clean?** A good pressure washing can make a tile roof look like new.

- **Is the vinyl siding clean?** A pressure washing can make an enormous difference in the home's appearance.

- **Is the garage door in good condition?** Replacing an old, ugly, banged-up door with a shiny new one (particularly if it's a two-car or larger structure) can really add to the look of a home.

- **Is the entryway to the home appealing and welcoming?** Adding features such as crown molding around the front door, replacing an annoying buzzer doorbell with a new, melodic one, and fixing any missing tiles on the walkway leading to the front door can spruce up a home's exterior. A fresh coat of paint can transform the front door into a welcoming asset.

- **Are the windows in good shape, or do they need to be replaced?** A complete window replacement can be costly, so if you don't have the budget for such a large project, try focusing only on the windows that are visible from the street, and replace those first. Then work your way around the home as your budget allows.

You can undertake dozens of different projects to make the outside of your second home look better. Condo owners are a bit luckier in that the homeowners' association is responsible for the exterior of the unit. But this means they're also more limited as to what they can do on their own. If you're a condo owner, consider using plants and attractive patio furniture on your lanai or deck to create a pretty exterior for your individual unit.

Updating the house for the 21st century

If you purchase a second home that was built within the last ten years, chances are good that it's already equipped with all the trappings of modern technology. Updating your house for the 21st century can definitely increase its appeal to buyers who want to be able to hook up their laptops and wi-fi adaptors quickly and easily. The more accessible your home is to today's technological innovations, the more attractive it will be for those who want to rent it, use it, and/or buy it. If your home is missing any of these high-tech delights, read on for info on how to upgrade your place.

Cable

Cable providers are always happy to come into a home without cable and wire it. These days, many homes have TVs in every room, which means you need to have a cable TV outlet (or satellite TV receiver) in several locations throughout the house. Expect to pay little or nothing for this wiring service. What you *will* pay is a monthly fee for service that will range from $40 to $150, depending on what types of channels and services you order.

When you're setting up your cable system, ask for a digital video recorder or digital video recorder (DVR) box. (Often, a DVR service can be switched on by using the same digital cable box without needing another piece of equipment.) These setups allow you to record and replay favorite shows, as well as pause and rewind live television. Both you and your renters will enjoy this perk, which you can use as a selling point when renting out the place.

Be sure to have the cable installed in all rooms where you expect to place a television, both now and in the future. Doing so saves you the trouble of having to add outlets later. Check your phone book for the names of the primary cable providers in the area and get a couple of quotes before selecting a provider. Check online forums and Epinions.com (`www.epinion.com`) for subscribers' opinions on your local company's performance.

Satellite TV

If you're unhappy with the pricing, features, or service of the cable company in the area where your second home is located, consider subscribing to satellite TV. Close to 30 million households in the United States now receive satellite TV services. And as with other technological amenities, satellite TV adds appeal to a home.

You purchase service from a satellite TV provider that provides the equipment and hooks up your TVs. You can buy outright the equipment and gear, or rent the equipment, similar to a cable box arrangement. The provider attaches the satellite signal receiver to the outside of your home and hooks it into equipment inside your house for receiving satellite TV signals. You pay a monthly fee that varies based on the service and channels you order.

The two biggest satellite TV providers are DIRECTV and the DISH Network. The DISH Network (www.dishnetwork.com) has the most channels. DIRECTV (www.directtv.com) has the most sports programming. Both offer a variety of packages; pricing ranges from under $20 to $100 a month.

High-speed Internet service

Internet access is as much a part of life these days as coffee in the morning, cellphones, and watching your favorite TV show. And hitting the Web with high-speed service has overtaken dial-up and is now the standard. As of March 2006, 22 percent of U.S. Internet users were still on dial-up, as compared with 42 percent who had broadband Internet access. So a high-speed connection is a definite renting point and adds appeal to a home. After all, the more conveniences the better.

You can purchase cable broadband service through your cable provider, you can go for DSL from the phone company, or you can buy service directly from your Internet service provider. Check with your cable provider and phone company for prices on these services; compare their offerings; do a little browsing online for comments, compliments, and complaints about each company's service record; and then make a decision based on your needs.

Many cable providers offer a *lite* Internet service (which has slightly slower download and upload speeds than full-blown packages) for a cheaper fee than the full-blown high-speed service. If you're only going to use your second home for a few weeks every year, and you don't have to consider renters' needs, you may think about this less expensive option.

Digital thermostats

A digital thermostat provides a much more accurate view of exactly how hot or cold it is in the home. This device allows you to make smart, energy-saving decisions that can save you money. Plus, your renters will love how easy it is to adjust and monitor the home's temperature. (One thing to consider: You should tell your renters the maximum temperature they're allowed to set the thermostat to or, better yet, if you have a programmable thermostat, show them how to program it. You don't want your ski chalet heated to 80 degrees all day while your guests are out!)

If the home you're buying has a traditional round dial thermostat, you may consider investing in a digital one that more precisely tells dwellers just how hot or cold it is in the house, while allowing you to adjust the unit to the exact temperature you want. Also, digital thermostats add to a home's appeal and perceived value. It's a terrific selling point.

Digital thermostats have a multitude of features, including programmability, remote control, frost protection, and even energy-use monitoring. Many allow you to program four different temperatures for four times of the day, for each day of the week, allowing total control of the home's interior environment. These are called *comfort levels* and use advanced technology to monitor and adjust temperature for — depending on how many heating/cooling zones are in your home — individual rooms or the whole house.

You can purchase a digital thermostat from a hardware store or online for $100 or less. If you can't install it yourself, expect to pay an HVAC professional another $100 or so to install it for you.

Deciding Whether You Want to Renovate

The case *for* remodeling is pretty simple: By upgrading kitchens and bathrooms, replacing flooring, and even adding features such as swimming pools and decks, second-home owners enhance the value of their homes — always a smart move. And if you're renting it out, the additional creature comforts and amenities can often justify a higher rent coming your way.

But do you want to renovate your own home? Seeing all the benefits in print is one thing, but actually doing the work and/or paying for it are definitely important factors to consider. Be sure to do the following when you're thinking of remodeling your home:

- ✔ **Make sure you have the money.** Remodeling a home can be an expensive undertaking, so be sure you have the financial resources to complete the job *before* you get started. Work up an estimate and then add a cushion (say, 20 percent) to protect you in case of cost overruns. (Prices go up, or you may change your mind and decide on a more expensive tile.)

- ✔ **Have an eye for design.** Remember that remodeling projects should improve the home's comfort and livability for you, while also increasing the property's sales appeal for potential renters and buyers. Make sure you plan the work before jumping into a project. (Check out the next section for more info on planning a project.)

- ✔ **Keep up with the times.** Updating kitchens and baths and undertaking other improvement projects in older homes can be particularly beneficial, especially if other homes in the surrounding area are newer or their owners have already upgraded them to more modern standards.

✔ **Concentrate on the kitchen.** Be sure to remodel wisely. Sellers often want to update the entire house before placing it on the market, but certain rooms need more attention than others. In most cases, the kitchen is the deal breaker. It's the heart of the home. An inviting, comfortable space is mandatory. (The "Remodeling kitchens" section earlier in this chapter has more pointers on freshening up this area in your home.)

By thinking like an investor, you can profit from your remodeling. Detach yourself emotionally and think of your second home as a business. Then pretend you're a stranger coming upon your place for the first time and doing a walk-through. This exercise can give you a good sense of the condition of various aspects of your home, and help you decide whether it's necessary, economically feasible, and advantageous in the long run to renovate.

Planning Your Renovations

A successful remodeling project starts with a well-thought-out game plan. Are you wondering what to include in your plan or even where to start?

A *renovation master plan* includes three things:

✔ **Your goals for your home:** List the *specific* changes you want to make during your renovation. For example, your goal list may include new wallpaper in the dining room, an above-the-stove microwave in the kitchen, new fixtures and a new vanity in the downstairs bathroom, and new carpeting in the master bedroom.

✔ **An estimated budget:** You need to figure out the costs of materials and the cost of contracted labor (for the work you can't or don't want to do yourself), and you also need to build in a surplus. Shop around online, make a few trips to local stores, and request estimates from contractors for the jobs to get an idea of how much you need to spend.

✔ **Short- and long-range timelines**: As always, be realistic, and do the math. If you plan on doing the wallpapering yourself, and you know from your research that your size dining room would take a professional three eight-hour days to complete, then add a "do-it-yourself" time factor (25 to 50 percent is a good start). For you, estimate it to be a 36-hour project. If you know you can put in six hours each Saturday until it's done, voilà! In six weeks your dining room will be finished.

You need to know these specifics before you start removing kitchen cabinetry, steaming off wallpaper, and tearing up carpet. In this section, I help you create such a plan, and then give you some advice on how to find the right people to carry it out as efficiently and economically as possible.

Developing a renovation master plan

Before you start any renovations, sit down and develop a plan. Doing so is important. If you do, although some things can go wrong, overall everything will run more smoothly and you'll be happier with the end result. Also bear in mind that even though defining your final goal when you're planning a project (new wallpaper in the dining room) is key, you also need to look at the smaller steps to take along the way to get there (cover the furniture, buy the wallpaper, lay down sheets, and so forth). Break down your overall vision into incremental, manageable steps, and you should be able to complete your remodeling projects without an overabundance of stress.

Use Figure 12-1 as a guideline for creating your own renovation master plan:

After you have this initial plan written down, you need to break down your "next three months" list into a more detailed overview, including:

- **What part of the home the project will take place in:** Bathroom, kitchen, bedroom, outside.

- **Exactly what needs to be done:** Be specific: Replace a leaky toilet, patch a roof leak.

- **Who is going to handle the work:** If you'll do it yourself, identify those projects; if you need a pro, do likewise.

- **How much you can afford to pay for it:** Be realistic. Don't allocate $200 for the installation of a new water heater when you know it'll be triple that at the very least.

- **What challenges or obstacles may come up during the process:** If, for example, you want to install a whirlpool tub in your master bathroom, and you know space is tight, it could pose a challenge.

If you decide to use a contractor, get at least three estimates for the project. Look not only at the bottom-line cost, but also at the array of services that the contractor offers and his reputation for doing good work, on time, and with no surprises. Don't forget to ask for and check a contractor's references, and if possible, visit one of the homes where work was done to see the contractor's efforts in person. Ask past customers about workmanship quality, timeliness, neatness, and follow-up service. Botched remodeling jobs are fairly commonplace. Be sure to check references before working with a contractor with whom you don't have a prior relationship. See the "Deciding to use a professional" section later in this chapter for more hints.

Home address: _____
When purchased: _____
Total budget for renovations: _____

Steps that need to be taken immediately and how much each project will cost: (List here only those things that you absolutely have to have fixed or replaced within the next three months or sooner.)

     Roof repairs: _____
     Plumbing issues: _____
     Broken appliances: _____
     Other critical needs: _____

Upgrades that you want to see completed within the next six to twelve months, and how much each project will cost: (These projects aren't urgent, but you're definitely interested in completing them within this timeframe. Examples include adding a new bathroom vanity, putting up new wallpaper in the dining room, or installing a digital thermostat. List them here along with the estimated amount.)

_____ : _____
_____ : _____
_____ : _____
_____ : _____

Projects that I really want to do now, but either can't spare the time or money to handle them right now: (List those upgrades that can reasonably be handled within the next one to five years as your budget and time allow. Examples include new kitchen cabinets, new flooring in a room, new heating and air conditioning, new windows, and so on. List them here with the estimated amount.)

_____ : _____
_____ : _____
_____ : _____
_____ : _____

Figure 12-1:
You can create your own renovation master plan. Use this one as a sample.

Figuring out how long you intend to own the property

Do you know how long you plan on owning your second home? You need to at least think about it, because your answer can have an impact on how much money, time, and effort you put into remodeling and upgrading the place.

Everyone's case is different, but here are a few scenarios that can help you gauge your own need to remodel your second home:

- ✔ **You're investment minded, and you plan to own your second home for a short while, improve it, and then resell it at a profit.** If so, you'll want to make improvements that truly increase your home's value, such as kitchen remodels and flooring replacements.

- ✔ **You're vacation minded, and you plan to own your second home for five to ten years, use it only once a year during that time, and then sell it.** If your home is just a getaway for your annual vacation, and you plan to rent it out for the rest of the year, then you'll want to make some minimal changes, but not break the bank trying to make the place look like Hearst Castle. Take whatever steps are necessary to make it comfortable for you and your guests, but stay away from the big projects.

- ✔ **You're retirement minded, and you plan to own your second home for five years and then move into it full time when you retire.** Outfit and upgrade the home in ways that are both pleasing and functional for you and anyone else who will be living with you when you retire. The bottom line: You come first in this scenario, because your second home will eventually be your retirement home.

Every situation is different. Use your best judgment when determining just how much money to pour into renovations. Also, be sure to talk to your real estate agent and/or other professionals about how much of your renovation investment you'll recoup. You need to know how much value certain upgrades will potentially add to your home.

Doing the work yourself

If you enjoy watching a designer tear down walls, put up wallpaper, and replace fixtures on television, and you automatically grab a shopping cart to load up with materials when you visit your local home improvement store, you just may be the perfect do-it-yourself homeowner — even if you're not totally confident about tackling certain projects.

Check out your surroundings

Too often, second-home owners, eager to update their abodes, ignore the basic rules of financing and contractor selection and, as a result, end up disappointed. Some neglect to look for the best equity loan package. And sometimes others simply throw restraint to the wind and go over the top with their changes, often ending up with extreme "improvements" that turn buyers off. Like an $88,000 bowling lane, or a $20,000 indoor pool, or a regulation-size basketball court on the grounds (all of which are real additions made to homes). Some of these improvements will never recoup their investment, but some second-home owners do them anyway.

To avoid these mistakes, first, be sure to shop carefully for your loan if you're using home equity to pay for the renovations. Also, check out the homes in your neighborhood and take note of how many have been upgraded in the past few years. If, for example, your home is the only one *without* an in-ground swimming pool, then that may be a good project to consider.

The reality is that if many of your neighbors have upgraded their kitchens and bathrooms, then such projects will likely pay off well for you. However, if every house on the block has a two-car garage, then adding a third or fourth bay to your own garage may not be the best move if recouping your investment is a priority.

Are you seriously considering doing some of the renovations yourself? When I say do it yourself, I don't literally mean that you'll be doing all the work totally by yourself (unless, of course, you want to). If you ask nicely, you can probably score some help from friends, family members, and neighbors who can assist with the projects and help you see them through to completion. If you plan to go the DIY route, keep some of the following points in mind before you turn your home into a construction zone.

Finding dependable help

Start by checking in with any friends or family whom you know are handy or — if you're lucky — even a pro skilled in certain areas of construction or remodeling. (My father is a general contractor, so guess who gets the first phone call when it's time to undertake a remodeling project?)

To persuade people to help, you may have to offer them an incentive. You may, for instance, offer to help them with their own projects in the future, such as moving or remodeling. You can also stock your second home with food and beverages for them to enjoy while working. Or pay for pizza or Chinese food for everyone. Whatever it takes to get the job done.

Don't bite off more than you can chew

Ever been to someone's house and are stunned by how many projects they have going on at once? The first thought that goes through your mind is, "How can they live like this?", right? When I have come upon these manic hives of activity, I've often wondered how the owners prevented themselves from getting completely overwhelmed by all the sawdust, paint, and plywood — not to mention how they didn't go completely nuts.

To avoid falling into this trap, carefully pore over the plan you drafted earlier in the "Developing a renovation master plan" section. (You did develop a plan earlier in this chapter, didn't you? If not, now is the time to do it!) You should decide on a practical, workable schedule that allows you to reach your goals — but without having to tear up your entire home at one time.

This approach also helps you stay within your budget. If you have three projects going at once, and if one or more suddenly require more money or time than you originally estimated, you can quickly find yourself grappling with unexpected financial concerns.

Deciding to use a professional

The typical homeowner just can't do some projects on his own. Replumbing bathrooms and installing new heating and air conditioning units, for example, are jobs that should definitely be turned over to the pros. And unless you or someone in your family or circle of friends is an electrician, you should leave any major rewiring or electrical-related projects for someone who is a licensed electrician. No joke: It's one thing to try to replace a toilet, make an ungodly mess, and then need to call in a plumber. It's quite another to risk electrocution or serious injury because you don't want to pay an electrician.

Finding a professional

Are you planning on major projects and need a professional to help? If so, use the following resources to find a good contractor or service professional:

> ✔ **Ask friends and neighbors for referrals.** The best place to start is with friends and neighbors who've hired and used specific pros. They can give you the lowdown on the person's performance and professionalism. Professionals in all fields rely on this type of word-of-mouth business and commonly try to cultivate it by leaving stacks of business cards behind when they leave a job site.

✔ **Call your real estate agent.** Do so if you can't get a good referral from a neighbor or friend. Most agents have a long list of reputable service providers in all fields and are happy to provide the names of one or two good ones whom you can call.

✔ **Go online.** Go to a search engine and type in a few keywords (and your town or county and state) to find professionals working in your area. Also, a search for a specific contractor after you're considering someone may turn up some valuable info.

✔ **Read your local newspaper's classified ads.** Contractors and professionals continue to advertise in their local newspapers, which remain a good source of potential candidates.

✔ **Try the Better Business Bureau or consumer organizations.** Folks at these groups (which include firms like Angie's List) can usually point you in the direction of a few good choices.

✔ **Open the phone book.** The Yellow Pages is a good place to look for pros, although a fancy display ad doesn't necessarily translate into a reputable professional. (In fact, the understated, two-line listing in the middle of the page may very well belong to the best contractor.)

Asking for references

If you've chosen a professional from anywhere other than a personal referral (the phone book, online listings, newspaper ads), use her references and check licenses before signing a contract for services.

When you call or visit the person providing the reference, ask the following questions:

✔ What are your overall thoughts on the contractor's workmanship?

✔ How well did the contractor meet the timeline?

✔ Why did you pick this contractor?

✔ How well has the project stood the test of time since its completion?

✔ Was the contractor available and receptive to follow-up customer service calls?

✔ Would you recommend this contractor to your mother, should she ever need remodeling work done?

Before you sign on the dotted line or hand over any deposits for work to be performed, do your homework. Even if you have to wend your way through a dozen different contractors before you find the right one to work with, do it.

The payoff will be well worth your effort when your project is completed professionally, on time, and within budget. In most states, contractors must be licensed to perform a specific type of work (such as drywall, HVAC, or electrical). Ask your contractor for his license number and check with your state board of licensing to make sure that the license is current and that no complaints or charges have been filed against this particular business.

Paying for the improvements

No matter if you do the work yourself or you hire a professional, you need to make sure you can afford the work. If you're doing the work yourself, then you only need to budget for the materials and supplies you'll need to get the job done. (The labor is gratis, thanks to you!)

If you're hiring someone to do the work, then their final quote will include the materials. (In some cases, you may be able to shop for and buy the tile, wallpaper, wood, and so forth, but most contractors will handle that for you. If you provide materials, then you only pay for the labor.)

Make sure that you budget carefully. You don't want to put yourself in a hole with your remodeling projects by not knowing what you'll be spending and where the money is coming from.

To come up with a budget, you need to know exactly how much *extra* money you can reasonably allocate to the project, be it from your monthly savings, income surplus, or perhaps a *home equity line of credit* (borrowed against the equity in your second home). If, for example, your home is worth $300,000 and your mortgage is for $250,000, then you can reasonably expect to borrow up to $50,000 to cover the improvements (but understand, of course, that you will also incur a new, monthly bill to pay off that loan).

To budget for a project, you'll need to divvy up the cash by the room or the job. For example, if the living room only needs painting, you can allocate whatever that job will cost and then move on to the bathroom, kitchen, and so on.

Keep these steps in mind when budgeting:

1. **Identify the job.**

   Do you want to reface the cabinets? Add a new vanity?

2. **Get a few estimates as to what each will cost.**

   Go to a store like Lowe's and ask a professional.

3. **On a piece of paper, make two columns, one for estimated cost and one for actual cost.**

   You can also create a Microsoft Excel document.

4. **As you tackle each remodeling job, deduct the costs of each job from your total budgeted amount for the entire upgrade.**

   If one job ended up costing more, you have the flexibility to juggle the other numbers to balance everything. For example, if the new fixtures for the bathroom vanity were 25 percent higher than you planned on, you may decide that a cheaper grade of tile for the foyer will do just fine.

The idea is to remodel or upgrade your second home in a way that makes it pleasing and comfortable for you (and any guests or renters), while at the same time adding to its value so that if and when it comes time to sell, you'll recoup your investment. Keep this in mind as you set and follow your budget.

How long will the renovations take?

As someone who was once promised that a quickie kitchen job was going to take five days to complete, and the job ended up taking a month (yes, a *month*), I'm here to tell you that *everything takes longer* than estimated when it comes to home remodeling and renovations.

A good general rule: Add a minimum of an extra 50 percent onto the original timetable developed by you and/or your contractor. For example, you may estimate that it will take two weeks to complete a bathroom remodeling project that replaces the flooring and installs a new tub, vanity, sink, and mirror. However, if you add a minimum of an extra 50 percent, then the more realistic completion time for this project is three weeks. By factoring an extra time cushion into your renovation schedule, you avoid any last-minute confusion and stress caused by unrealistic timelines.

Chapter 13

Handling the Maintenance and Upkeep on Your Second Home

· ·

In This Chapter

▶ Hiring a property manager to maintain your home

▶ Doing it yourself

▶ Keeping your home up to snuff, inside and out

▶ Closing your second home for the season

· ·

*B*ecause you already own a home, you're aware of all the time and money you spend maintaining it. Owning two homes doubles the amount of responsibility, and so protecting your investments is extremely important. For example, who'll mow the lawn and keep the grounds maintained when you're not around? And who'll deal with more pressing issues, such as when the toilet starts leaking or there's a sudden, small fire in the kitchen?

Some of these maintenance and upkeep questions are particularly important if you live several hours away from your second home. If you get a phone call in the middle of the night from your renter, you can't exactly hang up and drop by to handle the problem.

No matter how you maintain your home, whether by hiring a property manager to help with maintenance, upkeep, and emergency issues, or by doing it yourself, this chapter provides the helpful info you need. After reading it, you can have a good handle on exactly what it takes to maintain your second home and keep it in tiptop shape, year-round.

Deciding Whether to Maintain the Property Yourself: Yes or No?

Many second-home owners handle the maintenance, upkeep, emergencies, and other responsibilities of their second home. Whether you can successfully manage your own property depends on several factors. Ask yourself these questions to see if maintaining your second home is right for you:

- ✔ **How close is your primary home to your second home?** If it's less than a couple of hours away by car, you can probably visit every two weeks or so. Of course, this also depends on your schedule and other obligations. If you live far away from your second home and you want to maintain the property, check out "Managing Your Second Home from Afar" later in this chapter for specific info.

- ✔ **How handy are you?** If you and/or your significant other can patch drywall, repair pool filters, edge lawns, and change a faucet washer, then you can probably handle the upkeep of your place on your own. If, however, you have a lawn maintenance company, a pool guy, and a housecleaner at your primary home, and you have your plumber on speed dial, don't expect to do everything on your own at your second home.

- ✔ **How much can you afford to farm out?** If your budget allows you to hire a housecleaner (if you're renting out the home) and a lawn maintenance firm on your own, then you can probably get away with taking care of your second home without the help of a property manager.

- ✔ **What kind of home is it?** If your second home is a condominium that you can button up and leave without worrying too much about it, then forgo the property manager and do what needs to done on your own. But if you have a six-bedroom, five-bathroom single-family home with a pool and spa, then it may take a bit more elbow grease to keep your home in tiptop shape while you're not using it.

If you discover that maintaining your second home is just a tad too stressful, you may want to turn to a professional. If you want to hire a property manager to maintain your property, check out the next section for more specific info.

Relying on a Property Manager to Maintain Your Property

For most people, handling the maintenance on a primary home is more than enough work, thank you very much. At any given time, you have a lawn to trim, a fence to paint or repair, some major electrical or plumbing contraption to keep in good working order, one or more kitchen cabinets to clean (and sometimes adjust so the door doesn't come off in your hand when you open it), and a multitude of carpets to vacuum and clean. Add in a second home, and most people simply don't have the time, motivation, or financial resources to make themselves a full-time property manager or maid. And even if you did have the time, desire, or money to do it, wouldn't you rather invest it somewhere else?

Taking good care of your second home when you can't (or don't want to) is where a professional *property manager* can help. Even though hiring a property manager is an additional expense of owning a second home, it can be well worth the cost. A dependable property manager can save you money in the long run. For example, when she notifies you that several shingles blew off your roof during a storm, you can take care of the roof before the next storm. But the cost of a property manager is exactly why some second-home owners choose not to hire a pro.

In this section, I offer advice on hiring a property manager to oversee your second home's upkeep and show you how these whizzes can help you keep your second home shipshape. (Property managers can also help you market and rent out your place. See Chapter 11 for details.)

Asking the right questions

You want a property manager who can — and will — go the extra mile to truly maintain your second home and not just trim the grass once a week and hope the place stays intact until you come back. You want a property manager who is proactive and will make sure that more than the mere basics are done. What you want is a property manager with enterprise.

If you didn't hire a property manager to rent out your second home, check out Chapter 11 to help you locate good referrals. After you find a person or firm you believe may be able to handle what you need done, ask the following questions:

- ✔ **How much experience do you have managing second-home properties?** You want to work with someone who has experience working with and managing second homes, as opposed to rental apartment units or commercial buildings.

- ✔ **May I have the names of three or four other clients with whom you work?** Get feedback from these folks on what it's like doing business with the property manager. This type of info is valuable and enlightening.

- ✔ **How many other properties do you manage?** If they say, for example, 110, be sure to also ask how many employees they have. You want to be sure they have the staff to handle their workload.

- ✔ **Exactly what do you offer in terms of property maintenance and repair?** Do you, for example, offer the following:

    - Lawn maintenance and service.

    - Basic cleaning services.

    - Thorough cleaning services.

- Regular inspections (and if so, what is inspected and how often?).

- Repair and maintenance of major systems and/or exterior spaces. You want someone who will take charge and actually call the plumber when a leak is detected, not call you to report the problem.

✔ **When something goes wrong at my home, who will handle the repair?** If the property manager has someone on staff, all the better. However, many property managers probably call a third party, like a plumber, roofer, or HVAC professional, to handle it.

✔ **How do you charge for these services?** Even if he can't put a specific price on certain repairs, ask the property manager to quote an hourly labor rate, flat fee, and/or other ballpark estimate to help you determine whether you can afford his services.

✔ **How often will you report problems and concerns to me, and how will you contact me?** A phone call should be a property manager's first choice, and is usually the best way to reach you, even if he gets your machine or voice mail; then an e-mail if the situation isn't too urgent; then a fax. Megaphones shouldn't even enter the picture.

After you have the answers to these important questions, think about them and consider the idea of hiring a property management firm. Review your financial situation and decide whether using a property manager is a feasible way to handle the ongoing maintenance of your second home.

Going over the fine print

Before you sign a contract with a property manager, read the document in its entirety and make notes. If there's anything you're not clear about, or if any phrases or wording doesn't make sense to you, ask about it. You can also have your attorney review the contract to make sure you're getting a fair deal. And be sure the contract includes a few sentences outlining your right to terminate the agreement when warranted on 30 to 60 days' notice.

Figuring out how much to pay

After you've found a property manager who can handle your needs and you've decided to do business with him, then it all comes down to the money. See Chapter 11 for details on how much property managers charge and how much you should expect to pay. Understand that the property manager who helps you both rent out the home and maintain it, versus the one who only handles the maintenance, will likely charge more. And his monthly fees don't include the costs of repairs. Be sure to factor these monthly/quarterly costs into your overall cost of second-home ownership.

Considering a part-time property manager

After reading the fine print and considering the final costs, are you thinking that you can't afford to have a full-time property manager take care of your second home? Fear not. One option you have is to try to work out a part-time deal with a reputable company. Most companies should be willing — for a fee, of course — to come in on an as-needed basis to handle inspections, report problems, and even cut the grass. This is similar to keeping a company on retainer: You use them only when you need them. When the firm kicks into action, you'll be expected to pay for the services provided.

This way, when something big happens, you can have the firm mobilize and handle it without having to pay large monthly fees or commissions for ongoing service. If you establish a relationship with a property management firm, no matter how limited, then you're an established customer and they'll be there for you when you *really* need them.

Developing a working relationship with your property manager

If you've decided to trust someone to take care of your second home on either a part-time or full-time basis, make sure that you sow the seeds of a solid relationship right from the start. This is, of course, true with any professional relationship, like the one you have with your attorney, real estate agent, accountant, feng shui consultant, or doctor, and it should be standard operating procedure with your property manager as well. Establish open lines of communication with your property manager and agree on expectations.

Property management companies differ, but you can expect to have one or more key people with whom you work and whom you call with questions or for service problems. All firms keep accurate records of visits and the action taken, and your rep can discuss everything with you. You should also inquire whether they provide online access to management reports and other records pertaining to your property.

Communicating with your property manager

When working with a property manager, the first thing you need to do is come up with a good communication plan. Any professional relationship is a two-way street. Each side — no matter how busy one of them is — must do its part to make the relationship run smoothly. You need to be equally as available to your property manager as you expect him to be for you, and you'll be on your way to developing a great working relationship.

Here are the two key points you need to discuss with your property manager:

- **How will we communicate with each other?** Will it be by phone, in person, or by e-mail? The property manager who assures you he'll be calling you on a regular basis is a real pro.

- **How often will you be in touch with me?** Will we only talk when there is a problem? Or when I owe you money? Or will you set up a regular communication schedule (such as monthly chats or e-mails)? Again, the manager who keeps the lines of communication open is a winner.

You also need to decide under what specific circumstances, outside of regularly scheduled contacts, you want to hear from your property manager. For example, which incident would you consider important enough to warrant a call from your manager: a small hole appears in a screen door, the front porch light bulb goes out, the stove dies, or a neighborhood kid hits a baseball through the living room window?

Of course, you can tell your manager to take care of everything, up to a preset dollar amount, and bill you for the time and replacement costs. However, doing so can be risky, considering the slew of problems that can crop up at any given time with a second home. Then again, it can be a smart solution if your home is in fairly good condition from the beginning.

Nail down these details early in your relationship with your property manager. He should know precisely what he can do on his own and what you want to be notified about. And be specific. One way to do this is to set a dollar limit. Any repair or service that costs you, say, $100 or less, he can take care of without notifying you. Get this in writing so you don't get any surprises — like your property manager authorizing a $1,500 air conditioner repair and sending you the bill.

What to expect from your property manager

In today's busy world, property managers handle myriad tasks for second-home owners. If you're expecting him to manage the maintenance of your home, he can

- Handle tenant complaints and answer tenant questions

- Repair the property and keep it in good working order

- Contract and oversee lawn maintenance and gardening (although some property management firms have their own grounds people)

- Clean the home (after a short-term renter vacates the property, for example)

- Remove snow, leaves, and other debris that clutters the property

- Collect rent from short- and long-term tenants

- Handle payment of property taxes, expenses, and fees

✔ Check in with the owner periodically to update her on the property, discuss problems and issues, and assure her that the property is in good shape and well cared for

✔ Evict tenants (in the case of long-term rentals)

✔ Take care of other specific tasks that are discussed in advance and, preferably, written into the property management contract. A few examples:

- If your second home has its own pool, the property manager may coordinate the care of that pool and pay a pool company to maintain it.

- If you use the home twice a year but keep a lot of personal items and clothing at the house year-round, the property manager may oversee the professional storage of these items while you're not there, and take care of delivery of your possessions to the home when you arrive.

- If you own a home in a remote location — mountain, island, country — the property manager may set up increased security monitoring or housesitting on an as-needed basis.

Your property manager's primary responsibility is to *you*. If you rent your place, her secondary responsibility is to the tenant, with whom she also has to create and maintain a good working relationship. Keep this point in mind when you ask the property manager to do something that may upset your tenant. The tightrope your property manager walks has to balance out on both sides. For instance, refusing to authorize an immediate refrigerator repair will almost certainly put your property manager in a very uncomfortable situation with your tenants.

Checking on the property

Your property manager should conduct regular, in-person visits to your second home to make sure that it's still standing, that all systems are in good working order, and that it's in the same shape it was when you last left it.

In your contract, have the property manager include a specific checkup schedule for your home. In most cases, I recommend a minimum of once a month. During these visits she can walk through the home and around the outside looking for any signs of problems with your place. However, your property manager may offer you a different schedule. Common inspection schedules are quarterly or every-other-month visits, and it's up to you to decide whether this will work for you.

If, for example, you'll be using your second home every month, then quarterly checkups may be fine. However, if your home is in Europe, and you'll be there one month out of the year, and the property will be rented out for the other 11 months, then you should request — and spell out in writing — more frequent visits.

To ensure that the property manager does a thorough checkup, make detailed, written arrangements for an inspection and cleaning after each tenant leaves, and outline the specific preparations necessary for the next tenant to take possession. Also request an update on your property after each of these checkups, preferably in writing.

Dealing with emergencies

Emergencies are something no homeowner can avoid. From natural disasters and weather-related issues, to fires and structural catastrophes, to more common stuff like an overflowing toilet, Murphy's Law (anything that can go wrong will go wrong!) really applies quite frequently to homeownership.

Keep the following in mind when discussing with your property manager how to handle emergencies:

✔ **Ask your property manager how she's handled emergencies in the past, and ask her to be specific with real-life examples.** Discuss lots of "what could go wrong" scenarios with her. Decide what really constitutes an emergency (not a leaky faucet, for example) and together determine how to handle them. You may instruct her to call the police or fire department, for example, and then notify you. Then you'll ask her to deal with tenant concerns, report the incident to your insurance company, and handle any other details.

✔ **Always keep your property manager informed of your most current contact info.** This includes current phone numbers (home, cell, and work), e-mail addresses, and physical addresses. You don't want your property manager to get a "We're sorry, that number is no longer in service" message when she calls to tell you that an 8-foot alligator broke through your pool screen and is swimming in your pool. (That's a true story, by the way; it happened in my neighborhood about a year ago.) Be sure to give your property manager an emergency contact, just in case she can't reach you when the incident occurs.

✔ **Make sure that you have the proper insurance coverage to protect your investment and that your property manager is aware of this coverage.** If your home is located in an area where hurricanes, flooding, earthquakes, or other natural disasters seem to occur on a fairly regular basis, you need the proper insurance coverage to protect your second home. Talk to your insurance agent about your coverage, and purchase any additional insurance (such as national flood coverage) that will help you rebuild in the event of an emergency.

Covering these points in a conversation will help you develop a good working relationship with your property manager. Use open lines of communication and a detailed contract and plan for any and all events that could affect your property. Then take comfort in the knowledge that both you and your property manager are interested in keeping your second home safe and sound.

Who should the tenant call with problems?

Sooner or later, you'll get a frantic call from your tenant at an inconvenient time telling you that something has gone terribly wrong in your house. Maybe it's 2 a.m. on a Saturday when your tenant calls to say that the central air conditioning unit has broken down in the middle of a Texas heat wave. You can handle the situation in one of three ways:

✔ You can handle it yourself and schedule the repair by calling in your own cavalry, which usually is comprised of one or more area contractors qualified to handle the specific problem.

✔ You can have the tenant call the property manager, if you hired one.

✔ You can have the tenant call someone else who is handling on-site maintenance issues for the property. This can be a neighbor, relative, friend, or anyone else who has agreed to handle things like this on your behalf.

Understand that not all complaint calls will be about leaky toilets and broken stoves. Problems can range from noisy neighbors who are blasting music until 3 a.m., unwanted pests and insects that have invaded the home while you were away, and countless other issues.

By dealing promptly and courteously with these and other problems, you'll cultivate good tenant relations, and you'll probably minimize the number of late-night and weekend calls that come your way. Small problems can easily and quickly turn into big problems, so taking care of even minor nuisance calls with the same attention you'd give to emergencies will certainly pay off in the long run.

Be sure to leave clear instructions about "who to call, and for what reasons" prominently displayed on the refrigerator in your second home, especially if you expect to rent out the home to multiple vacationers over the course of a year.

Managing Your Second Home from Afar

If you decide to maintain your second home yourself and you live a fair distance away from your second home (or even if you only live an hour away), your busy life probably doesn't allow you to drop everything to deal with issues. You're certainly not alone; many people lead busy lives that preclude them from taking time away to maintain a second home.

Even though you may hate the idea (or even feel guilty about it), you should abandon the notion of achieving and maintaining perfection with your second home. If there's a small nick in a cabinet door, or a toilet that runs a minute too long, or an air conditioning unit that is just a tad louder than you would normally tolerate, remember that you're only spending part of the time there. Obsessing over these little details will drive you crazy. If, however, any of those little issues turn into larger problems, be sure to address them quickly. Strive to achieve a balance regarding your priorities and relegate your second home to second on your list when it comes to taking care of absolutely *everything* that can use some attention.

This section identifies the important areas you need to consider if you decide to tackle your second home's maintenance and upkeep yourself. I give you the lowdown on people who can help you maintain the property, discuss lawn maintenance and regular inside cleaning, and share some important points about safety. If something bad happens, don't worry. I have you covered as well, and I tell you how to handle mishaps and accidents.

Identifying who you can rely on

No matter if you live 300 miles or just 30 miles from your second home, you may not be able to drop by your second home whenever you feel like it. That's why having reliable people you can check in with about your home's condition is important.

If you're maintaining your second home, the following individuals can serve as your eyes and ears and make your job a lot easier:

- ✔ **Landscaper:** Landscaping and lawn maintenance crews can mow and edge the lawn and pull weeds. For a few extra bucks, most landscapers also trim hedges and trees as needed. (Check out the next section for more detailed info about lawn upkeep.)

- ✔ **Cleaning crew:** Second-home owners can use cleaning companies on an occasional basis to clean up the home after renters leave or spruce up the place after they themselves leave. This can give you peace of mind for your next trip, knowing that you won't be opening the door to a mess. (See the section "Cleaning your digs: Inside upkeep" later in this chapter for more detailed info.)

- ✔ **Handyman:** These folks can do the odd jobs around your house that you don't want to do or that you don't know how to do. If, for example, a permanent mirrored tile is lifting off the living room wall, or if some of the popcorn ceiling is shedding in one of the upstairs bedrooms, a handyman can fix it for you, and charge you by the job or by the hour.

- ✔ **Security:** If you're not going to be living in your second home full time, invest in a security system. These systems can be helpful in warding off potential crooks (sometimes the company's yard sign is enough to scare them off) and can alert you to any intrusions. I just had my security system overhauled for $700 and, for $50 a month, the security company monitors it closely enough that they once called the police to my home because my cat was jumping around and setting off the motion detectors. The money is well worth the peace of mind.

- ✔ **Neighbors:** Getting friendly with at least one or two of the folks who live close by your second home can be invaluable. They can make a quick phone call to you if they notice something that seems amiss. See Chapter 10 for more info on how to get to know your neighbors and a discussion of the rewards that can come from making new friends.

✔ **Attorney:** Some people like to do things on their own. Others like support, assurance, and reassurance. You may fall somewhere in the middle. When the time comes to sign an important agreement or make a key decision that can affect you legally, consult with an attorney for peace of mind. Expect to pay anywhere from $250 to $400 an hour.

You can ask the preceding service providers to call you if they see something that's awry — even if it has nothing to do with the service they're providing. Granted, the landscaper isn't responsible for notifying you if a couple of shingles blew off your roof, but professionals will almost certainly provide this courtesy if asked. It builds goodwill, and every businessperson knows how valuable that commodity is for long-term success.

Have a list of local service personnel on hand at all times at both your primary and second home. The list of phone numbers should include plumbers, HVAC repair shops, electricians, lawn care services, roof repair companies, and other firms that you can call on for help.

Keeping the lawn and garden looking good: Outside maintenance

Just because you're not at your second home year-round doesn't mean you can let the grass grow waist high, the free weekly newspapers pile up in the driveway, and the garbage cans roll around in the street. Doing so won't keep you on your neighbors' good sides. (If you own a condo, skip to the next section. Outdoor maintenance on such properties is generally the responsibility of the condo association and paid for through your monthly common charges.)

Start your own network

If you're going to be away from your second home for an extended period of time, and if you're not using a property manager, then you'll want to make friends with your new neighbors. Quickly. These folks can serve as your eyes and ears while you're away and can keep you informed of anything strange or worrying that may be going on at your property.

Provide these wonderful neighbors with an updated list of contact information, the dates that you plan to be at (and away from) your home, the names of anyone whom they can expect to see there while you're away, and descriptions of what they drive. (If Aunt May has a key and drops in once in a while, be sure to mention it.) Provide any other details that may be helpful to the people who will keep an eye on your place for you.

You may also want to leave a house key with a trusted someone nearby just in case access is required. If, for example, you're 1,200 miles away and someone needs to let service personnel in for an emergency repair, handling the call will be easier if a house key is nearby.

To keep your second-home investment intact and your neighbors happy, consider hiring a lawn maintenance firm to do the following tasks on a regular basis. They charge as little as $60 to $80 a month to mow and edge the lawn and pull weeds, plus a few more bucks for extra tasks.

- ✓ Maintaining the lawn weekly (mowing and edging)
- ✓ Weeding and trimming the hedges and trees monthly or bimonthly
- ✓ Checking the pool and spa filters and chlorine applications (weekly)
- ✓ Securing any trash cans in a designated area
- ✓ Pressure washing the driveway and adjacent concrete (yearly)
- ✓ Painting the exterior (every three to five years, depending on the weather and other elements)
- ✓ Removing leaves regularly in the autumn
- ✓ Maintaining the mailbox and any other outdoor fixtures (such as lighting — no dark bulbs!)

Your second home may have other outdoor elements that need regular attention, but by staying on top of these areas — either on your own or with the help of friends, neighbors, and local service providers — you'll have a good handle on exactly what needs to be done.

If you're not around your second home for a while, your lawn maintenance workers can also help with outdoor cleanliness. Ask them to keep an eye out for any garbage, free newspapers, or other items that may clutter your lawn and driveway. Explain that you're going to be away for a certain length of time and that you'd appreciate any extra cleanup help they can provide during that period.

Cleaning your digs: Inside upkeep

Keeping your property clean from across the miles is difficult to do on your own (unless, of course, you're a Jedi and can sense a disturbance in the Force from afar). Line up a combination of professional and personal help to ensure that your second home doesn't become an eyesore during the times that you're not in the house. This chore is particularly important for owners who are renting their second homes by the week or the month: It doesn't take long for daily usage to create a real mess in a home.

What if the tenant offers to do some of the maintenance?

Your tenant may offer to help around your second home and do some of the maintenance work. There's nothing wrong with having willing tenants handle some of the maintenance, as long as they know what they're doing. (And it certainly shouldn't take long to figure *that* out. "So *that's* what a lawnmower looks like! I've never seen one before!")

Short-term rentals (a week or two) probably won't be suitable for this maintenance approach, because you can bet that people who have a week at the shore aren't going to want to spend part of it cleaning your house. But many long-term tenants are often willing to handle at least some of the day-to-day tasks.

Lawn maintenance — mowing and edging — is a good starting point for three reasons: It needs to be done regularly, hiring someone to do it costs money, and doing it yourself takes time. Show your tenants the property lines, the equipment, and any special techniques you use to get the job done, and they should be on their way. And be sure to give them specific instructions if there's something you insist on: "The lawnmower blades must be wiped off after every mowing."

All interior cleaning should be the responsibility of the year-round tenant. Your tenants probably don't want you snooping around their living space every couple of weeks or so anyway. And that's perfectly understandable.

However, you should consider making regular, yearly, *announced* inspections to make sure problems don't pile up to a point where you have to spend tens of thousands of dollars to get things back in order after your tenants move out. You'll be looking for signs of problems with plumbing, leaks, and so forth. But a look around can also tip you off to the fact that your tenants now have five cats, along with their requisite litter boxes, and that your beloved second home now smells like cat urine.

Your tenants will probably resist helping with repairs (unless they're retired, super-handy, and enjoy the work). Most tenants feel that repairs absolutely are the owner's responsibility — and they're right.

You have a few choices when it comes to dealing with the odious task of cleaning:

- ✔ You can clean the place yourself. You clean whenever and however you want.

- ✔ You can hire a cleaning crew to come in regularly (for about $60 to $100 a week) and clean the home.

- ✔ You can hire a cleaning crew to come in and clean the house on an as-needed basis (for about $80 to $120 a shot).

To find outside help, ask friends and neighbors for referrals. Choose a service that's bonded and insured, and that has experience handling homes the size of yours.

Preventing accidents: Safety is key

Second-home owners sometimes overlook the issue of safety. A second home has more people in and out of it, especially if you're renting it. So maintaining your home safely is essential. What do you need to watch out for? Basically, anything that can cause injury. For example, a rug corner that's come loose and is sticking up can cause someone to trip and fall; a tub without a no-slip mat or decals is a danger zone; and missing or nonfunctioning smoke detectors and carbon monoxide detectors can result in a perilous situation.

When maintaining your second home, make your place as safe as possible. Take a walk through and around your house and run through some imaginary scenarios in your mind. Yes, someone could trip on that piece of carpet, right? And, yes, someone could fall in the pool inadvertently, right? Take the necessary measures to prevent accidents. Better to be safe than sorry.

Handling mishaps and accidents

You receive a phone call that something has happened on the property. You don't need to worry too much if you plan ahead and know how to handle the inevitable mishaps and accidents.

The best way to keep abreast of mishaps and accidents from afar is by having at least one trusted friend, neighbor, or family member within a few minute's drive of your second home. These mishaps can be as simple as a tree limb that snaps off and breaks a window, or as complex as a serious pipe break that floods the upstairs bathroom and sends water gushing out under the front door. (I've seen that one happen myself. The owners were away, and their neighbor noticed the problem and immediately called the condo management company, the fire department, the police, and the owners.)

Make sure that you inform this trusted person every time you or anyone else occupies or vacates the home, and tell him of any potential problems that may come up. Give him a copy of your service professionals' contact list (see the "Identifying who you can rely on" section for details) and authorize him to call anyone needed if something nasty comes up. Let your trusted contact know how to contact your tenants in case of a problem. Also consider how long you'll wait before entering the property in these situations. You should handle a big mishap (a tree through the roof after a tornado, for example) immediately, while you can take care of something minor (a small hole in the screen door) on your next visit.

> ## Putting a nosy neighbor to good use
>
> A friend of mine has a second home in a Florida community where "snowbirds" make their annual pilgrimage south, and then make the return trip home in the spring. But not everyone leaves. One woman lives there year-round and watches about 20 different homes for a small fee (about $200 for the season — everyone chips in). She keeps the owners informed of any problems.
>
> If you're buying in a community that's saturated with second-home owners, ask around to find out which of the year-round residents has the time and willingness to serve as a quasi property manager while you're away. If you can make this happen, it'll afford great peace of mind for a much smaller fee than what a professional would command.

If someone gets injured while on your property, call your insurance agent immediately. Keep this insurance agent's number handy, and share it with the trusted individual who watches your home while you're away. Your insurance agent will want to know the following:

- ✔ Who was injured and what is their address and contact info?

- ✔ A general description of the person's injuries: "Her knee was bleeding profusely and she may have broken her wrist."

- ✔ The exact circumstances of how she was hurt: "She was walking up the front steps, tripped, and fell onto her right knee and right wrist."

- ✔ Who witnessed the mishap?

- ✔ What medical attention the injured person received and where?

- ✔ Were the police called?

- ✔ Was an ambulance called?

- ✔ The name of the injured party's insurance company.

- ✔ Any damage to the premises and/or property as a result of the mishap.

- ✔ What, if anything, the injured party said to the homeowner.

Coping with theft or major property damage

Theft and property damage can happen at any home, but the second home left unoccupied for long spells is especially vulnerable. And because so many of these homes are in vacation spots (in Florida, for example, where hurricanes are a problem for a good portion of the year), they need a bit more attention when it comes to keeping them safe from theft and property damage.

No one likes to think about the frightening notion of someone breaking into their second home. The reality, however, is that it can and does happen, so take the following steps:

1. **Work to prevent a break-in.**

   • Get a monitored security system for your second home. You can get one for about $50 a month; it will be well worth the investment.

   • Be sure to have good, solid locks on the doors, and most important, *make sure they're locked* when you leave. (Lots of times, crooks do nothing but walk around trying doorknobs and then rob whichever homes were left unlocked.)

   • Install good lighting that features timers and motion detectors to help ward off would-be burglars who don't want to be in the spotlight.

2. **Be prepared to handle the situation if your home is broken into.**

   If your second home is broken into and you're the first one to discover the break-in, don't enter the home. Call 911 from your cellphone or a neighbor's house and wait for the police to arrive before going inside. If, on the other hand, you're notified of a break-in and your trusted friend, neighbor, or family member is at the home handling the police and securing the place, then the first person you need to call is your insurance agent.

If your second home is damaged due to weather, vandalism, or theft, you need to do the following:

1. **Call your insurance agent immediately to report the claim.**

2. **Secure the premises and protect the items inside and outside of the home.**

   For example, if a sliding glass door is broken, make sure the opening gets covered with plywood.

3. **Take any other measures necessary to safeguard your investment.**

   For example, you may need to use generators to provide electricity and/or light, or you may need to put tarps on the roof and lock any gates or doors that may become entrances for unwanted individuals.

Because you won't be living in your second home full time — and if you don't have a property manager, friend, or neighbor checking up on your home — you may not even know about the damage or theft for a while if you don't have an alarm system. For this reason, make arrangements with someone whom you trust to do regular drive-bys and internal inspections of the home while you're away. Also, notifying the local police that the house will be vacant for a specific time period is a good idea.

Closing for the Season

If you use your second home for a certain period of the year and then close it for the rest of the time, this section contains all you need to know about what you should do inside and out before you (cue lump in throat) kiss your getaway goodbye and fly (or drive) back to reality for a few months.

What needs to be done inside?

When leaving your home for an extended period of time, use the following checklist to make sure your home will be a pleasant place to return to. Many of these tips come from a friend of mine who lives in Michigan for part of the year and in a 55-plus Florida community the rest of the year. When he departs his second home, he spends at least a week preparing his home for vacancy. (Feel free to photocopy this list for your own use.)

- ❏ Call the cable company, telephone company, Internet service provider, newspaper delivery, garbage pickup service, and other utility service providers to let them know when to stop the service.

- ❏ Leave the water and electricity on while you're away.

- ❏ Have your mail forwarded back to your primary address. Do this a week early and have your primary home's post office hold the forwarded mail — doing so ensures a clean transition.

- ❏ Remove all food from the refrigerator and freezer and turn down the thermostat.

- ❏ Clean out the cabinets of noncanned food items that would go bad over the next few months.

- ❏ Clean the kitchen and put out insect or ant traps (to avoid a nasty surprise when you return).

- ❏ Open all the kitchen cabinets to keep air flowing through them and to avoid mold and odor problems.

- ❏ Straighten all rooms, make the beds, and clean the bathrooms.

- ❏ Turn the thermostat to a level that saves energy but also ensures that the home doesn't get too hot and/or damp from the humidity during the summer.

❑ Turn off the hot water heater.

❑ Talk to your neighbors about your departure and leave contact info for reporting any unusual activity.

❑ Lock all the doors and windows, and close the drapes or pull the blinds.

❑ If possible, use a lighting timing device that leaves on a light to let possibly troublesome passersby know that someone is home. Invest in those ultra-low-wattage spring bulbs to minimize energy consumption.

❑ Unplug expensive electronics like TVs, microwaves, computers, and other appliances to eliminate the possibility of damage from lightning strikes.

Your place doesn't have to be sparkling, but it should at least be neat and tidy for you when you return.

What needs to be done outside?

You have fewer chores to attend to outside when you're closing your house for the season, but you still want to take a few minutes to walk around the property. Here's what you should do:

❑ Bring all lawn and patio furniture into the home for storage in the garage or living room.

❑ Secure or bring inside all objects that may go flying in a strong wind or that people can walk off with. That includes flowerpots, garden hose reels, pool toys, barbecue grills, trash containers, and anything else that can turn into a projectile during high winds.

❑ If you use them, make sure any sprinkler systems are set to run automatically on their specified days.

❑ Make sure all doors and gates are locked.

❑ Take any other necessary steps that may be unique to your home to ensure that it will stay safe while you're away.

Chapter 14

What Uncle Sam Wants to Know: Important Tax Implications

In This Chapter

▶ Knowing what you need to know about taxes

▶ Taking all your key deductions

▶ Using depreciation to your advantage

▶ Making your second home your primary home: The tax implications

*P*urchasing a second home and using it for vacation or rental purposes (not as your primary home) can affect your tax return in the long term. You'll have additional income to report from renting it and additional expenses to deduct from the costs of maintaining it as an investment property.

When you become a second-home owner, you essentially become a business owner — but only if you're going to rent your home to others. If you don't rent your second home, then the effect on your taxes is relatively limited. Mainly, it gives you additional mortgage interest and property tax deductions, assuming you took a mortgage out on the place.

In this chapter, I walk you through the most important changes in your tax situation after you purchase your second home, and I offer some simple strategies you can implement to lower your final tax bill.

For more-detailed info that applies to your individual situation, always talk to a reputable accountant before making any assumptions or important decisions about your taxes or filing any tax returns. They know what they're talking about and have seen situations like yours countless times before. You can also pick up the latest edition of *Taxes For Dummies* by Eric Tyson, Margaret Atkins Munro, and David J. Silverman (Wiley) for help in understanding the latest tax-code changes and figuring out what forms you need to file.

Taxes 101: How Owning a Second Home Impacts Your Bottom Line

Uncle Sam defines a second home as any home other than your main home. So if you own more than one house, you have to select one as your main home and the rest become second homes. Second homes can be

- ✔ Single-family homes
- ✔ Condominiums or townhouses
- ✔ Cooperatives
- ✔ Mobile homes, trailers, or RVs
- ✔ Boats that include cooking, sleeping, and toilet facilities

The downside of owning a second home is that you have to pay property taxes on the home, no matter what, and you may have an increased income tax bill if you rent it. The upside is that no matter how you use your home, you gain some tax deductions.

If you're using your property solely as a second home (meaning that you're using it for your own personal vacations and visits), you can

- ✔ Deduct mortgage interest. But you can't deduct maintenance or other expenses associated with the property.
- ✔ Collect 14 days of rental income without having to pay taxes on that revenue.

If you use the home yourself for 14 days or fewer, and if you rent it out at *fair market value* (the price that an interested — but not desperate — renter is willing to pay on the open market to rent the home) at other times during the year, then you, my friend, have an investment property on your hands. That means that

- ✔ All the income the home generates is taxable.
- ✔ Most of the expenses associated with the home — including depreciation — are tax deductible.

Strategies to Lower Your Tax Bill if You're Renting Out Your Second Home

As a second-home owner, you can effectively lower your overall tax bills by claiming certain deductions associated with homeownership and rental property. And it's all perfectly legal, as long as you play by the IRS's rules.

In this section, I go over those deductions one by one, and help you understand exactly what you can — and can't — deduct on your tax return when you're a second-home owner and you're renting out your home.

I'm not a tax attorney or accountant, so if you have any questions after you read this chapter, I suggest you talk to a professional. For the most updated info on how to claim rental property income and expenses, get a copy of IRS Publication 527, "Residential Rental Property (Including Rental of Vacation Homes)." Call 800-829-3676 to get a hard copy of the publication, or scoot on over to www.irs.gov/formspubs and download a copy. The rules change all the time, and you'll want to have the most current information possible when you sit down to file your current year's return.

Renting a second home: My own story

While living in Florida, I owned a second home in Pennsylvania. I rented my three-bedroom, two-bathroom, two-story home to a couple who lived there from 1997 to 2004 (when I eventually sold it to them). It was a year-round rental based on the going rate in the area, which was about $700 per month.

During the seven-year period that I rented out the home, I claimed the rental income on the appropriate IRS form, and I deducted the following expenses associated with the rental:

✔ The mortgage interest payments

✔ The property taxes

✔ The homeowners' insurance

✔ The cost of repairing and maintaining the property

✔ The depreciation associated with the aging property

Every year, the home resulted in a slight loss, mainly because its historic age and upkeep requirements cost quite a bit each year. This loss was reflected on the front page of my 1040 tax return.

When it came time to sell the place, I had to pay back the following in capital gains:

✔ 25 percent of the total depreciation I had claimed over the seven years

✔ 15 percent of the remainder of the gain

But in the end, the taxes I had to pay were minimal compared to my tax savings over the seven-year period.

Figuring out whether your property qualifies as a rental for tax purposes

When you rent your second home, figuring out what you can and can't deduct on your tax return isn't always crystal clear. What you can deduct depends on how many days a year you rent the property. The friendly folks at the IRS consider a home to be a business entity under the following criteria:

- ✔ If you or another family member use the property for 14 days or fewer a year.

- ✔ If you or another family member use it for less than 10 percent of the number of days that the home was rented at fair market value.

  So if you rented the home out for 50 weeks, that's 350 days. If you and your family spent the remaining two weeks — 14 days — there, that's fewer than 35 days (10 percent of 350), so that year, the IRS would consider the home a business, with all the deductions that come with that designation.

  On the other hand, say you and your loved ones spent three months at your second home and rented it out the remaining nine months. The 10 percent rule wouldn't apply here because you spent 90 days at your place and rented it out for 270 days. In this situation, your 90 days in residence is well over the 27 days allowed to qualify the house as a business entity. You can't deduct expenses associated with renting the home.

Determining whether your second home qualifies as a business under IRS guidelines can get a little complicated, so it's always a good idea to have a tax accountant on your team who knows this stuff off the top of her head and can answer questions and steer you in the right direction.

Taking deductions on a rental property

So you have some income and expenses related to your second home, and you're ready to do your taxes. Table 14-1 summarizes whether you have to report rental income to the IRS and what deductions are allowed based on whether Uncle Sam and his team regard your second home as a business or a residence.

Depending on your individual situation, you'll likely fall into one of these categories and be able to figure out just what you can and can't deduct on your tax return. If your situation doesn't easily fit into one of these scenarios, be sure to talk to your accountant or other tax pro to find out exactly how to handle any rental income and expenses associated with your second home.

Table 14-1	Reporting Requirements and Allowable Deductions for Second Homes Used as Rental Property	
	You Rent Out the Home Fewer Than 14 Days a Year and Live There	*You Rent Out the Home More Than 14 Days a Year and Don't Live There*
Report rental income	No	Yes
Deduct rental expenses (such as maintenance, repairs, and so on)	No	Yes, up to the amount of income received
Deduct mortgage interest	Yes	Yes (in most cases; ask your accountant)
Deduct property taxes	Yes	Yes
Deduct homeowners' insurance premiums	No	Yes

The following sections look at the main categories of deductions that you may be able to claim on your second home. Be sure to keep the rules — 14 days or fewer, or 10 percent of the time the place is rented out — in mind when reviewing your options.

Property taxes

You can deduct property taxes on your tax return. If your home qualifies as a rental property (see "Figuring out whether your property qualifies as a rental for tax purposes" earlier in this chapter), you deduct the property taxes paid on Schedule E, Supplemental Income and Loss. This process is straightforward based on the exact amount of property taxes you paid on the home during the tax year.

So, if you have two mortgages, one for your primary home and one for your second home, and you rent out the second home, you file a Schedule A to deduct the property taxes paid on your first home, and a Schedule E to deduct the taxes paid on your second home. *Capiche?*

The moment you become a second-home owner, the amount of house-related paperwork that comes flying at you every month doubles. (Isn't that a pleasant thought? Not!) To deal with it, set up a separate file for each of your properties so you don't confuse your primary home's papers with your second home's papers. Start your second home file with a copy of your settlement statement that you receive at closing. Doing so makes it easy when it comes time to deduct the points (if you paid them) on the current year's return. Add to this file all 1098 mortgage interest statements, tax receipts, and proof of other expenses associated with your second home. And do the same for your primary residence. I suggest setting up and maintaining accurate, up-to-date, hard-copy files even if you use a software program to track household income and expenses. This way, when tax time rolls around, you have quick access to all the paper records associated with your expenses for each dwelling. Just throwing everything into a cardboard storage box isn't that great an idea. (And I know people who do precisely that. Tax time isn't a pretty picture.)

Mortgage interest

If you're using your second home as a rental property, then you can deduct your monthly mortgage interest on Schedule E, Supplemental Income and Loss, which has a space allocated to "mortgage interest paid to banks." (Check with IRS Publication 936, "Home Mortgage Interest Deduction," for details on how to deal with your specific home mortgage situation.)

Here's how mortgage interest works for second-home owners:

- ✔ If your home is considered an investment property, then you'll deduct your mortgage interest on Schedule E.

- ✔ If your home is considered a residence (you use it more than 14 days a year or for more than 10 percent of the total time it's rented out), then you'll claim the *mortgage interest only* (as reported to you on a form 1098 at the end of the year) on a Schedule A, Itemized Deductions, tax form. The only difference between how you report a primary versus a second home is in the form that you file with the IRS.

There are always exceptions to these rules, particularly when it comes to intricacies of the tax code, but most cases fall into one of these two categories. Remember rule number one: If you have any doubts or questions, consult your accountant or attorney!

Your mortgage interest may be limited if the total amount of mortgages taken out on the second home exceeds either of the following:

- ✔ The fair market value of the property

- ✔ $1 million (or $500,000 if you're married and filing separately from your spouse)

The mortgage interest deduction may also be limited if you have more than $100,000 ($50,000 for married filing separately) in home equity loans.

Don't forget to deduct the points paid on your second-home mortgage for the year that you paid them. A *point* is 1 percent of the mortgage amount, usually paid in cash at the time of the closing. Points are paid to score a lower interest rate on your mortgage. Points are essentially interest you're paying early to reduce the amount of total interest paid. If you buy a home in 2007, for example — and if you itemize deductions — when you file your tax return in 2008 for the prior year, you can deduct those points paid at closing.

Homeowners' insurance

If your second home is rented out for more than 14 days a year, you can deduct the cost of homeowners' insurance paid out to repair damage and replace the property. Stake your claim on line 9 of Schedule E.

If your second home is considered a residence — and not a rental property as defined by the criteria discussed in the "Figuring out whether your property qualifies as a rental for tax purposes" section — then you will *not* be able to deduct your homeowners' insurance costs.

Miscellaneous deductions

For your rental property, the IRS allows you to deduct certain expenses associated with running your business. You can claim the following expenses on Schedule E:

- Advertising
- Auto and travel
- Cleaning and maintenance
- Commissions (such as those paid to a real estate agent or property manager)
- Interest other than mortgage interest
- Legal and other professional fees
- Repairs
- Supplies
- Utilities
- Other

As you can see, the IRS provides a wide range of options for the rental property owner who incurs expenses throughout the year as a result of homeownership. Just keep in mind that this latitude has in the past caused many a homeowner to "take advantage," so to speak, of this ability to deduct various expenses, and, as such, makes the rental-property arena a red-flag area for the IRS. Avoid any potential issues by retaining receipts, avoiding over-deductions, and thinking twice before making any other moves that could send your tax return to an auditor's desk.

You can carry over any nondeducted rental expenses to later years (when, for example, expenses weren't as high). In other words, if you break even for two years in a row (your income equals your expenses and you show no taxable profit), you may end up with extra deductions (such as that $250 cleaning bill) that you can use for later years, when your second home produces a profit.

What you can't deduct now, but can later

You should be aware that some of the costs associated with buying a home are *not* tax deductible. Closing costs, for example, can't be immediately deducted from your tax return. However, you can recoup closing costs when it's time to sell your second home, so hang onto those settlement statements.

You can figure such expenses into the *adjusted cost basis* (the cost of the home *plus* any major improvements that added value to a property minus losses) of the second home. And what, specifically, are closing costs? These expenses include

- ✔ Appraisal fees
- ✔ Credit report fees
- ✔ Document preparation fees
- ✔ Other costs associated with the closing process

You can also deduct costly home improvements (new roofs and kitchens, for example) when selling your second home. Be sure to retain records of your improvements, and then talk to your tax preparer when you sell to ensure that all these issues are properly accounted for and squared away.

Taking advantage of depreciation

The IRS recognizes the fact that homes age and that keeping their value intact requires money and elbow grease. Because of this, second-home owners who rent out their properties for more than 14 days per year can deduct what is known as depreciation on their properties. *Depreciation* is a decrease or reduction in value that comes as a result of wear and tear or market conditions.

According to the IRS, only property used in a trade or business or for an income-producing activity can be depreciated. To qualify, the property must be something that "wears out" or becomes obsolete over time, and must have a useful life that extends significantly beyond the tax year. You recover the cost of income-producing property through yearly tax deductions and the depreciation (or deducting some of the cost) on your annual tax return.

Depreciation is a complex topic. For more information, refer to the IRS's Web site at www.irs.gov and read through Tax Topic 704, Depreciation. At the Web site, you can also access Publication 946, "How to Depreciate Property."

Claiming depreciation

Rental property (defined as property where a tenant stays for 30 days or more and where no medical or health care is provided) is depreciated over a 27.5-year schedule. To figure out the deductible depreciation on your second home, you use what is known as the *MACRS* (Modified Accelerated Cost Recovery System) method, which is used for properties placed in service after 1986.

To claim the depreciation deduction, you need the following info about your property:

- ✔ **Its recovery period:** For residential real estate, it's 27.5 years.

- ✔ **Its placed-in-service date:** Property is considered placed in service when it is ready and available for a specific use in that activity. That means if you buy your home in January 2008, and if you don't start renting it out until January 2009, then January 2009 is the place-in-service date.

- ✔ **Its depreciable basis:** As determined by an IRS table provided by the IRS in Publication 946, "How To Depreciate Property." Call 800-TAX-FORM (800-829-3676) or visit www.irs.gov for more info on how to obtain one.

Calculating depreciation

Are you scratching your head and wondering how in the heck depreciation really works? You're probably not the only one. Depreciation is no stroll in the park. It's difficult to understand, and I strongly suggest you talk with a tax pro for specific advice. The following simple example, however, can help you understand how depreciation works:

You purchase a home for $195,000 in January 2005 and immediately rent it out on a yearly basis for $1,000 per month. When you file your 2005 taxes, you fill out an IRS Form 4562, Depreciation and Amortization, on which you list the property type and location. For argument's sake, say the adjusted basis is $200,000. From Publication 946, you know that the percentage is 3.485 percent. You multiply that by the adjusted basis to come up with $6,970 as the depreciable amount that you can claim on your tax return.

If, at the time of the sale, your second home was rented out, then any monetary gain due to appreciation will be taxed at a maximum rate of 25 percent. To find out what's due, you'll have to take the yearly depreciation deduction and multiply it by a maximum rate of 25 percent. Any remaining gain will be taxed at 5 to 15 percent. The sale itself and these gains or losses are reported on IRS Form 4797, Sales of Business Property.

Pinning Down Property Taxes and Assessments

When you buy a second home in any state, you'll be required to pay property taxes — and the amount will be based on the government's determination of the property's assessed value. These taxes are used to support the infrastructure (schools, roads, bridges, public transportation, and so forth) in an area, and are paid by all property owners. Property taxes are deductible and in some cases (like when they are insanely high), they can impact the resale appeal of a property.

Because your second home may be in another state, and the odds are you'll probably retire there, knowing what taxes you'll pay — both before and after retirement — is important. An excellent source for this info is the Web site RetirementLiving.com (`www.retirementliving.com/RLtaxes.html`). There you'll find a complete overview of the tax situation in every state, from sales and fuel taxes, to property and retirement income taxes. (And even if your second home is in your home state, it's still a good idea to have a complete awareness of how your state taxes its residents.)

This section explains how your second home is assessed, thus determining your property taxes, how you can appeal an assessment if you think your taxes are too high, and what you can do to lower your taxes.

How are properties assessed?

How the assessor's offices come up with "assessed value" numbers for properties is a big mystery for most people. But it doesn't have to be. Most assessments use factors such as the home's size, square footage, location, and amenities to come up with the number. Sometimes they rely on building permits, which show new additions and renovations that may also affect the property's value.

Property assessors also factor in the following:

- What similar properties in the area are selling for
- What it would cost to replace the home
- How much it costs to operate and repair the home
- How much rent the property can generate
- Any other issues affecting its value

With this info in hand, the assessor will use one or more of the following approaches to come up with a number:

- **Sales comparison approach:** This involves comparing property in the same area to other like properties that have recently sold. The assessor analyzes the prices to see whether the sales were in line with what the market will bear. For example, if one 2,000-square-foot condo sold for $1 million, and another identical unit sold for $500,000 within a few months of the first sale, the assessor will investigate to see why there was such a large discrepancy.

  After those evaluations are done, the assessor will come up with what he believes is a fair valuation for your property.

- **Cost approach:** This is based on how much money it would take — factoring in today's land, material, and labor costs — to rebuild the property from the ground up. This approach works well for new or unusual homes for which there are no current *comparables,* or sales to compare the home to.

- **Income approach:** Here the assessor evaluates how much income the property would produce if it were rented as an apartment, retail store, or other type of business entity. This approach looks at how much rent the property would earn, the vacancy rates, the maintenance costs, and the operating expenses, as well as the current interest rate charged for borrowing money. All these factors are used to come up with an assessed value.

For a second home, you'll likely be dealing with the sales comparison approach most of the time, unless your tax assessor indicates otherwise. You can challenge the assessor's approach if you believe it will result in a higher assessed value than you believe is feasible.

Appealing an assessment

Tax assessors are usually required by the state they operate in to reassess property values every few years. If you receive one of their assessment notices — commonly called a *TRIM* or *truth rate in millage statement,* a notice which precedes an actual tax bill — and it's for a new value that doesn't sound right to you, you have the right to appeal the amount.

For example, say your neighbor's home is 1,000 square feet *larger* than yours, yet his tax bill is *lower* than yours. Aside from this fact driving you crazy (and, yes, it will, in fact, drive you crazy until it's resolved), you should use this disparity as an argument to have your tax bill lowered. You have every right to request that the county tax assessor reassess your home. (See the "How are properties assessed?" section for more basic info about the assessment procedure.)

There's no hard and fast rule for how to go about appealing your assessment. In many municipalities you file a written appeal within 90 days of receiving the assessment notice. You typically send the appeal to the county assessor's office or property appraiser's office, depending on what they call themselves in your community.

If you believe that you have a legitimate gripe with the tax assessor's office, *don't wait* until your final tax bill arrives. This is very important. By then it may be too late to do anything about the current tax year. Instead, file the appeal as soon as you receive the disputable assessment.

As you wind your way through the appeal process, remember that an appraisal is an *opinion of value* — an opinion that is handed down by a real estate professional. If your appraisal of your property's value doesn't match what the assessor says is its value, then you may have a case.

So, how do you win an appeal? That's the million-dollar question for any legal battle, but when it comes to an assessment appeal, there are a few ways to get the assessor to see your side of the story, which is, of course, "my house is not worth what you say it is. Sir. Or Ma'am." (And yes, politeness counts when dealing with any bureaucratic agency.)

If you decide to challenge the assessment, you'll have to attend a hearing where the issue will be reviewed. To strengthen your argument, bring as much evidence as possible to the hearing and be ready to clearly support your position. The following documents are all very effective in proving that your house has been assessed at a higher value than you're willing to accept as accurate:

- ✔ Information about any and all recent sales of the property in question

- ✔ A recent independent property appraisal by a qualified fee appraiser

- ✔ A sales comparison to properties that have sold recently and that are similar to yours in square footage and amenities

✔ A detailed outline of your original property cost (this is particularly applicable for new homes, which aren't always easy to assess because, in most instances, the cost of the land is only on the public record)

If you decide to appeal your assessment, talk to your real estate agent and/or appraiser. They can help you put together the necessary documentation and proof required to make your case at a hearing, and hopefully be granted a reduction in your assessment.

Lowering your property tax bill

Most states that tax residential land and buildings offer homeowners ways to reduce their tax bill to encourage homeownership and residency. Check with your local tax office for details on any and all tax relief benefits available to you.

In Florida, for example, full-time residents of the state can file for a *homestead exemption* that exempts the first $25,000 in assessed property value from taxes. Also, all 50 states offer some form of property tax relief based on age and, sometimes age and income combined. And some cities and municipalities offer property tax breaks for veterans.

Making the Transition: Your Second Home Becomes Your Primary Residence

You may not be looking to move into your second home permanently for several years, but that doesn't mean you shouldn't at least consider how it will affect your bottom line when the time comes to make that transition. Time passes quickly and, as the years go by, you get into a routine of spending a few weeks a year at your vacation place and collecting rent on the home the remaining time. You may think you have plenty of time to think about what you'll do with your primary home, but time flies, so give the following some thought. (Check out Chapter 16 for other issues you have to consider when your second home becomes your primary residence.)

The Taxpayer Relief Act of 1997 gave homeowners selling their primary residence a tremendous tax break: If you make less than $250,000 profit (up to $500,000 depending on your filing status — talk to your accountant) on the sale of your home, you don't have to pay tax on the profit, and you don't have to use the money to buy another home (like you did before the 1997 act). Profits above $250,000 are still subject to the standard capital gains tax.

If you sell your second home: A note on capital gains

Selling a second home can trigger a *capital gains* bill on your next tax return, so it's important to factor in this issue when you're thinking about selling. This is the difference in value between what you originally paid for a piece of real estate and the price at which it was sold (assuming the investment itself gained in value since it was purchased). This number is important because it can trigger what is known as a capital gains tax upon sale of the property. Talk to your financial advisor if you're unclear as to how the sale will impact your tax return.

If you own and use your second home as your primary residence for at least two of the five years immediately prior to the date of sale, you can exclude up to $250,000 of the capital gains earned from the sale of the home. You can exclude up to $500,000 if you're married and filing jointly, and if both spouses used the home as a primary residence for at least two of the last five years.

So if you purchased your home for $250,000 and sold it for a $100,000 profit, and if you lived in the home for two years before converting it into a rental property three years ago, then all the capital gains from the sale would be excluded.

If you don't meet those IRS requirements for excluding capital gains, the gains will be taxed at a rate of 5 to 15 percent, depending on your tax bracket. Such gains are reported on a Schedule D, Capital Gains and Losses, tax form.

And after you move full time into your second home, you have other tax implications to consider. For starters, you'll no longer be running your second home as a business and will no longer have to fill out Schedule E. Also, if you've been making improvements to your second home all along and deducting them, you'll no longer be able to do so, because your investment property is now your primary home.

You will, however, be able to continue to deduct any mortgage interest and property taxes paid as itemized deductions on your Schedule A. Your tax prep will be a little easier because you won't have to show that additional rental income and whatever expenses you had previously incurred with the home.

Part IV
Home, Sweet Home: Retiring to Your Second Home

The 5th Wave   By Rich Tennant

"Mr. Johnson, I think we've found your dream second home! By the way, how do you feel about ghosts, ancient burial grounds and curses?"

In this part . . .

Retirement may be a few years away, but there's no time like the present to start planning what role your second home will play during that stage of your life. This part helps you figure out how and when to sell your primary home and move into your second home. This part also includes a chapter that covers what you need to know when you do sell the place you now call home and a chapter that helps you plan for the future.

Chapter 15

From Landlord to Resident: Living Permanently in Your Second Home

In This Chapter

▶ Deciding on the right time to move

▶ Telling your renters it's time to go

▶ Transforming your second home into your full-time residence

▶ Dealing with the tax implications of your move

*W*hen you make the switch from landlord to resident, you have a lot to do. And packing is the least of it. When it comes time to move into your second home, you face a number of key decisions — decisions that can affect you both personally and financially.

For some people, the transition is easy. They pack up and sell the primary home, move into the second home, and voilá! Home, sweet home! But the transition isn't always this easy. Many people encounter problems, such as adapting to a smaller home, moving to a new state, climate, or country, or trying to sell an existing home in a saturated market.

This chapter helps you determine the right time to move and looks at the key factors to consider after you know when you'll be out of your primary home. This chapter wraps up with the best ways to tackle the financial and tax implications that arise when you shift from landlord to occupant.

Think of this chapter and Chapter 16 (which deals with selling your existing home) as ports in a storm during this important transition. Leaving the place where you've lived for so many years is a big deal. This house has been your home and it has tons of memories, but you can make this transition smoothly.

Deciding When to Move to Your Second Home

One day you'll wake up in the same house you've slept in for years and ask yourself: Shall I sell this place and move into my second home permanently? Is it time? Some of you may have been thinking for quite some time about when to make this move. But for others, a combination of factors will hasten your decision.

Before you figure out whether now is the right time to move to your second home, you need to take a close look at your current position. Think about when you plan to retire, your family and their lifestyle, the renters who are living in your second home, and the income the place is generating. You may have to factor in many different life scenarios before you make your decision.

Sit down and ask yourself if now is the right time to make the move. Analyze your family status, finances, work situation, and other factors that could affect your decision. Consider where you are in your life. Are you ready to stop working and live in the country? Are you leaning toward a second career and really looking to live near the city? Think about where you see yourself, your spouse, and your children being most comfortable for the next five to ten years.

This section explores some possible scenarios you may find yourself facing and helps you make the best decision.

Considering the impact of selling your primary home

Before you sell your home, you need to understand how your home's value and what you owe on it can affect your decision to move into your second home. (Chapter 16 specifically addresses what you need to know to help you sell your primary home.)

One way to figure out the financial side of the equation is by answering a few questions that will clearly show you exactly where you stand and help you decide on your next move (in both senses of the word!). As you decide whether you want to move into your second home, ask yourself the following questions:

✔ **How much did I originally pay for my home?** Cost is crucial, of course. Combined with your answer to the next question, what you paid will help you figure out you how much your primary home has appreciated since you purchased it.

✔ **How much the home is worth now?** A real estate agent can do a comparative market analysis (CMA) for you, or you can use an online resource like HouseValues.com (`www.housevalues.com`) or Zillow.com (`www.zillow.com`) to come up with your own numbers. If property prices in your area have skyrocketed in recent years, and you know you can make a killing if you sell your home right now, then now may be a good time to sell.

WARNING!

Don't base your own home's value on how much your new neighbor down the street paid for his place a year ago. The real estate market is in a constant state of flux, and the price someone in your neighborhood paid for a house 6 to 12 months ago may not be relevant today for your home. Avoid these "mis-estimates" by working with a real estate agent or other professional who, when it comes to your abode, can come up with an accurate portrayal of what the market will bear *right now* (because that's all that matters when it comes to selling and buying real estate — *right now*).

✔ **How much do I owe on my home?** You can check your most recent monthly mortgage statement for this information, or simply call your bank or mortgage company and ask for a payoff balance.

✔ **How much equity do I currently have in my home?** *Equity* is the value of the home less the total mortgage amount that you owe on the home. Calculate this figure by using the following simple formula:

1. **Take the current, realistic sale price of your home.**

   For example, you have determined that your primary house can realistically sell for $450,000.

2. **Subtract the total amount you owe from the price you expect your home to sell for.**

   Say you still owe $200,000 on your mortgage. Subtract that $200,000 from the expected sale price of $450,000 to come up with a figure of $250,000. That's your equity.

3. **Ask your real estate agent what your approximate closing costs and legal fees are likely to be, and subtract that number from the equity.**

   If your agent estimates the costs at $27,000, subtract that from the $250,000 equity figure. This number reflects an estimate of the greenbacks you'll pocket from the sale of your primary home.

   Before selling your primary home and moving into your second home, keep this final number in mind. Write it down somewhere so you don't forget it, but, frankly, I don't think you will forget it. If there's one thing most people never seem to forget, it's how much their home has appreciated over the years.

If you like what you see when you answer these questions — your home has appreciated well, your mortgage balance is low or nonexistent, your equity is high — then you're in a good position to sell your primary home and move to your second home. If the answers aren't quite as positive as you'd hoped for, now may not be the right time to sell your home. Be patient, keep paying that mortgage, and watch for home values to rise in your area. Look at these questions again in a couple of months, and you may be surprised at how your answers have changed for the better!

Moving before you retire

You may be wondering if you want or need to move into your second home *before* you retire. In some situations, like those in the following list, moving before retirement is a viable option

- ✔ **If your second home is near your place of work, and/or near your primary home.** This means accessibility to your existing workplace will be convenient, and you also won't have to deal with any type of "new area" culture shock.

- ✔ **If you're self-employed and your job isn't tied to any one place.** Writers, photographers, Web designers and merchants, consultants, and others who operate a home-based business, for example, can usually work from anywhere and aren't required to stay in one geographical location to earn an income.

- ✔ **If you're a few years away from retirement, but the value of your primary home is sky high and you'd like to cash in rather than take a chance on a drop in the market.** Timing is everything. The real estate market is a roller coaster of highs and lows, and sometimes the highs are breathtaking. We've been through periods when prices were incredibly high and, if you see that with your primary home and would like to cash in, then think about selling and moving to your second home before you're officially retired. (This assumes, of course, that you can still work your existing job from your second home.)

By making the move before you retire, you'll still have regular income coming in to cover expenses. That means when that $2,000 moving bill comes in, you won't have to dip into your nest egg to pay for it.

You may discover other reasons to continue working after you move to your second home. Carefully review your personal situation before making the move. Look at your family, finances, and living arrangement (still got a couple of kids at home? And so on). Also, be sure to think about your desire, or lack thereof, to continue working. Many baby boomers swear that they'll never succumb to the lure of retirement. Also, give some thought to what you'll do with yourself after you decide to jump off of the 9-to-5 train.

Moving after you retire

Are you tired of working and ready to slow down a bit? Are you ready to truly enjoy your second home? If so, you may be thinking about retiring and moving into your second home. Doing so offers several advantages:

- ✔ You will be free to enjoy life, every day, without the worries and headaches of having to go to a job.
- ✔ You can take full advantage of your surroundings and never again have to say, "Someday we'll go there when we have time."
- ✔ You can join the ranks of retired individuals who can avoid peak times at the grocery store and mall.

If you want to enjoy your retirement years in your second home, you need to make sure you're ready financially. First, you want to make sure that your pension, 401(k), and other sources of guaranteed income are adequate to cover all the housing expenses associated with your second home. To do this, list the income you expect to receive after you retire, using the following checklist:

- ✔ Pension
- ✔ Social Security
- ✔ IRA and/or 401(k) payouts
- ✔ Dividends and interest
- ✔ Life insurance annuity payments
- ✔ Income from a full- or part-time job
- ✔ Regular dips into savings

Make sure you factor in the profit that you'll earn when you sell your primary home. If you've been paying a mortgage on it for 20, 25, or more years, you may receive a nice chunk of cash from the sale because the long-term appreciation of homes is around 6 percent a year. (Check out Chapter 16 for more info on selling your primary home.) You can use this money for the move into your second home, as well as to create a decent nest egg for the future, no matter what your age is.

Compare the amount you'll bring in with the expense you're likely to have:

- ✔ The mortgage payment
- ✔ The property taxes
- ✔ The homeowners' insurance
- ✔ The homeowners' association fees
- ✔ The amount of money it takes to maintain and repair the home on an annual basis

Why you need to appreciate appreciation

Sometimes the appreciation in your primary home is stunning. (*Appreciation* is the increase in your home's value year after year.) I know a man who bought a lovely, two-family raised ranch in the mid-1960s for around $25,000. He sold it in 2005 for close to $400,000. Any way you look at it, that's some serious appreciation.

Because of the huge differences between houses bought 40 or so years ago and their

worth today, I hear the same exclamation all the time; whenever someone younger buys a car these days and pays, say, $27,000 for it, the person's parent, uncle, or older friend will inevitably comment, "That's more than I paid for my first house!"

Don't overlook the lifestyle changes that will come about as a result of your move. If, for example, you're an avid golfer who has lived in Michigan your entire life, then you can expect to be playing (and paying for) a lot of golf games at your North Carolina home that's situated two blocks away from a great city golf course. (Admit it: That golf course was one of the primary motivations you bought where you bought, right? Well, good for you.) If waiting a little bit for retirement ultimately means you'll be able to do more of the things you love (because it'll be easier to afford them), then it may well be worth the wait.

If, after doing these calculations, you discover that you don't have the finances you need to retire and move to your second home, don't despair. You may just have to stick around in the workforce a bit longer than you were expecting. And if you're already retired and think you may want to go back to work, *Working After Retirement For Dummies* by Lita Epstein (Wiley) can help you make that decision and find a job that's just right for you.

Are the kids out of the house?

If you and the Mister or Missus are empty nesters banging around a big ol' six-bedroom, five-bath house — of which you're only using one bedroom and one bath — then moving to your second home (particularly if it's smaller and easier to maintain) is probably a good idea.

If you find yourself facing one of the following reasons, then you may want to move:

- ✔ You just don't need all that space anymore — and it's a royal pain in the patootie to clean all those rooms and bathrooms.

> ✔ Paying for all that space and keeping up with the maintenance has been annoying your checkbook — and you're afraid she may blow.

> ✔ You'd like to be able to do your own lawn maintenance, cleaning, and repairs but you just don't have the time anymore.

Lots of moms and dads begin to consider downsizing when their kids go off to college, launch their careers, and/or start their own families. If this describes your situation, take a good look at your surroundings and lifestyle, and decide if now is the time to sell off the Ponderosa and move to Mayberry.

Are you renting your second home long term?

So you're seriously considering moving into your second home, but your renters still have six months left on their lease. You shouldn't just kick them out, but you can't let them live there forever. It's *your* house, after all.

The best approach is to talk to your renters early: as soon as you've decided to move into your second home full time. Let them know what your plans are They have rights as stated in their lease, and you have to follow them. Many leases state that as long as one party gives the other 30 days notice, and that both parties agree, then the lease can be terminated for any reason. But that's kind of harsh, if your tenants have been living in the home for years.

To avoid this kind of trauma, be completely upfront with your tenants *before* they sign a lease for the home and move in. So if you plan to retire to "their" home in five to seven years, tell your tenants. Plainly. And repeatedly, so there are no misunderstandings.

Besides preparing to break the bad news to your longtime renters that the dreaded move-out day is looming, you have to consider what impact losing that rental income will have on your finances. You'll also have to complete some paperwork to finalize the end of the relationship with your tenants. To make sure this process goes as smoothly as possible, check out "Giving your renters notice" later in this chapter for specific info.

Are you excited about moving to the area of your second home?

When you chose your second home, ideally you picked a location where you knew you would eventually want to live all the time (check out Chapter 4 for more info about your second home's location). Was it somewhere where the sand tickles your toes, where the golf course beckons every morning, or where the mountains and ski slopes seem to have been tailor-made just for you? Wherever it is, you knew it was a place you could call "home."

Moving to another country

Leaving the shores of the good ol' USA and planting roots in another country could be a book in itself, so this short sidebar just hits on some of the basic considerations that come into play when you become an expatriate and join those who have pulled up anchor and moved to another country (to gleefully mix metaphors!). (Flip to Chapter 9 for more specific considerations when buying a second home in another country.)

For starters, you want to be absolutely certain that your country of choice is indeed somewhere that you'd like to live full time. When you visit your second home monthly, quarterly, or annually, you should pay close attention to what life is like in the country.

Instead of being a tourist, be a *resident*. Take a good long look at the region and the country through the eyes of someone who lives there, and size up its strengths and weaknesses from that point of view.

Also, you must be aware of any and all paperwork associated with the move, including

- Rules for citizenship
- Visa requirements
- Passports
- Other documents that you'll need

If you've decided to live full time outside of the United States, you should talk to your financial advisor, as well as a lawyer who is experienced in naturalization and residency law. Do you want to remain a "visitor" to the foreign country and abide by periodic residency requirements? When will you be considered a naturalized citizen in the foreign country? Does naturalization have financial requirements, like establishing a bank account? Does it come with a passport or visa? Should you apply for citizenship in the foreign country? What are the tax consequences of carrying dual citizenship? Carefully consider your advisors' answers to these questions before deciding on what your official status will be in your foreign retirement country of choice.

It's also a good idea to pack light. Moving cargo overseas can be costly. And I mean costly with a capital C (even though it's got a lowercase "c," I'm making the point that . . . oh, you get it. Never mind). Check into this well ahead of time, and factor in the costs of moving items (such as automobiles, furniture, a piano, and other big things) to the new country.

As a second-home owner you have the luxury of testing the waters, both literally (if it's a beachy area) and figuratively, before moving. As long as you don't have a full-time tenant in your place, you can use your vacation time there to really dig deep and check out the surroundings. Your goal: to be absolutely certain the home is in an area where you would eventually like to live on a year-round basis.

If this isn't the case, then you may want to rethink your move. After all, the last thing you want to do is sell your primary home, pack up your stuff, move across the country, and find out that one or more of you really don't like where you've landed.

Think about all this carefully, and decide on a good time to move — or not to move — into your second home. If things don't feel *right* — and you will know that feeling, trust me — then you need to think about a different location or surroundings that are more conducive to your life and your lifestyle.

Turning an Investment into a Residence

If you've decided to move into your second home and you're currently renting it out, then it's time to turn your rental property into your home.

Although it sounds simple enough in theory — sell, pack, move, done, right? — you have to take a few key steps before you transform an investment into a home.

In this section, I help prepare you for the day when you have to wave bye-bye to your renters, give the place a good once-over, and prepare it for the day you move in.

Giving your renters notice

Longtime tenants hate to be booted out of the homes that they've funneled rent into for a year or longer. However, one day you'll want to make your second home your primary residence. When you do, remember that it's *your home,* and you can make any decisions about it you want to. You should not feel guilty about asking the renters to move. Do not fall into the trap of allowing your tenants to develop a sense of entitlement about *your place.* (It happens. I've seen it firsthand.)

When you make the decision to move to your second home (say, a year or so before you actually plan to move in), you need to gently remind your renters of the reality of their upcoming situation. This way, it won't be such a shock, and both parties will be able to handle it better. If you're friends with your tenants, or simply have a good rapport with them, then a phone call to talk things over is a nice first step and will allow you to make sure that they understand how the situation will unfold. Then follow up the call with a letter to protect yourself, in case you have to prove that you gave them ample notice.

Use the lease as a guide in giving renters notice, and remember that "too much" notice could result in an empty house that's producing no income, and "too little" could anger your tenants.

If you can't give fair warning

Unfortunately, life isn't predictable. You may face a situation where you need to move into your second home rather quickly and can't give the tenants as much notice that they have to leave as you might otherwise. For example, perhaps your primary home sold a lot faster than you thought it would, and your spouse will soon start a new job just down the street from your second home.

If you can't give fair warning, at least deal with the situation in a professional manner by trying a triple play of consideration:

✔ **Give your tenants ample time to find alternate living space.** I'd recommend at least 90 days, or whatever is specified in the lease. And even 90 days is, let's face it, not a whole lot of time to find a suitable place and move — especially if a family has become entrenched in a place for several years. For example, if you know that your tenants have talked about buying their own place, a little longer "notice" time would be a thoughtful consideration. Three months can fly by before you know it. Think about a six-month notice and put it in the lease. (See the next section for more details on this process.)

✔ **Tell your tenants that you appreciate their efforts in keeping your home neat, clean, and maintained during their time living there.** The tenants can then use this information (if you give it to them in writing) as a reference when getting a new place.

✔ **Offer to provide excellent references for them for their next landlord.** They'll need a few references, so offer up this goodwill gesture to ensure that they leave on a good note. There's nothing as convincing to a potential landlord than a rave review for the tenants from a former landlord.

In the meantime, you can rent a condo or apartment short term for your 90-day stint while you wait for your renters to vacate. Staying with family is another option, as are the new crop of "suite" hotels that offer hotel amenities with apartment-style living quarters.

Don't break the law — adhere to the lease

Just because you're the homeowner doesn't give you a right to kick out any renters on a whim. You probably signed a lease, right? (I hope you did to protect yourself and your property.) If you're ready to give your renters notice, make sure you refer to your lease.

Sixty to 90 days' notice is common, but for long-term, reliable tenants who are "settled in" this could be a tad brief. Use your best judgment for your and your tenants' situation. If you know they'd have no problem quickly moving into an apartment or another rented house, then the 60 or 90 days may work.

Talk to your real estate agent or attorney about landlord/tenant laws in your specific state. Find out what guidelines you have to follow when evicting tenants, and then follow them to avoid lawsuits during this process. Of course, you hope it doesn't come to actually needing to *evict,* but it's wise to know the specifics in case it comes to that.

As long as you don't violate the terms of the lease — or break any laws regarding landlord/tenant agreements — then you're free to move into your place whenever you want to. Sure, you can be nice and accommodating and considerate, but your and your family's needs and wants come first. It is, after all, *your* name on the mortgage, right?

Conducting post-rental inspections

After your renters have packed up and left for their new home, you need to see what condition they left your second home in by conducting a *post-rental inspection.* These inspections are important because you never really know how someone treats your home until you visit the place after they've vacated.

When you rented your second home, you should have had your renters give you a security deposit. A *security deposit* is a sum of money that you collect upon renting the home to pay for any extra cleaning or repairs required after the home is vacated. Now that you're ready to permanently move into the home and before you return the security deposit, you want to conduct a thorough inspection of your home — from the kitchen to the bathrooms to the patio — to make sure that there's no damage anywhere on the premises.

You should have your tenant(s) attend this inspection, which should take place within a few days of your tenants moving out — definitely no longer than a week. With them in attendance

- ✔ You can ask them questions on the spot about certain issues and problems you find.
- ✔ They can't say you broke the stuff after they were gone.
- ✔ They won't be shocked when you decide that you need to retain some of their security deposit.

The walk-through: Making the inspection

As you make your way through the home, ask yourself (and answer honestly): Is this damage normal wear and tear? If, for example, your tenants have been in the place for five or more years, a few smudges on the wall, a chip in the tile, an inoperable oven light, and a small stain on the carpet are just normal wear and tear and should be your responsibility to fix.

It's not fair to expect your tenants to pay to have the living room carpet cleaned with their security deposit because of a quarter-sized stain that will probably come out with spot cleaning. Be reasonable and put yourself in your tenant's position. It was their *home,* after all, not a museum.

As you make your way through the home, carefully check out the following areas:

- The front entryway, door locks, and windows
- The carpeting and flooring (and anything that may be "hiding" a problem on the floor)
- The paint (which you'll probably cover over anyway) and wall coverings
- The walls (look for excessive holes from pictures or other items) and anything that may be "hiding" a problem with the walls
- The kitchen and appliances
- All bathroom fixtures and toilets
- The home's exterior
- Any damage inflicted by pets or small children
- Anything else that catches your eye as being "just not right"

When you find damage

Create a document during the inspection process, and have the tenant sign and date it to acknowledge whatever damage you find. Make a note on this form as to who will fix the problem and where the money will come from. You have four choices:

- **The tenant's pocket:** The tenant may choose to pay for something small so she can receive the full amount of her security deposit.

  Before you hold some or all of that security deposit because of a broken dishwasher or a missing piece of tile in the bathroom, offer the tenant the opportunity to fix the problem herself. She may not want to, but you should at least extend that courtesy so she can't come back later and say you arbitrarily withheld her security deposit without giving her a chance to rectify the problem.

- **Your pocket:** You recognize the damage as coming from routine wear and tear and agree to take care of it.
- **The security deposit:** You and the tenant agree that you'll deduct an agreed-upon amount from the deposit to pay for any repairs.
- **Live with it:** Scuffed tiles, faded wallpaper, a nick in an appliance — you decide to blow off a few small things as no big deal.

Protecting an empty house

Depending on your circumstances, your second home may actually sit vacant before you move in. For example, your renters' lease expired and they moved out two months ago, but you don't retire for another two months and can't actually move in for three months. All in all, your second home will sit empty for quite some time. You'd like to avoid letting it sit empty for too long. A place empty for any length of time becomes more vulnerable to break-ins.

If your second home is going to stand empty for a while before you actually move in, make sure you do the following to protect your investment:

- ✔ **Tell your neighbors.** The more trusted souls aware that your home is vacant, the better.

- ✔ **Advise your real estate agent and/or property manager about the situation.** Both of these support people should be aware that the home will be vacant so they can help keep an eye on it for you. Even if you haven't spoken to your agent for a few years, you may want to keep him in the loop.

- ✔ **Give serious consideration to a monitored alarm system (if you don't already have one).** This is a good investment. For a few hundred dollars for equipment and installation charges, plus around $50 to $60 a month, you can have great peace of mind while living off-site.

- ✔ **Make it look like someone lives there.** Leave a low-wattage light on, and close any windows or blinds that, if left open, would clearly tell someone with nefarious ideas that this is a vacant home.

During this "empty" time, check on the home regularly — at least once or twice a month. If you can't do that, have a trusted neighbor or a real estate agent do it for you. This will help you nip any problems in the bud, instead of having to deal with a pile of problems when you're ready to move in.

I personally know of a condo owner who left his place vacant during December and January — and forgot to leave the heat on (and no one checked on the place). A pipe beneath the sink in the upstairs bathroom burst and flooded the entire unit. By the time one of his neighbors noticed water running down the outside of the unit and from under the front door, extensive damage had been done, ultimately requiring more than $100,000 in repairs.

Thinking about Remodeling and Settling In

What once looked like the perfect place for you to live during your retirement years may not be so perfect after you move in. That beach house may not really have enough storage space after all your stuff is moved in. And those "charming" old-fashioned faucets may quickly lose their charm when you begin using them all the time.

Luckily, an entire industry has sprung up to serve people like you: people who don't want to build a new house from scratch to get a home that satisfies their wants and needs.

You have several options when it comes to remodeling. These are the criteria as to how things will get done:

- ✔ How much work can you do yourself?
- ✔ How much money can you budget for the work?
- ✔ How many "handy" friends and relatives do you have? And how easily they can be coaxed (coerced? bullied? bribed?) into helping?

If you're seriously considering upgrading or remodeling your second home before you move in, this section can help by showing you how to take a second home that may not be all that conducive to full-time living and transforming it into a comfortable place to live.

Figuring out what you don't like about your second home

So you say your second home looked and felt perfect when you bought it, and it worked out well for vacations, but now that you have to live there full time, something (or, um, some *things*) just doesn't seem right?

Does the following ring a bell?

- ✔ The bathrooms feel small and cramped.
- ✔ The kitchen appliances are outdated compared to the ones you had "back home."
- ✔ The deck is showing its age.

✔ You hate the doorbell.

✔ The old-fashioned windows are no longer quaint, and, instead, have graduated to "very annoying" when you have to use them on a daily basis.

✔ The closets aren't big enough for all your stuff.

✔ You never noticed just how atrocious the carpet in the living room was.

✔ The paper towel holder in your old place was to the right of the kitchen sink, and the action of reaching to the right for all those years is now permanently imprinted on your brain — and it's driving you crazy because the paper towel holder in your new place is to the *left* of the kitchen sink. (Of such trivialities are breakdowns born!)

If the preceding items really get under your skin and drive you bonkers, you may need to consider upgrading, remodeling, or giving your second home a series of *adjustments*. Your second home is now your primary home. This is it. It's no longer "out of sight, out of mind," and so you need to do whatever is necessary to make the place as comfortable and livable as possible.

The first step is to flip to Chapter 12 for more about how to go about undertaking these types of projects no matter what your budget is. The same rules there apply when you're moving into your second home on a full-time basis, so check out that basic info.

Understand that by making these modifications now, rather than later, you'll get years of enjoyment out of your new home right away. Instead of complaining for years about the vinyl tile in the kitchen or lamenting about how you wish the home's deck were larger and better suited for entertaining, do something about it. You'll be glad you did.

Living a happy life in your second home: A checklist

Need help turning that second home into a comfortable and inviting primary home? This handy checklist of improvements and actions can help you create the perfect "home zone" for you and your family:

✔ **Clean the place up.** If you were dealing with renters, you *must* take the time to clean up after them. Renters are notorious for leaving places in somewhat of a shambles on their way out the door. Renters will mar the walls, mess up the carpeting, and put dings in your appliances. Paint the place, replace the carpeting, and fix any damage *before* you move in, if at all possible.

✔ **Put a little money into it.** There's no need to break the bank, but a few personal touches can make a rental property much more inviting and an all-around homier place. Invest in a few new pieces of furniture (both indoor and outdoor), replace those fake plants with real ones (because you'll now be on hand to water them), and take some other steps to make the home your own. Now's the time to bring out into the light of day all that stuff you've kept hidden for years in the *owner's closet* (that locked closet where you stored private belongings that you didn't want your renters to use or have access to).

✔ **Prepare yourself for the downsize.** If you're moving into a smaller home, prepare yourself by bringing only those items that you truly can't live without. Put the rest in storage or sell the stuff on eBay or at a garage sale (see Chapter 16). Otherwise, you'll find yourself crowded by piles of books, knick-knacks, accent tables, pillows, and antiques that simply don't fit in your new surroundings.

✔ **Create a lifestyle around it.** If the home you're retiring to is more than a few hours' drive time from your previous home, you may find yourself wanting for friends and family not long after moving away. To avoid this woefulness, schedule time for your friends and family to visit you, and also set up return visits "back home." Also, don't forget to get out and make new friends in your new neighborhood (see Chapter 16).

✔ **Tap your new area's amenities.** It's easy to get caught up in remodeling projects that take up 12 hours a day, but don't forget to take some time out to familiarize yourself with your surroundings, enjoy the sights, decide on a favorite grocery store, and locate the closest movie theater, museum, library, bookstore, and performing arts center. The sooner you find a few favorite haunts, the quicker you'll become acclimated and can enjoy your new *primary* home.

Considering Important Income and Tax Issues with Only One Residence

After you sell your primary home and move into your second home, you'll be free from having to pay two mortgages, two property tax bills, and two home-owners' insurance tabs every year. However, you'll also be losing any rental income that you've gotten used to over the years, as well as the tax deductions that were tied to the maintenance, upkeep, and insurance on your second home.

So the bottom line is that your financial situation will almost certainly change as a result of this move, so be sure to plan ahead. In this section, I advise you on what key financial factors to consider before making your move.

Losing the rental income

One of the first things you'll lose when you take your second home off the rental market is those lovely rent checks you've become accustomed to finding in your mailbox every month in exchange for letting others use your home.

As a second-home owner, you probably received a monthly rent check from a full-time, year-round tenant; a stack of weekly and monthly rental checks during the high season (and fewer checks during the low season); or a steady stream of checks throughout the year from tenants who rented from you during both the low and high seasons.

To offset your loss, keep the following pointers in mind:

- **Make the time between the last rental and your moving date as short as possible.** That way you won't have to cover two mortgages out of your own bank account for any longer than necessary.

- **Put your primary home on the market well in advance of the move.** Doing so assures that you're not suddenly paying out-of-pocket for two mortgages at once. (Yikes!)

- **Prepare adequately for the day the final rent check arrives.** Resolve yourself to the fact that you knew the day would come when that flow of checks would stop. Now it's time to pay for the mortgage on your second home (soon to be your first) on your own, without the help of a rent check. Before you make the break, go over your financial situation (income versus expenses) and be sure that you can cover the additional expenses every month.

To counter the expected loss of rental income, consider the two possible scenarios:

- **The right way to do it:** Give renters (or the real estate agent who is handling the short-term rental schedule) 90 days' notice to vacate your property (or however long you've decided to give your renters, based on the circumstances). Put your primary home on the market at the same time. This way, you'll have three (or more) months to sell your primary home, get your renters moved out, and get yourself moved in. (See the "Giving your renters notice" section earlier in this chapter for more details about this.)

  If this sounds too rushed, depending on your individual circumstances and your feelings toward your renters, add another month or two to the schedule. If you're in a hot real estate market and your house is guaranteed to sell within a week, then shorten the amount of time your house is on the market.

> ✔ **The painful way to do it:** Decide overnight that it's time to move, put your primary home on the market the following day, and ask renters to vacate within 30 days.
>
> I have nothing against spontaneity, but this approach can backfire on you pretty quickly and leave you stuck with an empty home in one hand and a home — possibly still carrying a mortgage — that's not selling in the other. In that case, you'll be standing there like blindfolded Lady Justice herself, a mortgaged house on each side of the scale, and no way to make things balance out.

Before you sell your primary home and move into your second home, give your finances an honest look. Consider what you're gaining and what you're losing, and make sure that things even out — or, ideally, work in your favor — before you make your move. That will help you avoid nasty surprises down the road.

Shifting your mortgage interest deduction from your first home to your second home

One of the income tax perks American homeowners enjoy is the *mortgage interest deduction*. (This deduction allows you to deduct the amount of mortgage interest paid to a lender in any given year. Check out Chapter 14 for more info.) It's so beneficial, in fact, that I know people who could easily pay off their mortgages in one fell swoop but opt not to because then they would miss out on the deduction.

But you're different. As a second-home owner who was renting out your home, you deducted the mortgage interest on your primary home on your Schedule A, Itemized Deductions form, and the mortgage interest you paid on your second home on your Schedule E, Supplemental Income and Loss form.

After you sell your primary home and move into your second home, this scenario changes. Now the mortgage interest you pay on your former investment property becomes a Schedule A deduction and you no longer file Schedule E — because you no longer have an *income-producing property*.

If you're unsure of how to make the switch on your returns, check with your accountant or tax attorney for details and the most current information available.

Chapter 16

Selling Your Primary Residence and Settling into Your Second Home

*Y*ou've circled the date in red marker on your calendar, you think about it every day, and you're doing everything you can to prepare for that time when your *second* home becomes your *only* home. But before you can make that clean break, you need to sell your existing home.

Depending on the state of the current real estate market, the condition of your home, and prevailing interest rates, selling your place could take as little as a week or as long as a year or more. I know the idea of a year's worth of showings is not a pleasant thought, but it's the reality of the cyclical real estate market, so it's important you know all the facts — and be prepared for whatever comes your way.

In this chapter, I discuss the process of selling your first home and coordinating the selling/moving so you don't have to rent an apartment for a month while waiting for the tenants in your second home to move out. I also explain home staging and how to use it to your best advantage so you'll be ready for the day the truck backs into your driveway to load up your stuff.

Putting Your Primary Home on the Market

Exactly when you put your home on the market, and how you do it, can influence how quickly it sells and at what price. If, for example, you wait until the last possible minute to sell — and if you opt to stick a FSBO (for sale by owner) sign in the yard — you may wind up negotiating hard with a buyer who knows that you're in a rush and that you don't have professional representation who can provide the solid reasons to stay as close to your asking price as possible. If, on the other hand, you plan your move carefully, work with an agent, and give yourself plenty of time to mull offers and make a decision, then not only will the process be less stressful, but you can stick to your asking price and not feel pressured to lower it because you're in a hurry.

In this section, I discuss some of the basics that you need to know when selling your primary home. For a more detailed discussion of all these points, pick up a copy of *House Selling For Dummies,* 2nd Edition, by Eric Tyson and Ray Brown (Wiley).

Using a real estate agent

If you've lived in your neighborhood or city for any length of time, you probably know at least one real estate agent who would be happy to list your home for sale. A real estate agent will hold open houses, advertise your home in the paper, submit the listing to the local Multiple Listing Service, snap photos, create virtual tours, and take other steps to get the home sold. Plus, she is always there on the other end of the phone when you have questions.

Uncovering the right agent to sell your house

Finding the right real estate agent who can help you sell your primary home is essential because they're not all alike. Some have more experience than others, some specialize in specific types of homes, some only sell commercial properties, and some are in the real estate business as a part-time job (rather than a full-time career). All this matters when it comes to deciding on who will represent your home.

If you don't know a real estate agent, ask friends and family for referrals, and take a walk or drive around your neighborhood and check out the "For Sale" yard signs. Make a note of which agents seem to be offering lots of homes in the area. This is usually a good indication of which agents are best to work with in a certain community or neighborhood. These folks know the area and will likely be a big help to you. (Chapter 6 provides more info about how agents work, how they're paid, and what to expect from this temporary, albeit very important relationship.)

After you have the names of a few real estate agents to contact, use this handy list of questions to interview at least three agents to determine what marketing efforts they use, their track record, and how you feel about working with them.

- ✔ **Are you a full-time real estate agent?** You don't want to work with someone who does real estate on the side. Why? Because it's common knowledge in the industry that the agent who isn't at her clients' beck and call 24/7 doesn't do the same volume of business as a full-timer, nor does she have the extensive expertise and scope of experience that a full-time agent does. Of course, there are part-time agents who are competent, reliable, and professional, and I'm not knocking them. I'm simply talking about opting for the most experienced agent, and they are almost always the full-timers.

- ✔ **How long have you been a licensed real estate agent?** Try to get someone who has been in the business for five years or more. The longer, the better.

- ✔ **Are you an MLS (Multiple Listing Service) member?** Today, most agents are, but ask anyway. (The *MLS* is the database in which all the agent-represented listings from a specific region are compiled.) Without a listing on the MLS, your home won't get the exposure you'll want and need to sell at the right price and within a desirable period of time.

- ✔ **How familiar are you with my community and neighborhood?** Someone who doesn't know the lay of the land probably isn't a good candidate because she won't know what types of homes have sold there recently, the differences between them, and the socioeconomic makeup of the area (all families, lots of kids; all retired, no kids; lots of singles; and so forth). If yours is the first home in the area she would be listing, keep looking.

- ✔ **How many homes did you sell in this area in the past year?** The average is 12 homes per year, although most top-selling agents far exceed that volume. Even during the slow times, a top-notch agent will move properties, so don't get hung up on the number of homes the agent has sold, but rather that she has been selling, period.

- ✔ **How frequently will you advertise and market my home?** What Internet sites will you list my home on? Will my home be highlighted with pictures, a banner ad, and standout headers? Will you have a virtual tour of my home on the Web site? Will it be listed on the MLS? Will you advertise it in the newspaper? Will it be listed in local homes magazines? Will you host an open house? How will you market my house to local agents? The more exposure, the better. Skip an agent who skimps on advertising.

✔ **How will you keep me apprised of my home's selling progress?** If you like regular phone calls, ask for them. If you prefer e-mail, ask for those. If the agent's answer boils down to, "I'll let you know when I have something to tell you, otherwise you'll never hear from me," move on.

✔ **Can you give me the names of three of your recent clients to call for references?** If the agent hesitates, say "Next!"

If you find an agent who fills the bill and whom you feel comfortable with, the next step is to sign a listing agreement with her. Most agents will ask for a six-month listing period, although you may be able to get a three-month stint. It doesn't hurt to ask. The benefit of a shorter contract is that the agent will know she may lose the listing at the end of the period if she's not performing. It's a motivational tool. The downside is that moving from agent to agent every three months until the house is sold doesn't give you a chance to develop a stable working relationship with any one agent. Twelve weeks go by in a flash.

Negotiating your agent's commission

Real estate commissions are negotiable and average about 5 percent nationwide. In some areas, they can go as high as 7 percent, and in others, they will be as low as 3 percent. Talk to your agent about the "going rate" first, and then negotiate down from there. Understand that agents usually have a "typical" commission rate in mind before they even start talking to you, and that *full-service agents* (those who handle the entire deal — from listing the home in the MLS to sitting next to you at the closing table) will probably insist on their full rate (and justify it accordingly, sometimes with a list of 100 or more tasks that they handle during the deal).

That said, however, you should definitely negotiate your agent's real estate commission, because the standard 6 or 7 percent rates don't apply in all areas anymore. Because of the Internet, there are no secrets about real estate commissions these days, which in this case can work to your advantage. A massive amount of industry information is available on the Web, and this has led to the growth of *discount brokers* who will list homes at a very low rate. Traditional agents are recognizing this competition, and yours may be willing to lower her commission as a result.

The practice of discounting agent commissions has become so prevalent that some agents are now putting the phrase "Full Service 3%" (or whatever rate they charge) on their signs. I have seen these signs, and their presence truly speaks to a sea change in the industry. Ten or 15 years ago, you would have never seen a commission rate advertised on a "For Sale" sign.

If you decide to use a discount broker, be sure to check what services the agent is offering you. Some states have recently adopted new disclosure laws mandating a written disclosure of the services a discount broker is waiving and the signed acknowledgement of these waivers by the seller.

Advice from every direction on setting your asking price

Where does the asking price on a home come from? How do you figure out what to ask? Prices come from many different sources — and some of these sources are not quite as knowledgeable and informed as others. For example:

- ✔ **Your real estate agent:** You should give her suggestion for a selling price great weight. Why? Because a savvy agent will generally *not* take on an over-priced homestead if she can help it. Her suggested price is usually based on actual sales of comparable homes in the area within the past year.

- ✔ **The guy next door:** He swears his home (which is almost identical to the one you're selling) is worth $750,000, so your home must be worth at least that.

- ✔ **A professional appraiser:** This person comes in and does a thorough, presale evaluation of the home's condition and size

and then compares it to recent sales. His price is probably the most accurate number possible.

- ✔ **A well-meaning parent:** Your mom and dad think your home is worth much, much more than the market will bear because, after all, you are incredibly special and that unquestionably applies to everything in your life — including the value of your home.

- ✔ **A free Web site:** Sites such as www. zillow.com provide home values for properties nationwide by street address. With a few clicks, you can find out what the house next door, across town, or across the country is worth based on prior sales. It's a valuable tool but not always spot-on regarding realistic values in terms of selling prices.

Negotiating an agent's commission is both a science and an art. You want to shoot for an agreement that entices your agent to agree to the lower commission and yet still work just as hard for you. Both sides want the best possible deal, so compromises are the tool when it comes to agreeing on a commission. Perhaps you find an agent you like, but you think her asking rate of 7 percent is too high. You base this opinion on what other agents are offering, or on the fact that Internet and discount brokers charge considerably less than their full-service counterparts. Talk to your agent about her commission. Maybe you offer her 3 percent. That's too low for her liking, so you split the difference and settle on 5 percent. Everybody's happy.

If, however, you're adamant about a 3 percent commission, and the agent simply refuses to work for that low a rate, then shake hands and say, "Thanks for your time" and find a discount broker. Bear in mind, though, that a stubborn attitude about fee ignores lots of other variables that are important, including the skills and experience of the agent. It's a cliché, but in many cases, you do get what you pay for.

FSBO: Selling your home on your own

If you've already bought or sold a home without the help of an agent, then you may want to stick a FSBO sign in the front yard and wait for potential buyers to come to your door. This is the for-sale-by-owner approach, and it's a strategy that many homeowners have opted for with good results.

It's not for everyone, but if you're game, just realize that when you go FSBO, you're your own agent, so to speak. With that comes all the work an agent would do for you, from showings and advertising to dealing with a potential buyer's real estate agent. However, if you've got the time, energy, and motivation, you can try it alone for a while and then call an agent if it doesn't work out for you.

It's a simple enough process to get started: Put the sign on your lawn. Then you can craft an advertising plan and prepare for potential buyers to get in touch. Make sure you've got plenty of time carved out for a few months when you go the FSBO route.

Considering important issues when selling

Whether you use a real estate agent or you sell your primary home on your own, you want to make sure you maximize your profit. You obviously don't want to lose money when you sell your place. At the same time, you also want to give yourself enough time to list your house, sell it, and move to your second home. As a result, you need to consider the following questions that can help you determine when you should put your home on the market.

When should you list your home?

Figuring out when exactly to list your home is a fine line to walk. If you list it too quickly and it sells while you still have tenants renting your second home, you may have to rent some temporary living space for yourself until your renters move out. If you wait to list your home until your tenants have moved out, and then it takes a long time to sell, you can put yourself in a financial pinch by having to pay two mortgages without any rental income coming in. No matter what, make sure you give yourself at least a 90-day window to sell your home.

So how do you walk this fine line? First, take a careful look at your local real estate market. Ask your agent for the latest news on the following points before you put your place on the market:

✔ **How quickly are homes selling right now?** Your agent can answer this question by checking the "days on market" numbers provided by the local MLS. FSBO sellers can get the most recent quarter or year's information from their local Board of Realtors. Find a listing of them at the National Association of Realtors Web site (www.realtors.org).

✔ **How close to asking price are these homes selling for?** This is an important point for anyone looking to score the maximum price within a specific or limited time frame.

After you have the answers to these questions, look at Table 16-1 to figure out which of the four categories your home falls into.

Table 16-1	Four Categories of Real Estate Markets		
Market Type	*Home's Time on Market*	*Home's Selling Price*	*When to List Your Home*
Hot: Low inventory; lots of competition among buyers	1–2 weeks	At or above asking price	1–2 months before you plan to move
Leveling or stabilizing: Inventory is increasing but not drastically; same number of buyers as sellers	1–2 months	At or just below asking price	3–5 months before you plan to move
Stagnant or soft: Many homes on market; sellers compete for buyers	6-12 months	At or below asking price	6–12 months before you plan to move
Declining: Inventory is high; buyers rule the roost	12-18 months	Well below asking price	Wait to sell your home, if you can

Based on market conditions, the advice of your agent, and your sense of how "in demand" your home will be when it hits the market (and you will develop this sense, trust me), you'll then need to decide on a time frame that meets your needs, but still works within the inevitable market forces that affect selling time, price, and your peace of mind.

If, for example, the market right now is favorable for sellers, and if you don't want to move out for another six months, then you'll want to put your house on the market in about two months. This gives your agent about 16 weeks to find a suitable buyer and close the deal, which should be plenty of time.

What if you sell your primary home before your second home is available?

Face it: Moving twice is a pain. So it's to your best advantage to try to time it so you sell your primary home and immediately move into your second home. But sometimes the right offer comes at the wrong time. What happens if your home sells more quickly than you anticipated, and your second home isn't ready for you? You can't exactly tell the prospective buyer, "no thanks," shrug off the situation, and wait for a similar offer to come along later when you *are* ready to move.

When you put your house on the market, you take the risk of having it sold before you're actually ready to move out. Sometimes this may be out of your control (the buyer's timetable figures into this, too, remember), but in many cases you can avoid this situation through good planning to figure out the best time to list your house. If you score a buyer and you're not ready to move, you can always consider short-term rental options or even bunking with family temporarily until your second home is available to you. (For information on how to prepare your second home and its tenants for your move-in date, flip to Chapter 15.)

If you do find yourself in this circumstance, you have to make a quick decision. You have to figure out what to do with your personal belongings and furniture — as well as yourself — while you wait for your second home to be ready for occupancy. You can

- ✔ **Put your stuff in mini-storage for $60 to $80 a month and stay with a friend or relative.** This solution is only short term. This plan works best for second-home owners whose place will be ready in under a month.

- ✔ **Rent an apartment short term.** If you have to wait longer than a month or two, you can move into an apartment and take your essential stuff with you. You can put the rest of your belongings in a mini-storage facility. Short-term storage is great, and you can use it as a staging area for when you finally do move.

Ideally, the length of time you have to wait to move into your second home won't exceed a month or two. Longer that that can make everyone testy.

How to determine whether to hold off on selling?

Although you're eager to move into your second home, sometimes you may want to wait to sell your primary home. For many, this option may be financially unrealistic, but for others, carrying two mortgages while the situation settles won't be a problem. Another option is to rent out your primary home and move to your second home, thus ensuring that you continue to generate rental income to cover at least one of your mortgages.

REAL LIFE EXAMPLE

Be careful about rushing into selling your home

Before you rush into selling your home, you may want to take a deep breath and think twice. I learned a valuable lesson a few years ago.

After I saw a large home for sale at the right price in a prestigious neighborhood, I made an offer and it was accepted. The sellers were in a rush, so the home closed within ten business days. On the other side of the move, my husband stuck a "For Sale" sign in the front yard of our existing home and sold it to a neighbor within an hour. Yes, I said within an hour: By the time I got back from the gym on a Sunday morning, the house was sold. To make things even more complicated, we were leaving for a one-month vacation in Hawaii in two weeks, so both transactions had to be wrapped up — at the seller and buyer's requests, not mine — quickly. It all worked out, though, and 14 days later my family and I were on a big bird flying to Honolulu.

The moral of the story is this: When you find the right home — or, if you're selling, the right buyer — go for it. Four years later I have no regrets. Sure, it was an insane two-week period of closing table visits and moving vans, but in the end, it was all worth it.

Everyone's situation is different, so here are a few scenarios that may warrant putting your home-selling plans in a holding pattern:

- ✔ **The real estate market is on the upswing:** If your agent tells you that home prices have increased 10 percent in the last three months, and that there's no end in sight, you should seriously consider selling at a later date. Set a target "For Sale" date based on your own timetable and finances. Keep your eyes open, though, and monitor the real estate market to avoid waiting *too* long and coming in at the tail end of the boom.

- ✔ **The real estate market is tanking:** If you know you'll take a loss on your home because the market has tanked, then hold off on selling during this period if at all possible. The market is cyclical, and it will bounce back at some point. It always does. How long you wait depends on what stage the market is at, so ask your real estate agent for some "from the front lines" advice on this one.

- ✔ **You're unsure about the move into your second home:** If you feel that you need a "trial run" at your second home, and if you can afford both mortgages and the associated expenses for a while, then by all means, wait to put out that "For Sale" sign. Be sure, though, to give yourself three to six months to get acclimated to your new place before you go running back home! If, after that period, you're still not happy there, then you'll know you made the right decision not to sell your primary home.

Your real estate agent is in business to sell homes, so don't rely solely on him to answer the question "Should I sell now?" with your best interest in mind. The odds are you'll hear, "Sure! Let's talk turkey!" Be sure to talk to other reliable sources, and look at the market and your situation carefully before signing that listing agreement.

Getting the Best Possible Price

Every seller wants the highest possible price for his home, and every buyer wants to pay the lowest possible price for the house she's buying. And as with all things, compromise is the name of the game. Working on opposite sides of the table, eager buyers and motivated sellers will slowly come to terms, hopefully creating a win-win situation for both parties.

In this section, I provide you with a few strategies to boost your home's value in the eyes of potential buyers. I also offer some tips on how to handle price reductions.

Determining a competitive price

When selling your primary home, do *everything you can* to score the best possible price for your place. Develop a close relationship with your real estate agent, communicate your needs, and take a proactive role. Do the following to ensure that you get top dollar for your home:

- ✔ **Conduct the necessary research (or have your real estate agent do it for you).** You want to determine what homes of the same size, age, and in the same general location are selling for. This will give you a good idea of exactly what is selling and for what price.

- ✔ **Verify that your house is "up to par" with those other homes before you decide on an asking price and post it on the MLS.** This will help you see exactly where your home will stand on the market.

As always, market conditions come into play. In a hot market, you may get away with selling a home at top dollar as is, even if it's in sore need of a paint job and new carpeting. In a flat market, however, that won't be as easy, and in a declining market, it'll be even more difficult. Keep all of this in mind as you put your home up for sale. (See the "When should you list your home?" section, earlier in this chapter, for more about the types of markets.)

The mother of home staging

Barb Schwarz, president of StagedHomes.com of San Francisco, came up with the idea of staging homes. Schwarz says she invented staging back in 1972 before anyone had assigned a label to the "home prep" process.

Today, Schwarz holds the registered trademark on the word "stage" as it pertains to preparing homes for sale. She speaks often on the subject

and, in 1998, developed an Accredited Staging Professional (ASP) course. The two-day course costs $295 and provides classroom-based instruction on anything and everything having to do with home staging.

For more info, check out `www.staged homes.com`.

Sprucing up your home

Real estate agents have been sprucing up homes and making helpful suggestions since the industry was born, but over the last few years, home staging has really caught on. *Home staging* is the deliberate sprucing up of a home to make it visually appealing to potential buyers. This includes steps like planting flowers in the front yard; removing clutter in each room; replacing drab bed coverings with new, attractive ones; replacing clunky old furniture with better-looking pieces; opening blinds, curtains, and shades during a showing; and adding stylish planters to the bathrooms and foyer. The focus is on space, light, color, and comfort.

Don't think you have to stage your home all at once. Make a few key changes, and then wait for agents to provide feedback from buyers after showings. For example, if more than one looker comments on the two small holes in the screen door, it's time to get it fixed.

Keep the following basics of home staging in mind as you prepare your home for sale. Just call them the three Cs:

- ✔ **Cleanliness:** Your home needs to be clean before you show it. To clean it properly, either hire a cleaning service or spend the weekend going from room to room cleaning any and all surfaces, floors, fixtures, bathtubs, ceiling fans . . . the list goes on.

  If your home needs a thorough top-to-bottom, every-nook-and-cranny cleaning, hire a cleaning service. The money will be well spent.

- ✔ **Clutter-free:** Pack up as much of your stuff as you can and put it in storage. One person's treasure is another person's clutter. You want to highlight your home and its architectural features, not your junk.

> ✔ **Color:** A few $5 cans of paint can make a significant difference in a home's appearance. You'd be amazed at the results you can get from a few coats of color. It's one of the cheapest DIY investments on today's real estate market!

By taking these relatively simple preemptive measures, you can effectively boost your home's value and make it stand out in a way that makes buyers sit up and take notice. Some of these projects can be completed for free, and in just a few hours, while others will take more time and effort. In the end, though, the time and energy you spend will be worth the effort when the offers start coming in — and they're as close to your asking price as the market will bear!

Compromising on the price

Your primary house is on the market, and you've done everything you can to ensure that you maximize your profit. However, sometimes you may need to compromise on your asking price if you really want to sell.

Ideally, you don't have to consider lowering the price until the *negotiation stage*. That's when you and the buyer negotiate, either one on one or through your respective agents, to come to an agreement on both selling price and terms.

Depending on the market, though, this compromise may come before you even receive an offer. For example, say that ten couples have walked through your place during the course of a month and you haven't received a single offer. Barring any other unforeseen factors, you may need to lower your price to a level that the market will bear.

Before you decide to compromise on the price, consider exactly *why* lower (or no) offers are coming in and what you can do about it. Listen to feedback from those who have walked through the house, pick your agent's brain (if you're using one), and use all this info to make smart decisions about how to improve the look and feel of your abode. This may help you get closer to your asking price. Of course, market forces will play a huge role, but you should work to make your house *worth* what you're asking. Then it'll simply be a decision as to how much less you're willing to accept, knowing that you've done all *you* can to maximize its perceived value.

Your real estate agent will probably ask you to review your asking price every four to six weeks and will likely ask you to reduce the price by 5 to 10 percent each time, again, depending on market conditions. If the house is in beautiful shape and in a hot market, you may not have to come down in price. But if the house isn't *showing well,* as we say in the biz, plus you're trying to sell in a faltering market, then you may need to reduce your price.

Looking good = $$$

One real estate agent I know shares the following tips with his home sellers whenever they ask him, "What can I do to get the best price for my property?" (Thanks, pal!)

Outside

✔ Put a new doormat at the home's entry.

✔ Put up a new mailbox and post, especially if yours is ratty or aged.

✔ Add mulch to your flower beds and around shrubs.

✔ Paint, stain, or varnish the front door, polish the brass, and install a new brass kick plate.

Foyer

✔ Make sure it's clean and not cluttered with furniture.

✔ Clean the light fixtures.

✔ Clean and polish the hardwood or tile floor until it shines.

✔ Add a small entrance table and a vase filled with fresh flowers.

Family/living/great room

✔ Put away all your collections, especially the fragile items such as pewter, crystal, or ceramic figurines.

✔ Store all political and religious mementos, as well as any business, sports, and personal awards. Remember: You want prospective buyers to easily imagine *themselves,* not you, living in the home.

✔ Remove as much "crowding" furniture as possible; open the room up and show lots of space.

Use the "rule of three:" Place no more than three items on any flat surface. This rule applies to every room in the house.

Dining room

✔ Take the extra leaf out of the table and put on a nice white tablecloth.

✔ Place a pretty fruit or flower arrangement in the center of the table.

Kitchen

✔ Remove all refrigerator magnets and "bulletin board" items.

✔ Take down your grandchildren's artwork. (Yes, I know you have some up there!)

✔ Stow in the cabinets all the smaller appliances that you normally leave out to free up counter space. Remember: space, space, space.

Bathrooms

✔ Downplay that dated ceramic tile with white towels, pretty window treatments, and colorful scatter rugs.

✔ Replace a rusted sink or, if that's not possible, touch up the rust spots.

✔ Repair or replace that defective exhaust fan or any cracked mirrors.

Bedrooms

✔ Remove as much bulky furniture as possible. Voilà! The room looks bigger!

✔ Clean out the closets so it appears as if there's lots of room to spare.

Garage/basement

✔ Remove as many stains as possible from the garage floor.

✔ Clean all the windows.

✔ Remove the cobwebs from the corners. (Yes, you have some. Trust me.)

Screened porch

✔ Repair all the holes in the screens, or replace the screens completely.

✔ Make sure that your outdoor furniture is clean and orderly and that the porch isn't overcrowded with tables and chairs.

Discuss all of your options and alternatives before reducing your price. Lowering your asking price indicates to potential buyers that you're more motivated to sell and that you may settle for an even lower price — even though you've already decided you're as low as you're going to go. Depend on the guidance of your real estate agent or another professional to determine which strategy will work best in your particular situation.

Moving Your Stuff

Moving an entire home from one place to another is disruptive, stressful, confusing, tedious, but it can also be worth all the hassle. When planning to move to your second home, you have plenty of decisions to make and factors to consider. For example, what are you going to do with your furniture and clothing, as well as household items and all that stuff that has piled up in the garage, and in the basement, and in the attic, and in the closets over the last few years? (And believe me when I tell you that you *will* ask yourself — more than once — "Where did all this stuff come from?!")

In this section, I give you some handy tips for packing up your primary home and moving everything to your second abode. I show you why list making is a good thing, tell you what to move yourself, and advise you on when you need to hire a mover. Also, I walk you through a handy moving-day checklist that will be a big help when you make your own move.

Purge what you don't need

Are you ready to jump into packing everything? Do you have tons of boxes and bubble wrap to protect your items? Before you do anything about your upcoming move, start with a big inhale, hold it, and then slowly exhale. Now it's time to start cracking. I want to reiterate the most important packing lesson I can offer you: *Purge before you pack.* That means throwing out, selling, or giving away everything that you no longer need or want.

Purging is particularly important if you already have a fully furnished second home to move into, because you simply won't need to duplicate all those end tables and dining room chairs that are already in place at your new home.

Determining what to purge

You know you have a lot of extra junk and stuff that you don't want to move, but how can you determine what to purge and what to keep? Work your way through your house, room by room, and consider the following:

✔ **Will this actually fit in my second home?** If you're downsizing, it may not, so now may be a good time to get rid of it.

✔ **Will it match the décor in my second home?** This may not be that big a deal, but you should think about it. A heavy, ornate, dark wood Elizabethan armoire may not look very good in the sunroom of a beach house, for example.

✔ **Is this something that I really want to keep?** Items with sentimental value will ultimately be given a pass regarding their likely "fit" — regardless of whether they match the rest of the décor. Grandma's mahogany accent table may be jarringly out of place in your new contemporary condo, but so what?

✔ **Is this something that I can sell at a garage sale or easily dispose of in another way?** If you know a particular piece would be snapped up if offered for sale, you may want to consider saying bye-bye to it.

✔ **Is this an old item that should have been replaced years ago?** If your answer is "It sure is!", then bite the bullet and put it out on the curb or schlep it to the dump.

✔ **Is this something that I haven't touched in years, and that I probably won't touch or use for at least another five years?** If your answer is, "I forgot I even had this thing!", then chuck it.

As you evaluate your belongings, put each item on a "yes," "no," or "maybe" list. Items on the "yes" list will get a new home; stuff on the "no" list is outta here (see the "What to do with your purged items" section for suggestions); and things on the "maybe" list just may get a second chance.

When you create your "yes" list, organize items by room. Have one page for the kitchen, another for the family room, and so forth. Then whoever is packing up each room can use the appropriate list as a reference.

Taking the plunge and purging your stuff

In the previous section, I suggested making lists of what to keep, what to toss, and what you weren't sure what to do with. Your lists will help you speed through the purging process:

1. **Grab some boxes, decide where each one will go (see the next section), and mark it accordingly.**

   You don't want any of the stuff you've already said *adios* to making an appearance at your second home, so it's especially important to label each box's end destination.

2. **Take your "no-go" list and go through the attic, garage, every closet and cabinet, the kitchen, bedrooms, bathrooms, and outdoor spaces gathering up what didn't make the cut.**

3. **Put items in their appropriate boxes.**

   You don't have to pack things by room when you purge. You can put all of your too-big clothes, the kids' old but useable toys, and that old iron in one box for Goodwill; put all of your unwanted books, video games, and DVDs in a box for your brother; and so on.

You can approach the purge process with enthusiasm — "Yay! Look at all the stuff I'm getting rid of (and maybe I can buy new, better stuff)." — or you can tackle it with sadness — "I'm gonna miss you, little Valentine's Day card from 1983." Either way, when you start moving boxes, ultimately you'll be glad that you decided not to save *everything*.

The kitchen is always the hardest room to pack, because you have to individually wrap *all* the breakable items (and there are, my friends, *lots* of breakable items in every kitchen!). By purging what you don't want, you'll have a much easier time packing up whatever remains when the time comes to do so.

What to do with your purged items

When you purge, you may be wondering what to do with all this extra stuff that you don't need or want. Well, you can

- ✔ **Donate it.** Groups like the Vietnam Veterans of America (online at `www.vva.org`) have a presence in most cities nationwide. These groups pick up household items, clothing, toys, games, and other items that you may not need or want but are still in good condition. They'll usually come right to your doorstep to pick up the goods. These types of groups typically work on a schedule — they pick up in certain neighborhoods on specific days — so contact your local chapter for more information. Be sure to ask for a receipt. Your donations are tax deductible!

- ✔ **Give it to friends and family.** If you're moving from Massachusetts to Florida, you can probably get rid of much of your winter clothing, although you'll want to keep a few important garments for visits up north.

- ✔ **Sell it.** If you wind up with enough good stuff to sell, you can put it in the local classifieds, list it on eBay, or have a garage sale. Don't ignore this way to raise a few bucks (it's even possible to generate enough cashola to fund your entire move) and unload some still-useable merchandise at the same time.

- ✔ **Store it.** You may have some items that you absolutely want to keep, but that you don't need right away and that won't fit into your new home, such as that extra set of golf clubs, your luggage set(s), and that extra-long surfboard. Mini-storage at $60 to $80 a month is a good option.

- ✔ **Throw it away.** That exercise bike with the broken chain that you've sworn you'll get fixed must go. You know you'll never fix it, and even when it was working, you know you never rode it.

Don't try to pack absolutely everything and then try to figure out what to keep, what to give away, what to toss, and so on when you get to your new home. This strategy will drive you crazy and add to the stress and confusion that comes with a major move. Instead, take the time to figure out early precisely what you want to do with your stuff.

Packing what you plan to keep

After you've decided the fate of most, if not all, of your belongings (see the "Purge what you don't need" section), use your "yes" list to start packing the furniture, household goods, clothing, personal goods, and decorations that you want to take with you.

Furniture is usually transported as is, or it can be wrapped in plastic for protection. How far it's traveling, in what type of vehicle, and just how valuable the item is will determine how you pack and ship it.

If you want to save your sanity, take a pencil and paper and make a scale drawing of each of the important rooms in your second home. Then measure the furniture you want to take with you and draw it in place on the appropriate room's page. Doing so not only assures you that the furniture will fit, but it will be a helpful guide when marking each piece and identifying it for the movers so they'll know which room to place it in at the new location.

You can pack the rest of your stuff in cardboard boxes (mini-storage facilities sell them for $3 to $6 a box, depending on size), or place items in large plastic totes (which come in all sizes but are a bit more expensive than boxes, ranging from $8 to $15 each).

As you pack your boxes, write on them what they contain and the room they'll go in at your new home. This way, when you and/or your movers get there, the boxes and items can be immediately placed right where they belong. Use a marker and masking tape (for totes and other items) or write directly on the cardboard boxes that you're transporting.

When you come to an item that's on your "maybe" list, put it aside until you figure out whether you'll have room for it. Take a second look at all the items at that point, and choose those that you truly want before putting them in the back of the van. Be hardhearted.

Moving yourself or hiring movers?

Whether you move all your belongings yourself or hire someone to help you depends on the following factors:

✔ How far away you're moving

✔ How much stuff needs to be moved

✔ How many friends and family you have (on both sides of the family and both ends of the trip) who are willing to help you load and unload the items

✔ Whether there are impediments (such as flights of stairs or elevators) on either end of the move

✔ Your own personal preference about hiring someone to do a job versus doing it yourself (Control freaks, you know who you are!)

If you're a do-it-yourselfer by nature, then by all means, rent the appropriate-size moving truck and start loading it up. (The number of rooms that you're moving determines truck size.)

If you're moving a relatively short distance, or in some cases, even to another state, doing it yourself is probably the most economical (but not necessarily the fastest) way to get the job done. If you're transporting heavy, bulky furniture, though, you're better off with a pro.

If you're moving a far distance and taking everything, hiring a professional mover can make moving easier. Movers fall into two categories:

✔ **Short-haul or "small" movers:** These folks usually work locally, moving people within a 10-mile radius (give or take a few miles) of their home base. These are the outfits that are usually local, and the company name is often a first or family name, like "Mike's Moving," or "Smith Brothers Moving."

To find these types of movers, check your local Yellow Pages, or use a Web site like www.emove.com, which will provide you with a list of short-haul movers in your area.

✔ **Long-haul movers:** These companies do exactly what it sounds like they do — they move residences and companies over long distances. Rates vary for their services, and you should get a quote from at least three companies before deciding on one to hire for your move.

These types of companies are also listed in the Yellow Pages, or you can check out a Web site like www.moving.com for more information on how to find a mover, get a rate quote, and hire a company to help you.

Moving companies offer a variety of services that go beyond just picking up and dropping off goods. For example, most also offer the following services for an additional fee:

✔ Packing up your primary home

✔ Unpacking at your second home

Get covered when you move

If you've decided to hire a moving company to move your household, be sure to buy an adequate amount of short-term insurance protection for your goods. Your options include:

✔ **Basic liability:** This coverage insures your household contents at 60 cents per pound, per item, no matter what its actual value. (In other words, don't expect your gold and diamonds to be fully covered under this protection.) This type of coverage is usually free and is provided by the mover as part of his fee.

✔ **Declared value protection:** This covers the replacement value of any lost or damaged items, minus the depreciation of those items. Your cost will be based on either the declared weight, per-pound value of the goods or their lump-sum value.

✔ **Replacement coverage:** This covers the cost of replacing an item at today's price. This insurance is more expensive and should be used only for expensive items that would be costly to replace. A Gibson classical acoustic guitar that's appreciated in value ten times since you purchased it would be an example of something you might want to protect with replacement coverage.

Be sure to talk to your mover about the coverage he provides, and then your insurance agent about taking out any additional coverage that you need to protect your home's contents during the move.

✔ Disassembling and assembling furniture and other items

✔ Storage facilities

✔ Cleaning services

✔ Rearranging homes and apartments

✔ Other services related to the home and moving

Check with the moving company you hire about these extra services and take advantage of them if you have the budget for it and if doing so will remove some of the pressure and make for a smoother transition to your new home. If you do use a moving company, also look into insuring your goods.

If you're moving into a second home in a foreign country, you should interview several moving companies and discuss the move in detail with them. A good place to start is the Web site 123Movers.com (www.123movers.com). There, you can plug in your zip code and the country you're moving to and get quotes from ten different companies. They also offer tips on international moving, one of which is "Let the pros pack your stuff." The distance and time makes it wise to not do it yourself.

Moving day: A checklist

Your moving day doesn't have to be the worst experience in your life. If you go into moving day with a plan (and another list), you can make the experience a lot less stressful and not quite as painful. To make your moving day just a tad smoother, keep this handy checklist close by.

- ✔ **Carve out the time.** Set aside one or more days to complete the entire move.

- ✔ **Buy some refreshments.** Keep an ample supply of beverages and snacks on hand for yourself plus anyone else who is helping you move. Chocolate is also a good idea for that midday slump.

- ✔ **Be considerate.** Don't block your neighbor's mailbox with the moving truck. Try not to leave furniture out on the driveway too long. Pick up any trash resulting from the move. Basically, put yourself in your next-door neighbor's position and act accordingly.

- ✔ **Have the directions ready.** If you've only flown to your second home and never driven to it, when moving day arrives, be sure to bring along a map or a printout from a site like MapQuest (www.mapquest.com) showing door-to-door directions to your new home.

- ✔ **Pack your plants carefully.** Find a place for these valued family members before you pull out of the driveway. Pots can be inserted in cardboard boxes and wedged into the car or truck in a way that prevents them from moving during transit.

- ✔ **Make appropriate arrangements for pets and children.** Kids and animals can be thrown off kilter by major life changes like moving. Make it easier for them by having some of their favorite things in the car they'll be traveling in, as well as ample snacks, drinks, and toys to keep them occupied during the trip.

- ✔ **Clean out your primary home *completely*.** Try to avoid leaving the place in disarray. You can hire someone to do this if you don't want to clean up after you're all packed.

- ✔ **Offer to reciprocate.** If friends and family are helping you with the move, be sure to offer your services for a future move. (And a little gift later would be a nice touch, too.)

- ✔ **Tip the mover.** If you use a mover, make sure you tip him. (Check out the preceding section, "Moving yourself or hiring movers?".) The amount is up to you, but when you get to your second home you should tip the individual movers a certain amount to show your appreciation (that is, of course, if you feel they deserve it!).

✔ **Embrace the experience.** The move itself will be over within a day or two, and within a few weeks, your life will be back to normal. Keep this in mind as you huff and puff your way up those stairs with a heavy television in your arms — and when you're tempted to snap at someone out of stress. As the Tao tells us, "Go with the flow!"

Making Your Second Home Feel like Home

You have been to your second home numerous times, and you're familiar with the surroundings. But living there is something entirely different. Your second home is now your primary home. To help make that transition as seamless as possible, keep the following in mind:

✔ **Make your arrival stress free by planning ahead.** Planning ahead includes packing one or two "must have" boxes and making sure you know where they are on the moving truck. In them, pack the essentials, such as bedding, utensils, toilet paper, towels, and such. (Check out the earlier section, "Moving Your Stuff" for more packing info.)

✔ **Get a good night's sleep the first night.** For many of you, your second home won't really be a *new* place, because you've likely spent many nights there already. But no matter whether it's your first night in your new primary home, or your 100th, it will be *different*. To get your mind off the moving and upcoming unpacking (even for a few hours; remember those boxes will be there in the morning), try to get some rest.

Pack some backup bedding so you know that you'll have at least a modicum of sleeping comfort in case your beds go AWOL. Don't forget the sheets, blankets, and pillows; pack the following and make sure you have easy access to them:

• **Inexpensive exercise mats:** These roll up, are padded, and are more than adequate for a few nights' sleep. Find them in any major department store that has a sporting goods department.

• **Air beds:** These are more expensive but are also much more comfortable and are as close to a real mattress as you're going to get. They're used in camping (the ones that can inflate off a battery-powered pump) and, after use, can be deflated and stored away until needed again.

• **Quilts:** A super-thick winter quilt can make a comfy sleeping surface in a pinch.

✔ **Put creature comforts first.** Having a few of your favorite things in your new home can make the transition go much more smoothly. Before you dive into unpacking that box of silverware that was last used when Aunt Bernice was over for dinner — three years ago — consider what you *really* need to be comfortable in your new surroundings.

✔ **Unpack all those boxes.** Wading through a sea of boxes is no fun and can easily make you feel overwhelmed. The following can help you make the unpacking process just a tad bit easier and a little less harried:

1. **Put your furniture in place first before unpacking any boxes.**

   Doing so gets the big stuff into the home first. It also helps you avoid having to navigate piles of smaller boxes and items the way you'd have to if you left the furniture for later.

2. **Organize as much as possible during the move.**

   Instruct your moving folks (whether they're hired pros or four of your wonderfully burly and charitable cousins) to put the labeled boxes where they belong in your new home.

3. **Unpack by priority.**

   Start with the bathroom, the bedrooms, the kitchen, the living room, and then the rest of the house. In the bathroom, make sure you unpack toilet paper, soap, and a towel first.

✔ **Meet or get reacquainted with the neighbors.** Try to take some time to meet your neighbors, especially if you haven't been vacationing regularly there over the last few years and you're essentially new to the area. If you've met the neighbors before, go over and get reacquainted if you haven't recently used your second home. Knowing the folks around you can provide a sense of security. Neighbors typically watch out for one another. This is a great comfort when you go away and your place is empty for a week or two at a time.

Chapter 17

Protecting Your Home for the Future

*I*f you sold your first home, then your second home is now your primary home. As you look toward a long and happy retirement, you want to make sure you protect your investment while you're still alive, as well as after you pass on.

This chapter looks at specific situations that you may encounter after you've retired to your second home. I explain how you can revitalize your future and tap into your home's equity with a reverse mortgage. I also discuss ways you can protect your second home, including changing the ownership structure and passing it along to your heirs.

Considering Reverse Mortgages as a Source of Income

During your retirement years, you may find yourself living on somewhat of a stretched income. You aren't working 40-plus hours a week and bringing in a regular salary. You may have limited retirement money and find that living on Social Security checks and your small pension isn't enough.

If you find yourself in this situation, you may want to consider a reverse mortgage as another financing tool for your retirement years. With a *reverse mortgage,* if you're 62 or older and your home is fully or almost fully paid for, you can get cash — a monthly payment or a lump sum — in return for a mortgage for part of the equity in the home. The property is used as security for the loan, and the reverse mortgage is paid off when the home is sold or when the owner passes away.

In this section, I talk about how this tool works. Reverse mortgages are somewhat complicated financial products. If, after reading this section, you want more details, pick up *Reverse Mortgages For Dummies* by Sarah Glendon Lyons and John E. Lucas (Wiley).

Tapping into equity to live

In order to tap equity in your home, you have to have equity in the home — preferably plenty of it. So if your (second) home is mostly paid for, you, Ms. Homeowner, may decide to go for a reverse mortgage. If so, you'll pay no monthly mortgage payments, but you'll still be responsible for property taxes, homeowners' insurance, and maintenance expenses. As long as you fulfill those obligations and reside in the home permanently, your reverse mortgage lender can't force you to leave or sell the place.

The amount of money available from a reverse mortgage is based on the following:

✔ The age of the youngest borrower (who must be 62 or older)

✔ The current interest rate (the total costs of the loan)

✔ The home's value (its current selling price)

✔ The specific type of reverse mortgage selected

These four factors are used to determine the maximum amount a homeowner can take in a reverse mortgage. Plus, federal guidelines protect the senior citizen by not allowing him to remove equity that would reduce the value of the home below a certain percentage. This amount is commonly capped at 40 percent of the equity. Thus, the reverse mortgage holder can be certain of never using up every cent of the house's worth. For example, a paid-off home worth $500,000 can carry a reverse mortgage of up to $200,000.

The current mortgage or mortgages on the property, any tax liens, and any major repair issues also affect how much you can get from the reverse mortgage. Any existing mortgages must be paid off with the proceeds from the reverse mortgage. A reverse mortgage must be the only mortgage on the property.

Property rich, cash poor

Real estate agents are fully aware of how burdensome basic necessities like food, medicine, heat, and utilities can be on a person living on a fixed income. I know an agent who is particularly attuned to this situation and routinely makes his clients aware of reverse mortgages as a way to provide relief. He works with seniors who already have substantial equity in their dwellings.

When volunteering his time with a Brooklyn home buyer-counseling nonprofit organization recently, he worked with an elderly homeowner who was running a monthly deficit. She was paying bills 60 to 90 days late and huddling in layers of blankets during winter months to save on heating costs — all in a property that was fully paid for.

The agent suggested a reverse mortgage. He explained to her that these are great for senior citizens who are "property rich and cash poor" — like her. His elderly client decided on a combination of payouts: She received a lump sum, a line of credit, and monthly payments.

She paid off all her bills that were past due, she reinstated her homeowners' insurance, and she was able to make repairs and keep up with the maintenance on her house. The monthly reverse mortgage check nicely supplemented her Social Security check and small pension. This agent made this woman's golden years shine again!

After an amount is determined, you can receive the cash in

- ✔ A monthly payment
- ✔ A lump sum
- ✔ A line of credit (you'll get a checkbook)
- ✔ A term payment (semiannually, annually, biannually, and so forth)
- ✔ A combination of these plans

If you decide to take the monthly payment, the amount computed on the day of closing is guaranteed as long as you permanently live in your home.

Benefits for you, drawbacks for your heirs

Reverse mortgages aren't for everyone. Before you consider a reverse mortgage, you need to understand the basic advantage and disadvantage of having one.

Reverse mortgages make the most sense for homeowners who have lived in and paid for their dwelling for a long period of time, and who are living on a fixed income and in need of extra cash to cover bills, medical costs, and living expenses. When people say that owning a home is an investment, this is what they mean. A reverse mortgage gives you the option of using all that money you've put into your investment while still keeping your home. For example, the 70-year-old homeowner whose home is paid off but needs more monthly cash to pay bills and live would probably benefit from the option. A reverse mortgage, however, would not be possible for a homeowner who owes more than 25 percent of his home's value.

However, reverse mortgages do have a significant disadvantage. The mortgages can become a problem when heirs don't like the idea of having to pay back the mortgage out of their inheritance. (The mortgage is passed on to whoever inherits the home.) Say you're a widow, your home is worth $400,000, it's paid for, and you decide to take out a $150,000 reverse mortgage with a monthly payment on a 10-year amortization schedule. (You're happy with a payment around $1,200 a month.) You end up living nine more years and, after you pass away, your son wants to sell the house he inherited, which is now worth $450,000. He will have to pay off the reverse mortgage (which will probably be close to $150,000 by then) at the closing, meaning he'll net around $300,000.

Changing the Ownership Structure of Your Home

Now that you're settled into your new home, you can relax a bit. However, you don't want to get too comfortable. Sometime soon you need to start thinking about your own demise, or at least your decline. That's right, now is a good time to figure out the best way to pass your property on to your *beneficiaries,* those near and dears — whomever they may be.

You need to think about the ownership structure of your home (and assets). The *ownership structure* is precisely what it sounds like: how your home is owned — whether it's in your and your spouse's names alone, or you and your kids, or you and other owners in a partnership. And there are different legalities involved with each one.

By changing the ownership structure of your second home, you can protect it in case something happens to you. For example, if you've changed the ownership status and four years later you have to enter a nursing home, you can protect the home from being seized as an asset by the nursing home to pay for its services.

In this section, I discuss the different types of ownership and give you a grounding in what's what. Deeds can be modified to add or remove owners, and you can even quitclaim (essentially, give) your home to your children or someone else if you choose to, and if it's in your long-term best interest. Ownership structure is a complex issue and differs from state to state, so consult an attorney for more info and if you have any questions not answered here.

Considering different structures

There are several types of ownership structures for real estate. Some are automatic. For example, in some states all married couples *hold* (or own) the property in the same way. And some ownership arrangements are deliberately set up a particular way for personal or financial reasons. Make sure you consult an attorney about these different structures.

Ownership structures include the following types. Talk to your attorney to find out how your property is held.

- **Sole ownership:** You own the asset by yourself, and you can sell it or give it away without having to ask anyone else for permission. A will is critically necessary here, or else the courts will decide who gets the house. (Check out "Making a will" later in this chapter.) If you solely own your second home and you don't have a will, the property could go into dreaded probate and get hit with high estate taxes.

- **Tenants in the entirety:** Reserved for married couples, this ownership structure requires approval from both parties before the property can be sold or given away. When one spouse dies, the other spouse automatically receives full title. (This type of ownership isn't available in all states.)

- **Joint tenancy with rights of survivorship (JTWROS):** You own an equal share of the property with one or more individuals. When an owner passes away, the property is automatically transferred to the surviving owners (even if your will states otherwise). That's right: A person's joint ownership can't be "willed" away, unlike when ownership is tenants in common.

- **Tenants in common (T/C):** You own shares in property with one or more persons. The shares of ownership don't have to be equal, and there is no right of survivorship. This means that when one owner passes away, that person's interest is passed along to his heirs, as named in a will. It doesn't go to the other owner(s).

✔ **Community property:** You and your spouse each have one-half interest in jointly owned property. If you get divorced, everything is split down the middle. If one spouse dies, the surviving spouse acquires the deceased spouse's half-interest in their community property. Remember, though, that community property is only recognized in nine states: Arizona, California, Idaho, Louisiana, Nebraska, New Mexico, Texas, Washington, and Wisconsin. Check with your respective state office for details.

The good news is that for married couples whose property is owned in joint tenancy, you can almost always avoid probate, court proceedings, and estate taxes when bequeathing a home, because full ownership of the home automatically reverts to the living spouse.

Adding your children to the deed

While you're reviewing your home's ownership structure, you may want to think about adding your children(s) name to the deed, thus assuring them control of (and responsibility for) the property at all times.

You'll have to work with an attorney or a title company to add children to your deed. Doing so may help stave off estate taxes that your heirs would incur upon your passing. It can also give you peace of mind about your property's ownership when it's time to pass it on to your children or even if the day comes when you're incapacitated and want to be sure your home is in good hands.

Once added, your children become *joint tenants*. That means that both you and they will share ownership rights to the property and also be liable for one another's debts, not just the mortgage. It also means that if one of the joint tenants (you or one of your kids) wants to sell the home, the other owner(s) have to agree to do so.

Any joint tenant who racks up debt risks having a lien put on the home to cover those obligations. So, if you and your daughter become joint tenants, and she gets buried in credit card debt that she can't (or doesn't) pay, the lender will pursue collection from your daughter's assets, which could include putting a lien on your house and even foreclosing. Remember that a lender can only foreclose if there's still a mortgage on the home.

So be sure to discuss this move with an experienced attorney (a chat with your accountant wouldn't hurt, too) before making any major decisions affecting the ownership structure and financial aspects of your home — and you. The legal and financial implications of adding your children to a home's deed are pretty sticky.

Should you quitclaim the house?

A *quitclaim deed* releases interest in a property to a specified person or persons without being compensated for the asset transfer. A legal document, the deed transfers rights to a property by a *grantor* — that's you — to a *grantee* — that's your child, your nephew, or your best friend.

That means you can quitclaim your home to anyone, anywhere, including your children. The drawback to this is that you're essentially giving away part or all of the home, and the recipients may be subject to a gift tax later on. Plus the grantees are then responsible for all financial costs associated with owning the house — property taxes, maintenance, insurance costs, and so on.

Using a quitclaim deed may be warranted in some situations, but for the best advice on this subject, talk to your attorney, accountant, and/or financial advisor, all of whom should be able to help you make the best decision regarding this legal move.

Leaving the Property to Your Heirs

Ultimately, the best way to bequeath a home is to plan well in advance for a time when the property transfers to one or more heirs, whether through a joint tenancy agreement, will, or other vehicle. Though the process can be fraught with both legal and financial implications, you should keep in mind the best interest of your heirs as you handle your estate planning.

Also, if you eschew planning ahead, then there's a very good chance that Uncle Sam will swoop in upon your death and snag a large chunk of what you've worked so hard to accumulate during your lifetime.

That means the planning should be less about how to draft the legal document, and more about how your children and/or heirs are going to enjoy the home when it's passed on to them. In this section, I explain how to make a simple will, how to divvy up your estate in a way that benefits everyone, and how to handle any disputes. (For more in-depth info on making out wills and passing on property, check out *Estate Planning For Dummies* by N. Brian Caverly and Jordan S. Simon [Wiley]).

Where there's a will, there's peace of mind

Making a will is one of those touchy subjects that many people don't want to deal with. But making a will is important and, when handled properly, can make an enormous difference in your loved ones' lives when you ultimately pass on.

A will is important for two main reasons. With a will

- ✔ Your estate can avoid lengthy probate periods and having to pay high estate taxes, or at least minimize them.
- ✔ You can ensure that your assets go to whom you want them to go to and with as small a cost attached as possible.

If you don't make a will, your worldly possessions and property may end up in *probate,* or in the government's hands, out of reach of the people whom you planned to leave them to, until a ruling is issued divvying up your estate.

Drawing up your will

Drawing up a will is a fairly straightforward process that you can do on your own, at a lawyer's office, or on your computer with one of the many software programs available today for about $30 or less. Try one of these will-making sites as a starting point: LegacyWriter (www.legacywriter.com) or LegalZoom (www.legalzoom.com). Both sites offer online downloads for their programs.

If you're confident you know what you want to bequeath, and to whom, and you don't have any complicated financial situations (like owning property with partners, for one), then you may not need a lawyer. Or you may want one to weigh in when you're done writing your will for reassurance that it's okay. If you're not sure whether your own situation is simple enough to do the will on your own, you can always take a swing at it yourself and then ask your attorney to review it, a service that would cost less than him doing the whole will from scratch.

If you decide to write your own will, stick to the following steps when doing so:

1. **List all your assets.**

   Assets are items or money owned by an individual. These typically include savings and checking accounts, investment accounts, property, life insurance policies, and personal property.

2. **Decide on who you want to inherit what and when.**

   You name *heirs* to inherit certain pieces of property. Your *beneficiaries* are the people designated to receive the *proceeds* (death benefits) of insurance policies or savings accounts when you die.

   For example, you may want to leave your son a gold ring that your father gave you when you were 16 years old. Or you want your brother to have your CD collection, library, or coin collection. Or you want to leave a certain amount of cash to your favorite niece. All of this is spelled out in your will and adhered to by its executor.

3. **Choose a guardian for your children (if any of them are under 18 at the time you're drafting your will).**

   A *guardian* is the person chosen to care for and raise your children in the event of your death. You also need to select an *alternate guardian* in case the first choice can't — or won't — take on the responsibility. When deciding who to name as guardian, consider each prospective person's suitability for raising children, their living and financial situation, and their moral and ethical makeup, and whether it agrees with yours. If you have an intuitive, heartfelt feeling that a specific person would raise and love your kids the way you do, that's your guardian.

4. **Select someone who can handle the assets that you leave to your children (if you think this will be necessary).**

   This person should be trusted and honorable, who you are reasonably sure will be able to accommodate your requests and take care of the details properly. A parent, brother, or sister may be your best bet, although an attorney may be better suited to handle the task. This doesn't necessarily have to be the same person you select as guardian, although it can be.

5. **Choose an executor.**

   The *executor* carries out your wishes, and handles all the paperwork (and there will be a lot of it!) and other administrative tasks upon your passing. Choose someone you know is smart, attentive to detail, trustworthy, and patient. All these traits will be necessary when executing a will.

6. **Print out the will and sign and date it in the presence of at least two witnesses, who must also sign.**

   An unsigned will, or an unwitnessed will, is, in most cases, an invalid will. You don't want to go through the effort of making a will and have it rejected when being filed because it wasn't legally signed, dated, and witnessed.

   Wills do not need to be notarized, but they do need to be witnessed. It's a good idea to check with your state laws to make sure you have enough witnesses sign it (some states require two, others require three). You can choose your own witnesses or have your attorney (if you're using one) provide them. Witnesses don't have the obligation (nor the right) to read the will. They are simply witnessing the will's signing by the will's maker. Also, the witnesses shouldn't have a stake in the will.

Storing (and reviewing) your will

Put your will in a safe place (such as safety deposit box at the bank, or in a fireproof high-security safe in your home), and make sure that the family member, trusted professional, or executor whom you designate to take care of things upon your death knows where it is and how to access it. (They don't need a copy in their possession while you're alive.) The will needn't be recorded with any government agency to be legal.

Because your financial situation will likely change from year to year, review your will annually. Make any necessary changes to your assets, beneficiaries, and other key elements. Sometimes you can make changes by simply adding a *codicil* (a document that details your revisions); other times you may need to draft a whole new will. This way, when the time comes that the will must be executed, the document will be up-to-date and accurate.

Considering estate taxes

When transferring real estate, in particular, you need to keep in mind the following points to protect your estate and your heirs. Estate taxes and those taxes incurred during real estate transfers (if and when your beneficiaries decide to sell the family home, for example) can be steep. Some can be avoided through careful planning, so be sure to discuss in advance any "divvying up" of your estate with an accountant or financial planner. That way, John won't get socked with a $100,000 IRS bill when he goes to sell your $650,000 home a year after your passing.

- ✔ **Look at your overall financial picture.** You can't just consider the home as a stand-alone entity — and then determine where the property fits into your complete estate plan. Is it the bulk of the estate? Or just a small part? Factor your home into your whole financial picture, which includes your savings, investments, IRAs, 401(k)s, and other assets. Talk to a financial planner for advice on how to ensure that the real estate transfer is being done in a way that doesn't adversely affect the entities that make up your complete financial portfolio.

- ✔ **Review your ownership structure.** Most couples own their homes in joint tenancy. If you don't own the home in joint tenancy — but you want to — talk to a title company or attorney as soon as possible about changing the ownership structure. See the section, "Changing the Ownership Structure of Your Home" earlier in this chapter.

- ✔ **Consider taking advantage of the $1 million that each individual is allowed to give away, tax-free, during his lifetime.** Those who use it are taking advantage of what is called the Gift Tax Credit, which allows an individual to claim a $1 million exclusion during his lifetime and used to, say, gift money to a child (to the tune of $12,000 or less per year).

- ✔ **Make sure that the title to the property is free and clear of any liens or defects before attempting to bequeath it to your heirs.** Think about any mortgages or debts on the home, and decide how those will be paid off. A *title search* (conducted by a title agent) can show whether a lien has been attached to the home. If any are found, they should be cleared up immediately by contacting the entity that attached the lien and resolving it (either having it corrected, or paying the debt, for example).

- ✔ **Avoid waiting until the last minute to get started on your estate planning.** Start the process now, and your heirs will be grateful for your efforts when their time comes to take over management of your financial assets.

Part V
The Part of Tens

The 5th Wave   By Rich Tennant

"Of course I could never afford a shoe this size if I weren't collecting rents from a tennis shoe across town and two espadrilles in Florida."

In this part . . .

Feel free to read these fun chapters when you have a few minutes. They may be short, but they're chock-full of helpful pointers. Want to know where to buy a second home, when to improve it, and how to orchestrate overnight visits from friends and family? Then this part is just for you. I break down these key aspects of second-home ownership into a simple-to-use format that you can put to work right now.

Chapter 18

Ten Popular Second-Home Locations

In This Chapter

▶ Choosing a location that suits your needs

▶ Looking outside the United States for a second home

*H*ow do you decide where to purchase your second home? For many people, this decision is a no-brainer. They buy where they have vacationed as renters for years. They buy in an area they know they love. For others, though, where they vacation isn't necessarily where they want to spend their retirement years, and this needs to be taken into consideration, because second homes also commonly end up being retirement homes. Maybe those ski vacations were great fun all those years, but someplace warmer may be a more appealing notion for retirement.

Certain areas of the country (and the world, for that matter) attract second-home buyers like bees to honey. For example, Florida is especially popular, in particular among those folks who live in the northern (colder) climes of the Northeast and Midwest. The Carolinas are also a popular choice for those northerners, and, ironically, for Floridians looking to escape their state's summer humidity and heat. Texas and other states in the Southwest also rank high on the list, as do cities like Las Vegas; Aspen, Colorado; and Cape Cod, Massachusetts, each of which offers its own appeal and its own unique activities and attractions.

If you don't yet have your heart set on an exact location and are thinking a bit further outside the box (and the States), or you're just aching to make a change from your usual vacation destination, then you've come to the right place. This chapter tells you about ten popular geographic areas for second-home buyers — including the pros and the cons of each — that you should definitely consider before making your final selection.

Florida

Ah, the Sunshine State. It's where scads of people in the United States want to be between November and March each year. Few other states can offer the combination of heat, sunshine, and beaches that Floridians bask in just about year-round.

But wait, Florida isn't quite so perfect. Throw in the risk of possibly devastating hurricanes, some major homeowners' insurance issues — regarding both cost (high) and availability of coverage (a challenge) — and the fact that many of the most popular areas for vacationers and second-home buyers are getting overcrowded quickly, and you may want to read the nine other suggestions in this chapter before settling on this one.

Even so, the state offers a wide range of options for the second-home buyer, from the laid-back style of **Key West** to the Disney-laden **Orlando** area to the sugary sand beaches of the **Panhandle.**

The Carolinas

North and South Carolina offer diverse vacation experiences that include beaches and mountains, rivers and lakes, and small towns and big cities. Because of these diverse features, both states are popular among second-home buyers.

Although the Carolinas get cold during the winter, they boast a number of great hideaways where you can find second homes for sale in areas that allow you to fully enjoy both states' many delights. The downside is that you're not going to enjoy bargain basement prices anymore: Both states have experienced high home appreciation over the last few years.

A few places to consider include South Carolina's **Myrtle Beach,** where the "Grand Strand" annually draws millions of visitors to its white sand beaches; **Beaufort**, also in South Carolina, whose seaside villages often find their way into best-selling novels; and North Carolina's gorgeous **Outer Banks,** where barrier islands span 130 miles.

Galveston, Texas

Situated in the Gulf of Mexico and connected to the Texas mainland by the 2-mile-long Galveston Causeway, the island of Galveston has become a popular spot for second-home buyers who want to own a piece of the 32-mile-long, 2½-mile-wide island.

Galveston exudes small, southern-town charm, yet is located only 40 miles away from Houston, making air travel to and from a second home on the island that much more feasible. The island's historic neighborhoods boast structures that are on the National Register of Historic Places, and the area is rich with late 19th- and early 20th-century architecture. Popular activities include windsurfing, boating, and fishing.

Keep in mind, though, that Galveston's seaside location means that it's vulnerable to hurricanes and inclement weather, and similar to what Floridians go through, obtaining homeowners' insurance for a property there may be challenging.

The American Southwest

The American Southwest — areas of Arizona, California, Colorado, Nevada, New Mexico, Utah, and Texas — boasts deserts, canyons, caves, and yes, even beaches, and the landscape is both beautiful and mysterious. The American Southwest offers perfect spots if you're looking for serenity in an environment very different from what most states offer. The Mojave Desert, for example, encompasses areas of Arizona, Nevada, and Southern California, all of which are popular among the vacation home-buying set. For individuals who live full time in the northern climates, the thought of owning a home in the Southwest and then retiring to it can be very enticing.

This region boasts lakes, scenic drives, volcanic craters, and of course, lots of deserts. If you like it very hot and sunny, and are enamored of history and ancient ruins (of which there are many in the American Southwest), then this region may be for you. If you find extreme heat to be unbearable, then you may want to steer clear of this area of the country and instead navigate toward a region where rain falls more readily and it isn't *always* summer!

The American Southwest is vast. To find the right place, you may first try renting one or more vacation homes (find them on a site like www.vrbo.com), before you buy. Also, if this region intrigues you, be sure to visit www.americansouthwest.net for info about everything the American Southwest has to offer.

Las Vegas

If glitz, glamour, and night life are on your second-home priority list, Vegas could be the place for your second home. The fact is, this city literally never sleeps. If you keep in mind that the odds at some of the nicest casinos leave a lot to be desired (you don't want to blow your retirement nest egg at the craps table), and you can handle living in Vegas as a temporary resident who only occasionally gambles, then you quite possibly can find a gem among the area's housing stock, especially if you're looking for a condo.

Over the last few years, developers have launched a large number of condo projects. This has created an ample inventory of new homes for second-home buyers who are looking for an urban getaway with undeniably adult attractions close by.

If you're looking for a family atmosphere, you may want to steer clear of Vegas for your second home. Even though Sin City has tried to clean itself up lately, I was there recently and saw very few children and families on the Strip.

Aspen, Colorado

Is swooshing down ski slopes right up your alley? If you have the money and are looking for that kind of outdoor activity right in your backyard, then Aspen, Colorado, is the place for your second home.

A chalet nestled on the snowy slopes with your name on it is waiting, but you'll probably pay a hefty price for it. Demand is high, and the location is desirable, so it's not unusual for $1 million to be the "low end" of the market here.

Keep in mind, too, that maintenance on a home in Aspen may be slightly to considerably more expensive than that of a beach location: Snow removal alone can set you back a few hundred bucks a month. After you and your family hit the slopes from your own villa, though, you'll almost certainly feel that it's all worth it.

Cape Cod, Massachusetts

Owning a waterfront home in Martha's Vineyard is something to brag about. And you should expect to pay the price for those bragging rights if you have your mind set on a place on this 413-square-mile peninsula of fields, forests, dunes, marshland, and beaches located off the Massachusetts coast.

From clam chowder festivals to cultural events to a thriving business economy, the Cape Cod area is a favorite for second-home buyers looking for an escape from the rat race. The area offers a beautiful traditional atmosphere, and during nonvacation periods, the area is typically only natives.

Specific areas to check out include **Falmouth** (for boating and fishing), **Sandwich** (for its famous glass products), **Nantucket Island** (for its art galleries and museums), and **Hyannis** (for its historic homes and sandy beaches).

Europe

You vacationed in Italy last year, and now you and your loved ones have decided that you want to visit Europe more often, but you don't want to stay in hotels. You would prefer to live in your own home, right? Well, you're in luck.

As a second-home buyer who is on the prowl for a new place, many options await you on the other side of that pond called the Atlantic Ocean. Whether you want to bask in the sun on the shores of the **French Riviera,** enjoy wine in the **Tuscan countryside,** or stand in the streets of **Spain** watching the bulls run, Europe may be just the ticket.

And speaking of tickets, be prepared to buy plenty of them if you're spreading yourself between a primary home in the United States and a second home based overseas. Also, expect to deal with nuances in the overseas real estate market and currency conversion issues, as well as adapting to life as a (temporary) local. (See Chapter 9 for more info on buying overseas.)

The Caribbean

The **Cayman Islands,** the **Virgin Islands,** and the **Bahamas** all present great second home-buying opportunities for Americans who want their own piece of paradise. Living on or near the beach is a draw in and of itself, and one that brings many new second-home buyers to these Caribbean islands every year.

I've visited all three countries over the last few years, and I can tell you that I've thought about taking the plunge and owning my own slice of each one. The islands are beautiful and enticing, but they also come with their own set of challenges.

All three locales have had run-ins with major hurricanes over the last decade, with Grand Cayman getting hit especially hard in 2004. All have since recovered, but the thought of future storms should cross your mind if you're going to buy in the Caribbean. As you may expect, insuring your new place may require extra effort to find adequate coverage at a price you're comfortable with.

On a positive note, the "for sale" signs are plentiful on homes throughout the islands, with single-family homes and condos making up the majority of the housing stock. If you plan to own a home here, check out Chapter 9 for help in buying beyond U.S. borders.

South America

Years ago, the average American second-home shopper probably wouldn't have even considered buying a home in a South American country, such as Argentina or Peru. But today, with the increasing interest in finding new, undiscovered places — and the fact that so many South Americans now reside in the United States — this thought is no longer so farfetched. In fact, places like **Buenos Aires, Argentina; Lima, Peru;** and **Montevideo, Uruguay** are among the hottest vacation spots for Americans these days. These areas are rich in culture, offer ample real estate opportunities, and provide a lifestyle that no U.S. city can mimic.

Remember that South America is not North America (with everything that goes along with that reality). Although prices can be good, politics and inflation can both affect your lifestyle.

When buying overseas, be sure to find a real estate agent who has worked with American second-home buyers in the past and who can guide you through the process. A good place to start is at domestic brokerages like Coldwell Banker or RE/MAX, both of which have international branches in South America. (Head to Chapter 9 for more advice on buying overseas.)

Chapter 19

Ten Ways to Make Your Second Home First-Rate

*Y*ou can easily lose sight of the fact that your second home needs the same attention as your primary home. After all, you probably don't have to look at it every day, right? That means you also don't have to contend with disapproving looks from neighbors when your grass grows too high, your stove's right rear burner that doesn't heat up, or the tub that drains too slowly, which would drive you nuts if you had to live with it on a daily basis.

But does that mean you can ignore those problems? No. You should do what you can — either on your own or with the help of others — to create a first-rate second home that you, your renters, your family, and others can enjoy for years to come. In this chapter, I show you ten ways to do that.

Look for Ways to Make Improvements

Tile floors chip. Old refrigerators don't refrigerate. Garage door openers stop opening. Doors squeak. Floors creak. Faucets drip. Paint fades. Drains don't. These are just some of the basic issues that homeowners deal with all the time, and you should address them as quickly as possible when they occur at your second residence, even though they're not in your face every day.

Not everything on your to-do list has to be expensive or take a great deal of time. If, for example, the faucet in the guest bathroom leaks and the fixture is from the Pleistocene Age, consider replacing it with a new $35 faucet that not only works correctly, but also looks much nicer. (And be sure to keep track of all repairs — even the little ones — by saving the receipts.)

Funnel the Profits Back into the Home

Successful business owners are always funneling money back into their businesses. Doing so is important, helpful, and smart. Because your second home is, in essence, a business until you move into it full time, you should consider putting at least some of your rental profits back into the place.

For example: Instead of pocketing that $2,000 monthly profit that you're making on your second home, allocate 25 percent of it ($500 a month) to home improvements. That doesn't mean you have to work on the house every month, spending exactly $500, but you will have $6,000 a year to reinvest.

Hire a Property Manager

A property manager can be your friend, especially if your primary home is more than a three-hour drive away from your second home. For a fee, these companies market the home to renters, inspect and report back to you, deal with tenants, and tackle the tasks associated with second-home ownership. If you go this route, the property manager can essentially serve as a second set of eyes watching your property and taking care of it. (Check out Chapter 11 for more on how a property manager can help you rent your home and Chapter 13 for more on how these folks can help you maintain the home.)

Use a Cleaning Service

Keeping your second home clean inside and outside is critical to attracting renters and keeping neighbors happy. No one wants to visit a dirty home or look out their window and see a ramshackle house in need of painting or power washing. Plus, making sure everything is neat and tidy shows respect for both your guests and your neighbors.

Unless you *really* enjoy cleaning toilets and showers, you should consider hiring someone to help you keep your second home sparkling clean and shiny. Expect to pay anywhere from $60 to $120 a month for the service, depending on the size of your home and how often you use or need the service. (Check out Chapter 13 for more helpful info on maintaining your home.)

Use a Lawn Service

Many neighborhoods these days have strict rules concerning overgrown yards. Because of this, you need to cut the grass yourself on a weekly basis or hire someone to do it for you. Much like a cleaning service, a lawn service can take a big load off your mind for only a small investment of $60 to $120 per month, depending on where your home is located and how large your yard is. Remember that a well-kept lawn and yard are the first things visitors and potential renters see. If your grounds are unkempt, you can be sure your place has dropped a notch or two in other people's perceptions. (Refer to Chapter 13 for more on the importance of the upkeep of your second home.)

Decorate like It's Your Primary Home

The best way to decorate a second home — particularly if you're going to be renting it out for part of the year — lies somewhere between Spartan and French castle. In other words, you don't want the place to look empty and sterile, but you also don't want to put so much of your personal stuff into it that it becomes uninviting for tenants.

Take the middle road when decorating your house. Dress the space and make it comfortable but not cluttered; contemporary, but not too modern; functional, but not crammed. Outfit it in a way that's comfortable and useful for you, your family, and your guests.

Make the Home Fully Functional

The last things a vacation renter wants to hear is that the hot tub is broken, the shower in the master bathroom doesn't work, the oven light is on the blink, and the downstairs toilet doesn't flush. Although you may not mind working around these things, your tenants are going to expect (and demand) the "best of the best" from their experience. That's what they're paying for.

You can't stay on top of every insect and missing tile, but do your best to keep your second home as functional as possible at all times. When in doubt, call a handyman to come in and knock off a list of items to fix or upgrade on a day when the place isn't rented out. It'll be well worth the effort.

Keep Tabs on Renters

"Treat our home like it was your own" is a common request by second-home owners who are renting their digs on a short- or long-term basis. Sounds good in theory, right? The reality is sometimes markedly different. Most tenants will happily shove an extra-large load of laundry into the washing machine to save time, because the average tenant probably doesn't care what happens to said washing machine, as long as her clothes get clean.

Not all renters are irresponsible. Either you or your property manager need to conduct regular inspections both before and after renters use the place. Ask for security deposits upfront, and don't return them until you know the place is in the same shape it was before the renters got there. Your renter's security deposit can fix any damaged items.

Personally Use It As Often As Possible

When you're in the middle of figuring out a year's worth of rental income and trying to schedule everyone for the weeks that they want, losing sight of the fact that you bought this home for *your* enjoyment is easy.

You and your family come first. Every September take a look at the year ahead. Use a calendar and a thick, red pen to mark off any days that *you* want to use the home. Then refer to that calendar when you're signing up renters. Unless something prohibits you from visiting your second home, don't give up any of the weeks you've called dibs for. By sticking to this strategy, you always get your first picks for vacation.

Invite Select Loved Ones to Your Home

Family and friends enrich your life. Thus, being able to spend time with them is a wonderful additional benefit of having a second home. You'll find that the atmosphere will be a lot more fun when you have cousins come to your beach house rather than to your primary home. So consider entertaining as a great way to enjoy the people closest to you.

Also, as word gets around that you've purchased a second home that sits unoccupied for part of the year, expect to get requests from friends and relatives who want to use it for their own vacations. As long as these individuals are trustworthy and responsible, and as long as they leave the place as they found it, allowing them to spend some time at your place shouldn't create many problems. See Chapter 20 for more details on how to set ground rules for friends and family who want to use your home.

Chapter 20

Ten Rules Your Friends and Family Must Follow When Using Your Home

In This Chapter

▶ Establishing who can visit when

▶ Making sure guests keep your home in good shape

A fter you become a second-home owner, the inevitable is bound to happen: Aunt Martha and Uncle George will be in dire need of a vacation, and it won't be long before you hear, "May we *please* stay at your place with George Jr. and our new beagles, Keanu and Cher?"

For many of you, the answer will be "Sure, Aunt Martha!" — and that's fine, as long as it doesn't conflict with your own plans to use your second home. But there are some things visitors need to know, and in this chapter, I discuss ten rules that you should lay down for friends and family who want to use your place. Feel free to post these rules in your house so your guests don't forget them. And if you don't think it would ruffle anyone's feathers, consider having your guests sign a copy of the rules, indicating that they've read them and that they'll adhere to them. (Although in the case of immediate family, asking may be a bit much.)

Tell your guests that they not only are expected to abide by *your* rules, but also by the rules of the condo development, neighborhood association, or co-op board when they're staying in your home. Condos, for example, often have rules about parking, speed limits, noise, and so forth, and when someone is in your unit, you're responsible for their behavior. Make sure your guests know this from the outset.

Visit on Our Schedule

As the homeowner, you determine who uses your second home and when. Set up a schedule of your own first, and *then* accommodate your guests. So if you and your family of four were set to use your two-bedroom, two-bath condo at the lake for Labor Day weekend, your aunt and uncle can't possibly be there at the same time — no matter how much they had hoped you'd allow it. If they insist, or even go so far as to get mad about it, politely explain that you booked yourself a year in advance (see Chapter 19 for details on making your own owner's calendar) and that changing it would be too much of an inconvenience for you and your family. Period. Case closed.

Offer guests a different weekend — or even the next free holiday if you're not planning on using your home then — instead, but don't ever feel guilty about not being able to accommodate "free" guests who can't work around your schedule.

Children, Pets, and Smokers Have Their Own Sets of Rules to Follow

In some families, a family vacation just isn't a family vacation unless the three kids, chain-smoking Uncle Ralph, Rover, and Miss Kitty all pile into the van for the getaway. But before you start opening the doors of your second home to friends and family, you should establish some basic rules regarding children, pets, and smokers. The big concern about these folks is that they'll potentially damage your precious second home. That's why you need to make rules and establish boundaries. After all, it is *your* house.

Consider posting and handing out a copy of the following rules to your guests. Feel free to modify these rules, based on your circumstances.

- ✔ No smoking in the home, on the lanai, or on the deck.
- ✔ No smoking in the home, but feel free to smoke out on the lanai or deck — but with the sliding glass door to the home closed.
- ✔ No children allowed on the deck alone. (Some lanais and decks are above the first level, and some owners forbid kids out there *at all.*)
- ✔ Please don't allow your children to eat in the living room. All eating must be done in the kitchen.
- ✔ Men must wear shirts while sitting on the furniture. (I saw this one posted in Hawaii; sweat and tanning oil can destroy fabric.)

> ✔ No pets allowed.
>
> ✔ Small pets (under 15 pounds) are allowed with notice and an additional add-on to the security deposit.
>
> ✔ Clean up after your pets.
>
> ✔ Clean up after your children.

Make up your own rules, and don't hesitate to add new ones when a new situation arises that you need to address.

Report Any Damage or Problems

Ask your guests to keep you informed of any problems or concerns that they see or experience while staying at your second home. Doing so is particularly important if you don't live near your second home because you can quickly find yourself up to your eyeballs in repairs and maintenance when problems aren't tended to.

If the snow is piled up past the windows, the cellar has a foot of water in it, or the oak tree on the front lawn is teetering at a weird angle, make sure your guests know that you want to know about it. Make this very clear to your friends and family both before and after their stay.

Treat the Home like It's Your Own

You would expect that someone would treat your second home as if it were their own, but it doesn't always work out that way. Although some guests are conscientious and rule abiding, others may feel as if the home is their playground. They may leave things in disarray or even broken.

You must lay down the ground rules early by telling guests exactly what your expectations are regarding how they treat your place. (Check out Chapter 1 for a list you can post on the fridge.)

Don't Cost Us Money

Owning a second home can be an expensive proposition if things like long-distance phone calls and $10 pay-per-view movies aren't treated with respect and used with discretion. Make your guests aware of "added expense" items, and indicate any areas where they may actually wind up costing you money.

All it will take is a few visits from friends or relatives to find out what areas are prone to these problems. One all-night, pay-per-view movie party and you'll have a good idea of exactly what to be on the alert for. (Of course, if one of your guests wants to order that new Al Pacino movie on pay-per-view and reimburse you for the cost, then that's fine.)

Clean Up After Yourself

Ideally, you want your second home to remain spic and span at all times. Sometimes it will be, sometimes it won't. Rather than let your guests have free reign over the place, make them aware upfront that you expect them to clean up after themselves.

Be specific in this request, and cover the following:

- Clean up the kitchen, clean out the fridge, and toss perishable foods stored in cabinets.
- Wash and dry all linens that were used (this can include towels and bed linens).
- Make the beds.
- Throw out all garbage.
- And so forth and so on . . .

You should also considering charging a deposit (the standard is $200 to $300) to cover accidents and any extra cleaning that needs to be done as a result of the guest's stay.

Don't Have Parties or Overnight Guests without Permission

Decide whether you'll allow your friends and family to have parties at your second home, and also whether you'll allow additional overnight guests. Sometimes this decision will hinge on the house itself. It's an important consideration for all second-home owners who want their abodes kept in the best shape possible and who don't want the hassle of having to clean up after an unapproved, 40-person New Year's Eve party.

If, for example, you have a five-bedroom abode in the middle of the Colorado Rocky Mountains, then an extra guest or two probably won't be that big a deal. But if you have a two-bedroom condo on Pompano Beach in Florida, then a raucous party or three extra people for a slumber party may be overdoing it.

Think about it, use your best judgment, and lay down the rules for such requests long before you allow anyone to use your home.

Expect Unexpected Visits from Us

If your second home is within driving distance of your primary dwelling, be sure to let your friends and family know that you may, ahem, "drop in" at any time to check up on the place. This probably won't be much of an issue if someone is staying for a few days over a long weekend, but if you're loaning your home out for a month or more, you'll probably want to make at least one or two trips there to make sure everything is shipshape.

If your guests know in advance that you may stop by, they'll likely take more care with the place and keep it neat, orderly, and maintained in case you pull one of your surprise inspections.

Leave the House and Its Contents the Way You Found Them

Don't let your guests get away with wrecking your home and leaving it for you to clean up. Although standard cleaning (toilets, bathtubs, clean linens, and so forth) is your responsibility, there's no excuse for marred walls, disorganized utility closets, and broken dishes. Accidents happen, but if they start to happen a little too often, it may be time for a reminder. Something along the lines of "We expect our house and its contents to be in the same shape they were in when you arrived for your stay" ought to do it.

Ask your guests to

- ✔ Put stuff back where they found it
- ✔ Clean up so the place is like it was when they arrived
- ✔ Throw out any garbage that they're responsible for
- ✔ Wipe down any smudged sliding glass doors

✔ Wipe off all surfaces, especially countertops and tables (both indoors and outdoors)

✔ Take whatever other steps are necessary to return the home to the condition it was in when they arrived

Don't expect a perfect job every time, but by giving clear instructions about all this before handing over the keys, you'll be doing what you can to make sure your second home is well taken care of.

Follow the Rules, and Come Back Again

Let your guests know that if they don't comply with your rules (no matter how loose or strict they are), they won't be using your place again.

Just as you would treat their second home with respect, you expect the same in return. Make this very clear, and enforce it when necessary.

Glossary

adjustable-rate mortgage (ARM): This type of loan features an interest rate and payment that can be adjusted upward or downward as frequently as every month in relation to market conditions. The interest rate is linked to the U.S. Treasury index or some other fluctuating financial index.

agent: A person licensed by the state to conduct real estate transactions. A real estate agent, for example, negotiates the transaction between a home buyer and a seller.

amenities: Parks, swimming pools, health-club facilities, recreational rooms, bike paths, community centers, and other outside features within close proximity to a specific home, group of homes, condominium development, or apartment complex.

amortization: The process of paying the principal and interest on a loan through regularly scheduled installments. Typically, the earliest payments are weighted heavily toward paying interest, so the amount of interest paid decreases and the amount paid toward the principal increases over the life of the loan.

annual percentage rate (APR): The cost of credit as a yearly rate or interest rate reflecting the first-year rate including certain points and credit costs.

appraisal report: A detailed, written report on the value of a property based on recent sales of comparable properties in the area and the replacement cost of the existing improvements (with the land value computed separately).

appraiser: An individual who is trained and experienced in the methods of determining a property's value through analysis of various factors, such as age, size, condition of the property, and current market conditions. In some states, a license is required, especially to appraise properties for government-backed mortgages.

appreciation: The increase in value of a real estate property. This includes land and structures.

assessed value: The value placed upon property for taxation purposes only.

buyer's market: When there are more homes for sale to choose from than a comparable number of buyers.

bylaws: The rules and regulations that a homeowners' association or corporation adopts to govern activities within the development of condos or homes.

closing: The final step in the home-buying process, wherein buyers, sellers, agents, attorneys, and a closing agent meet to sign all documents related to the home sale. In some states, an escrow agent, who manages the paperwork and files the necessary documents without the buyer and seller being present, handles this process. All signing is done before the date of title transfer.

closing costs: Expenses incidental to the sale of real estate, including loan, title, appraisal fees, and all prepaid fees that may be required.

commission: This is a negotiable percentage of the sales price of a home or a negotiated flat fee that is paid to the buyer and seller's agents in a real estate transaction.

community property: Property acquired jointly during a marriage by husband and wife.

comps: The recent sales prices, usually within the last year, of comparable properties in a specific area.

condo fees: An amount condominium owners pay every month toward expenses that all units pay for, including trash removal, landscaping, liability insurance, snow removal, outdoor electricity charges, common-area repairs, and maintenance.

condominium: Individual units in a building or development in which owners hold title to the interior space, while common areas, such as parking lots, hallways, and recreational areas, are owned by all the residents.

cosigner: A second borrower who signs in conjunction with the first borrower for the mortgage loan and who is equally liable for the debt.

credit scoring: A system of using recorded information about individuals (which includes what they owe and how timely they are in repaying their debts) and their loan requests to assess their future performance regarding debt repayment.

days on the market: The period of time that a property is listed for sale until it's sold or taken off the market.

deed: The legal document that transfers ownership of a piece of property from one person to another.

disclosure: A statement to a potential buyer from the seller listing information relevant to a piece of property, such as the presence of lead paint or a defective air conditioning unit. Some states have mandatory disclosure laws.

down payment: The difference between the home's value and the loan amount, to be paid by the buyer at closing.

earnest money: A sum of money given to bind an agreement, such as the sale of real estate.

empty nesters: Buyers who have raised their families and want to move into smaller homes that require less maintenance and upkeep.

equity: The difference between the market value of a property and the claims held against it.

escrow: The holding of funds or other property by an impartial third party for the participants in a real estate transaction.

Fair Credit Reporting Act: Designed to prevent inaccurate or obsolete information from remaining in a consumer's credit file, this federal law was passed in 1971 and regulates the activity of credit bureaus, requiring them to have reasonable procedures for gathering, maintaining, and disseminating credit information.

Fair Housing Act: In existence since 1965, this federal law makes it illegal to deny rent or refuse to sell to anyone based on race, color, religion, disability, ancestry, familial status, sex, or national origin.

feng shui: An ancient Chinese belief that the physical characteristics of a house and the positioning of the furniture in the home will affect its owner's fortune.

FICO: The Fair Isaac Company, the company that created the original credit-scoring model.

fixed-rate mortgage: A home loan in which the interest rate does not change during the entire term of the loan.

foreclosure: When a bank or lender "takes back" a home that hasn't been paid for by its owner for a set period of time, usually 90 days.

for sale by owner (FSBO): A property owner who acts as her own agent to avoid paying the negotiated sales commission that real estate agents command.

general warranty deed: A deed where the grantor guarantees that the property is free from claims, subject to specific exceptions included in the deed. The grantor warrants and defends the property to the grantee forever against the rightful claims and demands of all persons.

good faith estimate: An estimate from a lender that shows the costs a borrower will incur when buying a home, including loan-processing charges and home-inspection fees.

grantee: A person who acquires an interest in land by deed, grant, or other written instrument.

grantor: One who grants property or property rights.

home equity line of credit (HELOC): A secured line of credit, using the available equity in a property as collateral.

home equity loan: A revolving, open-ended loan extended under a line of credit and secured by the borrower's residential property.

home inspection: A thorough investigation of a home's structure, from the ground up. It typically includes examination of the home's foundation, framing, plumbing, electrical system, heating, air conditioning, fireplace, kitchen, bathroom, roofing, and interior.

homeowners' association: A group that governs a subdivision, condominium development, or planned community.

homeowners' insurance: Insurance that protects the homeowner from casualty losses or damage to the home or personal property.

house poor: A condition that occurs when someone puts too much of his monthly paycheck into housing payments and home upkeep and is left with no extra money to spend on other necessities.

interest rate: Expressed as a percentage, this is the sum charged by a lender for making a loan on a home.

Individual Retirement Account (IRA): An account that's used to save money — usually tax free at the time of contribution — for the future.

joint tenants with rights of survivorship (JTWROS): Ownership of real estate by two or more individuals where there is not specific fractional financial interest. In the event of the death of one party, the survivor(s) receives total ownership.

joint tenancy: Ownership by two or more people that gives equal shares of a piece of property. When one owner dies, the rights pass to the surviving owner or owners.

lease: A written contract with terms and conditions by which a landlord and tenant agree to a business arrangement involving a residence. For a monthly fee, for example, the tenant can live in the residence owned or managed by the landlord.

liability insurance: An insurance policy that protects owners against any claims of negligence, personal injury, or property damage.

loan-to-value (LTV) ratio: The relationship between the dollar amount of a borrower's mortgage and the value of the property.

maintenance fee: The monthly assessment members of a homeowners' association pay for the repair and maintenance of common areas. See *condo fees*.

manufactured housing: Prefabricated houses that range in scope from single-wide trailers to large, single-family homes.

millage rate: The tax due to a municipality or other governmental entity per dollar of the assessed value of a piece of property. One mill is one-tenth of a cent ($0.001).

mortgage: Debt instrument by which the borrower (mortgagor) gives the lender (mortgagee) a lien on property as security for the repayment of a loan.

Multiple Listing Service (MLS): A service created and run by real estate professionals that gathers all the property listings into a single database where buyers can review all available properties from one source.

open house: A marketing tool in which a listing agent opens a house for the public to come in and take a look.

option: A scenario in which a buyer puts a certain amount of money down in exchange for the right to purchase a piece of real estate within a set time period, but doesn't have the obligation to actually buy the property.

origination fee: A fee that most lenders charge for processing a loan. This is also presented as points, with one point equaling 1 percent of the total loan amount.

partnership: When two or more people pool their money, resources, and/or knowledge to run a business, which, relevant to this book, is the purchase, maintenance, and rental of a second home.

point: See *origination fee*.

PITI (principal, interest, taxes, insurance): Calculated by the lender, this is the principal, interest, taxes, and insurance on a home. The figure represents a borrower's actual monthly mortgage-related expenses.

private mortgage insurance (PMI): Insurance against a loss by a lender in the event of default on a mortgage by a borrower.

property manager: A person or firm charged with operating a real estate property.

property tax: Taxes levied by a local municipality and other governmental entities. These taxes are billed annually, although homeowners commonly pay them monthly along with the mortgage into an escrow account for when the bills come due. Property taxes are calculated at a certain percentage of a property's assessed value, called the millage rate.

property value: The value of a piece of property. It is based on the price a buyer will pay at a specific time.

purchase agreement: A document that details the purchase price and conditions of the transaction.

quitclaim deed: A deed that transfers ownership of real property from one individual to another, usually with no transfer of funds involved. The grantor doesn't warrant to defend any claims against the property.

rate lock: A written commitment issued by a lender to a borrower guaranteeing a specified interest rate for a specific period of time.

real estate: Land and anything permanently affixed to it, including buildings, fences, and other items attached to the structure.

real estate attorney: A lawyer who specializes in real estate transactions.

refinancing: Paying off one loan with the proceeds from another loan. Refinancing is often done when interest rates drop or if the borrower has built up quite a bit of equity in his home and would like to tap some of it as "new money."

reverse mortgage: A financial tool that provides seniors over the age of 62 with funds from the equity in their homes. No payments are made on a reverse mortgage until the borrower moves or the property is sold.

seller's market: An active real estate market in which sellers have the advantage during most negotiations, and multiple offers on a property are commonplace.

sole ownership: Ownership of property by a single person or entity.

tax deduction: Mortgage interest, loan points, and property taxes that can be deducted on a federal tax return. The deduction is made from the taxpayer's taxable income.

tenants in common: Property ownership where two or more people own property jointly.

tenants in the entirety: Only applies to husbands and wives. Through it, either party must obtain the consent of the other co-owner to deal with the property in any way that would affect the rights of the other.

timeshare: A vacation option through which someone owns the rights to use one or more weeks at a specific resort within a certain community. The weeks can usually be exchanged for use at other, participating properties.

title: The legal document that establishes ownership of a piece of real estate.

title insurance: A policy issued to lenders and buyers to protect any losses that could incur due to a dispute over the ownership of a piece of property.

transaction broker: A real estate agent who will, for a fee, handle the paperwork involved with getting a home sale transaction closed.

transfer of ownership: Any means by which the ownership of a property changes hands.

Truth in Lending Act: A federal law that requires lenders to fully disclose, in writing, the terms and conditions of credit, such as a mortgage, including the annual percentage rate (APR) and other charges.

underwriting: The process that lenders use to evaluate the risks presented by a specific borrower and to set appropriate conditions for the loan in question.

U.S. Treasury index: An index used to determine interest rate changes for certain adjustable-rate mortgages.

variable interest rate: A mortgage loan rate that fluctuates based on several factors, such as changes in the rate paid on bank certificates of deposit or treasury bills.

virtual tour: An online presentation that buyers can use to view a home's interior and exterior in a 360-degree view.

walk-out basement: A feature that allows an outside door to open to a lower ground level.

zoning: Regulations that control the use of land within a specific jurisdiction.

Index

• C •

BUSINESS, CAREERS & PERSONAL FINANCE

Fundraising For Dummies
0-7645-9847-3

Investing For Dummies
0-7645-2431-3

Also available:
- Business Plans Kit For Dummies
  0-7645-9794-9
- Economics For Dummies
  0-7645-5726-2
- Grant Writing For Dummies
  0-7645-8416-2
- Home Buying For Dummies
  0-7645-5331-3
- Managing For Dummies
  0-7645-1771-6
- Marketing For Dummies
  0-7645-5600-2

- Personal Finance For Dummies
  0-7645-2590-5*
- Resumes For Dummies
  0-7645-5471-9
- Selling For Dummies
  0-7645-5363-1
- Six Sigma For Dummies
  0-7645-6798-5
- Small Business Kit For Dummies
  0-7645-5984-2
- Starting an eBay Business For Dummies
  0-7645-6924-4
- Your Dream Career For Dummies
  0-7645-9795-7

HOME & BUSINESS COMPUTER BASICS

Laptops For Dummies
0-470-05432-8

Windows Vista For Dummies
0-471-75421-8

Also available:
- Cleaning Windows Vista For Dummies
  0-471-78293-9
- Excel 2007 For Dummies
  0-470-03737-7
- Mac OS X Tiger For Dummies
  0-7645-7675-5
- MacBook For Dummies
  0-470-04859-X
- Macs For Dummies
  0-470-04849-2
- Office 2007 For Dummies
  0-470-00923-3

- Outlook 2007 For Dummies
  0-470-03830-6
- PCs For Dummies
  0-7645-8958-X
- Salesforce.com For Dummies
  0-470-04893-X
- Upgrading & Fixing Laptops For Dummies
  0-7645-8959-8
- Word 2007 For Dummies
  0-470-03658-3
- Quicken 2007 For Dummies
  0-470-04600-7

FOOD, HOME, GARDEN, HOBBIES, MUSIC & PETS

Chess For Dummies
0-7645-8404-9

Guitar For Dummies
0-7645-9904-6

Also available:
- Candy Making For Dummies
  0-7645-9734-5
- Card Games For Dummies
  0-7645-9910-0
- Crocheting For Dummies
  0-7645-4151-X
- Dog Training For Dummies
  0-7645-8418-9
- Healthy Carb Cookbook For Dummies
  0-7645-8476-6
- Home Maintenance For Dummies
  0-7645-5215-5

- Horses For Dummies
  0-7645-9797-3
- Jewelry Making & Beading For Dummies
  0-7645-2571-9
- Orchids For Dummies
  0-7645-6759-4
- Puppies For Dummies
  0-7645-5255-4
- Rock Guitar For Dummies
  0-7645-5356-9
- Sewing For Dummies
  0-7645-6847-7
- Singing For Dummies
  0-7645-2475-5

INTERNET & DIGITAL MEDIA

eBay For Dummies
0-470-04529-9

iPod & iTunes For Dummies
0-470-04894-8

Also available:
- Blogging For Dummies
  0-471-77084-1
- Digital Photography For Dummies
  0-7645-9802-3
- Digital Photography All-in-One Desk Reference For Dummies
  0-470-03743-1
- Digital SLR Cameras and Photography For Dummies
  0-7645-9803-1
- eBay Business All-in-One Desk Reference For Dummies
  0-7645-8438-3
- HDTV For Dummies
  0-470-09673-X

- Home Entertainment PCs For Dummies
  0-470-05523-5
- MySpace For Dummies
  0-470-09529-6
- Search Engine Optimization For Dummies
  0-471-97998-8
- Skype For Dummies
  0-470-04891-3
- The Internet For Dummies
  0-7645-8996-2
- Wiring Your Digital Home For Dummies
  0-471-91830-X

* Separate Canadian edition also available
† Separate U.K. edition also available

Available wherever books are sold. For more information or to order direct: U.S. customers visit www.dummies.com or call 1-877-762-2974.
U.K. customers visit www.wileyeurope.com or call 0800 243407. Canadian customers visit www.wiley.ca or call 1-800-567-4797.

 WILEY

SPORTS, FITNESS, PARENTING, RELIGION & SPIRITUALITY

0-471-76871-5   0-7645-7841-3

Also available:

- Catholicism For Dummies
  0-7645-5391-7
- Exercise Balls For Dummies
  0-7645-5623-1
- Fitness For Dummies
  0-7645-7851-0
- Football For Dummies
  0-7645-3936-1
- Judaism For Dummies
  0-7645-5299-6
- Potty Training For Dummies
  0-7645-5417-4
- Buddhism For Dummies
  0-7645-5359-3

- Pregnancy For Dummies
  0-7645-4483-7 †
- Ten Minute Tone-Ups For Dummies
  0-7645-7207-5
- NASCAR For Dummies
  0-7645-7681-X
- Religion For Dummies
  0-7645-5264-3
- Soccer For Dummies
  0-7645-5229-5
- Women in the Bible For Dummies
  0-7645-8475-8

TRAVEL

0-7645-7749-2   0-7645-6945-7

Also available:

- Alaska For Dummies
  0-7645-7746-8
- Cruise Vacations For Dummies
  0-7645-6941-4
- England For Dummies
  0-7645-4276-1
- Europe For Dummies
  0-7645-7529-5
- Germany For Dummies
  0-7645-7823-5
- Hawaii For Dummies
  0-7645-7402-7

- Italy For Dummies
  0-7645-7386-1
- Las Vegas For Dummies
  0-7645-7382-9
- London For Dummies
  0-7645-4277-X
- Paris For Dummies
  0-7645-7630-5
- RV Vacations For Dummies
  0-7645-4442-X
- Walt Disney World & Orlando
  For Dummies
  0-7645-9660-8

GRAPHICS, DESIGN & WEB DEVELOPMENT

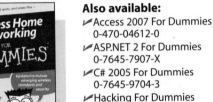

0-7645-8815-X   0-7645-9571-7

Also available:

- 3D Game Animation For Dummies
  0-7645-8789-7
- AutoCAD 2006 For Dummies
  0-7645-8925-3
- Building a Web Site For Dummies
  0-7645-7144-3
- Creating Web Pages For Dummies
  0-470-08030-2
- Creating Web Pages All-in-One Desk
  Reference For Dummies
  0-7645-4345-8
- Dreamweaver 8 For Dummies
  0-7645-9649-7

- InDesign CS2 For Dummies
  0-7645-9572-5
- Macromedia Flash 8 For Dummies
  0-7645-9691-8
- Photoshop CS2 and Digital
  Photography For Dummies
  0-7645-9580-6
- Photoshop Elements 4 For Dummies
  0-471-77483-9
- Syndicating Web Sites with RSS Feeds
  For Dummies
  0-7645-8848-6
- Yahoo! SiteBuilder For Dummies
  0-7645-9800-7

NETWORKING, SECURITY, PROGRAMMING & DATABASES

0-7645-7728-X   0-471-74940-0

Also available:

- Access 2007 For Dummies
  0-470-04612-0
- ASP.NET 2 For Dummies
  0-7645-7907-X
- C# 2005 For Dummies
  0-7645-9704-3
- Hacking For Dummies
  0-470-05235-X
- Hacking Wireless Networks
  For Dummies
  0-7645-9730-2
- Java For Dummies
  0-470-08716-1

- Microsoft SQL Server 2005 For Dummies
  0-7645-7755-7
- Networking All-in-One Desk Reference
  For Dummies
  0-7645-9939-9
- Preventing Identity Theft For Dummies
  0-7645-7336-5
- Telecom For Dummies
  0-471-77085-X
- Visual Studio 2005 All-in-One Desk
  Reference For Dummies
  0-7645-9775-2
- XML For Dummies
  0-7645-8845-1